The Merovingian Mythos

The Merovingian Mythos

AND THE MYSTERY OF RENNES-LE-CHATEAU

Tracy R. Twyman

Dragon Key Press
Portland, Oregon

ISBN: 0-9761704-0-X

Layout and Design:
Brian Albert.

Cover by:
Brian Albert.
Adam and Eve by Albrecht Duhrer

All graphics were retouched by Brian Albert.

Acknowledgements

The Author would like to extend thanks to Brian Albert, Martin Lunn, Nicholas de Vere, Rich Famous, Dwayna Wisdom, Amy Keller (for the *Le Serpent Rouge* translation), Paul Smith (priory-of-sion.com), George Moshanas, Tim Madison, the producers of Fox Television, and everyone else who kindly lent their assistance.

And of course, I would like to acknowledge BAPHOMET.

Frontispiece

The cover art is taken from Albrecht Durer's *The Fall of Man,* and represents the true DESCENT of the royal race. It is appropriate that it features the bull (representing Abel), and the goat (representing Cain). Esoterically, the serpent should be RED, and the apple, BLUE.

Table of Contents

Chapter One: The Enigma

"When Lucifer and the Trinity began to war with each other, those who did not take sides, worthy, noble angels, had to descend to earth to that Stone which is forever incorruptible. I do not know whether God forgave them or damned them in the end: if it was His due He took them back. Since that time the Stone has been in the care of those whom God appointed to it and to whom He sent His angel. This, sir is how matters stand regarding the Grail."
- Wolfram von Eschenbach's *Parzival.*

The Accursed Treasure

In Latin, the word "sacrum", from whence we derive the English word "sacred" has two apparently opposite connotations. One is "holy", or "consecrated", and the other is "accursed, horrible, detestable." You have to look at the context in which the word "sacrum" is used to determine whether the object being referred to is blessed by the powers of good, or cursed by the powers of evil. In the case of the object known as the "Holy Grail", however, and the related mystery of Rennes-le-Chateau, France, the determination is far from straight-forward.

As a researcher into the subject, I have often felt the spine-tingling sensation of the Devil himself breathing down my neck, and the presence of praeterhuman intelligences guiding me down the path towards revelation. That revelation was, for me, akin to the taste of the Tree of Knowledge Adam and Eve purportedly enjoyed in the Garden of Eden, giving them insight into the mind of God, a true divine illumination. As I continued down this path, following the twists and turns of the Holy Grail mystery wherever it led me, I discovered the answers to age-old questions, and revealed ancient secrets that have lain untouched in the dusty catacombs of dead history for thousands of years. Most of those secrets, I knew, would be of incalculable value to scholarship, and to humanity as a whole, once I was able to publish them. Other secrets I have learned are, as the saying goes, meant "only for the initiated." They are "to keep and conceal, and to never reveal", according to the well-known Masonic oath. For the legacy of the Holy Grail is the legacy of a forgotten race: the fathers of kings, builders of civilizations, and keepers of an arcane tradition meant only for an exclusive elite - the rightful inheritors of the secret doctrine of the Grail. To the initiated, a glimpse of the Grail is illumination, the sum of all desires, but to the profane unbeliever it is poison. Was I up to the perilous challenge of the Grail quest? Could I avoid the tricks, pitfalls and false roads that would greet me at every turn, and solve the riddle that hundreds of previous seekers had failed to? This book describes my adventurous quest, and the incredible results that it led me to.

The primary impetus for my interest in this mystery was, as it is for many Grail researchers, the publication of the best-selling *Holy Blood, Holy Grail*, by Michael Baigent, Henry Lincoln, and Richard Leigh. This book presented a radical new theory: that Jesus Christ did not die on the cross, but lived on to father children, whose descendants intermarried with what became the Royal House of France. And it all started with Henry Lincoln's investigation in the mystery of Rennes-le-Chateau.

The region of Southern France in which Rennes-le-Chateau is situated, called the Languedoc, has a long and fascinating history. During medieval times, It had been an important headquarters for the famous fighting monks known as the Knights Templar, the battle ground for the Catholic Church's crusade against the heretical Cathar sect, and the site of the capitol for France's first royal dynasty, the Merovingians - all subjects that I shall get to in due course. The tiny mountaintop village known as Rennes-le-Chateau had once been home to the Merovingian king-de-jure Sigisbert IV, and was quite possibly the home of his mother, Giselle de Razes, herself a Visigothic Princess. This village's central feature was, and still is, a little Catholic parish dedicated to Saint Mary Magdalene. To this quaint little church came, in 1885, a new cure, Berenger Sauniere, then 33, quite a learned man to be receiving such a seemingly lowly position. At that time, only about 200 people lived in Rennes-le-Chateau, and Sauniere's salary was a mere pittance - only a few dollars per year in today's rates.

In 1891, borrowing funds from the township, Sauniere began a restoration project for the church, on the encouragement of his friend, Abbe Henri Boudet, cure of a church at nearby Rennes-le-Bains. During these renovations, he had the altar stone lifted, which rested on two ancient Visigothic pillars. It was inside one of these pillars that Sauniere discovered four parchments, sealed inside wooden tubes, apparently written and deposited there by the parish's former cure, Abbe Antoine Bigou. Two of these parchments contained genealogies detailing the lineage of Dagobert II, the last effective king of the Merovingian dynasty. The other two parchments consisted of passages from the New Testament. But these were not mere pieces of scripture. They were written with deliberate spelling errors, misplaced truncated letters and spacing anomalies which revealed a clever coding system. Sauniere was sent by Monsignor Felix Billard, the Bishop of Carcassonne, to have the parchments interpreted by Father Bieil, Director of Saint Sulpice in Paris, as well as the priest's nephew, Emile Hoffet - an ecclesiastic scholar, closet occultist, and expert in cryptography. However, once deciphered, the parchments still did not make much sense, at least to the lay reader. The first one, which I will hereafter refer to as Parchment One, said:

"To Dagobert II, King and to Sion belong this treasure and he is there dead."

Parchment Two was much more cryptic. It read:

"Shepherdess - No temptation that Poussin and Teniers hold the key; Peace 681 by the cross and this horse of God I destroy this dæmon of the guardian at midday blue apples."

After the parchments had been deciphered, Father Bieil gave Berenger Sauniere copies of two paintings: one, an unspecified work by David Teniers, and the other, a work by the prolific Nicolas Poussin called *Les Bergers d'Arcadie - The Shepherds of Arcadia*. These facts help us to understand the reference in the parchments which reads: "Poussin and Teniers hold the key." Poussin's painting, although once thought to have been a figment of his imagination, is now known to have depicted an actual tomb that existed near the village of Arques at the time, six miles from Rennes-le-Château. In fact, Rennes-le-Chateau itself can be seen in the corner of the painting. The inscription on the tomb reads: "Et in Arcadia Ego", and is the title of an earlier work from 1618 by the painter Guercino, as well as another Poussin painting on the same theme made ten years previous. Often translated "Even in Arcadia I am", and taken to be a reference to the pervasiveness of Death, it means, more literally: "And in Arcadia I...", like an unfinished sentence. This sentence would take on an increasing significance as my investigation continued

When Sauniere returned from his trip to Paris, he is said to have exhibited strange behavior, continuing to renovate his parish, but now in a very strange bizarre fashion. For instance, he installed depictions of the Stations of the Cross on the church walls bearing some marked irregularities. Station XIV showed Christ's body being installed in the tomb at nighttime, in contrast to the traditional daylight depiction, causing the authors of *Holy Blood, Holy Grail* to question whether it was actually being *removed* from the tomb instead. Sauniere erected a large, Satanic-looking statue inside the doorway: a depiction of the demon Asmodeus, keeper of secrets and hidden treasures (and, according to cabalistic tradition, the true architect of Solomon's Temple). Above the door Sauniere placed a sign that read "Terribilis est locus ist", meaning "This place is terrible." He erected a Gothic-looking tower called "Tour Magdala" to house his library in, and a villa named "Bethania", after one of Christ's other disciples, Mary of Bethany. Sauniere could often be found up late at night, walking the grounds, digging in the graveyard and making excavations underneath the parish foundation. One interesting excavation involved lifting what was called "the Knight's Flagstone", which stood before the altar. No one knows exactly what he found under there, but he immediately told his workmen to put everything back, and had the stone (which bore a depiction of two knights riding the same horse, the seal of the Knights Templar) paved over.

Sauniere's behavior extended to the church's graveyard, where, without regard for the sanctity of human remains, he proceeded to desecrate a grave. It was that of the noble Marie, Marquise de Blanchefort, a descendant of the Merovingian kings, whose family had been deeply involved with the Knights Templar, providing them with their fourth Grand Master. The tombstone and plate had been designed by the parish's former cure, Abbe Bigou, who had been the Blancheforts' personal chaplain. The text of the tombstone's inscription contained spelling and spacing anomalies that turned out to be yet another code. When deciphered, it was found to be an exact replica of the coded text on Parchment Two, "Shepherdess - No temptation..." The plate was inscribed with a strange mixture of Greek and Latin letters that formed the words "Et in Arcadia Ego", along with a bizarre depiction of a spider, and again, the letters "PS." The inscriptions were removed by Sauniere, clearly in an attempt to cover up the "terrible" secrets he had learned from the parchments, but he did not realize that somebody had already made engravings, which remained in the town's archives.

At about this time Sauniere began receiving a large cash deposit from Archduke Johann von Habsburg, a cousin of Franz Josef, Emperor of Austria, and he proceeded to spend extravagantly - on food, wine, clothes, parties, trips to Paris, and more church renovations, using, at times, extremely rare and expensive materials. He was then, it seems, hired by Jean-Stephane Habsburg specifically to search for secret documents within the church. He also started carousing with a circle of occult initiates which included Emile Hoffet, opera singer Emma Calve (his suspected lover), and composer Claude Debussy. To all appearances, Sauniere had been converted to some strange occult sect, presumed by many to have been a Masonic-oriented secret society. But at the time, no one knew the name of this group. However, the answer may perhaps be found in an inscription placed on the Calvary in the church courtyard, "AOMPS" - which, as author Henry Lincoln theorizes, could stand for Latin words that translate to,

"Ancient Mystical Order of the Priory of Sion." This is perhaps also the meaning of the two letters, "PS", which can be found at the bottom of one of the parchments, along with the word "Sion", which is written backwards at the bottom of Parchment Two[1].

Sauniere continued his lavish spending and strange behavior for his remaining years, apparently keeping his secret within his circle of occult friends, including his friend Abbe Boudet, and his housekeeper, Marie Deneraud. Then on the 17th of January, 1917, the "Feast Day of Saint Sulpice", and the same date of death found on the tombstone of Marie de Blanchefort, the sixty-five-year-old Sauniere had an unexpected stroke - quite unexpected, considering that just five days previous, his parishioners had been noting how healthy he seemed for a man his age. Strangely, Marie Deneraud had already ordered a coffin for Sauniere.

For the next five days he lay on his deathbed. A priest from a nearby town was called in to hear his confession and administer Last Rites. But as witnesses state, the priest emerged from the bedchamber moments later, stricken with terror, and having refused to give Sauniere Extreme Unction. According to one witness, he "never smiled again", and his inexplicable state of mental anguish lasted for several months. On January 23, the day after his death, Sauniere's body was seated upright in front of the Tour Magdala, dressed in a red ceremonial robe with long tassels, which his parishioners proceeded to pluck off of his garment as they filed past, one by one, giving their respects. The meaning of this ceremony has eluded most researchers, but as I will later demonstrate, its roots are quite ancient.

When Sauniere's will was read, there were more surprises in store, for he was declared to be penniless, having given all of his accumulated wealth to Marie Deneraud. She continued to live off of this wealth until 1946, when a new French currency was issued. Frenchmen were required, while exchanging old franc notes for new, to give a basic account of how they had acquired their money. Rather than give any explanation, Madam Deneraud chose to burn all of her old francs in a bonfire outside of the Villa Bethania. This villa she then sold, and lived off of the proceeds for the next seven years. The villa's new owner, Neil Corbu, became her best friend, and she promised him that before she passed, she would reveal to him a secret that would bring him not only wealth, but "power." Unfortunately, she herself suffered a stroke before she could reveal it, and spent the rest of her short life in bed, having been rendered mute.

Over the years, much has been made of this mystery. The authors of *Holy Blood, Holy Grail* have suggested that the "he" referred to in the second parchment ("and he is there dead") might have actually been the big "He" - Jesus Christ, who, according to this theory, survived the crucifixion, faked his death, and was smuggled out of the Holy Land, allowing rumors of his ascent to Heaven to gather in his wake. Indeed a long-standing tradition embraced for generations in rural Southern France attests to this being the case. As the legend tells us, Jesus was not alone, but accompanied by his *wife* in this story - Mary Magdalene, the "reformed whore" of Catholic theology whom Jesus, to the consternation of his other disciples, loved above all others. She was also, of course, the patron saint of Rennes-le-Chateau. As *Holy Blood, Holy Grail* argues, Christ was a flesh and blood being, the biological son of his father Joseph, not some "Holy Ghost" merely inhabiting a human body. Furthermore, in the Gospels his disciples refer to him as "Rabbi", and rabbis were required to be married, encouraged to have families so as to set a proper example for the rest of the Jewish people. As the theory goes, Christ was no peasant, no mere beggar, but literally the King of the Jews, with a rightful claim to that title through his descent from King David. And as it happens, the local French legends state that Mary was pregnant at the time with Christ's child, the royal heir to the throne of Jerusalem. Southern France already included a large Jewish population that would have welcomed them. Thus the legends state that "Mary Magdalene brought the Holy Grail to France" - the Holy Grail, in this context, being a symbol for Mary's womb, pregnant with the royal blood of the Holy Family. This blood became, through Christ's descendants, intermingled, they say, with that of local nobility, and eventually ended up flowing through the veins of the Merovingian kings of France.

This tale, along with a number of other, more ancient mythological elements, eventually evolved into the Grail myths of the Middle Ages. One of the most convincing pieces of evidence for this is that fact that the French word for "Holy Grail" - "Sangreal", is remarkably similar to the French words for royal blood, "Sang Real." As perhaps confirmation of this, the authors of *Holy Blood, Holy Grail* did receive, while researching their book, information from a priest with connections to Emile Hoffet stating that that treasure which Sauniere discovered, and which led to him receiving cash payments ensuring his secrecy on the matter, consisted of "incontrovertible proof" that Christ survived the crucifixion, only to die years later in Southern France. Presumably, therefore, Christ's body would be interred there, perhaps elaborately so, by his loyal Visigothic subjects, who would have passed down the story in allegorical form to the generations that followed. Was this, then, the meaning behind the allegory of the tomb in Poussin's painting, *The Shepherds of Arcadia*? Did it, perhaps, depict an actual tomb clearly visible near Rennes-le-Chateau while at the same time pointing metaphorically to another, more important tomb that still lies hidden within the region's voluminous mountains?

In fact Henry Lincoln has discovered an amazing correspondence between *The Shepherds of Arcadia* and the landscape of Rennes-le-Chateau - specifically, a pentagram which he found implied in the painting's geometry[2]. The same pentagonal geometry can be found on a map of Rennes-le-Chateau, formed by five mountain peaks that make, seemingly against all odds, a mathematically perfect pentagram. Perhaps this pentagram acts as the proverbial "X" marking the spot of the sacred tomb. Thus the painting, which may be a coded message from a Renaissance painter clued in to the mystery, could actually be a map to buried treasure, the remains of the most popular man in history (Jesus) and the link between the French Merovingian kings and the biblical House of David. Could Poussin have known all this, enough to encode such a message in his picture? As it turns out, in 1656, Poussin was visited in Rome by Abbe Louis Fouquet, brother of Nicolas Fouquet, Louis XIV's superintendent of finances. After the meeting, while still in Rome, the Abbe sent a letter to his brother saying:

"He and I discussed certain things, which I shall with ease be able to explain to you in detail - things which will give you, through Monsieur Poussin, advantages which even kings would have great pains to draw from him, and which, according to him, it is possible that nobody else will ever discover in the centuries to come. And what is more, these are things so difficult to discover that nothing now on this earth can prove of better fortune nor be their equal."

Shortly after receiving this, Nicolas Fouquet was arrested, imprisoned, and

held "incommunicado" for the rest of his life. The letter was confiscated by Louis XIV, who later went to great efforts to obtain *The Shepherds of Arcadia*, which he hung at his private apartments in Versailles. But what was it that Poussin and the Abbe discussed? What had he discovered "which even kings would have great pain to draw from him"? Was it, perhaps, "incontrovertible proof" of the tomb of Christ in France?

But why, many have asked, if he was not the son of God, and did not die on the cross for our sins, should his bloodline be so important? If the people who ascribe to this theory do not believe in his divinity, why should they care about his descendants? And why did Sauniere erect that demonic statue in the doorway of his church, with the inscription outside that said "This Place is Terrible?" Why was it that when Sauniere lay on his deathbed, the priest assigned to administer Last Rites refused him Final Unction, and exited his bed-chamber white as a ghost, terrified out of his wits? What secret was it that Sauniere divulged on his deathbed which caused this priest to be thereafter a changed man, who reportedly "never smiled again?" It is illogical that the prospect of Jesus Christ being married and having children would, at the close of the 19th century, illicit such a response. Such an idea is heretical, but certainly not demonic, and not the kind of thing that would cause a person to lose his sense of humor for the remainder of his life. Furthermore, why would the Catholic Church and the hidden hierarchy of Europe be willing to kill, as they purportedly had in the past, to keep a such a secret, the implications of which would seem to be purely theological and academic? It did not make sense to me when I first to write a book about this mystery. But as I discovered, throughout history, the Holy Grail has played a pivotal role, and the powers of the Grail are both sacred and demonic.

What is the Holy Grail?

As I have shown, it was the position of the authors of *Holy Blood, Holy Grail* that the "Sangreal", or "Holy Grail", as described in the stories that emerged from the courts of Europe in the early part of this millennium, is actually a veiled reference to the bloodline of David, a play on the words "Sang real", or "royal blood." In the Grail stories of the Middle Ages, the custodians of the Grail are the "Grail family", headed by the Fisher King. They trace their lineage back to Joseph of Arimathea, who, along with Mary Magdalene, was supposed to have brought the Grail (often a cup filled with the "blood" of Jesus) from Jerusalem after the crucifixion. The Grail family, in the Grail stories, is romanticized as being chosen directly by God to guard the Grail (just as King David was chosen by God to rule over the Kingdom of Judah) and one of its members, Sir Galahad, is described as "a scion of the House of David." Galahad is traditionally said to be the grandfather of a real-life character, Godfroi de Bouillon, who led the First Crusade and in 1118 founded, as we shall soon relate, the Order of Sion and the Knights Templar. The Grail guardians are described in the romances specifically as Templars. The Knights Templars were also at that time very influential in the French royal courts that commissioned most of the romances, so it is possible that they might have had an indirect effect on the content of the stories. Wolfram von Eschenbach states explicitly in the Grail romance *Parzival* that the Grail is the source of kingship. "And if anywhere a land loses its lord", he writes, "if the people there acknowledge the Hand of God, and seek a new lord, they are granted one from the company of the Grail."

However, there are many different versions of the Grail myth, and many different interpretations of what the Holy Grail actually was. But I do not see these interpretations as conflicting with one another. Rather they fit together to form a pattern, revealing that the Holy Grail is not merely a single object, but a network of related traditions as old as history itself.

A Stone

In Eschenbach's *Parzival*, the Grail was a magic stone that could create things out of nothing, bring the dead back to life and cause those who looked upon it to never age another day. It also communicated. Written messages would appear on its surface detailing the names and lineages of those chosen to seek the Grail, and Parzival actually talked to it. It is called *"lapsit exillis"* - "stone from the heavens." Indeed, in the story it states that angels had "left it on earth and then rose high above the stars, as if their innocence drew them back." There are also versions of the story where these are described specifically as "fallen angels" who descended to Earth after the biblical "war in Heaven."

The Grail is sometimes identified as the "stone of light" knocked from Lucifer's crown during this war in Heaven. Others have claimed that the stone from Lucifer's crown was actually a meteorite, perhaps the one revered by Muslims at the Dome of the Rock in Jerusalem, a sacred black stone which they believe "fell from Heaven" as well. In fact, the Koran says that Muhammad stood upon this stone when he was taken to Heaven on a "ladder of light" by the Angel Gabriel. (This "ladder of light" will take on greater relevance later on in this book.)

Another candidate for the "Grail as stone" is the Emerald Tablet of Hermes, a slab of crystal engraved with ancient wisdom by the Greek god of writing. The stone upon which it is written supposedly "fell from Heaven", and the wisdom it contains is alchemical in nature, detailing a ten-step process, both chemical and spiritual, that results in the creation of the "Philosopher's Stone." Also called the "Elixir of Life", this "stone" bestows enlightenment and immortality upon those who partake of it. It is symbolized in alchemy by the Sun, and in equated with the Grail.

The stone from Heaven upon which all of this alchemical wisdom was purportedly engraved is often specified as the stone from Lucifer's crown. In these versions, Hermes is equated with the biblical prophet Enoch, and is said to have passed the Tablet on to his grandson Noah, who took it with him on board the Ark.

A Cup

As previously mentioned, the Grail is traditionally thought of as the cup that caught Jesus Christ's blood as he hung upon the cross. This legend was first found in Chretien de Troyes' *Perceval*, written in 1182. The Grail is also said to be the cup used by Christ at the Last Supper. One popular candidate for this artifact is a crumbling hunk of olive wood which rests at the Nanteos Mansion in Glastonbury, England, supposedly brought there by Joseph of Arimathea. Richard Wagner visited the mansion once and there conceived the idea for his opera *Parsifal.*

But there are many other stories surrounding the Grail cup. Some have said that this is the same cup used by the priest Melchizedek while serving Abraham bread and wine on Mount Moriah. From the Grail cup, sometimes described more as a bowl or a serving dish, one could obtain whatever kind of food one wished, in limitless abundance. In this way the legend is obviously based on ancient Celtic myths about Bran the Blessed's "cauldron of rebirth" and the magical "Horn of Plenty." This accords with earlier prototypes of the Grail story from Mesopotamian cultures that refer to a mystical bowl which, coincidentally, is covered with sacred writing. The word "grail" is said by some scholars to come from the Old French word "gradale", a dish used to serve successive courses in a meal, but I have discussed in a later chapter how this word could have a much older antiquity. When not filled with blood or food made from thin air, the Grail was empty, and its emptiness was heavily stressed, perhaps because emptiness is the supreme state of being and enlightenment - the annihilation of the ego.

Mystical Union

This brings us to another point of view concerning the Grail: a spiritual experience. It is described as the most worthy thing that one can seek, and those who embark upon the quest for the Grail must be completely pure of heart. One does not merely "find" the Grail: one "achieves" it, and at that point is initiated into its secrets. Just seeing it causes an overwhelming, trance-like state of awe and reverence, and the experience brings a complete transformation of the soul. "Upon a green achmardi she bore the consummation of heart's desire", writes Eschenbach, "its root and its blossoming - a thing called 'the Gral', paradisal, transcending all earthly perfection!" In the story of *Parzival* the Grail has been lost, causing a state of infertility called "the Wasteland." The Fisher King, Parzival's uncle, is wounded in the crotch, and the festering sore, along with the Wasteland, cannot be cured until the Grail is found - an obvious metaphor for spiritual redemption. This is the redemption that, mystics relate, occurs when one's inner polarities (male/female, light/dark, etc.) are aligned, equalized, and transcended, creating a feeling of sublime nothingness that leaves one receptive to divine influence. It is union with God, the Great Void, the state of Samadhi that is the goal of yogic meditation.

Bodily Secretions

Famed magician Aleister Crowley had quite a different take on the meaning of the Grail. Noted for his work in the field of sex magic, he combined Tantric theory learned in India with methodology learned from the German Ordo Templi Orientis. He believed that sex performed ritually could result in transcendence of the ego and union with the Godhead. This was possible if one was "in conversation with the Holy Guardian Angel" at the moment of orgasm, and the process for reaching that state is detailed in *The Book of the Unveiling of the Sangraal*. Afterwards, all fluids created during sex must be consumed in full by the magician, so as to retain their potency (in the same way that Tantrics retain their semen so as to prevent a loss of energy). Crowley referred to semen as "red tincture", vaginal secretions as "white tincture", and the mix of the two, the Elixir of Life. He also called it significantly, the "Magnum Opus" or "Philosopher's Stone." The holy vessel (vagina) from which one drinks the Elixir of Life he called "the Sangraal." This is an important connection, because according to my research, sex magic appears to have been part of a long-standing tradition in which many members of the Grail family and their close associates participated. Interestingly, when Crowley wrote about his own sex magic rituals he referred to himself as "the Great Beast" and his consort as "the Whore of Babalon." I am reminded of a passage in Saint John's *Revelations* describing the Whore of Babalon thusly:

"And the woman was arrayed in purple and scarlet colour, and decked with gold and precious stones and pearls, having a golden cup in her hand full of abominations and filthiness of her fornication" (Revelation, 7:4-5).

Does that golden cup symbolize the same idea as the Holy Grail? As I was soon to find out, the concept of a "Scarlet Woman" is directly related to both the practice of sex magic and the Holy Grail tradition, so the answer to that question is most probably "yes."

The Ark

In his book *The Sign and the Seal*, Graham Hancock argues that the Grail might have actually been the Ark of the Covenant, the revered Judaic relic designed by Jehovah and built by the Hebrews to absolute geometric perfection. This was the 1 cubit x 1 cubit x 2 cubit wooden cedar box into which Moses placed the Tablets of the Testimony: tablets of stone engraved by the finger of God[3]. It was overlaid with the purest of gold, and crowned with two mysterious winged objects called cherubim who each had two faces: of a lion and eagle, a man and an ox, respectively. Between their outstretched wings stood the Mercy Seat, where God would literally sit and talk to the priest. In fact, God was referred to as actually *living in* the Ark. "The Lord reigneth; let the people tremble: he sitteth between the cherubim; let the earth be moved[4]." The prophet Samuel was said to have seen and conversed with a "form", which he took to be God, in the vicinity of the Ark. Later, King Solomon had a temple built for it, in which he used the Ark to conjure up not only Jehovah, but a host "demons" and "archangels." The Ark "smote" those who touched it, moved objects at will and produced "manna" for the Israelites to eat while they were starving in the desert - all attributes shared by the Grail. The Ark had to be obscured by a veil at all times lest those who looked upon be killed, and only the sons of the High Priest Aaron were allowed to actually see it, protected by a "breastplate of judgment" made from gold and precious stones.

Graham Hancock bases his argument on the fact that the Knights Templar, "guardians of the Grail" according to tradition, were believed to have excavated a treasure from the caverns underneath Solomon's Temple which made them extremely rich and powerful. They were rumored to have taken this treasure to the mountain of Montsegur in the Languedoc region of France, which was the prototype for the setting of most of the Grail romances, "Montsalvat." It is also quite close to Rennes-le-Chateau.

Each of these explanations of the Grail is equally intriguing. I eventually came to the conclusion that they may all be correct, and that the Grail is really a combination of all of the above, each providing a piece of the puzzle known as the "Grail mystery." This mystery, I believe, has now finally been cracked, and one of the first keys that helped open up the mystery to me was the existence of the "Grail bloodline." My study of this subject began with the legendary Merovingian kings.

Blood Royale

It is not known when the Merovingian dynasty began, for their rule over the Frankish kingdom seems to have already been well-established by the time of Meroveus - the source of the line's name and the first king of that line to have made his way onto the historical record. Before this there is no other line of Frankish kings whom the Merovingians would have usurped: they simply had always been the royal family as far back as anyone could remember. Meroveus was, however, worthy of being called the progenitor of the dynasty, for his conception was in no way natural. Meroveus was, according to the legend, the spawn of two fathers: one, the Frankish King Clodio, the other, a mysterious sea creature called "the Quinotaur." This beast raped his mother, already pregnant, as she was swimming in the ocean, and managed to magically inject his own seed into the developing fetus, co-mingling his own inhuman blood with that of the Frankish kings. This is why Meroveus' name bore within it the French word for "sea", and why his descendants, the Merovingian kings, were believed to possess magical, super-human powers. As *Holy Blood, Holy Grail* states:

"According to tradition Merovingian monarchs were occult adepts, initiates in arcane sciences, practitioners in esoteric arts - worthy rivals of Merlin, their fabulous near-contemporary. They were often called the sorcerer kings or thaumaturge kings. By virtue of some miraculous property in their blood, they could allegedly heal by the laying on of hands; and according to one account the tassels on the fringes of their robes were deemed to possess miraculous curative powers. They were said to be capable of clairvoyant or telepathic communication with beasts and with the natural world around them, and to wear powerful magical necklaces. They were said to possess an arcane spell that protected them and granted them phenomenal longevity - which history, incidentally, does not seem to confirm."

Other rumors about the Merovingians were very specific. For starters, each supposedly bore a birthmark that consisted of a red equilateral cross, either above the heart or between the shoulder blades. They were called "the long-haired kings", because they refused to cut their hair, which purportedly contained the essence of their magical powers. At death, it would appear that they partook of the ancient ritual of trepanation, allowing the "soul" to escape to the afterlife through a hole drilled in the deceased's skull. They were also ritually entombed with strange, occult artifacts, much like the Egyptian Pharaohs. In the tomb of Meroveus' son, King Childeric, there was interred a severed horse's head, a golden bull's head, a crystal ball, and three-hundred golden bees - a symbol of the Merovingian line. (These bees were later attached to the coronation robe of Napoleon Bonaparte, who had married a Merovingian princess, in order to connect himself symbolically with the ancient kingly line.) There was another similarity between the Merovingians and the Egyptian Pharaohs: both were considered to be priest-kings, and living incarnations of the divine. This was seen by the authors of *Holy Blood, Holy Grail* as evidence for a Merovingian descent from Christ, and a long-standing local tradition does indeed link them with said blood, making them, by definition, a "Grail family."

The knowledge of this remarkable ancestry was purportedly the impetus behind the pact made between Meroveus' grandson, King Clovis I, and the Roman Catholic Church in the year 469, bestowing upon him the title "New Constantine", and control over a vast kingdom which provided the prototype for the "Holy Roman Empire." This title was, according to the pact, to be passed down to his descendants from that moment on, in exchange for his conversion to the faith. (Yes, the presumed "children of Christ" were themselves, until that time, not Christians.) The idea, according to *Holy Blood, Holy Grail*, was that by employing the Merovingians and allowing them to spread their empire, the Church could keep the priest-kings "under their thumb", so to speak, and silent about their divine lineage, which could be devastating for the hegemony of the Roman faith. For several generations, this agreement was observed, and the baptism of Clovis was a fondly remembered event, commonly depicted in ancient seals with the king being submerged in a Grail-like cup. But in the year 679, the Church broke their very own pact, in the most devastating of ways.

By the time the Merovingian King Dagobert II was born, in 651, the power of the throne had already been weakened, with authority increasingly being usurped by court chancellors known as "Mayors of the Palace." On the death of his father, the five-year-old Dagobert was kidnapped by then Palace Mayor Grimoald, who tried to put his own son on the throne instead. Human compassion saved young Dagobert from death, and he was exiled to Ireland, only to return years later and reclaim the throne in 679. But the problems of the Mayors of the Palace continued. Apparently displeased with Dagobert's lack of allegiance and devotion to the faith (a problem noted in previous Merovingian kings as well), the Roman church entered into a conspiracy with Mayor Pepin the Fat. On December 23, supposedly while on a hunting trip in the haunted and sacred wood called the "Forest of Woevres", Dagobert was lanced through the eye, on Pepin's orders, they say. With Roman Catholic endorsement, Pepin passed political power onto his son, Charles Martel, thus beginning the Carolingian dynasty that would later become so famous. After that, the Merovingian bloodline faded into obscurity. All subsequent Merovingian kings were essentially powerless, and they were officially thought to have died out with one of Dagobert's grandsons, Childeric III. Forty-nine years later, Charles Martel's grandson, Charlemagne was anointed Holy Roman Emperor. The church had finally washed its hands of the Merovingian problem, or so they thought.

And what was the problem, exactly? According to the claims, the Merovingians, as his blood descendants, knew the truth about Jesus and his actual significance as King of the Jews. They knew that the Roman church had stolen their birthright, usurped their role as the priest-kings of the "True Church", co-opted the idea of Jesus and created a fictionalized version of the messiah to further their own agenda - world domination, both secular and spiritual. The Merovingians knew that the fantasy of Christ as a virgin-born deity who suffered willingly for our sins and ascended to heaven was just that - an "opiate of the masses" used by the Romans as an excuse to set themselves up as the arbiters of God, and thus perpetuate their faltering empire. And with the death of Dagobert II, they thought they had eradicated this threat for good.

But according to the sources used in *Holy Blood, Holy Grail*, the Merovingian bloodline continued on in secret, via Sigisbert IV, son of Dagobert II and his second wife, Giselle de Razes. Historians have assumed Sigisbert to have been another casualty of his father's assassination, but there is actually no record of this. Legend says that Sigisbert IV was taken by his sister after his father's assassination and sent to the Languedoc, then ruled over by his mother. This occurred in the year 681, a possible explanation for the use of this number in one of the coded messages from Sauniere's parchments. He also took on the name of "Plantard", meaning "ardent flowering shoot", a reference to the continuation of the Merovingian line, and took on his uncle's titles "Duke of Razes" and "Count of Rhedae." From this, the family names Plantard, Plantavelu, and Plantagenet (the name of one of Britain's most famous royal lines) can be traced. It is also likely that Sigisbert's descendants were the rulers of a independent kingdom encompassing the region of Razes and Rennes-le-Chateau that came into being in the 8th century. The rulers of this land included Theodoric, Guillem de Gellone (a famous figure of his time who was mentioned in Dante's *The Divine Comedy*) and Prince Ursus, listed by some genealogies as Dagobert II's grandson, Sigisbert VI. Somewhere around 879, he was declared "King Ursus" by his supporters, who attempted to usurp King Louis II and place Ursus on the French throne. Although the insurrection failed, Ursus married into the Breton ducal house, and his descendants took on the duchies of Brittany and Aquitaine. They also brought the bloodline to England, beginning the Planta family line that eventually resulted in the Plantagenets. One member of this Planta line was Bera IV, also called "the Architect." There is a possibility that he and his descendants may have been involved in the formation of Freemasonry. Interestingly, according to Masonic scholar Albert Pike, the Craft is sometimes referred to as *"Frankmasonry."*

Genetic descent is not the only way in which the Merovingians have passed on their heritage to future generations. The other was in the form of a cult - a cult which cherished Christ and, in particular, Mary Magdalene, as progenitors of the Merovingian "Grail blood", which they deemed sacred. This cult also recognized another divine ancestor, represented by the Quinotaur, whose genetic essence was intermingled with that of the blood of Christ in the bodies of the Grail kings. Essentially, it was what we would call the cult of the Holy Grail. Certainly this cult was responsible for the way Dagobert II's relics were treated after his death. While the Roman Catholic Church and the Carolingian hierarchy were attempting to excise Dagobert II and his heirs from the history books (so much so that any chronicle of French kings written before 1646 fails to even mention him), Dagobert's body was exhumed in 872 from the royal chapel of Saint Remy in Stenay and moved to a new church, where it became the center for the worship of "Saint Dagobert", for he had been canonized by a local "metropolitan conclave." The relics were believed by the local cult to protect the town against intruders, and they began to observe a feast on every "Saint Dagobert's Day" - December 23, the anniversary of his martyrdom. The Pope later canonized Dagobert in 1159, not the last time the Church would mark for sainthood a person who had been martyred by the Church itself.

Years later, the Church would turn martyring those of the Grail cult into a full-time job.

The Albigensian Crusade

In the year 1209, the Catholic Church began its first and only crusade against fellow Christian Europeans, the Cathars. The word "Cathar" came from "Cathari", meaning "the Pure Ones", although they were also called "Albigensians" because they had first been publicly condemned by an ecclesiastical council at the Languedoc town of Albi. The Cathars were a heretical Christian sect who believed that one could commune with the True God through the spiritual experience of "gnosis" - direct knowledge of the divine. They did not believe in the crucifixion or honor the cross. They also believed that the "Jehovah" of the Bible was actually a demiurge: "Rex Mundi", the King of the World, who had created the corrupt world of matter in order to entrap men's souls. The goal of gnosis, then, was to free oneself from the bonds of creation, much like the Buddhist concept of "nirvana." They were fish-eating vegetarians, and practiced birth control to prevent innocent children from being brought in to the corrupt world of matter. Oh, and one other thing: they were rumored to have possessed a vast treasure that included the "Holy Grail."

The Languedoc region of France was a bastion of Cathar thought, where it had threatened to become the dominant religion. Nearly 30% of all Cathar priests were drawn from Languedoc nobility, and even non-Cathars in the region usually maintained a cold attitude towards the Church of Rome. The Languedoc was at that time an independent principality, with a distinct culture of esoteric thought and higher learning. So when the "Albigensian crusade", as it came to be called, began, even many non-Cathar locals defended their home-grown heretics to the death.

For the next forty years, the Church attempted to wipe out the Albigensian menace. The destruction of Catharism, which tended to run in families, was so complete that the Crusade is now considered by historians to be Europe's first genocide. Those who were not killed in the fighting were arrested and tortured by the Dominican Order's Holy Inquisition. The Church's army spared no one, not even non-Cathars, who stood in the way of their stated goal. When Pope Innocent III was asked how the soldiers should know the heretics from the true Christians, he responded with the oft-quoted line, "Kill them all. God will know His own."

And that they did. The Cathars and their defenders fought bravely, but in the end it was no use. Some of the few remaining Cathar strongholds, towards the end, were those in Arques, Narbonne, Toulouse, Carcassonne, and Rennes-le -Chateau. But the final fortress to capitulate was that of Montsegur, "poised", as *Holy Blood, Holy Grail* relates, "like a celestial ark above the surrounding valleys." It was besieged by the invaders for ten months, and finally fell in March of 1244.

On the first of March, the less than 400 remaining defenders, 180 of them actual Cathars, and the remainder mercenary soldiers, were offered terms for surrender. The soldiers would receive full pardon, and the heretics would only have to renounce their beliefs and make a full confession. The Cathars agreed to a two-week truce while they considered the terms, with the understanding that if anyone tried to escape, they would be immediately executed. They took the whole two weeks, but in the end, the Cathars refused, and were immediately burned to death.

Yet according to the legends, the night before the end of the ceasefire, a small group of Cathars managed to sneak out of the fortress carrying some unnamed treasure - one quite separate and distinct from the famed hordes of gold and other booty the heretics possessed, which had been smuggled out safely much earlier in the siege. Given the importance of the date, which was Easter, March 14, the day of the Spring Equinox, the authors of *Holy Blood, Holy Grail* assumed that the "treasure" must have been some sort of holy relic, which they had needed to hold onto until that point for use in their Spring Equinox ritual. Records indicate that an equinox ritual did indeed take place. Whatever it consisted of was in all probability the reason why at least twenty of the mercenary soldiers who were defending the Cathars converted to their religion at the last moment, thus sealing their death warrants. The writers of *Holy Blood, Holy Grail* have theorized that the ritual had more to do with the equinox than with the Christian Easter, since Easter celebrated Christ's resurrection after the crucifixion, and the Cathars did not believe that Christ had died on the cross. But could it not have been both an observance of the equinox *and* an Easter ritual - one that actually repudiated the crucifixion? A letter written by Jean de Joinville, friend to French King Louis IX during the 13th century, stated that , "The king once told me how several men from among the Albigenses had gone to the Comte de Montfort... and asked him to come look at the body of Our Lord, which had become flesh and blood in the hands of their priest." Perhaps the Cathars did possess the true Body of Christ, and perhaps something about that body provided proof that Christ had not been crucified. Then again, as we were later to discover, Christ was not the only being whom the Cathars may have called "Lord." Nor were they the only possible possessors of the Holy Grail and the secret traditions of Christ whom the Catholic Church would decide to root out in the coming years.

The Knights Templar

According to chroniclers of their early years, the Knights Templar were founded in 1188 by Hughes de Payen, a vassal of the Count of Champagne. This occurred after they had presented themselves to Baldwin I, King of Jerusalem, whose older brother, Godfroi de Bouillon had led the crusaders to victory in the Holy Land almost twenty years previously. They proposed themselves as a order of fighting monks, who would protect the roadways for pious pilgrims journeying to Jerusalem. They were immediately given an entire wing of the royal palace as their headquarters - a wing that had been built upon the foundations of the Temple of Solomon. Thus they received their name, the Knights of the Temple.

For the next nine years they admitted no new members to their order - strange since the nine founding members hardly seem like they would have provided an adequate number of staff to protect all of the roads to the Holy Land. Furthermore, there is no evidence from contemporary chroniclers indicating that they even engaged in such activities. Guillame de Tyre, the chief chronicler of the age and an intimate associate of King Baldwin, does not even mention them, causing the authors of *Holy Blood, Holy Grail* to suspect that he had been silenced by the royal muzzle to cover up for the Templars' actual activities - excavating the Temple Mount. The authors speculate that when the Roman legions sacked the Temple in 70 A.D., they took only the most obvious loot, unwittingly leaving behind the most valuable treasure, chief among which would have been the Ark of the Covenant, and perhaps, the artifact which came to be known as the Holy Grail. This could have been secreted away by the Temple priests in any of the numerous tunnels known to exist beneath Solomon's Stables on the Temple Mount - stables which the Templars made use of during their nine-year stay. This could have, in fact, been the purpose behind the foundation of their order - a mission based upon knowledge that had been passed down from Christ's descendants to the Merovingians, and then on to the Templar founders. The main figures involved in the Templars' foundation (King Baldwin, the Count of Champagne, Andre de Montbard, Hughes de Payen, Bertrand de Blanchefort and Godfroi de Bouillon) were all descendants of Merovingian blood, and if they had been in on the family secrets, that could explain why they willingly pledged themselves, their money, and in the king's case, the royal quarters to the cause. If they had been successful in their mission, it could explain how they acquired the capital with which they eventually created a vast empire.

During their first nine years they became famous throughout Europe as the selfless "Militia of Christ." By 1127, most of the knights had returned to Europe, and in the following year, Saint Bernard of Clairvaux, Andre de Montbard's uncle, published a pro-Templar tract entitled *In Praise of the New Knighthood.* At the Saint Bernard-inspired Council of Troyes, the Church officially recognized the Templars as a religious and military order dedicated to the defense of Christendom. Saint Bernard then assisted in the drawing up of their rules of conduct, based upon those of the Cistercian order of monks, another group upon whom Bernard had much influence. Templars were sworn to poverty and celibacy. They wore white mantels to symbolize their purity, emblazoned with the red cross patee. And just as the Merovingians were forbidden to cut their hair, the Templars were likewise forbidden to cut their beards. The Templars' reputation for bravery was well-earned. They were not allowed to retreat from battle unless the odds outweighed them three to one, and when they were captured they were obliged to fight to the death rather than beg for mercy or ransom. They were also pledged to secrecy about the orders workings, and were inducted with a strange initiation ceremony about which there were many rumors. A few years later, there was another interesting development in their rule. In 1139, a former student of Saint Bernard's, Pope Innocent II, issued a papal bull stating that the Knights Templar would owe allegiance to none except the Pope himself, making them immune to the political whims of all authorities, both religious and secular.

As their fame grew, so did their ranks, and thus, their property holdings. The sons of European nobility swelled their membership, and the vast amounts of money and property donated by the new recruits swelled their territory and their coffers - for new recruits, as per their vow of poverty, were required to relinquish all property upon admittance to the order. Soon they stood at the helm of a huge, international empire over which they held complete independent sovereignty. During Christendom's Second Crusade, the Templars accompanied France's King Louis II into battle, and played a decisive role in preventing the war from becoming a total disaster. Over the next century, they secured their important role in international politics by utilizing their influence upon a number of kings, nobles, and ecclesiastic authorities. Many of these kings were financially indebted to the Templars, and some actually resided with them. The Grand Master of the Temple even stood by England's King John as he signed the Magna Carta. At times, it appeared that the Templars possessed the power to make or break a monarch's career according to their desire.

Their political influence spread in direct proportion to their huge banking operation. In fact, the modern institution of banking, in which money can be deposited in one location and withdrawn in another, is a Templar invention, along with the "cheque", likely named after the "chequerboard" pattern that was one of the Templars' most well-recognized motifs. This made it possible for pilgrims and travelers to journey safely without fear of roadside robbers, and the cheques were unforgable, as they were written in sophisticated secret codes for which the Templars became known. Almost every king or queen in Europe banked with them, as well as a number of Muslim leaders whom they dealt with on a regular basis. As *Holy Blood, Holy Grail* puts it, "The Templars thus became the primary money changers of the age, and the Paris preceptory became the center of European finance."

The Templars' enterprises put them in the position of being conduits for new forms of art, science, and craft, as well as new forms of thought and belief. They had access to new advances in agriculture, armaments, surveying, mapmaking, and navigation, and they were one of the first groups of people to employ the magnetic compass in their seafaring. They ran their own hospitals to treat wounded soldiers, and were at the forefront of modern medicine, bringing to the field a scientific point of view unusual among their contemporaries, including an unprecedented understanding of the principals of hygiene. They even made medical use of mold extracts, similar to the widespread use of penicillin as an antibiotic today. Their mastery of architectural principles, including the understanding of advanced mathematics (such as was used in the building of the Giza pyramid, for example), along with their patronage of the stonemasons' guilds, led to the development of Gothic architecture.

They were equally influential in bringing new religious and philosophical ideas into vogue throughout Europe, including blends of Islamic, Judaic, and Gnostic threads of thought, setting the stage for Europe's cultural Renaissance, which followed the medieval era and incorporated these same themes. Their ambiguous relationship with the Saracen enemy in the Holy Land, with whom they maintained a respectful peace whenever possible, led to the incorporation of a number of these new thought systems and scientific techniques, for Arab culture was still, at that time, a high civilization. There were even rumors of a close relationship with the Order of the Assassins, called by some authorities the Islamic equivalent to the Knights Templar. Like the Templars, they took oaths of secrecy, conducted strange ceremonies, and were obliged to fight with the same fanatical bravery.

But when their relationship with the Muslims began to deteriorate, the Templars' foothold in Jerusalem began to slip. King Baldwin IV of Jerusalem died in 1185. In the battle over the succession that resulted, the current Grand Master of the Knights Templar, Gerard de Ridefort, was said to have betrayed some oath made to the deceased king, initiating a near-civil war amongst the Europeans living in the Holy Land. He also managed to destroy the long-established truce between the Christians and the Saracens, and led the Christians into a battle at Hattin in 1187 that resulted in the end of their 100-year-long reign in Jerusalem. By 1291, almost the entire Holy Land was under Saracen control. The last Christian fortress, Acre, fell dramatically in May of that year.

The Templars set up new headquarters in Cyprus, but without the Holy Land to protect, or new territory to capture on behalf of Christendom, they lacked any clear-cut goals. The authors of *Holy Blood, Holy Grail* suggest that at this point, the Knights Templar turned their attention towards a new ambition: creating their own independent European state. Other authors, such as Alan Butler and Stephen Dafoe, have suggested that Switzerland is a likely candidate for the planned Templar state, and even suggest that the Swiss nation is a direct result of this. Evidence they give includes the extensive Templar holdings that existed there, the Templar-style equilateral cross on their national flag, and the well-established role that Switzerland plays as a center of European finance. Also, in Valais, Switzerland, the capitol is called "Sion", and is the center of a modern-day Templar order (the Grand Swiss Priory) dedicated to controlling the world by controlling its finances. However, the authors of *Holy Blood, Holy Grail* believe that the land which the Templars had picked to be the "New Jerusalem" was, in fact, the Languedoc region of Southern France - land of the Merovingian kings, whose descendants included the Templars' founders. It was also the realm of the Cathar heretics, who, as it turned out, were closely associated with the Knights Templar as well.

It has been written that one of the Templars' founders was a Cathar, and that their fourth Grand Master, Bertrand de Blanchefort, was from a "Cathar family." So too were many of the order's dignitaries. And although the Templars were officially neutral in regards to the Albigensian crusade, they did accept a number of Cathars into their ranks at that time, providing them with immunity from prosecution. They even allowed Cathar refugees to take shelter in their preceptories, and on some occasions did defend them militarily. According to *Holy Blood, Holy Grail*, "In the Languedoc, Temple officials were more frequently Cathar than Catholic", and, "The Grand Master at the time... declared there was in fact only one true crusade - the crusade against the Saracens."

But the Catholic crusade against heresy would soon be turned against the Templars themselves, and the Holy Inquisition, which had been formed to deal with the Cathar problem, would soon be torturing their knights. For by 1306, the Templars had made a most powerful enemy: King Philippe IV of France. He did not merely resent them because they owed no allegiance to him, being obliged solely to the Holy See, and constituted a military threat greater than his own armed forces. He also owed them a lot of money, which he could not afford to repay, but which he knew they held in great abundance. Furthermore, they had insulted him in the past by refusing him admittance to their ranks. Perhaps he had even heard about the treasure from Jerusalem that they supposedly possessed. Whichever the case, he had decided that he would do away with the Templars, not only in his own domains, but everywhere altogether. And the only other power he knew of that held the amount of international clout needed to execute the plan was the only power that held command over the Templars: the Papacy. But manipulating the Papacy was nothing new to King Philippe the Fair. He had already, as most historians will attest, played a guiding role in the kidnapping of Pope Boniface VIII and the poisoning of Pope Benedict XI. The current pope, Clement V, owed his very throne to Philippe, who had been responsible for his election. Even as the son of Ida de Blanchefort, from the same family as the Templars' fourth Grand Master, Clement V still could not resist pressure from Philippe the Fair. Philippe wanted to persecute the Templars for heresy.

The drama which unfolded thereafter gave rise to numerous legends, including the superstition surrounding "Friday the 13th." Philippe had drafted a list of charges, largely based on evidence gleaned from spies, and from a defected Templar who agreed to be a witness. He then issued secret orders to his seneschals throughout France, sealed, with instructions that they were to be opened at dawn on Friday, October 13, 1307, and implemented immediately. All Templars were to be arrested at once, and all of the order's property seized.

Despite the trouble the king went through to keep the plan secret, the Templars still seemed to have received some sort of warning, for the vast majority of their wealth, along with whatever holy relics they presumably possessed, had already been spirited away into trusted hands far from the king's reach. (Most of this could be achieved through their highly sophisticated network of banks.) The order's current Grand Master, Jacques de Molay, had just had all of the order's books burnt for no apparent reason. And one Templar who left the order had been told by the treasurer that this was a "wise" move, as danger for the order lurked around the corner. Also, a memo had been given to all of the Templar preceptories in France warning their members not to divulge any information to anyone about the order's customs and rituals. The Templars who were arrested went without struggle, as if they had been instructed to submit.

However, not all Templars were arrested. It is known that a group of them, all closely associated with the treasurer, escaped, taking with them, presumably, all the wealth and treasure they could carry. According to the legends, the Templars loaded the loot onto wagons, which they then transported to the coast, where eighteen ships awaited them at the Templar naval base at La Rochelle. These ships vanished without a trace shortly before the arrests.

The fate of the arrested knights varied. All were interrogated, and many were tortured into confessing. The confessions, as well as the accusations, all revolved around similar themes. A list of charges drawn up by the Inquisition on August 12th, 1308 reads:

"Item, that in each province they had idols, namely heads.
Item, that they adored these idols.
Item, that they said that the head could save them.
Item, that it could make riches.
Item, that it could make the trees flower.
Item, that it made the land germinate.
Item, that they surrounded or touched each head of the aforesaid idol with small cords,
which they wore around themselves next to the shirt or the flesh."

They were also accused, among other things, of homosexual rites, of baby sacrifice, of committing abortions, and of ritually trampling upon the Christian cross during their initiation ceremony. A widespread interpretation of this ritual, repeated often throughout the confessions, is that they were expressing their denial of the crucifixion, presumably because they had come across evidence that Christ did not die on the cross. This ritual could also have served as an introduction to a spiritual discipline that was older than Christianity. One aspirant, during the initiation ceremony, was supposedly told that he should not believe in Christ, but in a "higher God." A crucifix was then displayed, and he was told, "Set not much faith in this, for it is far too young." The accusations regarding this ritual, however, had been floating around the rumor mill since at least 1249.

The most widespread and consistent aspect of the confessions, however, involved the worship of one head in particular, specifically an idol named "Baphomet." Some said it was a man's head, some a woman's head. Some said that it was bearded, some that it was made of glass or crystal, and some said that it had two faces. A popular tale held that it was the head of the Templar's first Grand Master, Hughes de Payens, or that of John the Baptist. The latter seems a likely rumor to have been circulating amongst the Templars, for one of the theories surrounding the order is that they ascribed to the Johannite belief that John the Baptist was the true messiah, and Jesus a false prophet. Some even said that Baphomet was not a mere head, but a demon, perhaps the Devil himself - half male, half-female, half-human, and half-beast. This was the source for the 19th century occultist Eliphas Levi's well-known depiction of Baphomet, now incorporated into the Waite tarot deck as "the Devil." This popular image, sometimes referred to as "the Sabbatic Goat", was made to embody symbols of conflicting dualities. Thus the beast bears the breasts of a woman and the sex organs of a man. He is shown poised between the waxing and waning moon symbols with his right and left hands pointing up and down, respectively. Levi designed a sigil depicting an inverted pentagram with Baphomet's goat face super-imposed onto it, and called it the "Goat of Mendes." This symbol was later used by Anton LaVey's Church of Satan.

Yet there was another idolatrous head found during the raid on the Templar's Paris preceptory which presents an intriguing possibility about Baphomet. According to the written account, it was, "a great head of gilded silver, most beautiful, and consisting of the image of a woman. Inside were two head-bones wrapped in a cloth of white linen, with another red cloth around it. A label was attached, on which was written the legend "Caput 58 M." Given the evidence that the Templars knew of and believed in the Grail family, descendants of Christ, and Mary Magdalene, some think that this idol contains the relics of Magdalene herself. After all, 5 +8 = 13, and M is the thirteenth letter of the alphabet, so "58M" could be a code signifying the name "Mary Magdalene." However, there is another important detail to consider as well. The "M" was actually written as "♍", the astrological sign for "Virgo." There is a symbolic connection between the figure of Mary Magdalene and the figure of Virgo. There is also a connection between Mary Magdalene and the goddess Venus, or Isis, upon whom "Virgo" is based.

As it turns out, Isis figures into a popular legend regarding the origin of Baphomet. According to the tale, a Templar called "the Lord of Sidon" was in love with a young woman named Yse (possibly derived from "Isis") who died suddenly. On the night of her burial, he dug up her body and copulated with it. Nine months later a voice "from the Void" told him to go back to the grave, where he would find his son. There he discovered a head resting on a pair of leg bones (perhaps the origin of the Templar's famous skull and crossbones symbol.) The voice told him that if he was careful to guard the head, it would be "the giver of all things." He took it with him and for the rest of his days it protected him. Later on, the tale relates, the Templar order got a hold of it and incorporated it into their rituals.

Despite the severity of the charges leveled against them by the Papacy, most Templars were able to confess and go on with their lives. A number of them escaped persecution altogether. In England, for instance, King Edward IV (Philippe's son-in-law) took a protective stance towards the Templars, only pursuing them under extreme duress from the Pope, and then after most of them had already escaped. Those that were arrested often received light sentences involving a few years of penance in a monastery - not unlike the life they were used to living anyway. Their lands were given to the Knights Hospitaller of Saint John, now known as the "Knights of Malta", and the military wing of the Vatican. It was an order that reportedly had much in common with the Templars, perhaps even certain belief systems, and there is evidence that some of the escaped Templars simply joined this rival order.

Where did the escaped English Templars go to? Most likely, Scotland, which provided a haven for renegade Templars from all over Europe. Scotland was at war with England at the time, so pressure from King Edward would have been useless, and Scottish people at that time did not care much what the Pope thought of them either. Escaped Templars played an integral role in the history of Scotland, where the order was never officially dissolved. They are said to have fought by the side of Robert the Bruce during 1314's Battle of Bannockburn. They purportedly survived in Scotland at least until 1689, when, during the Battle of Killiecrankie (part of a revolt against the deposition of Scottish Stuart king James II by William of Orange) an ancient Templar device was found on the body of John Claverhouse, Viscount of Dundee.

In the province of Lorraine, which was then part of Germany (and now part of France), the region's duke exonerated all Templars of heresy, instructing them to array themselves in the clothes of common people and blend in with the populace. The Templars were openly defiant in both Germany and Spain, where they were proclaimed innocent by their judges, and went on to live normal lives in other orders, such as the Teutonic Order, or the Knights Hospitaller. In Portugal, the order itself was cleared of all charges, and merely had to change its name, becoming the Knights of Christ[5]. This order was devoted specifically to sailing, and sponsored a number of history's most well-known explorers. Vasco de Gama was a member of the order, and Prince Henry the Navigator, speculated as having been among the few to explore (albeit secretly) the New World prior to Christopher Columbus, was a Grand Master. Most importantly, however, Christopher Columbus himself was the son-in-law of a Knight of Christ, and may have used his relative's maps to navigate his way to America, where his ships sailed under flags bearing the order's insignia, the red equilateral cross. The Templars also reputedly used their influence in the Teutonic Order to exact a measure of revenge against the Catholic Church, when they decided to support the Protestant Reformation of Martin Luther.

Revenge was something that was definitely on the minds of escaped Templars, especially in regards to what happened to their last known Grand Master, Jacques de Molay. Although he had confessed to the charges, he later repudiated them, claiming that the confession had been made during torture, and was therefore not valid. He was thus consigned, in March of 1314, to be slow-roasted upon an open fire in a public square. Before he died, de Molay is said to have called on both Pope Clement and King Philippe to join him in death within a year. Clement died of dysentery within a month, and about eight months later, Philippe died of unknown causes. This, of, course, lent credence to the rumors that the Templars were adept at witchcraft.

Nor did the revenge end there. In 1789, the dying curse of de Molay re-emerged in the actions of French Freemasons, heirs to the traditions (and perhaps the secrets) of the Knights Templar. These Freemasons were responsible for orchestrating the French Revolution against both the Catholic Church, and the current political state. King Philippe's descendant, Louis XVI, was beheaded before a cheering crowd. As the king's head rolled off the guillotine, a man reportedly leapt onto the scaffold and flung Louis' blood all over the crowd, shouting "Jacques de Molay, thou art avenged!"

In many other ways, too, the Templars lived on. Their secrets and traditions were taken up by the Order of Freemasons, a secret society, derived partially from medieval stonemasons' guilds, which has included many of Europe, England and America's most influential political figures from the seventeenth to the nineteenth centuries. They have largely been given credit for both the French Revolution and the American Revolution, and are thought by many to constitute an international conspiracy that continues to this day. The Freemasons do indeed seem to have embraced ideas that would tend to be associated with the Templars, including "secrets" regarding Solomon's Temple, the Ark of the Covenant, the Holy Grail, and alternative interpretations of both the Old and New Testament, embracing a lot of so-called "apocryphal" legends. They also use a number of the same symbols that the Templars used, including the skull and crossbones, the equilateral cross, and the double-barred Cross of Lorraine. And of course, the Freemasons' approach in general tends to be "occult" and "Gnostic", just like the

Templars, derived from secrets that have purportedly been passed down from ancient Egypt and even earlier, just as the Templar wisdom is said to have been derived. The Freemasons even have entire degrees dedicated to the mythos of the Knights Templar.

Through the aforementioned stonemasons' guilds, which eventually evolved into Masonic lodges, the Templars communicated to the world the secrets they had learned from their excavations of Solomon's Temple - secrets involving sacred geometry and architecture. This resulted in the stunning array of Gothic cathedrals that sprung up across Europe during the Middle Ages and immediately afterward. These cathedrals are like music expressed in architecture, based upon the principle of the Golden Mean, nature's most perfect mathematical proportion, which will be discussed at length later in this book. Within the dimensions of the cathedrals were contained, so they say, the ancient secrets of alchemy, and by the looks of them one can easily imagine that to be true.

Because of their renowned esoteric wisdom, the legend of the Templars has been utilized by a number of other occult groups throughout the centuries. The Rosicrucian Order, an influential element of the Renaissance soon to be discussed, based its own mysteries upon theirs, as did the "Order of New Templars", a neo-pagan white supremacist organization that played a part in the rise of the Third Reich, before being obliterated by that Reich's ironic anti-occult efforts. Even the inner order of the S.S., known as the Black Sun, was patterned after the Templars. Other, more innocuous occult figures have embraced the teachings of the Templars as well, such as H.P. Blavatsky and Rudolf Steiner. Then, of course, there are the numerous neo-Templar orders that proliferate throughout the Western world, mostly social clubs for middle-aged men, all of whom claim a direct pedigree derived from the original order. Without a doubt, the legend of the Templars will live on to seed the fertile plain of the human imagination well into the twenty-first century.

The Templar Conspiracy

For a number of reasons, several books, including *Holy Blood, Holy Grail*, have suggested that a conspiracy has contrived to distort the historical facts regarding the Knights Templar, and indeed, that the creation of the Templars themselves was the result of a conspiracy. One of the facts that seems to have been distorted is the date of the Templars' foundation: 1118. If the historians are correct, the Templars started in that year with nine knights, and did not add to their membership for another nine years. But it is known that by 1126 they had added four new members, so either the date of their foundation is wrong, or the bit about them admitting no new members for nine years is wrong. If the last piece of information is correct, then they would have actually been founded in 1111 or 1112. And there just so happens to be much evidence supporting that idea. For instance, in 1114, the Count of Champagne is known to have received a letter from the Bishop of Chartres regarding his intention to join "The militia of Christ", a nickname for the Templar order. Clearly, then, the existence of the Templars was already well-established.

This count of Champagne seems to have been at the center of the social circle that created the Templars. One-third of the nine knights who founded the Temple were vassals of the Count of Champagne, including Hughes de Payen, their first Grand Master. When the Count himself finally joined in 1124, he was therefore, in a reversal of traditional authority roles, pledging allegiance to one of his own vassals. There are other strange inter-connections as well. The Count also demonstrated his patronage to the Templars' sister order, the Cistercian Monks of Saint Bernard, when in 1115 he donated the land onto which Saint Bernard's Abbey of Clairvaux was built. Saint Bernard was also the nephew of one of the Templars' original nine knights: Andre de Montbard. The court of Champagne, located in Troyes, was furthermore the location of a number of activities with which the Templars were also associated. It was a center for cabalistic studies throughout the Middle Ages, birthplace of the earliest versions of the Grail romances, and the site of some of the Templars' most important holdings.

The authors of *Holy Blood, Holy Grail* indicate that this conspiracy revolved around the treasure of Solomon's Temple - a treasure that they suspect included the so-called "Holy Grail" - and that this conspiracy was primarily composed of descendants of the Grail family, the Merovingians. These are the people who may have been in possession of hereditary secrets regarding the location of the treasure, which must have been the main purpose behind creating the Templars. It was also the reason why King Baldwin II gave them quarters on the Temple Mount, and why they kept so few members for the first nine years - so that it would be easier to protect the secret. The suggestion seems to be that the conspiracy officially began in 1104, during a meeting between the Count of Champagne and a number of nobles from the Brienne, Chaumont, and Joinville families, as well as the "liege lord" of Andre de Montbard. It was immediately after this that the Count of Champagne left on his first trip to the Holy Land. He made another such trip in 1114, apparently desiring to join the Templars, who were already in existence. Upon his return, he donated that land to the Cistercian order mentioned previously. Following this, the holdings of both the Templars and the Cistercians expanded exponentially. The authors of *Holy Blood, Holy Grail* theorized that a conspiracy had been behind the formation and rapid growth of both orders, and that this conspiracy in fact constituted a third order in itself.

This third order, they surmised, seems to have been preoccupied with the Languedoc region of Southern France (where Rennes-le-Chateau is located), and around the Templar preceptory in nearby Bezu. Templar activities in this region came to a head at around 1153 with Bertrand de Blanchefort, whose ancestral home was located in that region. The authors of *Holy Blood, Holy Grail* describe Blanchefort as "the most significant of all Templar Grand Masters", and as a protege of Andre de Montbard. Under Blanchefort's leadership they became highly-trained and organized, as well as a force to be reckoned with in European finance and politics. It was Blanchefort who donated to them the lands near Rennes-le-Chateau and Bezu upon which they built their preceptories. And in 1156, under Blanchefort's direction, a group of Germans were imported into the region by the Templars, purportedly to work in the region's numerous gold mines. As *Holy Blood, Holy Grail* states, "These workers were supposedly subjected to a rigid, virtually military discipline. They were forbidden to fraternize in any way with the local population, and were kept strictly segregated from the surrounding community." But what was all of this secrecy actually for - especially since the gold mines that they were supposedly working in had been emptied by Roman miners during the previous millennium? According to Cesar d'Arcons, an engineer hired to write up a report on the region's mineral deposits some time later, these Templar-employed German miners were not actually mining anything, but were excavating a subterranean crypt.

Whatever it was for which they were digging, they continued to take great pains to preserve the secret for many decades. By the end of the next century, the Templars had been invited by the lord of Bezu and Rennes-le-Chateau to dispatch a special contingent of Templars from Rousillon to Bezu, where they built a lookout post at the top of the mountain. No one knows why, however, since the pilgrim routes that ran through the area were already adequately protected. But as the locals will tell you, even unto this day, the Templars were actually there to guard a treasure - one clearly connected with what those German miners had been doing nearly a century earlier.

It is curious to note, with this in mind, that for reasons unspecified, the Templars stationed at Bezu and Rennes-le-Chateau were the only ones in France who went completely unpersecuted during the raid of 1307. Obviously, these knights had something up their sleeves that rendered them untouchable - a secret of some sort. And this secret was undoubtedly shared by that third, hidden order which I previously mentioned. That order is called the Priory of Sion.

The Priory of Sion

The "Prieure de Sion", or "Priory of Sion (Zion)" first began publicizing itself, in modern times, at least, in 1956, when an explosion of written material regarding Rennes-le-Chateau, the Templars, and the Merovingians began to appear in France. The majority of this material appeared to the authors of *Holy Blood, Holy Grail* to have originated from the same group of people - although credited to divergent and supposedly unrelated authors. Most of these authors appeared to have inside knowledge of the Rennes-le-Chateau affair, and this information was leaked systematically through tantalizing tidbits that served to whet the reader's appetite, and increase the aura of mystery already surrounding the whole affair. In short, it appeared to be "propaganda" which promoted the subject of Rennes-le-Chateau and the Merovingian monarchy on the part of this shadowy organization.

Some of the material appeared in mainstream books, newspapers, and magazines. For example, there was a series of best-selling paperbacks by Gerard de Sede, including *The Accursed Treasure*, written by a man who turned out to be an agent of this shadowy organization. His books were largely based on an informant named Pierre Plantard, the organization's leading figure. The rest of this explosion of materials, which are referred to in *Holy Blood, Holy Grail* as the "Priory Documents", took the form of papers, pamphlets, and privately-published limited edition books and magazines deposited quite purposefully in France's national library, the Bibliotheque Nationale in Paris. Each of these would provide certain pieces of the puzzle which, when put together with the others, would begin to form a fuller, albeit still bewildering picture. Many of these were authored under obvious pseudonyms of symbolic significance, such as Antoine l'Ermite, named after Saint Anthony the Hermit, or "Madeleine Blancassal", derived from the French spelling of "Magdalene" and the names of the "Blanque" and "Sals" rivers, which converge at the village of Rennes-le-Chateau. The work of Ms. Blancassal was said to have been published by Switzerland's foremost Masonic lodge, Grand Loge Alpina. Strangely, the lodge itself denies this, although a researcher hired by the authors of *Holy Blood, Holy Grail* spotted it on the lodge's library shelves.

Other "Priory Documents" (as *Holy Blood, Holy Grail* refers to them) were published under the names of actual people, some of whom died mysteriously shortly after their publication. For instance, there was *Dossiers Secrets* (*Secret Dossiers*), a strange collection of purported data pertaining to the Merovingians and the Priory of Sion. It contained genealogies, letters, newspaper clippings, and other scraps all thrown together, along with commentary from the author, "Henri Lobineau", and some other unnamed commentator. However, within the *Dossiers* themselves it was revealed that "Lobineau" was a pseudonym, and it was claimed that the real author was one Leo Schidlof, who died in 1966. The authors of *Holy Blood, Holy Grail* talked to his daughter, who denied that he had written the *Dossiers*, but said that during his life and especially on the day of his death a number of people had tried to contact him on the subject, which he swore he knew nothing about. Yet *Secret Dossiers* asserted that he had not only written or compiled most of the material in the book, but had also possessed a leather briefcase filled with secret documents pertaining to the Rennes-le-Chateau between 1600 and 1800. The *Dossiers* claimed that shortly before his death M. Schidlof passed the briefcase onto a courier named Fakhar ul Islam, who was supposed to meet in East Germany with an "agent delegated by Geneva" in February 1967, in order to transfer the briefcase to him. However, it is claimed that Fakhar ul Islam was expelled from East Germany before this could occur, and went back to Paris to "await further orders." His body was found on February 20 on the railway tracks at Melan, France, having been thrown from an express train. The details of Mr. Fakhar ul Islam's death turned out to be true, as the discovery of his decapitated body had been reported in the papers the following day. The briefcase, of course, was gone.

One of the most significant "Priory documents" is *Le Serpent Rouge*. This consists of a prose poem, thirteen stanzas in length, each dedicated to one of the houses in the thirteen-house zodiac system used by the Priory of Sion (which I will discuss more later on). It also contained a Merovingian genealogy, two maps of medieval France, and a map of the grounds of the Seminary of Saint Sulpice. The poem, although cryptic, made clear allusions to Rennes-le-Chateau, Mary Magdalene, January 17th, Freemasonry, alchemy, and a host of other subjects pertaining to the mystery at hand. It appeared to provide, in coded language, step by step instructions for discovering the secret of Rennes-le-Chateau. The authors were purported to be named "Louis Saint-Maxent, Pierre Feugere, and Gaston de Koker", three men who, just days after the poem was deposited in the library, were found hanged without explanation.

According to the "Priory Documents", especially those found in the Bibliotheque Nationale, there was indeed another order behind the foundation of the Knights Templar: the Priory of Sion. The purpose of the Priory, which has continued, unlike the Templars, intact unto the present day, was and is the preservation, support, and eventual restoration to the throne of the Merovingian bloodline. In fact, not only are the Merovingians considered by the Priory to still be the rightful kings of France, they are also considered to be eligible for other thrones throughout Europe, as well as that of Jerusalem. This is by virtue of the fact that they passed their divine lineage on, though dynastic intermarriage, to many of Europe's leading royal and noble houses, and most especially to a certain few, including the lines of Blanchefort, Gisors, Saint-Clair/Sinclair, Plantard, Hapsburg, and Lorraine. The Priory, according to the documents, possessed in its day a great deal of clout in the realm of international politics, and it still does today, secretly commanding the allegiance of a number of key individuals in politics, diplomacy, banking and finance - especially in Europe, and especially in France.

The authors of *Holy Blood, Holy Grail* found that there was in fact an Ordre de Sion which resided in Jerusalem at least as early as the turn of the twelfth century - a mere ten years after the supposed foundation of the Order, according to the documents, in 1090. Furthermore, their headquarters was the Abbey of Notre Dame du Mont Sion, an Abbey founded by Godfroi de Bouillon. The Priory Documents state that the Knights Templar were created specifically by the Ordre de Sion, with the help of guiding lights Hughes de Payen, Bisol de Saint Omer, Hughes, Comte de Champagne, and Andre de Montbard (said to have been made a member of the Ordre de Sion, in 1111, the same year in which *Holy Blood, Holy Grail* speculated the Templars to have actually been founded). In 1117, Sion supposedly had Baldwin I, who, they say, "owed his throne" to the Ordre de Sion, negotiate the constitution of the Knights Templar. But as we know, the Templars had already existed in a rudimentary form prior to that.

Baigent, et. al. did find evidence that the historical Ordre de Sion had connections to the Templars, including charters bearing the signature of Hughes de Payen along with those of known members of Sion. Even more convincing, the list of Templar Grand Masters included in *Secret Dossiers* was even more complete and correct than any previously published list, as if drawn from inside information. The authors also found evidence that the group which eventually became the Ordre de Sion had a hand in starting the Crusades in the first place. This group consisted of monks from the Southern Italian region of Calabria who in 1070 migrated to the Ardennes forest, then owned by Godfroi de Bouillon. This same group is mentioned in the works of Gerard de Sede as having been led by the Merovingian Prince Ursus. They were patronized by de Bouillon's aunt and foster mother, Mathilde de Toscan, duchess of Lorraine, who gave them land at Orval, near Stenay, and the site of Dagobert II's assassination. But then in 1108 they vanished completely, and nobody knows where they went. *Holy Blood, Holy Grail,* however, speculates that they may have followed Godfroi de Bouillon on his crusade to the Holy Land, where "he is known to have been accompanied by an entourage of anonymous figures who acted as advisors and administrators." Further, Gerard de Sede wrote that Peter the Hermit, de Bouillon's tutor and one of the main figures behind the undertaking of the Crusades, was a member of the Calabrian monks.

In the *Secret Dossiers*, there is a quote from historian Rene Grousse stating that the kingship of De Bouillon's brother, Baldwin I, rested upon a "royal tradition", itself "founded on the Rock of Zion", which was described as "equal" to that of all European dynasties. This is strange, considering that at that time, Baldwin's office as "King of Jerusalem" was an elected position. But if Baldwin was indeed a descendant of the Merovingians, and thus Christ and King David, this would explain the allusion to the "Rock of Zion", a reference to the sovereignty of David's god-ordained kingship and the divine right of his bloodline to rule. Further, if Baldwin had in fact been installed in his office by an organization which represented that bloodline, it would explain how he "owed his throne" to the Ordre de Sion. This is certainly what it sounds like when contemporary chronicler Guillame de Tyre writes that as soon as Jerusalem had been captured, a secret group of unknown men, one "a certain bishop from Calabria", met to offer the throne of the new kingdom to Godfroi de Bouillon. For whatever reason, he declined the "King" title, but accepted that of "Defender of the Holy Sepulcher", and when he died in 1100, his brother Baldwin gladly accepted the crown.

After this point, the Ordre de Sion is not mentioned again in history until 1152, when King Louis VII of France brought them ninety-five new members and gave them the priory of Saint-Samson at Orleans. Says *Holy Blood, Holy Grail*, of these new members, "twenty-six - two groups of thirteen each - are said to have entered the 'small Priory of the Mount of Sion', situated at Saint-Jean le Blare on the outskirts of Orleans[6]."

In 1188 there was a rift between the Order of Sion and the Order of the Temple. The Templars' current Grand Master, Gerard de Ridefort, had recently lost the Holy Land to the Saracens, and had also committed some kind of unspecified "treason." So in that year, during a ceremony called the "Cutting of the Elm", the Order of Sion officially disavowed the Templars and cut themselves off from them. As the Priory documents state, an event known as the "Cutting of the Elm" did occur at Gisors during that year, although the historical record of this event does not contain any reference to either the Order of Sion or the Knights Templar. It also does not appear to have ever been fully explained. Supposedly, there was an elm tree located in the "Champ Sacre", or "Sacred Field" at Gisors. The authors of *Holy Blood, Holy Grail* write that, "According to medieval chroniclers the site had been deemed sacred since pre-Christian times, and during the twelfth century had provided the setting for numerous meetings between the kings of England and France." The Elm was, as the story goes, the only source of shade on the field. It was more than 800 years old, and "so large that nine men, linking hands could barely encompass its trunk." In 1188, during one of those historic meetings between the French monarch, Philippe II, and the English monarch, Henry II, a skirmish broke out between the two men's armies over the shelter provided by this tree. After three days of negotiations, *Holy Blood, Holy Grail* states that a "full-scale onslaught" ensued. The English "took refuge within the walls of Gisors itself, while the French are said to have cut down the tree in frustration. Philippe II then stormed back to Paris in a huff, declaring that he had not come to Gisors to play the role of woodcutter." Other accounts of the story include some other bizarre details. They say that Philippe announced to Henry that he intended to cut down the tree, and Henry's response was to reinforce the trunk with bands of iron. *Holy Blood, Holy Grail* tells us that:

"...the following day the French armed themselves and formed a phalanx of five squadrons, each accompanied by a distinguished Lord of the realm, who advanced on the elm, accompanied by slingsmen, as well as carpenters equipped with axes and hammers. A struggle is said to have ensued, in which Richard Coeur de Lion, Henry's eldest son and heir, participated, attempting to protect the tree and spilling considerable blood in the process. Nevertheless... the tree was cut down."

After the Cutting of the Elm, the Order de Sion selected a new Grand Master, Jean de Gisors, changed their name to "Prieure de Sion", and adopted an odd nickname, "Ormus", again with the "M" written as the sign for Virgo, with the other four letters written inside of the symbol. "Ormus" is also the name of an Egyptian sage from Alexandria, who in A.D. 46 created an initiative order with the Rose Cross as its insignia. It is significant, then, that in that same year of 1188, the Prieure de Sion also adopted the subtitle "Order de la Rose-Croix Veritas." They kept that bizarre nickname, Ormus, until 1306, the year before the downfall of the Knights Templar in France. In that year, 1307, Sion's Grand Master, Guillaume de Gisors, received the golden head called "Caput 58 ♍" from the Order of the Temple. Apparently then, there was still some degree of cooperation between the two orders. However, it is strongly implied in *Holy*

Blood, Holy Grail that only *some* members of the Temple at that time continued to receive Sion's support, and that the Priory may have actually been involved in the persecution of the Templars. Guillame de Gisors was also close friends with Guillame Pidaye, who participated in King Philippe's raid, indicating that he may have been acting as a double-agent, facilitating the raid on the one hand, and tipping off select Templars in time to escape on the other.

As the years progressed, the Priory itself became the target of Roman Catholic hostilities, albeit in a far less drastic fashion. In 1619, the Priory of Sion was evicted from their house at Saint-Samsom. They had incurred the wrath of the Pope and the King of France for spending extravagantly, boycotting Catholic services and being generally irreverent towards all authority. From that point on, they disappear from the pages of history, at least apparently, until their reemergence in the twentieth century. But in the meantime, the Priory of Sion, according to their own literature, experienced an illustrious series of Grand Masters, or "Nautonniers" (Navigators). Some of these names may be quite familiar to you. The list published in *Secret Dossiers* is as follows:

Prior to "Cutting of the Elm"
Hughes de Payen: 1118 - 1131
Robert de Bourgogne: 1131 - 1150
Bernard de Tremblay: 1150 - 1153
Bertrand de Blanchefort: 1153 - 1170
Janfenders Fulcherine: 1170 - 1171
Francois Othon de Saint Arnand: 1171 - 1179
Theodore de Glaise: 1179 - 1184
Francois Gerard de Ridefort: 1184 - 1190

After the "Cutting of the Elm"
Jean de Gisors: 1188 - 1220
Marie de Saint-Clair: 1220 - 1266
Guillaume de Gisors: 1266 - 1307
Edouard de Bar: 1307 - 1336
Jeanne de Bar: 1336 - 1351
Jean de Saint-Clair: 1351 - 1366
Blanche d'Evreux: 1366 - 1398
Nicolas Flamel: 1398 - 1418
Rene d'Anjou: 1418 - 1480
Ioland de Bar: 1480 - 1483
Sandro Filipepi: 1483 - 1510
Leonardo da Vinci: 1510 - 1519
Connetable de Bourbon: 1519 - 1527
Ferdinand de Gonzague: 1527 - 1575
Louis de Nevers: 1575 - 1595
Robert Fludd: 1595 - 1637
Johann Valentin Andrea: 1637 - 1654
Robert Boyle: 1654 - 1691
Isaac Newton: 1691 - 1727
Charles Radclyffe: 1727 - 1746

Charles de Lorraine: 1746 - 1780
Maximilien de Lorraine: 1780 - 1801
Charles Nodier: 1801 - 1844
Victor Hugo: 1844 - 1885
Claude Debussy: 1885 - 1918
Jean Cocteau: 1918 - 1963

One can see that this list consists of a mixture of noblemen and women, some famous, some not, all of whom possessed Merovingian blood, along with a number of well-known artists, intellectuals and occultists, some of whom are among the most important in history. The authors of *Holy Blood, Holy Grail* were able to identify in each purported Grand Master strains of unorthodox religious thought, as well as other activities consistent with Priory membership, and were also able to establish definitive personal links between each Grand Master, his predecessor, and his successor. According to the Priory's statutes, published in the "Priory documents", the grand mastership is hereditary by default, and electoral in case of vacancy, explaining how even non-bloodliners could obtain the office. However, it is also possible that we do not know the true family history of each of these individuals, and that there may indeed be some "Grail genes" residing within their blood, for it seems unlikely to us that they would have chosen leaders completely outside of the family. This perhaps explains why some of the Grand Masters are listed as having taken office at ages as young as six, and why, of the famous ones, many assumed office prior to achieving their fame. Perhaps it is worth considering whether or not the Priory may have had a hand in the accomplishments that made these people famous. Perhaps these men allowed themselves to be used as pawns in the Priory of Sion's strategic plot for world domination. Once the light of the Holy Grail is shined upon the works and activities that encompassed these men's lives, we can see that behind the familiar facade of history are the unseen hands that have guided the destiny of civilization, manipulating hearts and minds in accordance with some obscure grand plan.

Endnotes

[1] Another word found in that parchment was "Rex Mundi", meaning "King of the World." Rex Mundi was considered by the heretical Cathars who had once occupied the area to be the evil demiurge that had created existence. The significance of this will soon be understood.

[2] The pentagram, of course, is a symbol of Venus, and one of the most recognizable symbols of the occult.

[3] *(Exodus 31:18.)*

[4] *(Psalm 99.)*

[5] For a number of years, most of Portugal's early kings were Grand Masters of this order.

[6] See Appendix A for the significance of the numbers 26 and 13.

Chapter Two: The Underground Stream

"Beneath this marble shaft, as black as coal rises the Fountain of Fortune. He who drinks of it will suffer dire misery. For this spring was brought forth by the sorcerer Vergil, who laid his curse upon it.
- Rene d'Anjou
Le Coeur d'Amours Espris

Nicolas Flamel

The first figure on the list of Grand Masters who is not known to have had royal blood was Nicolas Flamel, owner of a small Parisian bookshop who became one of the fifteenth century's most renowned alchemists. Flamel was intrigued by the concept of alchemy, and longed to get his hands on the fabled *Sacred Book of Abraham the Jew, Prince, Priest and Levite to that Tribe of Jews Who by the Wrath of God were Dispersed Amongst the Gauls* - a book which purported to disclose the secret of the Philosopher's Stone. One night he dreamt that an angel came to him and bequeathed him this book, with the promise that he would "see in it that which no man will be able to see." Shortly afterwards, a cash-strapped student walked into his shop and offered to sell him a copy of the very book in question. Flamel, of course, snapped it up right away.

At first he did not know what to make of it. Bound in copper plating and covered inside and out with symbols completely foreign to this advanced master of the occult, it proved, at first, indecipherable. It remained so for the next twenty-one years, torturing the aging bookseller, until he finally resolved to seek out a Jew conversant in the Cabala who would be capable of reading it. Jews had been expelled from France at that point, so he went to Spain, then a safety zone for both Jewish and Muslim esotericists, under the guise that he was taking a pilgrimage to the Cathedral of Saint James of Compostela. He found no help there, but on the way back, he met a Jewish Cabalist named Maestro Canches, who was able to elucidate for him the key to the book's code. Flamel had not brought the entire book, however, but only a few pages, and agreed to bring the old Jew back with him so that they could decode the rest of the book. Flamel even had him converted to Christianity so that he would not technically be guilty of smuggling a Jew into France. Unfortunately, Maestro Canches died on the trip to Paris. But he had given Flamel the information he needed to be able to decode the rest of the book, and on January 17th (there's that date again) Flamel is said to have transmuted mercury into gold with the use of the Philosopher's Stone.

From that moment on, Flamel lived a comfortable, but not extravagant lifestyle, well beyond the means of most small bookshop owners, obviously having discovered in the Philosopher's Stone the source of perpetual wealth. He and his wife Pernelle opened a new store and founded a number of churches and hospitals, which they decorated with strange, occult symbols derived from *The Book of Abraham the Jew*. He spent the remainder of his life writing treatises on alchemy. But it was only to his wife and his nephew Perrier that he left his testament revealing the secret of the Philosopher's Stone, and then only after his purported death at age 80, in 1418. He was buried at Saint Jacques la Boucherie, where his bookshop was located. On his tombstone were carved a sun, a key, and a closed book. These, along with the other alchemical symbols represented on his various properties, were removed over time by treasure hunters, who attacked his grave and former domains searching for his secrets. One of these persons was said to have found, beneath the foundations of Saint Jacques la Boucherie, vials full of red "projection powder."

As the generations passed, one of the descendants of Flamel's nephew, "Dubois", came into possession of the projection powder, an used it in a magic show he put on for King Louis XIII in which lead balls were changed into gold. Immediately afterwards he was interrogated by an important historical personage named Cardinal Richelieu, who was trying to wrench from him the secret of alchemy. All this resulted in was Richelieu's frustration and Dubois' execution, whereupon Richelieu seized all of his property, as well as that of his illustrious ancestor. Richelieu had Flamel's houses turned inside out in search of secrets and treasure, even opening the man's coffin - which, according to rumor, was found empty. (Indeed, "Flamel sightings" occurred numerous times throughout the centuries following his death.) Richelieu successfully got his hands on *The Book of Abraham the Jew*, and built an alchemical laboratory in which he tried out various experiments. But he was unable to fully interpret the book, and failed to transmute anything. After that most of the text of *The Book of Abraham the Jew* became lost, leaving only the diagrams, which have been published numerous times since.

What is there to indicate that Nicolas Flamel was in fact a member of the Priory of Sion? Well, for one thing, the manner in which he *just happened* to come across *The Book of Abraham the Jew*, which he had been searching for his entire life, and then *just happened* to run across the right man to help him interpret it, is indicative of involvement in a secret society. It was rather like the way in which Berenger Sauniere came across the parchments, and then had them interpreted at Saint Sulpice, after which he, like Flamel, became inexplicably wealthy. Then there is the title of the book itself, *The Book of Abraham the Jew, Prince, Priest and Levite to that Tribe of Jews Who by the Wrath of God Were Dispersed Amongst the Gauls*. This indicates a Prince of a Jewish tribe that became *dispersed* in Gaul, now France. Jesus supposedly fled to Gaul after the crucifixion partially because there already existed a large Jewish and semi-Jewish population in that region, perhaps the remnants of one of Israel's lost tribes. Then there is the fact that Flamel learned the book's secret on a pilgrimage to Saint James of Compostela, the purported burial place of Jesus' brother James. More interesting is that fact that the pilgrim route to Saint James of Compostela passes very near Rennes-le-Chateau. Then, of course, there is the date of the first presumed alchemical transmutation, January 17th - the date of Sauniere's stroke, Marie de Blanchefort's death, and the Feast Day of Saint Sulpice. Then there is the absolute secrecy with which Flamel guarded the key to the Philosopher's Stone, only divulging it to family - his wife and his nephew. And finally, there are the actions of Cardinal Richelieu, indicating that he knew for a fact that Flamel was in the possession of a real secret.

Interestingly, Cardinal Richelieu is discussed extensively in *Holy Blood, Holy Grail*. During the 1600s, he constituted the real power behind Louis XIII's throne. And in 1633, out of a desire to wrench Southern France from the influence of Spain and Austria, he brought France into the Thirty Years War against those two nations (who represented the Catholic side of the conflict), in favor of the Protestant armies of Sweden and Germany (whose leader, Elector Frederick, Palatinate of the Rhine, was strongly supported by the Rosicrucian thinkers of the time). This is a strange position for a Catholic

Cardinal to take, and the authors of *Holy Blood, Holy Grail* indicate that Richelieu may have been a Rosicrucian himself – which might mean that he was connected with the Priory of Sion for whom the Rosicrucian order may have been simply a front. Perhaps when Richelieu raided Flamel's domains, he was just acting as an agent of the Priory, attempting to repossess property that was rightfully theirs. Or perhaps he was a double-agent.

Rene d'Anjou

The next *Nautonnier* on Sion's list worth examining is Rene d'Anjou. Though little known today, Rene d'Anjou was one of the most influential figures of the Renaissance, and came to assume a huge collection of titles, including: Count of Bar, Provence, Piedmont and Guise, Duke of Calabria, Anjou, and Lorraine, and King of Hungary, Naples, and Sicily, Aragon, Valencia, Majorca, Sardinia, and Jerusalem; the last being titular, inherited from his ancestor, Godfroi de Bouillon through the House of Lorraine. Rene has been credited with inventing the double-barred Cross of Lorraine, associated with his ruling house and later the French Resistance movement, but the Templars were known to have used it at least 200 years earlier, and it can probably be traced back further as well. Rene was born on January 16, 1408, in the Lorraine castle at Angers. In 1419, at the age of ten, he was married to Isabel of Anjou, then nine. It was also at this time that Rene was installed as Grand Master of the Priory of Sion. Given Rene's Angevin ancestry, it is natural that he would have been chosen for such an august position, even at a tender age. His uncle, Louis, Cardinal of Bar, was his regent for another ten years, until he was ready to become the helmsman of the order than would become the most influential factor in his hugely significant life. Rene also belonged to some other fraternal orders, including the Order of the White Greyhound, the Order of the Fidelity, and his own self-created chivalrous Order of the Ship and Double Crescent (a revision of the Order of the Crescent created by Louis IX) - which for some reason was suppressed by the Pope.

In 1415, Rene's sister Mary was married to the Dauphin of France, later King Charles VII. Charles' father had been recently overthrown by King Henry V of England, who then proclaimed himself Regent of France and married the Dauphin's sister, Katherine de Valois. The French were under the domination of the English, but a ray of hope came in the form of Jeanne d'Arc[1]. She first appeared in 1429 at the fortress of Valcouleurs, announcing her divine mission to deliver France from the English overlords, thereby fulfilling an old prophecy by Merlin about a maid from Lorraine who would be sent by God to liberate France. This, she claimed, would require her to visit the Dauphin at his court at Chinon. Instead of requesting that the commandant at Valcouleurs escort her there, she specifically asked for Rene d'Anjou, entreating his father-in-law, the Duke of Anjou, for "your son, a horse, and some good men to take me into France." This implies that she already had Rene in mind. It was Rene's mother, Iolande d'Anjou, who took Jeanne d'Arc under her wing, convincing the court and the Dauphin that she was in fact the prophesized "Maid of Lorraine." Iolande even officiated over the examination to ensure her virginity, which made a very dramatic scene in the Joan of Arc film, *The Messenger*. In the end, it was Rene who accompanied Jeanne to Chinon, and he is said to have been by her side at the siege of Orleans. He also led the main battle at Senlis and was one of Jeanne's captains at the siege of Paris. Some contemporary chroniclers even wrote that the two were lovers. It was Rene whom King Charles VII sent to inform a deflated Jeanne that the siege of Paris was being withdrawn. Afterwards she was captured, sold to the English, convicted of heresy for claiming to speak to God, and then burnt at the stake. It is said that she clutched a Cross of Lorraine at her breast as she prepared to die. All of this seems to indicate that the appearance of the Maid of Lorraine was something orchestrated by the House of Lorraine from the very beginning, with full consent from all parties. But as the authors Michael Baigent, Richard Leigh and Henry Lincoln write, "In the centuries that followed, a systematic attempt seems to have been made to expunge all trace of Rene's possible role in Jeanne's life."

In 1431, Rene inherited the Duchy of Lorraine from his father-in-law, but was imprisoned in Dijon when the Duke of Burgundy staked a rival claim to his inheritance. He was eventually freed with the help of his wife, Isabel, but not before leaving his own two children behind as hostages for the next three years! Rene developed an interest in painting that would last a lifetime, and is known to have decorated one of the rooms in the castle that was his prison. Later, when Rene and Isabel became the Duke and Duchess of Lorraine, court was held at their castles throughout Anjou and Provence. These courts included Jewish cabalists, astrologers and even the physician Jean de Saint-Remy, grandfather of Nostradamus. In fact, Christopher Columbus was a member of the court for a while, and Rene was the person who gave him his first ship's commission to Tunis.

Rene's court would hold constant soirees, poetry readings, mystery plays, and "allegorical" knightly tournaments called "pas d'armes", a combination of battle and pre-scripted play. Rene established rules and traditions for knighthood, chivalry and jousting which are still observed by chivalrous orders and anachronistic societies today. He wrote a couple of books on the subject, one being *Livre des Tournies,* or *Manual for the Perfect Organization of Tournies,* which includes things like how to make a challenge, how to correctly display banners, and how to show ladies proper respect. The other was called *Battles and the Order of Knighthood and the Government of Princes.* Today this rests in the library of Lord William Sinclair and bears the names "Jesus - Mary - John" on the cover - names, we now know, of some of Rene's biblical ancestors. The court manifested a fairy tale-like legend around itself, as it perpetuated the stories of the Holy Grail, King Arthur, Tristan and Isolde, etc. Rene was preoccupied in particular with the Grail story, and is known to have collected "Grail cups." His favorite possession was a red crystal goblet of Egyptian origin which he believed had been used by Jesus and Mary Magdalene during their wedding at Cana. An inscription on the side of the cup read: "He who drinks well will see God. He who quaffs at a single drop will see God and the Magdalene."

Rene d'Anjou's influence on the European culture of the Renaissance was so great that we might wish to call it the "Rene-sance." He befriended Cosimo de Medici while in Italy, and many believe him to have been the impetus for a number of important decisions made by de Medici during this time. These include: the founding of Europe's first public library in San Marco in 1444, which was loaded with rare manuscripts on neo-Platonic, Pythagorean, Gnostic and Hermetic thought; the instruction of the University of Florence to begin teaching Greek; and the creation of an academy for the study of Pythagoras and Plato, which sparked a number of other, similar institutions. Rene is also credited with introducing into this intellectual renaissance the theme of

"Arcadia", the Greek Paradise. In his court at Tarascon, Rene staged *The Pas d'Armes of the Shepherdess*. The Shepherdess in the play was his mistress at the time, who, according to Baigent, et. al in *Holy Blood Holy Grail*, was, "an explicitly Arcadian figure, embodying both romantic and philosophical attributes." She presided over a tournament fought by knights who represented conflicting ideals which must be reconciled - a very Hermetic concept. Rene also displayed other Arcadian themes in his famous paintings, depicting himself standing next to a tombstone[2]. The presence of a tomb is also implied in his painting *Le Fountaine de Fortune*, which was an illustration from his illuminated manuscript, *Les Coeur d'Amours Espris* (*The Book of the Heart Possessed by Love.*) In this picture, the "fountain" mentioned in the title looks distinctly like a tombstone, and it is the source of an "underground stream", Alpheus (from the Greek for "source"). Alpheus is a real river in Arcadia, Greece, and it really does go underground, re-emerging at the Fountain of Arethusa in Spain. Hermetically, this river represents an "underground stream" of secret knowledge passed down through the "subterranean" Grail families and the organizational offshoots of the Priory of Sion.

Rene married his second wife, Jeanne of Laval, in 1454, and stayed with her until he died at Aix-la-Chappelle on July 10, 1480, leaving behind a huge and carefully organized library. The tombstone that he had chosen for his burial at the Church of Saint Maurice was rather odd, as it was surmounted by a painting he had made showing a dying, half-skeletal king sitting on a throne, holding a scepter and orb, his crown slipping off of his head as it leans to the side. It is fitting that a man who had much worldly power, and yet was so spiritually adept, was so comfortable with his own inevitable mortality.

Iolande de Bar

Rene's daughter, Iolande de Bar, followed him as Grand Master of the Priory. She had married Ferri, Lord of Sion-Vaudemont, who was also a member of Rene d'Anjou's Order of the Crescent. Iolande turned Sion-Vaudemont into a holy site for the region of Lorraine - or rather, she returned to it the holy status it had enjoyed since pre-Christian times. It had once been the location of a statue of the Teutonic goddess Rosemerthe, and during the early Christian era it was known by the Judaic-sounding name Mount Semita. During the reign of the Merovingians it had housed a statue of the Virgin, and this statue had once been declared "Sovereign of the Comte de Vaudemont", as well as the "Protectress of Lorraine." A festival for the "Queen of Heaven" was held there every year, and at least as early as the 14th century there was, centered in Sion-Vaudemont, a secret society called the "Confraternity of Chevaliers of Sion", which originated at the abbey on Mt. Sion in Jerusalem, and would appear to be the same as the Priory of Sion.

Sandro Filipepi

Following Iolande on the list of Nautonniers is Sandro Filipepi, better known as the artist Botticelli. He is most famous for his much-copied depiction of *The Birth of Venus*, garbed with nothing but her flowing red hair, rising from the half-shell. One of his biggest patrons was Georges Antoine Vespucci, tutor to Rene d'Anjou's grandson Rene. He also studied under two masters whom Rene d'Anjou had patronized, Filippo

Lippi and Mantegna - as well as under Verrocchio, an alchemist and Hermeticist whom Leonardo da Vinci (the Grand Master who followed Botticelli at the Priory) would himself study under. And although Botticelli is not known to have had Merovingian blood, those who patronized him did, including members of the Medici and Gonzague families.

Botticelli was part of the "neo-Platonic" movement popular during his age, which sought to resurrect classical aesthetics and revitalize the myths of ancient Greece and Rome, as well as the ancient precepts of Hermeticism and sacred geometry, by incorporating them into new art forms, often depicting them under the guise of Roman Catholic symbolism. He also repeatedly featured the theme of the "underground stream" in his work. In the center of *Madonna of the Magnificat* is a winding river issuing from a clearly subterranean source. Similar streams are prominently displayed in *Celestial Annunciation*, and hidden in the background of *Adoration of the Magi*. Botticelli was clearly an occultist, and based most of his paintings on a pentagonal grid. He is also a likely candidate for the designer of the first deck of tarot cards - the other being his tutor, Mantegna.

Leonardo da Vinci

One of the most audacious claims made on the list of Priory Grand Masters is that Leonardo da Vinci followed Botticelli in the assumption of that office. As one of the most brilliant minds in known history, this accomplished painter, sculptor, sketch artist, architect, scientist and inventor embodied the definition of the term "Renaissance man", and would make a proud addition to any organization's membership. He had been friends with the previous Grand Master, both having been apprenticed to Verrocchio and patronized by the Medici, Este and Gonzague families. Leonardo also had a patron in Francesco Sforza, a founding member of Rene d'Anjou's Order of the Crescent, and one of Rene's best friends.

It is now known, and was known at the time, that Leonardo was a bit eccentric in his religious and philosophical beliefs - heretical, even. He appears to have endorsed an old Christian heresy stating that Jesus had a twin brother named Thomas. This belief would seem to be illustrated in Da Vinci's *The Last Supper*, where one of Christ's disciples is depicted bearing an uncanny resemblance to Christ himself. Also, the depiction of Saint John sitting next to him looks decidedly female, perhaps a covert acknowledgement of Christ's marriage to Mary Magdalene. The authors of *Holy Blood, Holy Grail* also felt that this theme was illustrated by a sketch of Da Vinci's called *The Virgin with Saint John the Baptist and Saint Anne*. In the book *The Templar Revelation*, authors Lynn Picknett and Clive Prince further ascribe to Leonardo a belief in the Johannite heresy, which states that John the Baptist was, in fact, the true Christ, and Jesus a usurper. This cult they identified with a gesture, made with the right index finger pointing skyward and the palm facing inward, which can be found depicted in numerous works of Da Vinci's, and in the works of other Renaissance artists as well, always associated with John. In the same book the authors theorize that Leonardo may have, in fact, created the famed relic the Shroud of Turin as a hoax, using a then unknown photographic technique which he may very well have invented.

The Campaign Against the House of Valois

During the sixteenth century, the Priory of Sion and the Grail families, including the houses of Guise and Lorraine, embarked on a conspiracy to oust the ruling Valois dynasty and reclaim the French throne for Merovingian blood. The conspiracy spanned three generations, and the terms of three Priory of Sion Grand Masters: Connetable de Bourbon (a.k.a. Charles de Montpensier), Ferdinand de Gonzague, and Louis de Nevers. The plot came closest to fruition between 1550 and 1570 due to the efforts of Charles, cardinal of Lorraine, and his brother Francois, duke of Guise. They were both cousins of Connetable de Bourbon and relatives of the Gonzague family, each of which provided financial and moral support for the Lorraine cause. Although historians have characterized the two brothers as cruel and fanatical Catholics, *Holy Blood, Holy Grail* describes them as opportunists who took advantage of both Catholic and Protestant factions whenever it suited them. As the book describes, "In 1562... the Council of Trent, the cardinal of Lorraine launched an attempt to decentralize the papacy - to confer autonomy on local bishops and restore the ecclesiastical hierarchy to what it had been in Merovingian times."

By the following year, Francois de Guise was within reach of the French throne, when he was quite suddenly assassinated. The cardinal of Lorraine died a dozen years later, but the conspiracy continued with the next cardinal of Lorraine and the next duke of Guise. At the helm of this conspiracy was Priory of Sion Navigator Louis de Gonzague, duke of Nevers, and the banner they employed was the Cross of Lorraine. The conspirators succeeded in exterminating the Valois line, but ironically, by that point the House of Guise was itself near extinction, and could not bring forth a legitimate candidate for kingship.

Nostradamus

Besides the known members of the Priory of Sion, there were others who throughout the generations lent their hands in assistance to their cause. According to the Priory documents and Gerard de Sede, this included the famous prophet Nostradamus, astrologer to the French court, and an advisor to Catherine de Medici (the mother of Mary, Queen of Scots). He most certainly would have been in a position to: (a) pass along sensitive information to the Priory that he may have been told or overheard, and in particular (b) provide the French court with faulty astrological predictions that would have worked to the conspirators' advantage. In fact, Nostradamus' famous quatrains may not even have been prophecies, but instead secret messages for the Priory of Sion, descriptions of past events, or plans for future machinations pertaining to their conspiratorial plot. As *Holy Blood, Holy Grail* puts it:

"...there is no question that some of Nostradamus' prophecies were not prophecies but referred, quite explicitly, to the past - to the Knights Templar, the Merovingian dynasty, the history of the house of Lorraine. A striking number of them refer to Razes - the old comte of Rennes-le-Chateau. And the numerous quatrains that refer to the advent of 'le Grand Monarch'... indicate that this sovereign will derive ultimately from the Languedoc[3]."

Nostradamus seems to have been admitting that there was more than met the eye in regards to his gift of prophecy when he described it as, "An emotional tendency inherited from a line of ancestors." Perhaps his ancestors and the ancestors of the Merovingians were one and the same.

Gerard de Sede had a number of details to add regarding Nostradamus' relationship with the Grail families and the Priory of Sion. He says that before Nostradamus became famous as a prophet, he spent a great deal of time in the Lorraine region, and that this was a sort of probationary period, following which he was initiated into the Priory's secrets. As the story goes, he was shown a very secret, very ancient book, which provided the basis for his subsequent "prophecies." This book was shown to him at the Abbey of Orval, which had been donated by Godfroi de Bouillon's foster mother, and which, according to *Holy Blood, Holy Grail*, was the birthplace of the Priory of Sion. Up until the period of the French Revolution, books of prophecies attributed to Nostradamus continued to issue from Orval.

Robert Fludd

The next Nautonnier on the list after Louis de Nevers was Robert Fludd, known as the "John Dee of the 15th century[4]." He was one of the more formative influences on the body of esoteric thought that is now called "Western magic": including alchemy, cabala and Hermeticism. Although not publicly known to have been a member of the then-developing Rosicrucian brotherhood, he did write that that the "Magia, Cabala and Alchymia of the Brothers of the Rosy Cross" was of the "highest good." He was a prominent member of the London College of Physicians, and was patronized by both James I and Charles I, from whom he rented land in Suffolk. And perhaps most amazingly, Fludd was on the committee that determined the translation of the King James Bible.

Robert Fludd's father had been friends with the Priory's previous Grand Master, Louis de Nevers, and had sent Robert to study at Oxford, which John Dee had attended and there formed a secret society of student occultists. After Oxford, Fludd traveled the continent, and met with a number of influential members of the Rosicrucian movement. Then in 1602, he was commissioned to tutor Henry of Lorraine's sons, especially Charles, duke of Guise. He continued his relationship with Charles for the next twenty years. By then Charles had married Henriette-Catherine de Joyeuse, whose possessions included Couiza and Arques, right near Rennes-le-Chateau.

It was during and immediately after this time that the Priory plot to seize the French throne for Merovingian blood took a new turn - with the new claimant to the office issuing not from Guise, but from its sister house: that of Lorraine. Their candidate was Gaston d'Orleans, Louis XIII's younger brother, who had married the duke of Lorraine's sister. Among his supporters was Charles, duke of Guise. Although the attempted deposition of King Louis failed, the monarch confronted another problem, which favored his opposition - his inability to produce a child. But then in 1638, twenty-three years into a childless marriage, his wife, Anne of Austria, suddenly became pregnant. According to both contemporary and subsequent rumors, the true father was also the true power behind the throne: Cardinal Richelieu, mentioned previously in the section on Nicolas Flamel. Another theory states that it was Richelieu's successor, Cardinal Mazarin, and that he and Anne were secretly married after Louis XIII's death.

The Fronde and the Compagnie du Saint-Sacrament

The birth of the "king's son" ruined Gaston d'Orleans' bid for the throne, but it sparked the beginning of a civil war that would continue off and on for the next decade, known as the Fronde - an attempt to remove Cardinal Mazarin and Louis XIV from their positions. This civil war, consisting largely of highly-orchestrated "popular uprisings", was sponsored by the same families associated with the Grail blood and the Priory of Sion that have consistently been the instigators behind our entire story. And for their headquarters these "frondeurs" chose the ancient Merovingian capitol of Stenay, near the location of Dagobert II's assassination, as though they were making the statement that the ultimate aim of the plot was in fact the avengement of Dagobert's death.

The "Priory documents" state that during the Fronde years, the Priory "dedicated itself to opposing Mazarin." As the documents say, it did so under the facade of another fraternal organization, one acknowledged by history to have been at the forefront of the Fronde - the Compagnie du Saint-Sacrement. The documents state that the Priory of Sion *was* the Compagnie de Saint-Sacrement.

History tells us that the Compagnie was formed around 1629 by a close associate of Gaston d'Orleans, although he is the only founding member who is known. The rest of the group's upper hierarchy were anonymous, and even the low-ranking members did not know who they were. Of these lower-ranking members, some of them have been named: the duchess of Longueville's brother, the bishop of Alet (near Rennes-le-Chateau); Charles Fouquet (brother of the Superintendent of Finances, whose other brother wrote that letter to Nicolas Poussin mentioned previously); Saint Vincent de Paul (to be discussed later); and Jean-Jacques Olier, founder of the Seminary of Saint Sulpice, which was used as the Compagnie's headquarters. The members did not understand or question the orders they were given, and they were not permitted to communicate with one another. The main thing that bonded them together was a mysterious and elusive secret, what chroniclers referred to as "the Secret which is at the core of the Compagnie." The order's own statutes state that, "The primary channel which shapes the spirit of the Compagnie, and which is essential to it, is the Secret."

The purpose behind the Compagnie has been, to historians, completely confusing. On the surface, it claimed to be devoted to charitable work, but underneath the surface, it was much more devoted to spying on behalf of the frondeurs, and infiltrating the upper echelons of government, nearly dominating, at times, the parliament, judiciary, and police, as well as holding key positions in the king's cabinet. Saint Vincent de Paul was made confessor to Louis XIII, and Anne of Austria was, for a period, completely malleable in the hands of the Compagnie, who managed to turn her against Mazarin for a brief span.

Another ambiguous aspect of the Compagnie was their religious affiliation. Historians present the Compagnie as representing rigidly conservative Catholicism, and as being devoted to eliminating "heresy." Yet many of the group's known members were Protestants. Furthermore, why should such an organization be opposed to arch-Catholic Mazarin? And if it was heresy they were against, why did the Catholic hierarchy of the time refer to the Compagnie as heretical it itself? They were charged, quite reminiscent of the Templars, of "impious practices", and bizarre, unnatural initiation ceremonies. Some of them were even threatened with excommunication, a threat which did not seem to faze these supposed "arch-Catholics."

Even though Cardinal Mazarin and Louis XIV had rallied against them for years, the Compagnie du Saint-Sacrement carried on as normal, well past 1660, when the king finally ordered their dissolution. But in 1665, they concluded, according to the "Priory documents", that they could not continue in their "present form", and withdrew from public light, recalling all of their official documents and sealing them away in Saint Sulpice. The authors of *Holy Blood, Holy Grail* point out that these documents would then have been available to the decoder of the Rennes-le-Chateau parchments, Emile Hoffet, later on. But in one form or another, the Compagnie is known to have operated into the next century, tormenting Louis XIV, and some say it continued into the 1900s. They were mentioned in a negative context by the royally patronized writer Moilere in his play *Le Tartuffe*, and the Compagnie actually used its conspiratorial ties to have the play suppressed for the next two years. Meanwhile, the Compagnie had its own literary propagandists in La Rochefoucald and La Fontaine, both known members of the Fronde and the Compagnie who used allegorical satire to attack the king. And in the case of La Fontaine, the king attacked back, attempting to bar his entrance to the Academie Francaise, the French literary academy. Interestingly, La Fontaine was patronized by the duke of Guise, the duke of Bouillon, and Gaston d'Orleans' widow.

Johann Valentin Andrea and the Rosicrucians

Holy Blood, Holy Grail theorizes that the Compagnie may also have been connected to the then-developing Rosicrucian brotherhood, which was at that time being led by current Priory of Sion Grand Master, Johann Valentin Andrea. The flames of Rosicrucianism were then being fanned by Andrea's *Rosicrucian Manifestos*, and *The Chemical Wedding of Christian Rosenkreutz*, both published anonymously, although Andrea later confessed to writing them "as a joke." *Chemical Wedding*, however, reads less like a joke and more like a complex web of Hermetic, alchemical and astrological symbolism, coupled with veiled allusions to political and religious conflicts then occurring. Written from the perspective of the Rosicrucian brotherhood's legendary namesake, it incorporates neo-Platonic allegory, elements of the myths of Osiris, Venus, Deucalion, Atlas, and many others, as well as allusions to a mysterious "Princess" whose office must be restored. And like the Knights Templar, Rosenkreutz supposedly wore a white tunic and mantle with a red cross.

As a whole, the *Rosicrucian Manifestos*, which allegedly issued from an "invisible" secret society in France and Germany, predicted a new golden age of Heaven on Earth, an Arcadian paradise worthy of Rene d'Anjou's imaginings - a world order reflecting harmonious cosmic laws in which the spirit of man would be freed to pursue its God-given destiny. They also, sometimes allegorically, sometimes not, railed against the Roman Catholic Church and its worldly kingdom, the Holy Roman Empire. For this reason, Rosicrucianism was hated and suppressed by the Catholic hierarchy, while the Protestant movement embraced it.

Rosicrucianism was embraced by another figure associated with Protestantism. whom Johann Valentin Andrea was related to by blood: Frederick of the Palatinate, a man whose genealogy tied in with those of the Grail families, and whose ideals would seem to be identical to theirs. After marrying Elizabeth Stuart, daughter of James I of England, he established a court in the capitol of Heidelberg, which was formed, shall we say, along "Hermetic lines." Frances Yates, as quoted by *Holy Blood, Holy Grail*, explains what developed from this:

"A culture was forming in the Palatinate which came straight out of the Renaissance but with more recent trends added, a culture which may be defined as 'Rosicrucian.' The prince around whom these deep currents were swirling was Friedrich, Elector Palatine, and their exponents were hoping for a politico-religious expression of their aims... The Frederickian movement... was an attempt to give those currents politico-religious expression, to realise the ideal of Hermetic reform centered on a real prince... It... created a culture, a 'Rosicrucian' state with its court centered on Heidelberg."

It was Frederick's actions on behalf of the Rosicrucian movement, becoming the monarch of the rebelling nation of Bohemia, against the wishes of the Holy Roman Empire, that led to the Thirty Years' War between the Catholics and the Protestants - a war which would devastate Europe. It was in the midst of all of this that Johann Valentin Andrea organized a network of "Christian Unions", made up of groups of thirteen individuals per union. Each member was expected to be an expert in one or another field of knowledge. The aim of the Unions was to preserve science, philosophy, Hermeticism, and other knowledge threatened by a Catholic church then busy persecuting heretics. They also provided safe houses for the heretics themselves, and acted as smuggling rings, helping those Protestants, freethinkers and esotericists then fleeing the Inquisition escape to England. There they found a refuge, for British Freemasonry was just then in its formation, and many of the exiled heretics fell in with the "Invisible College" of occultists, including Robert Moray, Elias Ashmole and Robert Boyle, which is yet to be discussed. There is even evidence that Freemasonry itself was partially derived in structure from the Christian Unions, and in substance from the Rosicrucian mysteries. To this day there is a degree in Scottish Rite Freemasonry called "Knight Rose Croix."

Chateau Barberie

Another bone of contention that the Grail families had against Cardinal Mazarin, according to the "Priory documents", was his razing of Chateau Barberie, near Nevers, in the Nivernais region. It had been the official residence of the Plantard family after Jean de Plantard, a direct descendant of Dagobert II, married Marie de Saint-Clair of the aforementioned Saint-Clair/Gisors family in 1548. But by 1659, Mazarin, who had an unexplained obsession with possessing Nevers, finally bought the entirety of Nivernais on July 11, the date on which the "Priory documents" state that Chateau Barberie was burned to the ground. The authors of *Holy Blood, Holy Grail* found evidence to substantiate this story, but they also found evidence to suggest that Mazarin had taken lengths to remove these facts, and the existence of Barberie itself, from the historical record.

Nicolas Poussin and Nicolas Fouquet

Cardinal Mazarin found another enemy in the figure of Nicolas Fouquet, the aforementioned Superintendent of Finances to Louis XIV who, according to *Holy*

Blood, Holy Grail, was "the wealthiest and most powerful individual in the kingdom", and "was sometimes called the true king of France." He also planned to take over Brittany and become the duke of an independent duchy. His mother and brother Charles were both members of the Compagnie du Saint-Sacrement, and Charles was the archbishop of Narbonne, located in the Languedoc. In 1656, Nicolas Fouquet, for some unknown reason, sent his brother Louis, a priest, to Rome. It was on this occasion that Louis wrote the letter quoted previously, alleging that he had learned a secret from Nicolas Poussin which "even kings would have great pains to draw from him."

Whether or not kings managed to draw the secret from him, King Louis XIV certainly caught wind that something was up, and that it had something to do with Nicolas Poussin. For in 1661, he had Nicolas Fouquet arrested on murky charges of "sedition", and "misappropriation of funds." He seized all of Fouquet's property, and insisted on solely, personally, privately going through Fouquet's papers and documents himself.

Meanwhile, the prosecution of Fouquet became the "trial of the century", lasting for four years, with public opinion split, during which time the brother, Louis Fouquet, died. The Compagnie du Saint-Sacrement used all powers available to them, including the membership of one of Fouquet's judges in their order, to try to get the charges dismissed, or the sentence demanded (death) diminished. The court finally decided on eternal banishment as an appropriate punishment. King Louis, furious, had the entire panel of judges replaced with those he found more compliant. They still refused to put Fouquet to death, and sentenced him instead to life in prison. The king then dictated the conditions. He was kept in what we would now call "solitary confinement", where he could neither write nor speak, and the soldiers guarding him were forbidden to talk to him on penalty of death. Some authors theorize that Fouquet was in fact the "Man in the Iron Mask."

Coincidentally, in 1665, the same year in which Nicolas Fouquet was imprisoned, Nicolas Poussin died. For the next twenty years, King Louis jockeyed for possession of what he regarded as Poussin's most important work: *The Shepherds of Arcadia*. When he finally got a hold of it, he did not put it on public display, but hid it away in his private quarters, and let no one view it without his expressed permission.

Curiously, although Nicolas Fouquet went down in disgrace, his grandson became the Marquis of Belle-Isle and, as *Holy Blood, Holy Grail* puts it, "the single most important man in France." In 1718 he traded Bell-Isle to the King of France, and received in return the duchies of Longueville and Gisors, both locations associated with families of Merovingian blood. Twenty-four years later, Gisors, with Fouquet as its duke, was declared a "premiere duchy."

Not far from Gisors is Les Andelys, the small town in which, in 1594, Nicolas Poussin was born. Early in his career he moved to Rome, only returning once to France, in the 1640s, under orders from Cardinal Richelieu, who had hired him to do a special job. Poussin's correspondence and papers reveal that, from the safety of Rome, he was heavily involved in the Fronde. He was also a keeper of secrets. His personal motto, with which he would sign his autograph, was "Tenet Confidentiam."

The Poussin work in question, *The Shepherds of Arcadia*, did not just spontaneously generate. It was based on an earlier painting of his, *Et in Arcadia Ego*, containing the same elements, which was itself based on a painting also called *Et in Arcadia Ego* by Giovanni Francesco Guercino, dating from 1618. Poussin's version of *Et in*

Arcadia Ego includes the river god Alpheus, also the name of the "underground stream" of Rene d'Anjou's Arcadia, which set the precedent upon which both of these artists had designed their paintings. All three works - the two *Et in Arcadia Ego*s and *The Shepherds of Arcadia* - contain the shared elements of a tomb, shepherds, and the phrase "Et in Arcadia Ego."

In his own illustrations Rene d'Anjou had depicted the underground stream in Arcadia issuing from something that looks somewhat like a tomb. The skull in Guercino's painting is a motif used, among other things, in the mysteries of the Knights Templar and the Freemasons. Interestingly, in the painting, the skull appears to have been trepanned in the manner of the Merovingian kings. It is also interesting to note that Masonic themes can be found throughout Guercino's other works, even though Masonry as a formal institution was not yet in existence. One, called *The Raising of the Master*, even depicts the story of Hiram Abiff, architect of Solomon's Temple, who is such an important figure in Freemasonry.

The phrase "Et in Arcadia Ego", seemingly ambiguous in meaning, would appear to have been a sort of code during this time period for those "in the know" - members of the Priory of Sion and those with knowledge of their secrets. The concept of Arcadia as a Hermetic ideal seems to have been implicit, symbolizing the hope for a new order based on cosmic principles of divine order, the kind of world of which the Rosicrucians spoke. It is always associated with a mysterious ancient tomb of unknown import, as if the world for which they hoped was in fact the rebirth of a world that had once existed in the far-distant past, the "golden age" of which the ancients spoke. The phrase "Et in Arcadia Ego" has also been, according to the "Priory documents", on the official device and family crest of the house of Plantard since around the 13th century, when Jean de Plantard married Iodine de Gisors.

Robert Boyle

Johan Valentin Andrea's grand mastership was followed by that of Robert Boyle. He was the so-called "father of modern chemistry" who was among the earliest to theorize upon the existence and structure of the atom, and who was one of the most renowned intellectuals of the Age of Enlightenment. His father was the Earl of Cork, and he himself was offered peerage, but turned it down. His provost at Eton College, which he attended, was part of the circle surrounding Frederick of the Palatinate. After completing school, Boyle toured Europe, including the Medici dominated city of Florence, then a haven for esotericists, scientists and philosophers persecuted in more Catholic-dominated lands. He also spent nearly two years in Geneva, where he studied demonology and occultism. There he acquired a book called *The Devil of Mascon*, which he hired his friend Pierre du Moulin, son of Catherine de Bar's personal chaplain, to translate.

When his European tour was completed, he returned to England, and there fell in with a social set surrounding Johann Andrea's good friend, Samuel Hartlib. It was at this time that he began to write letters to friends referring to the "Invisible College", which sounded, from his description, like a powerful secret society of initiates into the occult mysteries, much like the Rosicrucians. He even specified in one letter that, "the cornerstones of the Invisible College or (as they term themselves) the Philosophical College, do now and then honour me with their company." It is entirely possible that this was a reference to his induction into the Priory of Sion.

In the 1650s, Robert Boyle spent much time at Oxford with Frederick of the Palatinate's former chaplain, John Wilkin. In 1660, with the dismantling of Oliver Cromwell's anti-monarchist Protectorate, the monarchy was restored and the Stuarts of Scotland, direct descendants of Merovingian blood, were once again the kings of both Scotland and England. It was around this time that, as *Holy Blood, Holy Grail* theorizes, the Priory of Sion might have transferred the bulk of its efforts and loyalties away from the French branches of the Grail family, like the House of Lorraine, and onto the House of Stuart. When Charles II came to power, Robert Boyle was one of his first and most outspoken supporters. Charles II also became the Head of the Royal Society, a conclave of scientists and intellectuals with official royal patronage. Most of the members of the Royal Society were Freemasons, and most coupled their scholarly pursuits with esoteric ones, making the Royal Society appear to be much like the "Invisible College" which Robert Boyle, one of the society's most prominent members, had previously described. He became an even more prominent member of the society after 1668, when he moved permanently to London, residing with his sister - wife to one of Johann Valentin Andrea's good fiends, John Dury. Here, Robert Boyle entertained some very important guests, such as Cosimo III de Medici, soon to be ruler of Florence and grand duke of Tuscany.

But Boyle's most frequent visitors were the philosopher John Locke and the scientist Isaac Newton, the latter of whom would follow him as Grand Master of the Priory of Sion. With Newton, the relationship revolved largely around alchemy, which Boyle had supposedly taught Newton the secrets of. For John Locke, commonly thought to have been a member of the Rosicrucians, meeting Boyle inspired him to take a long vacation in Southern France. He specifically visited Carcassonne, Narbonne, Toulouse, and perhaps even Rennes-le-Chateau. These were all important sites in the history of the Cathars, which Locke was particularly interested in studying there, as well as the legends in Southern France about Mary Magdalene and the Holy Grail. He even visited Saint Baum, where Magdalene was supposed to have lived, as well as the graves of Nostradamus and Rene d'Anjou. He also consorted, while in France, with none other than the duchess of Guise.

Boyle, on the other hand, was busy exchanging letters with a fellow alchemist in France, Georges Pierre. These letters reveal Boyle's involvement in an occult fraternal order to which also belonged the duke of Savoy and Pierre du Moulin. Boyle published a couple of alchemical texts called *Incalescence of Quicksilver with Gold* and *A Historical Account of the Degradation of Gold.* Then in 1689 he announced in writing that he would no longer entertain guests on certain days that he had scheduled to conduct alchemical experiments, which he described as, "less simple and plain than those barely luciferous ones I have been wont to affect... though the full and complete uses are not mentioned, partly because, in spite of my philanthropy, I was engaged to secrecy."

The details of Boyle's experiments were never publicly revealed, but when he died in 1691, he left to his friends John Locke and Isaac Newton all of his papers, as well as an unknown "red powder" which was integral to his experiments - perhaps the same red powder mentioned previously in the account of Nicolas Flamel.

Isaac Newton

If Robert Boyle was the father of modern chemistry, Isaac Newton was certainly the father of physics as a serious study. He is known mostly today for his Theory of Gravity, Theory of Light, Laws of Motion and Laws of Thermodynamics, as well as the invention of the Calculus. He claimed to be a descendant of "ancient Scottish nobility", and as benefits an aristocratic Brit, he attended school at Cambridge. He was inducted into the Royal Society in 1672 at age thirty, where he met Robert Boyle in 1673. He met their mutual friend, John Locke about sixteen years later. It was around this time that he also encountered a Genevan aristocrat named Nicolas Fatio de Duillier, a former spy against Louis XIV. According to *Holy Blood, Holy Grail*, de Duillier "appears to have been on intimate terms with every important scientist of the age", and he immediately struck up a close friendship with Newton that lasted for ten years.

Six years after meeting de Duillier, Newton was made warden of the Royal Mint, and was therefore involved in fixing his country's gold standard, an interesting occupation for a practicing alchemist presumably capable of creating gold at will. He was elected president of the Royal Society four years later, and also became acquainted with a Frenchman and Royal Society member named Jean Desaguliers - whom, as I shall soon discuss, was instrumental in the spread of Freemasonry across the continent.

Although I have no proof that Isaac Newton was a Freemason, he did belong to a quasi-Masonic organization called the Gentleman's Club of Spalding, to which the poet Alexander Pope also belonged. And Newton was clearly interested in the subjects to which Freemasonry addresses itself. For instance, he considered Noah to have been a far more important source of God's wisdom than Moses - a common theme throughout Freemasonry and a detail that will assume greater importance when I later discuss the relationship between the biblical Flood and the mystery of the Holy Grail. He also wrote a very interesting book called *The Chronology of Ancient Kingdoms Amended*, which traced the origins of the institution of monarchy, especially the Jewish monarchy of King David. As *Holy Blood, Holy Grail* describes it, Newton "attempted to establish... the primacy of Israel over other cultures of antiquity." Like many Freemasons, Newton believed that the ancient Jewish mysteries contained true revelations and divine secrets, but that they had largely been corrupted over time by the editors of the Torah and the Holy Bible. He had great interest in the theories of Pythagoras, especially the "music of the spheres", which he considered to be an analogy for his own gravitational theories. He was interested in the Masonic and Pythagorean science of sacred geometry, and believed that there were numerological connections between music and architecture. In fact, an even more overtly Masonic belief he held was that the secrets of alchemy were embedded into the precise dimensions of Solomon's Temple. His favorite alchemical metaphor was the myth of the Quest for the Golden Fleece. He believed this story to be key to properly dating the events described in both classical and biblical myth, which he considered (as I do) to be real historical records. Newton's library contained copies of *The Rosicrucian Manifestos* covered in his own scribbled notes, and over a hundred books on alchemy. One of these alchemical texts was written by none other than Nicolas Flamel, and had been hand-copied by Newton himself. Newton continued to correspond with his friends Robert Boyle, John Locke, and Nicolas Fatio de Duillier about alchemy for the remainder of his life, even at times writing these letters in cryptic codes.

As if it was not obvious from what I have already discussed, Newton was an enthusiastic embracer of heresy. He denied the existence of the Trinity, the divine nature of Jesus, and the veracity of the New Testament. He also avidly studied and wrote about Gnosticism, rejecting the mechanistic theories of the universe held dear by his fellow scientists in favor of a material world that derived itself from the spirit. There was another Gnostic-oriented, Cathar-like group in whom Newton, along with his friend Fatio de Duillier, held considerable interest: the Camisards, also known as the "Prophets of Cevennes." This group had arisen out of the same areas of Southern France as the Cathars, and just like their predecessors had been driven out by the Vatican with military force, escaping into Geneva and London in the early part of the eighteenth century. They too hated the Catholic church and denied the divinity of Jesus, and just like both the Cathars and the Knights Templar, they dressed themselves in white tunics.

As interesting as Isaac Newton's life was, his death was, perhaps, even more so. Sensing his impending doom weeks ahead of time, he and his closest friends set about cremating large portions of his private papers, presumably to preserve the secrets of alchemy, as well as the secrets of the Priory of Sion. And in an eerie parallel to the death of Berenger Sauniere, who was refused Last Rites, Newton specifically requested that he not receive Last Rites.

Although there is little doubt about the depth of Isaac Newton's genius, there are some, shall we say, "interesting" circumstances surrounding his two greatest discoveries: the Theory of Gravity, and the Calculus. We are all familiar with the story of the apple that supposedly fell on Newton's head as he sat under a tree, providing the inspiration for his Theory of Gravity. Is this story a metaphor for divine inspiration, or for receiving the "forbidden fruit" of secret knowledge? The apple is certainly emblematic of the fruit of the Tree of Knowledge consumed by Eve in the Garden of Eden, and the story of it falling from the tree onto Newton's head brings to mind the story of the Grail stone falling from Heaven. The tale surrounding Calculus is even more suspicious. As it turns out, Newton had been working on the Calculus for some time, and he was not the only one. He was in a neck-and-neck race with a German mathematician named G.W. Leibnitz. In either a bizarre twist of fate or a bizarre conspiratorial plot, he and Leibnitz completed their formulas for the Calculus on the same day. To Leibnitz's great dismay Newton went down in history as the man who "invented" Calculus. However, the German may have gotten the last laugh, for it is his far more simply expressed equations which are used in mathematics today.

Charles Radclyffe and the Scottish Rite

Following Isaac Newton as the Head of the Priory was Charles Radclyffe, son of an illegitimate daughter of the Stuart King Charles II. Radclyffe was, according to *Holy Blood, Holy Grail*, from "an influential Northumbrian family", who since the time of James II had been the earls of Derwentwater. He was thus cousin to both Bonnie Prince Charlie, the Stuart king de jure who never made it to the throne, and to the Earl of Lichfield, George Lee, also the son of one of Charles II's bastards. Charles Radclyffe and his older brother James became key figures in the "Jacobite movement." After Charles II's successor, James III was sent into exile, this movement attempted to reestablish and secure the Stuart throne[5]. That year, in 1715, there was a Jacobite Scottish rebellion in which both Charles and James Radclyffe participated, and there were arrested and imprisoned. James was executed, but Charles managed to escape, and fled to the protection of Jacobite sympathizers in France. He immediately became secretary to James II's successor as king-in-exile, Bonnie Prince Charlie. It took thirty years, but finally Bonnie Prince Charlie and his ranks arrived in Britain in an attempt to retake the throne. Charles Radclyffe was captured on his way to join them, and the following year, when the Jacobite attempt was crushed, he was beheaded at the Tower of London.

But there was more than just Jacobite politics on the minds of Charles Radclyffe and his compatriots. They were also deeply involved in Freemasonry, particularly Scottish Rite Freemasonry, believed to have been inherited from the rituals of the Stuart dynasty. This brand of the Craft included many more degrees than regular "York Rite" masonry, which of course meant that it contained greater, deeper and more voluminous secrets. These mysteries were supposedly derived from Scotland, and from there, some even older source. The Scottish Rite rituals included more overtly "occult" material - Hermetic, cabalistic, Rosicrucian and alchemical material - and initiates were taught specifics about the origin and history of their organizations' practices. Furthermore, as *Holy Blood, Holy Grail* blatantly states, "It is probable that Scottish Rite Freemasonry was originally promulgated, if not indeed devised, by Charles Radclyffe." Charles also founded the first European Masonic lodge in Paris. He was shortly thereafter declared "grand master of all French lodges", which he remained for at least a decade more. Therefore the authors of *Holy Blood, Holy Grail* state that, "The dissemination of 18th-century Freemasonry owes more, ultimately, to Charles Radclyffe than to any other man." But Radclyffe did not work alone, nor did he accomplish everything hands-on, but worked through middlemen and accomplices, such as Chevalier Andrew Ramsay.

To a large degree, Ramsay associated with the same crowd as Isaac Newton, including Jean Desaguliers, who was one of the Royal Society's "two curators of experiments" and one of the age's leading proponents of Freemasonry in Europe, as well as a friend of Charles Radclyffe's. Ramsay was further the master of the lodge at the Hague, where, in 1731, under his leadership, the first European prince to join Masonry was initiated: Francois, duke of Lorraine, soon to be Holy Roman Emperor through his marriage to Maria Theresa of Austria. Ramsay also studied math under Newton's best friend, Nicolas Fatio de Duillier. As for Newton himself, Ramsay practically worshipped him, regarding him as the era's leading sage. And like both Newton and de Duillier, Ramsay had a keen interest in the heretical Camisards. He was also a member of a Masonic-like secret society called the Philadelphes.

Ramsay moved to Cambrai in 1710, where he became part of the close circle surrounding Fenelon (the former cure of Saint Sulpice who was famous as an occult philosopher, and whose name pops up repeatedly in regards to this mystery). He became a dedicated Jacobite shortly after meeting Charles Radclyffe, and even worked for a period as tutor to Bonnie Prince Charlie. Although he was a known enemy of the presiding government in England, he returned there in 1729 with no problem, and almost immediately joined the Royal Society, as well as the aforementioned "Gentleman's Club of Spalding."

The following year he returned to France to campaign for Freemasonry. Here he was patronized by relatives of Frederick of the Palatinate, the House of Tour d'Auvergne, viscounts of Turenne and dukes of Bouillon. The duke of Bouillon in particular was a cousin of Bonnie Prince Charlie and an outspoken champion of Freemasonry.

Ramsay became his son's tutor, and was given property to live on by the duke. However, Ramsay's greatest contribution to the growth of Masonry came in 1737, when he delivered his *Oration*, which specifically detailed the origins and history of the order. This *Oration* later became incorporated as an official Masonic document, and its claims have become part of Masonry's basic tenets. As *Holy Blood, Holy Grail* states, "On the basis of this *Oration*, Ramsay became the preeminent Masonic spokesman of his age." But, they continue, "Our research convinced us ... that the real voice behind Ramsay was that of Charles Radclyffe." It was, after all, Charles Radclyffe who, as master of the lodge at which Ramsay gave his *Oration*, presided over the event. It was also Radclyffe who acted as chief signatory at Ramsay's funeral in 1743. And there was another contribution to Masonry, particularly the Scottish Rite, that Radclyffe was to make as well.

In 1742, four years before Charles Radclyffe's death on the chopping block, a German-born man named Karl Gottlieb von Hund was initiated into the mysteries of Freemasonry. But this initiation was far from ordinary. According to Von Hund, it was presided over by three "unknown superiors" who conferred upon him a new system of Masonry as yet unrevealed called "the Strict Observance", so named because of the stringent oath of obedience it required. These unnamed initiators claimed that the Strict Observance was a direct inheritance of the Knights Templar, specifically the ones who had escaped King Philippe's persecution and settled in Scotland. Moreover, Hund had been a large contributor to the Scottish Jacobites, and he believed until the end that the man in charge of his initiation had been either Bonnie Prince Charlie himself, or one of his close associates. The authors of *Holy Blood, Holy Grail* concluded that the man in question was in fact Charles Radclyffe, which would mean that the Rite of the Strict Observance, derived from the rituals of the Knights Templar, was installed in the degrees of Scottish Rite Freemasonry by none other than the Priory of Sion.

Unfortunately for Von Hund, no one in his own time believed his tale about the "unknown superiors", who, although they had promised to contact him in the future and initiate him further, never did so. The authors of *Holy Blood, Holy Grail* theorized that what had actually happened was that the Jacobite cause had collapsed, and that his initiators, Charles Radclyffe and friends, had all been either killed, imprisoned, or sent into exile.

But there is more evidence to confirm Baron von Hund's story, and the involvement of the Priory of Sion. One of the few pieces of information von Hund did manage to obtain from his sole contact with the "unknown superiors" was a list of the Grand Masters of the Knights Templar - a list identical to the one provided in *Secret Dossiers*. This list, as I have said, was established by the authors of *Holy Blood, Holy Grail* to be more accurate than any other list of Templar Grand Masters they had previously seen. But Von Hund's list was written when most of the vital documentation on the Templars that would have made such a list researchable was still hidden away in Vatican vaults, proving that Von Hund's sources had access to inside knowledge.

Charles de Lorraine

After the Jacobite cause was put to rest, Von Hund was patronized by the current Holy Roman Emperor, Francois, duke of Lorraine. And Francois' own brother, Charles de Lorraine, became, according to the "Priory documents", Grand Master of

Sion following Charles Radclyffe's death. It was Francois whom I mentioned previously as the first European Prince initiated into Freemasonry. Not long after his initiation, he went for a lengthy visit to England, where he promptly joined the Gentleman's Club of Spalding.

Thereafter Francois de Lorraine was one of continental Freemasonry's leading figures, and, as *Holy Blood, Holy Grail* puts it, "His court in Vienna became, in a sense, Europe's Masonic capitol and a center for a broad spectrum of other esoteric interests as well." As per example, Francois had an alchemical laboratory installed in the Hofburg, his imperial palace. When he inherited the title of grand duke of Tuscany from the Medicis, he became instrumental in protecting the Freemasons of Florence from harassment by the Inquisition.

However, in order to receive the archduchy of Tuscany, Francois had been forced to abdicate his claim to Lorraine, which was ceded to the French crown. His brother Charles, however, refused to recognize this, and instead presumed to take on the mantle of the duke of Lorraine himself. In 1742, he raised an army and marched on Lorraine in an attempt to reclaim it. Only the distraction of a French invasion of his territory in Bohemia prevented him from doing so.

Charles' chief military adversary was Frederick the Great, himself somewhat of a mystic who, despite their differences, maintained considerable respect for Charles, about which he was very outspoken. Nevertheless, Frederick defeated Charles at the dramatic Battle of Leuthen in 1757, marking the end of Charles de Lorraine's military career.

After his retirement, Charles set up court in Brussels, where he became the region's chief patron for the arts. His court very much reflected that of his esteemed forefather, Rene d'Anjou. He also became, in 1761, Grand Master of the Order of Teutonic Knights. Nine years later, he appointed his favorite nephew, Maximilien coadjutor of the Order. Maximilien was as close to his uncle as could be, and when a magnificent equestrian statue of Charles was unveiled in Brussels, on the specifically chosen date of January 17, Maximilien was in attendance. Not surprisingly, then, Maximilien followed his uncle as Grand Master of the Priory of Sion.

Shugborough Hall

There is another connection to Charles Radclyffe which has left a significant mark on the mystery of the Holy Grail and Rennes-le-Chateau. It pertains to the House of Anson, present earls of Lichfield. When Radclyffe escaped from Newgate Prison in 1714, avoiding the fate of his brother, James, his escape was assisted by his cousin, the earl of Lichfield. Although that particular line became extinct later in the 1700s, the title of earl of Lichfield was bought by the Anson family, and is retained to this very day. Their family seat currently rests at Shugborough Hall in Staffordshire. It had once been the home of the brother of George Anson, who was famous for circumnavigating the globe. And when the old "nautonnier" George Anson died in 1762, a curious poem was read aloud by in Parliament by friends of his - one which appeared to refer to the very elements of Poussin's painting, *The Shepherds of Arcadia*. It read:

> *"Upon that storied marble cast thine eye.*
> *The scene commands a moralising sigh.*

E'en in Arcadia's bless'd plains,
Amidst the laughing nymphs and sportive swains,
See festal joy subside, with melting grace,
And pity visit the half-smiling face;
Where now the dance, the lute, the nuptial feast,
The passion throbbing in the lover's breast,
Life's emblem here, in youth, and vernal bloom,
But reason's finger pointing at the tomb!"

What makes the connection to Poussin even more explicit is that right there on the Shugborough Hall property stands a marble bas-relief bearing a mirror-reversal of Poussin's *The Shepherds of Arcadia*. Called "the Shepherd's Monument", it was made by Peter Scheemakers in the 1700s, and beneath the relief we find written a code which, until recently, had not been deciphered. It said:

O.U.O.S.V.A.V.V.

D.   M.

The likeliest explanation has come from an 18th century poem by Anna Seward called *The Swan of Lichfield*, which contains two lines that, apart from a single letter, the above code is a perfect abbreviation for. They read:

"Out your Own Sweet Vale, Alicia
Vanisheth Vanity Shepherds of Arcadia
'Twixt Deity and Man thou Shepherdeth the Way."

Charles Nodier

The next to take the helm of the Priory of Sion was Charles Nodier, a prolific and hugely famous writer during the nineteenth century whose fiction has been compared to that of Edgar Allan Poe. Nodier was the son of an apparently orphaned girl named Suzanne Paris, who married a solicitor in Besancon. His father was also a member of the Jacobite Club who later, during the French Revolution, became the town's mayor and president of their revolutionary tribunal. He was also a known and outspoken Freemason.

Nodier was something of a child prodigy, and had achieved celebrity status as a writer by age eighteen. He continued to write on a non-stop basis for the rest of his life. In addition to his fiction, he also wrote nonfiction on a wide variety of subjects, including art, literature, law, travel, etymology, zoology, psychology, archeology, and of course occultism, as well as a body of personal musings. Esoteric subjects, however, appear to have been a distinct preoccupation of Nodier's.

In Nodier's prodigious eighteenth year, he was made the chief librarian at the Arsenal Library, which was, according to *Holy Blood, Holy Grail*, "the major French depository for medieval and specifically occult manuscripts." These included a large collection of works by Nicolas Flamel, as well as Cardinal Richelieu's entire library, which was rich in Hermetic and cabalistic texts. There were also a number of manuscripts taken from French monasteries during the Revolution, and a large portion of the

Vatican's archives, which had been plundered by Napoleon. This contained numerous records pertaining to heresies, the Inquisition's information on the Knights Templar, and books on a variety of occult subjects.

It was to this material that Nodier, along with his friends Eliphas Levi and Jean Baptiste Pitois devoted much of their attention. Levi, whom I have mentioned previously, was then and is still now one of the most highly-regarded authors on the subject of the Western magical tradition, whose contributions include the modern conception of the Devil as the Templar idol, Baphomet. Pitois has a similar reputation, and his *History and Practice of Magic* is still cherished by occultists today. (It also includes a dedication at the front to Charles Nodier.) It was to these three figures that the "occult revival" of their age can be attributed.

One of Nodier's published works during this time was a series of books about interesting historical sights in France, in which he includes a considerable amount of material pertaining to the Merovingian era, as well as the Knights Templar, and Gisors. He was especially intrigued by the cryptic "Cutting of the Elm" event which took place there and purportedly constituted a ceremonial separation of the Templars from the Priory of Sion.

Nodier gathered around him a flock of young disciples, or "aesthetic potentates" as he called them, to whom he played the role of mentor. This group included Balzac, Delacroix, Dumas, and Victor Hugo. It was Hugo who was Nodier's closest friend, and Hugo followed him as Grand Master of the Priory of Sion. His friends also included a man with the curious name of Francois-Rene de Chateau-briand, who had visited Nicolas Poussin's tomb in Rome and there placed a stone reproduction of *The Shepherds of Arcadia*. The writings of Nodier's salon set bear specific references to the mystery of Rennes-le-Chateau and related subjects, such as a book from 1832 by Auguste de Labouisse-Rochefort called *A Journey to Rennes-le-Bains*, which, as *Holy Blood, Holy Grail* states, "speaks at length of a legendary treasure associated with Blanchefort and Rennes-le-Chateau." This person also wrote a book called *The Lovers - To Eleonore* which bears the phrase "Et in Arcadia Ego" on the title page.

Like everything else in his life, Charles Nodier became involved in secret societies at a very early age. By the time he was ten, he had joined the Philadelphes, and created his own version of the group at age thirteen. It was to this group that one of its members, a close friend of Nodier's, addressed an apparently coded essay which exists in the archives of the Besancon Library, titled *The Arcadian Shepherd Sounds the First Accents of a Rustic Flute*. Later, in 1802, Nodier admitted belonging to a secret order which he in writing described as "Biblical and Pythagorean." Fourteen years later he wrote an anonymous text called *A History of Secret Societies in the Army Under Napoleon*, in which he attributed a number of historical events to the covert action of these organizations, including Napoleon's fall. Nodier wrote in this book that all secret societies were under the control of a single, supreme secret society, which he names as being none other than the Philadelphes. He also wrote, though, about an "oath that binds me to the Philadelphes and which forbids me to make them known under their social name", indicating that this may have been just another front for the Priory of Sion. In this book he quotes a speech that he claims was made at a meeting of the Philadelphes by one of the leading plotters against the regime of Napoleon - interesting because Nodier's self-made group of Philadelphes from his childhood supposedly included a young man who would later become one of Napoleon's biggest enemies. The quoted individual, speaking in regards to his newborn son, purportedly stated:

"He is too young to engage himself to you by the oath of Annibal; but remember I have named him Eliacin, and that I delegate to him the guard of the temple and the altar, if I should die ere I have seen fall from his throne the last of the oppressors of Jerusalem."

Nodier's book succeeded in fanning the flames of an already-persistent secret society paranoia that abounded during the post-Napoleonic era. In fact, Nodier seems to have gone out of his way to establish a reputation as a dangerous conspiratorial plotter himself. He had at first, because of his family's affiliations, had a favorable attitude towards the French Revolution, but later changed his mind, and had the same transformation of attitude about Napoleon. In 1804 he wrote an anti-Napoleonic satire call *Le Napoleone*, then made great efforts to try and gain attention from the authorities for having written it. They were sluggish to react, and only after much prodding, including a letter to Napoleon himself by the guilty party declaring his deed, did they arrest and imprison him for a month, leaving him to continue his actions against the emperor. He at once became involved in the anti-Napoleonic plots of 1804 and 1812.

The Catholic Modernist Movement

Charles Nodier's disciples continued his writing tradition after his death. Take, for instance, Jean Baptiste Pitois, who in 1833 went to work as an administrator in France's ministry of education. The ministry immediately undertook a plan to publish all documents pertaining to French history that had, up until that point, been censored. Two committees were formed for the occasion, upon which sat none other than Victor Hugo, as well as two influential authors, Jules Michelet and Baron Emmanuel Rey. Under the ministry's auspices Michelet published a compendium of records from the trials of the Knights Templar by the Inquisition, called *Proces de Templiers*. Also under the ministry of education Baron Emmanuel Rey published books about the Crusades in which he presented, for the first time, the Priory of Sion's original charters. More charters were printed in the *Revue de l'Orient Latin*, the official journal of Baron Rey's archeological foundation, the Societe de l'Orient Latin, published from their headquarters in Geneva.

The ministry of education instigated a fresh approach to scholarship that spread throughout Europe, especially Germany - an approach that relied on rigorous analysis and the comparison of multiple source materials to establish clear facts. This approach had led to such philosophies as Darwinism and atheism, which became serious threats to the church. Even more threatening was when such scholarship techniques were turned on the Bible itself, the result of which was a veritable crisis of faith among many of the Church's former devotees.

To combat this, the Church sponsored the "Catholic Modernist Movement", an attempt to train a new breed of clerics who could strike down anti-biblical arguments with the same rigid reliance on fact that the arguments themselves purported to be based on. But the results of this attempt actually worked against the Church. When armed with the techniques and background knowledge of 19th-century scholarship, these "Modernist" clerics could see for themselves the flaws in the Church's traditional interpretation of the scriptures. By the turn of the century, Modernism had itself become the heresy it had been formed to combat. Modernists were placed on the Vatican's official watch list, and all clerics forbidden to associate with the movement, even forced to take an oath not to embrace any Modernist ideas. The Modernists were even, interestingly enough, accused of being "Freemasons" by the Roman authorities. But Modernism continued to proliferate, spreading throughout Europe and Britain as it grew fashionable with the era's intelligentsia. And the center for the dissemination of Modernist thought was the Seminary of Saint Sulpice.

Victor Hugo

There are some other details about the life of Victor Hugo, besides what we have already gone over, that are worth mentioning. Best known for his plays *Les Miserables* and *The Hunchback of Notre Dame*, Hugo came from a purportedly "aristocratic" lineage stemming from Lorraine. He was born in Besancon, home of the Nodiers and center of post-Revolutionary occult conspiracies. His father appears to have been acting as a double agent during Napoleon's reign, serving a general under the emperor while at the same time consorting with those who plotted against him. One of these consortees was, in a bizarre and kinky twist, his wife's adulterous lover, who lived with the family and was godfather to young Victor.

As a teenager, Victor Hugo became one of Charles Nodier's proteges, from whom he appears to have acquired an appreciation for Gothic architecture, which would later figure into his writing. At age seventeen Hugo, along with his brother and Charles Nodier, started a publishing house that produced a magazine which Nodier edited. He was later married at none other than Saint Sulpice. In 1825, Hugo and Nodier took their wives on a lengthy tour of Switzerland and then attended Charles X's coronation. Hugo continued to model his life on Nodier's, even forming his own salon in the Nodier tradition which included many of the same people. At Nodier's funeral in 1845, Hugo was one of the pallbearers.

Hugo's esoteric interests and heretical beliefs were undeniable. Like his predecessor Isaac Newton, he rejected both the Trinity and the divinity of Jesus. And of course, as a disciple of Nodier, his thinking was saturated with Gnosticism, Hermeticism, and cabalistic concepts. He even joined a version of the Rosicrucians to which Eliphas Levi also belonged.

It is interesting to note that Victor Hugo was, throughout his life, a devoted monarchist, although he maintained an affection for Napoleon, who had married into the Merovingian bloodline, and who had attempted to link himself to that dynasty by attaching King Childeric's golden bees to his coronation robe. Although Hugo supported the restoration of the Bourbons to the throne, this would appear to have been merely an outgrowth of his desire for the trappings of monarchy. His attitude towards the Bourbons themselves was a bit wishy-washy, and in the case of Louis XIV, downright negative. He did, however, support the cause of the so-called "Citizen King", Louis Philippe, who had married the niece of Maximilien de Lorraine.

Claude Debussy

The Grand Master to follow Hugo at the helm of the Priory was also the Grand Master who led them during the years of the Berenger Sauniere saga - the renowned composer, Claude Debussy. From humble beginnings, Debussy nonetheless achieved fame, like many Priory Grand Masters, at an early age, and was performing for the mistress of the President of France by the time he was a teenager. He had already established contact with the President himself, as well as a number of other powerful people and well-known socialites. At age eighteen, a female aristocrat from Russia who had also patronized Tchaikovsky decided to adopt him, and took him on tours throughout Italy, Russia and Switzerland. He won a much esteemed music award in 1884, and then continued his travels throughout the continent. During this time, he established an inner circle consisting of men and women from noble families whose names he went to great lengths to keep secret.

However, a greater turning point in his life was meeting Victor Hugo, to whom he was introduced by the poet Paul Verlaine, and he shortly afterwards put to music a number of Hugo's best works. At this time, Debussy also fell in with a group of "symbolists", then one of the dominant art movements in Paris. Among this circle: Berenger Sauniere's mistress and dedicated occultist, opera singer Emma Calve; Emile Hoffet, the cleric from Saint Sulpice who deciphered Sauniere's parchments, and who introduced Sauniere to Debussy; poet Stephane Mallarme, who wrote the poem upon which Debussy based one of his most famous works, *L'Après-Midi d'un Faune* (*The Afternoon of a Faun*); Maurice Maeterlinck, who wrote a "Merovingian" play called *Pelle et Melisande*, which Debussy transformed into a hugely successful opera; and Comte Philippe Auguste Villiera de l'Isle-Adam, who wrote *Axël*, a play of "Rosicrucian" content that was warmly embraced by the symbolists and which, originally, Debussy had planned to turn into an opera as well. Also included: famous writers Oscar Wilde, Stefan George, Paul Valery, Andre Gide, Marcel Proust and W.B. Yeats; the founder of the Cabalistic Order of the Rose-Croix, who was also friends with Emma Calve; Satanist Jules Bois, again friends with Emma Calve, who helped S.L. MacGregor Mathers establish the Hermetic Order of the Golden Dawn; and the famous mystic Papus, spiritual advisor to Nicolas and Alexandra of Russia.

Papus was also involved with Jules Doinel, a librarian at Carcassonne who started a "neo-Cathar" church that included both he and Papus as bishops, and which was situated in the Languedoc. He declared himself to be "Gnostic bishop of Mirepoix and Alet", counting both the parishes of Montsegur and Rennes-le-Chateau among his domains. The church was consecrated at the home of Lord James Sinclair's wife. Their "neo-Cathar" movement raised alarm at the Vatican, and the Papacy even issued an official condemnation of the church for promulgating "the ancient Albigensian heresy." Doinel was well-acquainted with Emma Calve, as well as the cure of Rennes-le-Bains, Abbe Henri Boudet. He was also a frequent visitor to the region of Rennes-le-Chateau, so he may indeed have known Berenger Sauniere.

Debussy had a friend in Josephin Peladan, as associate of Papus and Emma Calve who, towards the close of the 19th century, proclaimed that he had discovered the true tomb of Christ while visiting the Holy Land. The location he gave was not the Holy Sepulcher, which is the traditionally acknowledged site, but underneath the foundations of the Mosque of Omar, which had at one point been under the control of the Knights Templar. Of Peladan's discovery, one of his disciples wrote that it was, "so astonishing that in any other era it would have shaken the Catholic world to its foundations", indicating that something about the tomb itself revealed some earth-shattering secret. Perhaps it provided the basis for Peladan's insistence that Jesus had been a man, not divine.

Peladan founded his own Hermetic order in 1890, which he called "The Order of the Catholic Rose-Croix, the Temple, and the Grail." He also decided to embark upon a career as an artist, playwright, and composer. He summed up his artistic approach as that of "a knight in armor, eagerly engaged in the symbolic quest for the Holy Grail." The theater company which he created specialized in particularly Arcadian themes, including, as *Holy Blood, Holy Grail* states, "Orpheus, the Argonauts, and the Quest for the Golden Fleece, the Mystery of the Rose-Croix, and the Mystery of the Grail." Claude Debussy was one of the company's chief patrons. Peladan also initiated a series of annual art exhibitions titled "Salon de la Rose + Croix." His mission with these salons was, "to ruin realism, to reform Latin taste, and create a school of idealist art." Certain styles and themes were explicitly disallowed at these salons, including, "all landscapes except those composed in the manner of Poussin."

Finally, another friend of both Peladan and Debussy was Maurice Barres, who had once belonged to a Rosicrucian order with Victor Hugo. Barres' most successful novel was *La Colline Inspiree* (*The Inspired Mount*), which, it has been theorized, is partially allegorical of the story of Berenger Sauniere. Interestingly, though, the actual location in which the story takes place is the aforementioned village of Sion in Lorraine.

The Protocols of Sion and the Hieron du Val d'Or

Around the turn of the century, a controversial document was published, the effects of which reverberated well into the middle of the next century: the notorious *Protocols of the Learned Elders of Zion*, long held by scholars to have been a hoax. As the czar and czarina's involvement with the occult and reliance on mystical advisors grew, so too did the paranoia in Russia about secret societies and their influence on national politics. The mystical advisors in question - Rasputin, Papus, and a mysterious figure named Monsieur Philippe - also had a powerful enemy: Grand Duchess Elizabeth, who wished to see her own hired puppets acting as advisors to the throne. One such puppet was Sergei Nilus, who in 1903 presented to the czar *The Protocols of Zion*. These were documents purporting to be the minutes of the World Jewish Congress, a Jewish conspiracy that supposedly intended to take over the world. Unfortunately for Nilus, the czar recognized it as a fraud, declared that all copies of the document were to be destroyed, and banished Sergei Nilus from the court.

Over the years, however, the document was published again and again, becoming a cult classic among anti-Semites, who fervently believed in the document's authenticity. The *Protocols* were used to fuel the fire of anti-Jewish hatred after the Russian Revolution of 1917, as well as by the Nazis a few years later. Although at times a bit over-dramatic, there is something inherently believable about the *Protocols*. They lay out in straightforward rhetoric the Machiavellian steps which an international conspiracy would go through to take control of the world's governments and institutions, and to maintain power, largely through the manipulation of the masses, as well as those already in power. It recommends the proliferation of dangerous creeds, philosophies, religious and political ideas such as Marxism, Anarchism, Atheism, and Darwinism, all to sow discord and cause the breakdown of traditional institutions, clearing the way for the new hierarchy of which the *Protocols* speak. It is bone-chilling to read such a document as this, written in the 19th century, which predicts perfectly the results of a conspiracy that in every way resemble the world in which we currently live.

But what the *Protocols* outline is much more than your typical paranoid New World Order scenario. They speak of a global monarch, the "King of the blood of Sion", of "the dynastic roots of King David", who as ruler of a new "Masonic kingdom" will be both the "King of the Jews" and "the real Pope", acting as "the patriarch of an international church." Of him, the *Protocols* state, "Certain members of the seed of David will prepare the Kings and their heirs... Only the King and the three who stood sponsor for him will know what is coming." Finally, the *Protocols* end with a curious postscript: "Signed by the representatives of Sion of the 33rd Degree."

The authors of *Holy Blood, Holy Grail* presented a theory regarding the *Protocols* with which I overwhelmingly concur. They proposed that the "Learned Elders of Zion" were in fact the Priory of Sion, and that this document had been, originally, the minutes of one of *their* meetings, which fell into the wrong hands and was subsequently transformed into a weapon for anti-Semites. It certainly bears all of the earmarks and catch phrases for a "Priory document", and overall the goals that are set forth within, as well as the methods proposed for achieving them, fit my conception of the Priory's own objectives, although I imagine that in certain sections of the document the original version might have been phrased more delicately. Furthermore, there is circumstantial evidence to indicate that this was indeed the case. The earliest known version of the *Protocols* was actually written in French, and most scholars believe it to have been partially based on a political satire written by Maurice Joly against Napoleon II which was published in Geneva in 1864. Maurice Joly was also a member of the Rose-Croix order, and good friends with Victor Hugo. But perhaps it was the other way around. Perhaps the *"Protocols of Sion"* and the anti-Napoleon satire were themselves based on the same Priory of Sion document, which Joly, as a potential member of the Priory, could possibly have had access to. We cannot know for sure, but it is known that in 1884, copies of the *Protocols of Zion* were found circulating amongst the members of a Masonic lodge to which Papus himself belonged - the lodge where the aforementioned legend of the wise Egyptian sage named Ormus (whom the Priory of Sion called themselves after) first surfaced.

Furthermore, there was during this period in time a secret society with stated goals very similar to those enumerated in the *Protocols of Zion*, and they were in fact, apparently, an auxiliary order of the Priory of Sion. They were called "The Hieron du Val d'Or", which, *Holy Blood, Holy Grail* notes, contains an anagram of the place-name "Orval", a location that frequently crops up throughout this mystery. Notably, the word "Orval" contains the syllables which, in French, mean "gold" and "valley." Thus "Val d'Or" means "Valley of Gold." In his 1979 book *Le Tresor du Triangle d'Or* (*The Treasure of the Golden Triangle*), Jean-Luc Chaumeil (a one-time spokesman for the Priory of Sion) states that the Hieron practiced a version of Scottish Rite Freemasonry, and the upper degrees of this order constituted the lower degrees of the Priory of Sion itself. Chaumeil describes the group's disposition as "Christian, Hermetic, and aristocratic." They proclaimed themselves to be Catholic, even though the Church of Rome condemned them. Their mystic teachings contained, according to *Holy Blood, Holy Grail*, "a characteristic emphasis on sacred geometry and various sacred sites... an insistence on a mystical or Gnostic truth underlying mythological motifs", and "a preoccupation with the origins of men, races, languages, and symbols... ." The order was, "simultaneously Christian and 'trans-Christian.' It stressed the importance of the Sacred Heart... sought to recognize Christian and pagan mysteries", and "Ascribed special significance to Druidic thought - which it... regarded as partially Pythagorean." The Hieron du Val d'Or was also unabashedly pro-monarchist, and sought a restoration of the Holy Roman Empire. But this one would be built, unlike the previous one, on an ultimately spiritual basis - a vision specifically echoed in the Priory of Sion's own literature, which I will soon discuss. The new empire would have been a reflection of Heaven on Earth, that specifically Hermetic Arcadian ideal. Jean-Luc Chaumeil described the Hieron's ideal state as:

"...a theocracy wherein nations would be no more than provinces, their leaders but proconsuls in the service of a world occult government consisting of an elite. For Europe, this regime of the Great King implied a double hegemony of the Papacy and the Empire, of the Vatican and of the Habsburgs, who would have been the Vatican's right arm."

The authors of *Holy Blood, Holy Grail* were quick to point out that this envisioned scenario accords with the Nostradamus prophecy about the "Great King" who would issue from Lorraine, since the Habsburgs essentially *were* the House of Lorraine. At the same time, though, this vision accords with that shared by numerous other cultures throughout the world and throughout history who have embraced the myth of the King of the World, an archetypal quasi-divine global monarch who appears in many ancient legends. It further accords with the "King of the blood of Sion" image discussed in the *Protocols of Zion*.

Perhaps even more shocking, Chaumeil claims that Berenger Sauniere, Abbe Henri Boudet, Emile Hoffet, and the Bishop of Carcassonne were all members of this organization, and that it was a political scuffle within this organization which led to Sauniere's premature death. Chaumeil describes Sauniere as a pawn in the Priory of Sion/Hieron du Val d'Or's bizarre plot regarding Rennes-le-Chateau and the surrounding area. According to this version of the story, Sauniere had been involved with the order since before his arrival at the parish of Rennes-le-Chateau, and had actually been dispatched there by them for the purpose of finding the parchments. But in 1916 he is said to have had a falling out with the order, which supposedly explains his mysterious death the following year. Chaumeil states that Sauniere's "handler" with regard to lodge business was actually the cure of Rennes-le-Bains, Abbe Henri Boudet, who is said to have orchestrated all of Sauniere's activities, including the remodeling of his church and the surrounding domains. Boudet was also purportedly the middleman who passed along Priory of Sion hush money - not to Sauniere, but to his housekeeper, Marie Deneraud, who was also in their employ and to whom all checks were made payable. She also, says Chaumeil, was the agent through which Boudet transmitted all of his highly specific instructions for Sauniere. And Chaumeil tells us that Sauniere did not even know true nature of the "treasure" and "secret" which he protected until 1915, one year before his supposed falling out with the order, when Boudet made a deathbed confession to his fellow cleric and conspirator. What exactly that was we may never know.

Jean 23

Following Claude Debussy, the next Grand Master of the Priory of Sion was

Jean Cocteau (1889-1963), an influential poet, playwright, novelist, artist and film-maker from the early half of the twentieth century. He was a contemporary of people like Pablo Picasso, Igor Stravinsky, and Marcel Proust. He was born on July 5, 1889[6] in Maisons-Laffitte, a Parisian suburb, to a cultured, aristocratic family. As *Holy Blood, Holy Grail* states: "Cocteau was raised in a milieu close to the corridors of power - his family was politically prominent and his uncle was an important diplomat." His father, a painter, shot himself when Cocteau was only nine years old, and so he clung to his mother, maintaining an unusually close relationship with her for the rest of her life. As is the case with many geniuses, Cocteau did poorly in school, and dropped out in the equivalent of high school. He ran away from home at age fourteen, and spent his time in Venice, as well as the "red light district" of Marseille. He was soon ingratiating himself with the salon crowd of Paris, impressing some of the world's most well-known artists and intellectuals with the brilliance of his work. He presented his first poem to his salon friends at age fifteen.

Before long, Cocteau was patronized by some of Europe's most wealthy and respected nobility. His fame and reputation grew, and by the latter part of his life, he had been elected to the prestigious Academie Francaise, inducted with a ceremonial sword that had been designed by Picasso. He had also been named "Poet of the Year", made a "Chevalier of the Legion of Honor", and was invited to Oxford to become an honorary Doctor of Letters. Once, he was even invited by Charles de Gaulle's brother to give a national address on the general state of France. Though some think otherwise, there is no doubt in my mind that Jean Cocteau had every attribute required to be the Priory of Sion's Grand Master, and had accomplished everything necessary to be listed among the greatest poets and artists of all time.

Cocteau consorted with a number of people who, if they were not actually members of the Priory of Sion, made superb candidates. Picasso, for instance, to quote John Richardson, "was of noble lineage; what is more, his uncle Salvador had married into the Malagueño aristocracy. 'I'll dine with the duke' is how he ends one of his notes." In 1917, he even had an audience with the King of Spain. His art, too, shows his interest in Hermetic subjects: his obsession with the bull symbol, his use, on more than one occasion, of the alchemical symbol of the Black Sun, and his undeniable use of pentagonal geometry in many, if not most of his cubist paintings. Another candidate was Salvador Dali, whose "surreal" and "cubist" works often centered around strangely Hermetic religious themes, and the two films that he worked on, *The Andiluvian Dog* and *The Golden Age,* both used the classical Grail-themed works of Richard Wagner as a soundtrack. They were even financed by the same noble family - the Noailles' - that financed Cocteau's first film, *Blood of a Poet*. Furthermore, Dali's bust was once sculpted by the same artist - Arno Breker - who also sculpted a bust of Jean Cocteau.

But besides these two, Cocteau had connections to people who were almost undeniably members of the Priory. Cocteau was good friends with Jean Hugo, grand-son of the one of the Priory's Grand Masters, Victor Hugo. He was also on close terms with Jean's wife Valentine Gross Hugo, whom he called "my swan." Together they collaborated on countless projects. Cocteau was quite enamored with the late Victor Hugo himself and even made a film adaptation of Hugo's *Ruy Blas*. Cocteau also had a direct, public relationship with the man who purportedly preceded him as Grand Master of the Priory of Sion: composer Claude Debussy. In 1962, one year before his death, Cocteau was commissioned to design the set and costumes for a production of *Pelle et*

Melisande.

In addition, Cocteau maintained a life-long respect for Leonardo da Vinci, another Priory Grand Master, and quoted him often. It was from da Vinci that Cocteau obtained his theory of the use of line in his artwork, which was one of his main methods for communicating the secrets he had learned from the Priory of Sion, using sacred geometry and symbolism. Cocteau's lines were often subtle, implied - which, he believed, made the statements encoded in them all the more powerful.

Although he displayed a lifelong interest in Hermeticism and pagan mythology, and although he had never been particularly pious, Cocteau re-converted to Catholicism, the religion of his birth, in 1925. With a seemingly libertine lifestyle saturated by opium and young boys, Cocteau might have seemed an unlikely convert, but, in a way, that might have been part of what drove him back in the first place. Then again, it could have been something far more complicated.

Cocteau's 1925 re-conversion came he when met the poet Jacques Maritain, a Catholic who "sought a reconciliation between Christianity and the twentieth century." Maritain had first become acquainted with Cocteau's work when a disciple named Charles Herion gave him a copy of Cocteau's pamphlet *Le Coq et l'Arlequin*. Herion soon became ordained as a priest, and it was from him that Cocteau took the sacraments for the first time since his childhood, during the Feast of the Sacred Heart. This "Sacred Heart" symbol played a large part in Cocteau's passionate conversion. According to William Emboden, when Cocteau was introduced to Father Herion, he:

"...looked at the swarthy priest wearing a cloak with a red cross above a red heart - the symbol of his order - and all but swooned as he dropped into the arms of the church. When he wrote afterwards of Father Herion as an angel in costume, we cannot help but look back to the opium drawings of only months earlier with the theme of the angel with the heart on his chest. ...Cocteau was now in the same 'club' as Picasso and Stravinsky; he had converted back to Catholicism."

Indeed, it would appear that Cocteau was already a member of a club that included those two - specifically, the Priory of Sion. The Sacred Heart symbol which so attracted him, and which had been a theme of his art even prior to his conversion, was a symbol used by the Hieron du Val d'Or, and would appear to be an adaptation of the rose-cross.

Cocteau's beliefs were, and always had been, highly unorthodox - much like those beliefs held by other members of the Priory of Sion. For instance, the Priory of Sion reserves a special reverence for the biblical figure of Mary Magdalene (or "Madeleine" in French), who seems to have significance for them both as the mother of Christ's children and as an embodiment of the Venus goddess archetype. Cocteau, too, seemed to bear a similar reverence for this figure. As William Emboden writes, "[Cocteau] spoke of a mystical effluvium of the Madeleine Church [in Paris], like the emanations from some antique temple, that kept him in the region of that edifice." The Priory of Sion has, in the past, purposely used the letters "MM", or sometimes just "M" to symbolize Magdalene, and Cocteau used them as well. In the Church of Notre Dame de France ("Our Lady of France") in London, which Cocteau decorated with fantastic murals, this letter "M" is mysteriously placed on the altar, directly beneath the depiction of the crucifixion.[7] To the left are depicted the dice thrown by the Roman soldiers, who according to the Gospels, cast lots to determine who should get Christ's clothing after he died. The number of dots that are shown on the dice is fifty-eight, a significant number. The skull of Baphomet, which the Templars and were said to have possessed was referred to cryptically as "Caput 58M", and I have already shown how this could be a coded reference to Mary Magdalene.

The same statement is being made in Cocteau's mural at Notre Dame. This statement is further reinforced by the fact that the "M" on the altar is directly below a rose that Cocteau has placed on the cross, precisely beneath Christ's feet. Not only does that make it a "rose-cross", but the rose is directly above the initial "M" for "Mary." The term "Rosemary" is used in occult parlance to refer to the female consort of a God or demon (thus the title for the film *Rosemary's Baby.*) This is exactly what Magdalene's symbolism entailed. The fact that the rose, as well as the blood drops beneath it, are colored both red and blue may indicate the "blue blood" of the Grail bloodline. Given all this, the Church's title "Notre Dame De France" is interesting. Most would assume this to be a reference to the Virgin Mary, who is referred to by Catholics as "Our Lady." But the true "Lady of France" is the goddess Marianne, their national symbol. Perhaps "Marianne" and "Magdalene" are representations of the same archetype. Cocteau did indeed make a number of drawings and sculptures featuring Marianne. One of the drawings even ended up on a national French postage stamp.

Notre Dame de France is located in London's red light district. Cocteau had always, for some reason, held a special place in his heart for prostitutes, who had taken him in when he ran away to Marseille at age fourteen. William Emboden writes of Notre Dame that: "This church was dear to Cocteau because it was French and because it was in an area frequented by prostitutes and the poor of London. After his mural was completed, the local prostitutes took up a collection and bought a blue rug in honor of the Virgin and as a tribute to Cocteau's work." The irony of a group of pious Catholic prostitutes paying homage to a *virgin* cannot be ignored, and perhaps someone was making a veiled reference instead to Mary Magdalene (the real "Notre Dame" honored in Cocteau's mural) under the guise of the Virgin Mary.

Another heretical belief posited by the Priory of Sion seems to be present in Cocteau's work: the idea that not Christ, but a substitute died on the cross, while the real Jesus went on to raise his royal family in the south of France. This concept is illustrated in the Notre Dame mural, where only the feet of the crucified man can be seen, leaving his identity undetermined. Looking on, with a scowl on his face, and tears of blood dripping from his eye (which has been made to resemble a fish) is a man who is unmistakably Christ - the real one. On the opposite side of the cross, Cocteau has depicted himself, with his back turned to the crucifixion, as if to show that he rejects the orthodox version of the story. The theme is picked up at the Chapel of Saint Blaise, which Cocteau decorated and was buried in. Here we see two Christs depicted. We see only the head of the central one, wounded with his head slumped over as though he has just died on the cross. Above him, however, is another Christ, wounded in the hand, but perfectly alive. On either side of the two figures are two identical crowns of thorns, repeating the "dual Christ" theme. Finally, in the Chapel of Saint Peter that he painted, Cocteau has made another unorthodox statement on the nature of Christ. In his own words: "I concealed the image of Christ in a curve of the Roman vaulting. You can't see it as you enter the chapel. You have to get close to the altar to spot it. The construction of the vaulting reveals it only to the Priest, unless you go up and look." In other words, the true nature of Christ is concealed to all but the initiated, and is not to be found in the man who died on the cross.

The belief that John the Baptist was the true messiah, and not Christ, is one that, it has been posited, is also held by the Priory of Sion. Because of the special reverence that they seem to hold for him, all of their Grand Masters since the Cutting of the Elm have taken the title "Jean (or, if female, "Jeanne") upon assumption of the office. It has been noted by authors Lynn Picknett and Clive Prince that a hand signal associated with John the Baptist (a raised forefinger) can be found at the mural at Saint Blaise being made by Christ.

The authors of *Holy Blood, Holy Grail* have also made the point that Jean Cocteau, as the twenty-third Grand Master of the Priory of Sion since the Cutting of the Elm, would have been "Jean 23." In 1958, during Cocteau's Grand-Mastership, a new Pope came to power - Angelo Roncalli - who also called himself John XXIII. It was this Pope that finally revoked the ban on the practice of Freemasonry for Catholics, making members of the Priory of Sion (which has described itself as a "Hermetic Freemasonry", legitimate Catholics again. What is more, the 1976 book *The Prophecies of Pope John XXIII*, allegedly written by the Pontiff himself, stated that he was secretly a member of the Order of the Rose-Croix, with whom, to quote *Holy Blood, Holy Grail*, "he had become acquainted while acting as papal nuncio to Turkey in 1935." Stranger still, in *The Prophecies of Malachi*, written by a 12th-century Irish monk, the assumption of the papacy by a "John XXIII" was predicted, and the descriptive motto he gave to this Pope was "Shepherd and Navigator." Well, "Navigator", of course, is the official title given to the Grand Masters of the Priory of Sion. Furthermore, Jean Cocteau identified himself with the Greek mythological figure of Orpheus, who was the subject of many Cocteau paintings, drawings, poems, plays and films. Orpheus was, traditionally, both a shepherd and a seaman. This tends to indicate that Pope John XXIII was a member of the Priory of Sion, and had a very close relationship with Jean Cocteau. The authors of *Holy Blood, Holy Grail* suggest that, "Cardinal Roncalli, on becoming Pope, chose the name of his own secret grand master - so that - for some symbolic reason, there would be a John XXIII presiding over Sion and the papacy simultaneously." What could this symbolic reason possibly have been?

The Priory of Sion, as we know, has always been presumed to be at odds with the Catholic Church for a number of reasons. First, there is the fact that the Church had stolen the mythos of Christ for its own use, and the way the Church had purged the Bible of any reference to Christ's marriage, children, or real patrilineal ancestors. Then there is the fact that the Church has censored any interpretation of Christ other than its own faulty version, and "cleansed" the Bible of all texts that presented evidence to the contrary. Then, of course, there is the pact that the Church made with the Merovingian descendants of Christ, making them the perpetual heirs to the title "New Constantine" in exchange for their silence about their divine lineage. This pact was broken when the Church conspired to assassinate Merovingian King Dagobert II, and drove the Merovingians virtually out of existence.

But the Priory has often been composed of members who were nominally Catholic, and many of them have even been clerics. Furthermore, the Priory had, by Cocteau's time, begun calling itself "an order of Catholic chivalry", and Cocteau had taken care to make a public show of his re-conversion to Catholicism. The Priory had also recently announced its intention to create, through covert manipulation, a United

States of Europe - much like what the European Union is becoming, and what the Holy Roman Empire (which the Merovingian bloodline first presided over) used to be. Such a feat would be as impossible today as it was back then without an alliance with the Catholic Church, which still holds the allegiance of much of Europe's citizens.

Yes it would - an alliance, or a coup. Evidence indicates that such a coup was attempted with the placement of John XXIII on the papal throne - a coup for which that other John 23, Jean Cocteau, was at the helm. Chillingly, John XXIII died in the same year as Jean 23 - 1963 - a mere five years into his papal reign, indicating that the attempted coup was snuffed out by the Vatican before it accomplished its ultimate goal: a reform from the inside of the corrupt Church of Christ, by those who possessed his true teachings, and his blood. But they certainly tried. The authors of *Holy Blood, Holy Grail* state that:

"...more than any other man, Pope John XXIII was responsible for reorienting the Roman Catholic Church - and bringing it, as commentators have frequently said, into the twentieth century[8] ... And in June 1960, he issued a profoundly apostolic letter. This missive addressed itself specifically to the subject of "the Precious Blood of Jesus." It ascribed a hitherto unprecedented significance to that blood."

This would be the blood whose bearers, in the form of the Grail family, the Priory of Sion was sworn to protect

It is interesting that both John 23s were thought of as prophets. Pope John XXIII's papacy had been predicted by the prophecies of Malachi, and there were a set of prophecies attributed to John XXIII as well. Cocteau had also been named "the Prophet" by the sculptor Arno Breker, for reasons that remain unexplained. But there is a clue in the first syllable of Cocteau's name - a symbolism which Cocteau himself emphasized in his work. He called himself "le Coq" ("the Cock"), and published a folded broadside of the same name with Raymond Radiguet in 1920. According to William Emboden, "Cocteau liked the concept of a bird alter ego. ... It is a symbol of the soul's flight." Cocteau referred to changes in his artistic style as "moltings", and his young disciples were referred to by others as "geese." The poet Apollinaire characterized Cocteau in writing as, "The bird that sings with its fingers", a line that was later used in Cocteau's film *Orpheus*. But it was the cock specifically, Emboden writes, in which Cocteau saw himself, "as a bird that calls the morning hour, and calls his name in part." A cock is an announcer of things, just like a prophet[9], and thus he used the crowing of the cocks in his films *Blood of a Poet* and *Testament of Orpheus*. He also used the cock in the murals of the Chapel of Saint Peter, where the bird watches the Denial of Saint Peter from atop of a ladder.

Recall that it was Peter who was said to have denied Christ thrice, by the third crow of the cock, on the morning of the Crucifixion. There is a further symbolic significance here. Saint Peter is regarded by the Catholic Church as the first Pope, and yet he denied the true Christ, as the Church still does today. They consider Peter (who was consumed with jealousy for Mary Magdalene's relationship with Christ, and who mischaracterized them both in his teachings) as their rock of foundation. Indeed, Peter's name means "rock", and it is also very close to "Pater" ("Father"), the title assumed by all Catholic priests upon ordination. In another mural at Saint Peter, entitled *Saint Peter Walking on Water*, Christ is shown standing with his right foot upon a white rock, presumably the "Rock of Zion" upon which he said his messiahship was founded (i.e., the bloodline of King David). Yet Christ also called Peter "my rock." On the left side of the picture is Saint Peter supposedly "walking on water", with the help of heavenly angels. But examination shows that he is not walking on the water so much as being held aloft by the angels while his feet are dipped into the water. The rites of baptism as practiced by the likes of John the Baptist involved the immersion of the feet in water - not the entire body, as is practiced today. This mural, completed in 1957, one year before John XXIII's assumption to the throne of Saint Peter, may have been Cocteau's way of prophetically announcing a reconciliation between the Rock of Zion (the Priory of Sion) and the Rock of Saint Peter (the Catholic Church), pronouncing that the Church, symbolized by Saint Peter, was about to be re-baptized.

But what exactly *were* Cocteau's religious beliefs, if they were not orthodox Catholic? To explain, I will quote a letter from one of Cocteau's friends, Jean Bourgoint (a monk also know as "Brother Pascal") to another of Cocteau's friends, Madame Jeannette Kandaouroff, apparently in response to a letter she had written him after Cocteau's death in 1963. He wrote:

"... I want to correct your mistake concerning Cocteau's death, which - quite the opposite of what you think, touched me profoundly... One thing I should like to clear up at once is the word <u>Satan</u>, which you think you remember and which I do not remember having used concerning him. Isn't there confusion here? Didn't I speak of <u>Lucifer</u>, bright name of the 'most beautiful of the Angels' before his fall? (In fact, don't you have a magnificent photograph of him, part of my 'estate', signed by him with that name?)"

Perhaps this identification with Lucifer is the source of what William Emboden calls, "Cocteau's preoccupation with angels, and the belief that all persons are angels in borrowed costume." Cocteau also repeatedly drew a figure called the "angel of flaming cheek", which could easily be identified with Lucifer. And of course, we should consider Cocteau's signature, with which he always included that perpetual symbol of Lucifer, the pentagram, complete with a little dot in the middle. Cocteau's explanation of his use of this star was that it represented a head wound that Apollinaire had received during the Great War. This may be a lie, but it represents an interesting metaphor: that of the divine ray of Lucifer entering into the brain of one who has just become enlightened. Henry Lincoln has pointed out that there is a geometrically implied pentagram in the mural at Notre Dame de France which radiates from the center of Cocteau's forehead. Does this represent a Luciferian epiphany? What, then, were Cocteau's plans for reforming the Church? Whatever these plans were, his work on them ended with his death in 1963. But they were to be carried on by his successors – among them Pierre Plantard de Saint-Claire.

Endnotes

[1] A statue of Jeanne d'Arc can be found on the grounds of Sauniere's church at Rennes-le-Chateau.

[2] Recall that a tomb, a shepherdess and Arcadia are the main elements of the Nicholas

Poussin painting *The Shepherds of Arcadia*, mentioned in the parchments found at Rennes-le-Chateau.

[3] The importance of this reference will become obvious later on when I discuss in greater detail the concept of the "King of the World."

[4] John Dee, inventor of "Enochian magic", is one of the most influential figures of Western occultism

[5] Interestingly, while James III was in exile, he resided with the duke of Lorraine at Bar-le-Duc.

[6] Cocteau's full name was Clement-Eugène-Jean-Maurice Cocteau, but he enjoyed using "Jean Cocteau" because it could be initialized as "J.C.", the same initials as "Jesus Christ."

[7] Another, similar-looking and oddly-placed M. can be found on Cocteau's glass sculpture entitled *Stele*, and numerous Ms have been found in his mural at the Chapel of Saint Peter.

[8] The second most influential figure in liberalizing the Church was Cocteau's other friend, Jacques Maritain.

[9] In this sense, then, "Jean the Birdman" could be code for "John the Prophet." In other words, Cocteau was again identifying himself with Saint John the Baptist, and all that he represents.

Chapter Three: A Hermetic Freemasonry

"The Candidate must renounce his personality in order to devote himself to a higher moral apostolate."
- Article 7, *Statutes of the Priory of Sion*

In the year in 1956, during the grand mastership of Jean Cocteau, the Priory of Sion underwent considerable change. The order's statutes were rewritten, and the order's structure revised. The membership was increased five times, and they officially registered themselves with the French government. Their stated objective, according to the government's *Journal Official*, was "studies and mutual aid to members." At this time they took on the subtitle of "C.I.R.C.U.I.T.", which stood for "Chevalierie d'Institutions et Regles Catholiques d'Union Independente et Traditionaliste" (Chivalry of Catholic Rules and Institutions of the Independent and Traditionalist Union). *C.I.R.C.U.I.T.* was also the name of a magazine published by the order for its members.

It was at this point that the Priory began publishing the aforementioned "Priory documents" which, fifteen years later, had fomented into a firestorm of gossip about the Priory of Sion and Rennes-le-Chateau that proliferated throughout the country's popular magazines and newspapers. For instance, a 1973 article from *Midi Libre* purported that the Priory had chosen a candidate for the throne of a future Merovingian France by the name of M. Alain Poher. He had been the Provisional President of France both after the resignation of President Charles de Gaulle and after the death of President Georges Pompidou. He does have a possible connection to the Merovingian bloodline via an ancestor named Arnaud, Count of Poher, who married into the Plantard family. He was also a decorated hero of the French Resistance. As we shall see, members of the Priory of Sion played a number of key roles during the German occupation of France, and their true loyalties were not always clear-cut. Furthermore, the Priory of Sion would seem to have been manipulating French politics to a very high degree during this tumultuous period, in an apparent effort to further their long held goals of remodeling Europe according to their divinely-inspired ancient plan: a new Holy Roman Empire, or, as they now called it, a "United States of Europe."

At the head of this new empire would be a "Grand Monarch", a king whose throne had always been in existence, recognized by those who had been initiated into his secret, and was soon to make his power externally recognized as well. According to one Priory document:

"The King is shepherd and pastor at the same time. Sometimes he dispatches some brilliant ambassador to his vassal in power, his factotum, one who has the felicity of being subject to death. Thus Rene d'Anjou, Connetable de Bourbon, Nicolas Fouquet... and numerous others for whom astonishing success is followed by inexplicable disgrace - for these emissaries are both terrible and vulnerable. Custodians of a secret, one can only exalt or destroy them. Thus people like Gilles de Rais[1], Leonardo da Vinci, Joseph Balsamo, the dukes of Nevers and Gonzaga, whose wake is attended by a perfume of magic in which sulphur is mingled with incense - the perfume of the Magdalene."

If the Priory documents are correct, the Priory of Sion used such vassals as these throughout the twentieth century to manipulate affairs of state, across Europe and all over the world, to bring about their "United States of Europe." In accordance with the blueprint laid out in the *Protocols of Zion*, and in accordance with the Priory's past behavior, the Priory documents indicate that the Priory has been playing all sides of the political spectrum, sewing the seeds of discord by promoting not only monarchist senti-ments, but also Socialism, Communism, Fascism, Catholicism, anti-Catholicism, and Freemasonry. A document written by S. Roux in a self-published pamphlet asserts:

"One cannot say that the Church is ignorant of the line of the Razes [the Merovingian line from Dagobert II], *but it must be remembered that all its descendants since Da-gobert have been secret agitators against both the royal line of France and against the Church - and that they have been the source of all heresies. The return of a Merovin-gian descendant to power would entail for France the proclamation of a popular mon-archy allied to the USSR, and the triumph of Freemasonry - in short, the disappearance of religious freedom."*

Another Priory document, called *Le Cercle d'Ulysse* by Jean Declaude, de-clares that since the death of Jean Cocteau, an Abbe Ducaud- Bourget had been at the helm of the Priory, and that the order had since become, "a power capable of confront-ing the Vatican in the days to come. Monsignor Lefebvre is a most active and redoubt-able member, capable of saying 'You make me Pope and I will make you King.'"

Abbe Ducaud-Bourget had been trained as a priest at Saint Sulpice. He was both a conventual chaplain of the Vatican's Templar-like Sovereign Order of Malta, and a well-known Resistance hero. He was an accomplished poet who had been admitted, like so many other members of Sion, to the Academie Francaise. But he was also known to lean to the right politically. He liked Mussolini and once voiced his desire for France to "recover its sense of values under the guidance of a new Napoleon."

As for "Monsignor Marcel Lefebvre", that would be Archbishop Marcel Le-febvre, a fanatically traditionalist Catholic who openly defied Pope Paul VI, labeling him as too liberal, resulting in a brush with excommunication. Abbe Ducaud-Bourget was a member of Lefebvre's Traditionalist camp, and even led protests against the cur-rent leadership of the Church. He was also threatened with excommunication. Le-febvre had been a member of Action Francaise, considered to be an extremely right-wing organization, and had complimented Argentina's fascist regime publicly. How-ever, in 1976, when Lefebvre appeared to be on the brink of excommunication, the Pope changed his mind. According to an article from London's *Guardian*, on August 30, 1976:

"The Archbishop's team of priests in England... believe that their leader still has a pow-erful ecclesiastical weapon to use in his dispute with the Vatican. No one will give any hint of its nature, but Father Peter Morgan, the group's leader... describes it as being something 'earth-shaking.'"

Later, around 1980, an article ran in the popular French magazine *Bonne Soiree* linking both Ducaud-Bourget and Lefebvre with the Priory of Sion, and claiming that they had both recently visited the site of Chateau Barberie, which was so precious to the Priory.

Pierre Plantard de Saint-Clair

Another article in *Bonne Soiree* from 1981 stated that Pierre Plantard had been elected the new Grand Master of the Priory of Sion in 1981, by a "Convent" of the Priory's 121 dignitaries. As the article described it, "The 121 dignitaries of the Prieure de Sion are all *eminence grises* of high finance and of international political or philosophical societies." It also stated that Pierre Plantard was the direct descendant of Dagobert II, which:

"...has been proved legally by the parchments of Queen Blanche of Castile, discovered by the Abbe Sauniere in his church at Rennes-le-Chateau (Aude) in 1891. These documents were sold by the priest's niece in 1965 to Captain Roland Stansmore and Sir Thomas Frazer, and were deposited in a safe deposit box of Lloyd's Bank Europe Limited of London."

The authors of *Holy Blood, Holy Grail,* in an interview with Plantard associate Philippe de Cherisey, were told that, "Francois Ducaud-Bourget had not been elected by a proper quorum." One possible explanation for this is a rift that occurred in the Priory around 1956, centered on Cocteau's new statutes. In addition to increasing the order's membership by five times, these articles, among other things, required that members provide the order with a notarized copy of their signature and birth certificate, and that they always admit to their membership with the Priory upon being asked about it by an outsider. Failure to do so would be considered resignation from the order. Many members were enraged because they felt that they were being "deprived of their anonymity." Perhaps Bourget was elected by a segment of the Priory that had broken off from the main group in protest, and which was no longer recognized by that main group. Indeed, such a schism does seem to have occurred, one which assumed proportions similar to the Cutting of the Elm, but which "was averted by the diplomatic skill of Pierre Plantard.

M. Plantard's biography is nothing short of fascinating, and more than a bit confusing. In addition to being a direct descendant of Dagobert II, he is also a direct descendant of the owners of Chateau Barberie, and in an interview with Gerard de Sede once mentioned an "international secret" that is hidden at Gisors. In fact he seems to have been de Sede's main source of information for his books about Rennes-le-Chateau and the Priory of Sion. Plantard's grandfather was purportedly a friend of Berenger Sauniere, and Pierre Plantard owned a great deal of land near Rennes-le-Chateau, such as the ruins of the Blanchefort Chateau, and the land upon which the Church of Saint Dagobert once stood. A bizarre little biography of Pierre Plantard, which was written by his first wife, Anne Lea Hisler, in *C.I.R.C.U.I.T.* reads as follows:

"Let us not forget that this psychologist was the friend of personages as diverse as Comte Israel Monti, one of the brothers of the Holy Vehm, Gabriel Trarieux d'Egmont, one of the thirteen members of the Rose-Croix, Paul LeCour, the philosopher on Atlantis, the Abbe Hoffet of the Service of Documentation of the Vatican, Th. Moreux, the director of the Conservatory at Bourges, etc. Let us remember that during the Occupation, he was arrested, suffered torture by the Gestapo, and was interred as a political prisoner for long months. In his capacity as doctor of arcane sciences he learned to

appreciate the value of secret information, which no doubt led to his receiving the title of honorary member in several hermetic societies. All of this has gone to form a singular personage, a mystic of peace, an apostle of liberty, an ascetic whose ideal is to serve the well-being of humanity. Is it astonishing therefore that he should become one of the eminence grises from whom the great of this world seek counsel?"

A researcher working for the authors of *Holy Blood, Holy Grail* contacted writer Jean-Luc Chaumeil, another associate of Pierre Plantard, on the Priory's political intentions. As they described it, he told them that:

"...in a few years... there would be dramatic change in the French government - a change that would pave the way for a popular monarchy with a Merovingian ruler on the throne... Sion was ... intent on presiding over a restoration of true 'values' - values, it would appear, of a spiritual, perhaps esoteric character. These values ... were ultimately pre-Christian..."

Chaumeil also said something very peculiar, making the abrupt and unsolicited comment that "not all members of the Prieure de Sion ... were Jewish", implying that the majority of them in fact were.

Vaincre and the French Resistance

The authors of *Holy Blood, Holy Grail* arranged a series of interviews with Pierre Plantard himself. In the first interview he claimed that the Priory possessed the treasures of Solomon's Temple, which would be "returned to Israel when the time is right." He also repeated Chaumeil's assertions about the coming political changes in France. Over a series of subsequent meetings, dealt with extensively in *Holy Blood, Holy Grail* and *The Messianic Legacy*, the authors learned much about both Plantard's intentions and those of the Priory of Sion. They also undertook their own investigation of Pierre Plantard. They discovered that he had indeed been very active in the French Resistance. Between 1941 and 1943, he had edited what purported to be a "Resistance journal", a strange little magazine called *Vaincre*. Between 1943 and 1944, he had supposedly been imprisoned by the Gestapo in Fresnes, although the authors were not able to confirm this.

They did, however, manage to track down copies of six issues of *Vaincre*, which they described as "printed on high-quality paper, which was difficult to obtain in France at the time." It was published by the company of Poirier Murat, a French Resistance hero and friend of Plantard. The first issue had a press run of 1,379, which had grown to 5000 by the sixth issue. "On the whole", *Holy Blood, Holy Grail* concluded, "*Vaincre* represented a venture that could not possibly have been undertaken without some knowledge on the part of the authorities. It also represented a venture with substantial money behind it."

Although *Vaincre* proved to be an actual publication, it was not what one would think of as a "Resistance journal", and more of a new age publication, dealing with mythology, mysticism, Hermeticism, cabalism, etc. There were articles about Atlantis, the fabled underground city of Agartha, lost races, and talk of "secret masters" hidden in the mountains of Tibet. Most of these themes, interestingly enough, were also those embraced by the secret societies that spawned the Nazi movement. And there was indeed a secret society behind the publication of *Vaincre*: Alpha Galates.

Alpha Galates purported to be a chivalric order. It promoted the value of chivalry as a means for revitalizing spiritual values, and creating a new spiritual order throughout the world. As *Vaincre* stated, "...chivalry is indispensable because our country cannot be reborn except through its knights." It also emphasized the need for chivalry, including the bestowal of knightly titles, to be based on spiritual and moral achievements, as they had been in the beginning of the chivalric era. Honors should not, as they later were, be handed out in return for political favors. *Vaincre* declared that, "The chevalier cannot live without the spiritual ideal, which is the reservoir for moral, intellectual, and spiritual force through coming generations."

Vaincre reveals some direct links between Alpha Galates and the Priory of Sion, indicating that, if they were not the same order, they were at least sister organizations. *Vaincre* states that the order is divided into the "Legion", who conduct "philosophical research", and the "Phalange", who train future members. This is exactly the divisional structure given to the Priory of Sion in Cocteau's 1956 statutes. However, Plantard had previously stated that his membership in the Priory began in 1943, and his involvement in Alpha Galates began a year earlier. Yet one would think he had already been involved for some time by 1942, as he was already editing their official magazine, billed in the first issue as "Pierre de France." By the fourth issue he had lengthened his name to Pierre de France-Plantard, and was named in *Vaincre* as the Grand Master of Alpha Galates, which was now headquartered at his own address in Paris.

Vaincre states that Alpha Galates had been registered with the *Journal Official* in 1937, but this was not recorded, and the French Ministry of Defense denies any knowledge of the order, as did the French Prefecture of Police, even though they did in fact have records showing that they had investigated the group. They definitely had reason to investigate, for the political bent of *Vaincre* would seem, on the surface at least, to be considerably right-wing. For instance, one of its frequent contributors was Professor Louis le Fur, who had been a well-known writer and journalist during the Occupation, and was appointed by Petain to a prominent educational post. Le Fur states in one of his articles in *Vaincre* that he has belonged to Alpha Galates for eight years.

Even more damning is the content of the magazine itself, which extols the virtues of Petain and the Vichy government. A romantic and patriotic hymn to Petain was even published in the first issue, and the Order of Alpha Galates was proclaimed to be "in the service of the homeland." Also, what would a right-wing journal be without anti-Semitism, of which *Vaincre* contains plenty. One line reads, "To restore our homeland to its rank... it is necessary to eradicate... false dogmas ... and the corrupt principles of the formerly democratic Jewish-Masonry."

The authors of *Holy Blood, Holy Grail* theorized that this might have been just a front, a cover for *Vaincre*'s real intentions. And Pierre Plantard, when confronted, told them the same. As they described it, "He hinted that beneath its pro-Vichy Petainist patina, *Vaincre* contained coded messages that would have been decipherable only to the Resistance." Indeed, it is hard to reconcile the exoteric messages of *Vaincre* with the fact that so many of its contributors, and so much of the membership of Alpha Galates, including Pierre Plantard had been closely allied with the Resistance, along with Abbe Ducaud-Bourget, who may have presided over the Priory of Sion and is said to have inducted Pierre Plantard into the group. Furthermore, Pierre Plantard later served as an assistant to Charles de Gaulle, who is on record as having refused to work closely with former collaborators. Also, in November of 1942, a pro-Vichy and pro-Nazi publication called *Au pilori* published an attack on Pierre Plantard, Alpha Galates, and *Vaincre*, which would have been unlikely had they in fact been on the same side.

The commentary from *Au pilori* was obviously taken very seriously, for *Vaincre* dedicated an entire issue to rebutting it. It was announced that a member of Alpha Galates had been removed from the order, apparently for leaking information to *Au pilori*. *Vaincre* also clarified its mission: a "United States of the West."

This idea is one of the predominant themes throughout *Vaincre*, and is illustrated by a drawing that ran in the first issue. This drawing depicts a mounted knight riding down a road upon which is written "The United States of the West." This road divides areas labeled "Brittany" and "Bavaria." The horse is galloping towards a rising sunset marked with "1946" and the sign of Aquarius, indicating that the birth of the United States of the West will be the dawn of a new age.

For Alpha Galates, this was not merely a dream. It was a plan. Alpha Galates member Louis le Fur later founded a group called "Energie" that included Robert Schuman, another man who dreamed of a United States of Europe, and who later became an instrumental figure in the drafting of the plans for the European Economic Community. And it was not only the men of Alpha Galates and the French Resistance that were dreaming of a United Europe. The dream was alive in Germany, with both the Nazis *and* with the German Resistance.

The German Resistance movement was largely centered on an aristocrat named Claus von Stauffenberg, a nobleman and monarchist with a large and loyal following of acolytes called "the Kreisau Circle." Stauffenberg was responsible for the famous "Bomb Plot", the attempt to assassinate Hitler on July 20, 1944, now celebrated as Stauffenberg Day in Europe. Among his circle were his cousins Count Helmut James von Moltke and Hans Adolf von Moltke, the latter of whom was apparently a member of Alpha Galates. In the article in *Vaincre* in which it is announced that Pierre Plantard has been elected Grand Master, Hans Adolf von Moltke, who is described as "a great German, one of the Masters in our Order", is quoted as stating:

> *"I have the pleasure to say, before my departure for Spain, that our Order has at last found a chief worthy of it in the person of Pierre de France.*
> *It is therefore with total confidence that I depart to perform my mission; for while not deluding myself about the perils I run in discharging my duty, I know that until my last breath my watchword will consist of recognition of Alpha Galates and fidelity to its chief."*

Von Moltke had been the German ambassador to both Poland and Britain, and had just been appointed ambassador to Spain. His cousin Helmut James von Moltke had been attempting to circumvent Hitler by negotiating a peace deal with the Allies himself through associates in Sweden, and it is likely that Hans Adolf von Moltke was on a similar mission in Spain. Von Moltke died in Spain later that year, and although the Allies won the war, the peace that followed was not at all what the Kreisau Circle had in mind. Had they been successful in negotiating their peace deal, Europe may well have turned out much differently that it is today.

This link between the Kreisau Circle and Alpha Galates represents the first definitive link between the French and German Resistance movements yet known. And the relationship between the two groups seems not to have begun until 1942, the same year that *Vaincre* began publishing. Like the members of Alpha Galates, the Kreisau Circle became involved in the planning of the EEC through their associates in the Swiss branch of the British Foreign Office, and through Allen Dulles, then head of the Swiss station of the OSS - which later became, with Dulles at the head, the CIA. As I shall discuss, the Priory of Sion appears to have a special relationship with the CIA as well.

Charles de Gaulle and the Committees of Public Safety

During the mid-1950s, about the same time that a schism within the Priory of Sion was occurring, France was brought to the brink of civil war as a result of the fact that Algeria, which was under French control, was jockeying for independence. Coalition governments were collapsing at an alarming rate, and the situation, which lasted for eight years, appeared dire. Within the French Army stationed in Algeria, a network of secret societies was formed with the aim of keeping Algeria under French control. They were called the Committees of Public Safety, named and modeled after a similar network of secret societies formed during the French Revolution. These groups, which included a number of former Resistance leaders, embraced Charles de Gaulle (alleged by the Priory documents to be a pawn of the Priory of Sion) as the only man they felt could lead France out of the mire towards victory.

In the Spring of 1958, the French government decided that it would cut its losses with Algeria and grant their independence. In reaction to this, the Committees of Public Safety staged a coup d'etat, declaring their own government, meanwhile pleading with Charles de Gaulle to seize the French government and reunify the country. Within a couple of months, Committees of Public Safety began to appear in mainland France. One Committee took control of Corsica by force while another based in Algeria busied itself propagating a peculiar message: that the citizens of France must "choose between the star of Moscow and the Cross of Lorraine." In this brewing conflict former Resistance fighters and Vichy collaborators found themselves on the same team: French nationalism

Then all of the sudden, their dreams came true. In fear of a widely spread rumor that a coup was being planned in Paris, the ruling government simply resigned on May 28. The following day, the Committees of Public Safety organized marches throughout Paris in support of De Gaulle. Hours later, De Gaulle accepted the Presidency, and began forming a government that included many of the key figures in his rise to power. Among them was Andre Malraux, an associate of Jean Cocteau and an alleged member of the Priory of Sion.

But now that De Gaulle was in control, he was expected by the Committees, who had orchestrated his rise to power, to maintain Algeria's colonial status. Yet what they did not know was that he had no intention of doing so. As soon as they caught wind of this, many members of the Algerian Committees, feeling betrayed, formed the OAS (Organisation de l'Armee Secrete - Secret Army Organization), which for years afterward staged numerous assassination attempts on De Gaulle. However, none of them were successful, nor was this group considered a serious threat. The French Committees, though, *were* a threat, and De Gaulle feared that, like the Committees of Public

Safety during the French Revolution, they might turn on him at any time and march him off to the guillotine. What De Gaulle wanted was for the Committees to be disbanded entirely. And with that, we once again come to the subject of Pierre Plantard.

According to Plantard himself, he had been asked by Charles de Gaulle to take control of the Parisian Committees, see to it that they completed their task of installing De Gaulle in power, and then dissolve them once this had been done. Presumed confirmation of this appears in a pamphlet by Anne Lea Hisler which was deposited in the Bibliotheque Nationale in 1964. In this she states that the headquarters of the French Committees was in the Parisian suburb of Aulnay-sous-Bois, directed by Michel Debre, Andre Malraux, Marshall Alphonse Juin, and Pierre Plantard, whom she calls "the Way.", she states). She then quotes a letter purportedly written by De Gaulle to her husband on August 3, 1958. It says:

> *"My dear Plantard,*
> *In my letter of 29 July, 1958, I said to you how much I appreciated the participation of the Committees of Public Safety in the work of renewal I have undertaken. Now that the new institutions have been established, which will enable our country to rediscover her rightful status, I believe the members of the Committees of Public Safety can regard themselves as released from the obligations they have until now assumed, and can demobilize."*

Further confirmation came from the Institut Charles de Gaulle. Although they were unable to find any mention of Pierre Plantard in their own archives, they did manage to scrounge up some references to him in France's leading newspaper, *Le Monde*. One article, dated June 6, 1958, quoted a communique that had been issued from the headquarters of the French Committees of Public Safety, stating:

> *"The Committees of Public Safety must express the wishes of the people, and it is in the name of liberty, of unity, and of solidarity that all French citizens must present today to aid Charles de Gaulle... Patriots, to your posts, and have confidence in the man who has already saved France..."*

The author of this statement was signed as "Captain Way", one of Pierre Plantard's pseudonyms. Then two days later, another article appeared quoting another communique about the Committees, which was signed by "M. Plantard", who also said that he could be called on his home phone by dialing "WAY-PAIX" (Way-Peace). Finally, on July 29, the day that de Gaulle wrote the aforementioned letter to Plantard, another article ran in *Le Monde* quoting yet another communique signed by "Captain Way", this one announcing the dissolution of the committees. The article goes on to say that Captain Way is, in fact, "M. Pierre Plantard... who, together with certain friends, took the initiative of establishing this Committee." It further states that Plantard will be "secretary in charge of propaganda" for "the 'Movement' which will comprise the successor to the Committee."

C.I.R.C.U.I.T

Following *Vaincre*, Pierre Plantard lent himself to another publishing venture, the aforementioned *C.I.R.C.U.I.T*, which first appeared in 1956, that crucial year for the Priory. Actually, this was only the first series of *C.I.R.C.U.I.T.*, the second of which appeared in 1959. The first series does not mention either Pierre Plantard or the Priory of Sion, and on the surface, at least, reflects little of the interests of either. Other than an article about a thirteen-house zodiac system used by the Priory (which I discuss in Appendix A of this book), the rest of the magazine appears to have been published by a low-cost housing association. It contains unremarkable articles about housing, and other seemingly extraneous materials such as, according to *The Messianic Legacy*, "crossword puzzles, contests for children on a housing estate, advertisements for pencils." The meaning of this is unclear, but it is quite possible that, like *Vaincre*, *C.I.R.C.U.I.T.* was operating on two levels at once, and that secret messages were being communicated through cryptic words inserted into otherwise uninteresting articles.

The second series of *C.I.R.C.U.I.T*, which began in 1959, while not at all straightforward, was at least an obvious organ of the Priory of Sion. Pierre Plantard is listed as Editor, though the Priory of Sion is not specifically mentioned. Instead, the magazine purports to be published by an organization called "The Federation of French Forces", for which an address and phone number is provided. Unfortunately, researchers have determined that neither the address nor the phone number were correct, and they have not been able to find any information on the Federation of French Forces. But the street name mentioned in the address, "Aulnay-sous-Bois", is the same street from which the central command of the Committees of Public Safety operated, indicating that the Federation of French Forces were somehow a continuation of the Committees. As if to verify this, the second issue of the 1959 *C.I.R.C.U.I.T.* series mentions yet another letter that Plantard supposedly received from Charles de Gaulle.

The second series of *C.I.R.C.U.I.T* resembles *Vaincre* in many ways, and even makes reference to the other magazine. Like *Vaincre*, it covers topics related to the occult, mysticism, chivalry, French nationalism, and European unity. Many of these articles are written by Pierre Plantard, who here, as in the pages of *Vaincre*, uses the pen name "Chyren." Some articles are also, as in *Vaincre*, written by his wife Anne Lea Hisler. There is again an emphasis on the importance of a thirteen-house zodiac, and Pierre Plantard uses this system to predict France's destiny for the next few decades.

There are other, more cryptic topics discussed in *C.I.R.C.U.I.T* as well. There is an entire article dedicated, seemingly out of place, to the details of viticulture and wine selling. Particular emphasis is put on something called "the grafting of vines", which apparently is a coded reference to the intermarrying of royal bloodlines. Another peculiar line from one of Plantard's articles is worth quoting, and its importance will become clear in the pages to follow. Philosophizing about the destiny of human civilization, he writes:

"...all is accomplished in accordance with well-determined cycles. A 'Nautonnier' guides the ark ('arche') in the flood."

In regards to the politics of state, *C.I.R.C.U.I.T* does not confine itself to mere statements of opinion. They predict what they believe will inevitably occur. They argue for the abolition of the French system which carves the country's geography into departments. They then lay out their own blueprint for the restructuring of the French government. It would include nine sections: "Council of the Provinces; Council of

State; Parliamentary Council; Taxes, Work, and Production; Medical; National Education; Age of Majority; and Housing and Schools." This doesn't seem terribly radical.
But then, in another article by Plantard, he enunciates plans for the restructuring of the
entire world:

*"...the creation of a Confederation of Lands becomes a Confederation of States: the
United States of Euro-Africa, which represented economically (1) an African and European community of exchange based on a common market and (2) the circulation of
wealth in order to serve the well-being of all, this being the sole stable foundation on
which peace can be constructed.".*

The United States of Europe

One of the most consistently-stated goals of the Priory of Sion, and those associated with it, is a United States of Europe. According to *Holy Blood, Holy Grail*: "The
Prieure de Sion seeks a United States of Europe partly as a bulwark against the Soviet
imperium... a self-contained and neutral power bloc capable of holding the balance of
power between the Soviet Union and the United States."

The idea of a united Europe was, as we know, popular amongst the French
Resistance. It was espoused by people such as Andre Malraux, who advocated a
"European New Deal" allied against the USSR. In 1942, Winston Churchill was quoted
as saying, "I trust that the European family may act united as one under a Council of
Europe. I look forward to a United States of Europe." Organizations such as Pan Eu-
ropa, founded by Count Richard Coudenhove-Kalergi, began to pop up in the 1940s.
Pan Europa included Jean Cocteau's friend Paul Valery, and is currently directed by
Otto von Hapsburg. They employ a Celtic cross as their insignia.

Other groups that were interested in seeing European unity were the Western
intelligence agencies, especially British and American intelligence, who sought to build
a pro-European network amongst militant Catholic and right-wing political groups.
When the OSS (Office of Strategic Strategies), precursor of the CIA, was under the control of William Donovan, they attempted to infiltrate the Vatican and put priests in top
positions on their payroll. They made use of Father Felix Morlion, founder of Pro Deo
(For God), a European Catholic intelligence agency which the OSS funded and installed
first in New York, then in the Vatican itself. They also made use of the Society of Jesu-
its, which had been involved in Catholic espionage for years.

In 1948, the same year that the Congress of Europe met at the Hague, the OSS
became the Central Intelligence Agency. Immediately the CIA began funding European
political parties, particularly the Christian Democrats, in an attempt to manipulate European governments and pull them to the right. The following year, the ACUE (American
Committee on a United Europe) was formed, and William Donovan was made its chair-
man. Allen Dulles, former head of the OSS in Switzerland, friend of the Von Moltke
cousins and future head of the CIA, was Vice-President. The Director of the Council on
Foreign Relations, and the future coordinator of the Trilateral Commission, George S.
Franklin, was the Secretary. They even had another CIA agent, Thomas Braden, as
their Executive Director. It was because of these men that the decision was made for
the State Department to fund the European Movement. Following this, Joseph Retinger
proceeded to collaborate with Prince Bernhard of the Netherlands and others to create

the now infamous globalist think tank, the Bilderberg Group.

Meanwhile, the CIA busied itself funding organizations and newspapers all over Europe that were pro-Catholic and anti-Communist. A major recipient was Italy's Christian Democrat party, which had been started by the father of future Pope Paul VI, who was also on their payroll. He had been working as a spy and liaison for the OSS, then later the CIA, since during WWII. It has also been said that Pope John Paul II has been receiving weekly intelligence briefings from the CIA since 1978, although it is unknown whether that continues to occur given the Pope's current state of deterioration.

It was during the 1960s that the CIA began distributing funds to its favored groups through the Vatican's own bank. This was done with the help of a shadowy, pro-Catholic, anti-Communist Masonic lodge known as "P2", which allegedly had lodges not only in Italy, but also France, Portugal, Switzerland, the United States, Nicaragua, Bolivia, Paraguay, Argentina, and Venezuela. As author David Yallop has written:

"[P2] interlocks with a number of the military regimes of Latin America, and with a variety of groups of neo-Fascists. It also interlocks very closely with the CIA. It reaches right into the heart of the Vatican. The central common interest of all these elements is apparently a hatred and fear of Communism."

All of this came out in the Italian press when a massive banking scandal broke involving the official Vatican bank, Banco Ambrosiano, and P2. The main figures implicated were P2 members Michael Sindona (a high ranking official in the bank and P2's financier) and the lodge's Grand Master Licio Gelli. Gelli was a man with far-right viewpoints who, after the scandal broke, was found hanging from the Blackfriar's Bridge in London in 1982, in a manner consistent with Masonic ritual[2]. It also led to the murder of an Italian investigator, Giorgio Ambrosoli, and later that of Michael Sindona himself, who was the chief suspect in the other two killings.

It is known that P2 was under the direction of an even more powerful organization, which one former member, Mino Pecorelli, named as being the CIA. (Pecorelli was murdered after making this acknowledgement.) But there is another possibility as well. Supposedly, "P2" is short for "Propaganda Due", the meaning of which is not elaborated on. However, we have received one suggestion from an informant that "P2" simply means "Priory 2", and that it is a break-off group of the Priory of Sion.

Certainly it is interesting to note that P2 began in the 1960s, just about four years after the "schism" within the Priory caused by Jean Cocteau's new statutes. Perhaps P2 is made up of part of that group which never got reintegrated into the order after the schism was resolved. This idea is further corroborated by a bizarre book called *Scandals of the Prieure de Sion*, written under the pseudonym "Cornelius."

Cornelius states unequivocally that the murder of Giorgio Ambrosoli was ordered by a well-known Italian politician who was also one of the senior dignitaries of the Priory of Sion. He states that both Michael Sindona and a number of banks in the US have been involved in questionable financial deals with the Priory of Sion. He says that the Priory was intimately involved with the Italian Mafia, and with P2. Another person Cornelius alleged to be involved was Cardinal Jean Danielou, who was, according to *The Messianic Legacy*, "the Vatican's chief spokesman at the time on clerical celibacy." He was found dead in a scene that involved a female stripper and a large amount of cash - purportedly killed by a heart attack. Interestingly, Danielou had been a friend of Jean Cocteau, and had made a Latin translation of his play, *Oedipus Rex*. Cornelius implicates Danielou in the financial transactions between the Vatican, P2, and the Priory of Sion, and intimates that the Cardinal's death was somewhat less than natural.

Finally, Cornelius says that in 1981, Pierre de Plantard, having recently been elected Grand Master of the Priory, had a meeting two days later with P2 Grand Master Licio Gelli at a cafe called "La Tipia" in Paris. This just so happens to be the same place where Plantard insisted on meeting the authors of *Holy Blood, Holy Grail* for some of their interviews.

The Knights of Jerusalem and the Knights of Malta

When the P2 scandal broke in 1981, and Licio Gelli's property was raided, they discovered links between P2 and other organizations that were very highly ranked within the Vatican. These included a Vatican intelligence agency called "Opus Dei", which controls Vatican Radio, and another group that actually claims descent from the Knights Templar: the Sovereign Military Order of the Temple of Jerusalem. This order, which dates back at least to 1804, claims to have been created by the Templars' last Grand Master, Jacques de Molay, who purportedly drew up a charter prior to his execution which named his successor. They are a genuine continuation, they said, of the original order, and they were now dedicating themselves to "antiquarian interests." However, when the authors of *Holy Blood, Holy Grail* met with one of their representatives in 1982, and then did some research on their own, a much more complicated picture emerged.

The representative told them that they had just undergone a schism in which members of their group broke away to form their own, now headquartered in Switzerland. From this another group had spun off calling itself "Grand Prieure de Suisse", led by a man named Anton Zapelli, which made its headquarters in the Swiss city of Sion. This organization included a number of members who also belonged to the Grand Suisse Loge Alpina, and Zapelli had been named by one of the informants interviewed for *Holy Blood, Holy Grail* as being, "The real power behind the Prieure de Sion." In their subsequent research, the authors came across internal documents from the Grand Prieure de Suisse. They dealt largely with two themes: international banking and European unification, specifically "the role of modern Templars in the reunification of Europe."

If the ancient order of Templars lives on in the Sovereign Military Order of the Temple of Jerusalem, so too does their ancient rival, the Knights Hospitaller, live on in the Sovereign Military Order of the Knights of Malta. They were first organized as the Order of Saint John in Jerusalem in 1070, three decades before the Crusades began, to provide medical care for pilgrims to the Holy Land. Over the next 60 years they transformed themselves into an impressive military and financial power on par with the Knights Templar and the Teutonic Knights, both of whom they had an antagonistic relationship with. Even while the other two orders, which both practiced similarly "heretical" rituals, were being persecuted by the Church, the Hospitallers were favored by the Pope, and were given many of the Templars' former holdings after their dissolution. Over the years they moved their headquarters from Cyprus to Rhodes, which, as *Holy Blood, Holy Grail* describes, "they governed as their private principality." It was later transferred again to the Isle of Malta. *Holy Blood, Holy Grail* states that, "In the mid-sixteenth century, they were still one of the supreme military and naval powers of the Christian world, with strength and financial resources comparable to most kingdoms."

They were ousted from Malta by Napoleon in 1798, but reestablished themselves in Rome, taking on the name "the Knights of Malta" to avoid confusion with other organizations in Germany and Britain that were called "The Knights of Saint John", but were actually Protestant. They still held a considerable amount of political power as the world entered the twentieth century, and they were actually named as potential candidates to take control of Jerusalem after WWII. Today they maintain, from their seat in Rome, a prominent organization that spans the globe. Further, they are still recognized by international law as presiding over "an independent sovereign principality", as states *Holy Blood, Holy Grail*:

"The Grand Master is recognized as a head of state, with a secular rank equivalent to a prince and an ecclesiastical rank equivalent to a cardinal. The Order maintains formal diplomatic relations with a number of countries, especially in Africa and in Latin America, and in those countries its ministers enjoy standard diplomatic privileges."

The leadership of the Knights of Malta is in no way democratically chosen. All members of the upper degrees must come from an aristocratic family with a coat of arms that is at least 300 years old. The membership includes not only high-ranking members of the Church, but also high-ranking members of international business and politics. Not surprisingly, they are deeply entangled with Vatican intelligence units, and are described in *Holy Blood, Holy Grail* as being "one of the primary channels of communication between the Vatican and the CIA." Its membership is saturated with people from intelligence agencies the world over, and the American contingent is rather substantial. Among its ranks have stood CIA directors John McCone and William Casey, as well as Alexander Haig, Colin Powell, William Bennett, and William F. Buckley. CIA director William Colby was invited, but responded, "I'm a little lower key." Also among the Knights of Malta have been a number of members of the P2 lodge: Licio Gelli, Umberto Ortolani (Gelli's closest associate), Chiefs of the Italian Secret Service General de Lorenzo and General Allavena, General Giuseppe Santovito, once Chief of Italian Military Intelligence, and probably many others.

One of the Knights of Malta's primary activities in the last 20 years has been the fight against Communism in South and Central America. It is through them that the CIA has often funneled money to right-wing military groups in these areas to help them crush the left. As it just so happens, the one-time head of the Knights of Malta in the US, J. Peter Grace, also ran the Americares organization. This group was dedicated to the same right-wing cause. They are suspected of having funded the World Anti-Communist League with money provided by the Knights of Malta and, ultimately, the CIA.

Acknowledgement of a relationship between the Knights of Malta and the Priory of Sion came from Pierre Plantard himself, who admitted that a number of his order's members were also Knights of Malta. Abbe Ducaud-Bourget, the man who had brought Plantard into the order originally (and who has been cited by some authors as Grand Master of the Priory after Jean Cocteau), was Magistral Chaplain of the Knights of Malta for fourteen years.

A series of events surrounding some falsified documents which pertained to the present location of the Sauniere parchments convinced the authors of *Holy Blood, Holy Grail* that the Priory's relationship with the British and American intelligence network did indeed exist. It also led to yet another schism within the order. At one of the authors' many meetings with Pierre Plantard at La Tipia, he told them that this schism was caused by an "Anglo-American contingent" within the order who were trying to move the Priory's focus away from restoring monarchy in Europe and towards more practical and immediate goals. They were led to believe that this "Anglo-American contingent" consisted of spies from the CIA, MI5, and the Knights of Malta. Then he appeared to - almost - make an astounding proposition. As they described it:

"...M. Plantard paused and began to muse. There were, at present, two vacancies in the Order, he said reflectively. It would be a great advantage to have those vacancies occupied by 'foreigners' who would be sympathetic to the French and continental position. That would serve to counterbalance the influence of the 'Anglo-American contingent.' There was a long and pregnant pause. We said nothing. The conversation drifted to a different topic. But for a moment, it actually appeared as if M. Plantard had been about to offer us membership in the Order."

The offer was never accepted, however, and to my knowledge, the "Anglo-American contingent" was never defeated. At the authors' last meeting with Plantard, he expanded upon the Priory of Sion's political goals for the immediate future. He remarked, according to *The Messianic Legacy*, that "Mitterand... had been a necessary stepping stone", but, "had served his purpose, and was expendable." He said that for some of the Priory's members, their ultimate aim was a United States of Europe, to balance the power exercised by the Soviet Union and the United States. They also desired a larger "common market" of the Occident, which would include both Europe and the United States. About the involvement of the Vatican in this grand plan, Plantard said that Rome was "cooperating" in accordance with their "ongoing policy" on such matters, a policy "to which individual popes were bound." Also, *Holy Blood, Holy Grail*, he said, had "caused quite a few ripples" within the Vatican.

Compared to the carefully-scripted trickles of information that they had received from the Priory thus far, Plantard was practically spilling his guts. A few weeks later, they learned why. They received a letter from him, addressed to the membership of the Priory, and dated two and a half months prior to the authors' last meeting with him, stating that he was resigning not only his grand mastership, but his membership in the order. This was done "for reasons of health", and "for reasons of personal and family independence." Furthermore, his resignation was prompted by "certain maneuvers" made by "our English and American brethren", and because of the numerous "false or falsified documents" about him that had been published "in the press, in books, and in duplicated pamphlets deposited in the Bibliotheque Nationale."

With Plantard's resignation, the Priory of Sion apparently went into hiding again. But the exposure of its mythos to pubic consciousness has caused the Priory of Sion's legend to expand exponentially in popularity. The primary reason is this: within the saga of the Priory, the Merovingians, the Grail, and Rennes-le-Chateau resides a mystique that all of us subconsciously relate to. Deep within or ancestral memory, we can all recall a time when the sacredness of certain bloodlines was innately understood, and the concept of a king as an incarnation of God needed no explanation. In our sub-conscious minds, we all know that there is a pattern to the events of history; that this is no random collection of occurrences, but rather, in many instances, the result of a highly-orchestrated plot perpetrated by the unseen hands of the elite. Within ourselves, we know that there must be some reason why the elite are who they are, and why they do what they do. Most of all, every one of us responds on an instinctive level to the religious and mythological symbolism, including the diabolical symbolism, employed by the Priory of Sion, which is the key to understanding their mysteries, as well as their grand political plan. In order to fully comprehend the enigma surrounding the Priory of Sion, we must begin by understanding their heretical religious beliefs.

Endnotes

[1] Gilles de Rais, a noble who was instrumental in the campaign of Jeanne d'Arc, was later convicted of raping and killing dozens of young boys in Satanic rituals.

[2] (When initiated, the Masonic candidate takes an oath swearing his loyalty and secrecy, on penalty of ritualized murder such as this.)

Chapter Four: The Golden Age

"...When a stream is polluted it is necessary, if you are to find pure water, to go back to the source. It's the same with tradition - it only remains pure at its origin."
- Paul Le Cour, *The Age of Aquarius*

The Ancient Origins of Christianity

The membership list of the Priory of Sion and its related auxiliary orders is about as heterodox as one can imagine. It has included devote Catholics, Protestants, Christian heretics, occultists, atheists, even avowed Satanists and Luciferians, as well as adherents of some of the most extreme right and left-wing political causes of history. But despite their wide differences, they all seem to hold certain elements in common – namely an infatuation with the mythology of the Grail, and an insistence on the importance of certain royal bloodlines, most especially the Merovingian. The authors of *Holy Blood, Holy Grail* determined that the Priory revered the Merovingians because they believed them to be descendants of Christ – carriers of his sacred royal blood, and guardians of the true teachings of Christ. *Holy Blood, Holy Grail* implied that the true Christian church, perpetuated by Christ's offspring, held religious beliefs shockingly heretical when compared with the dogma of the Catholic Church. In short, they asserted that the heresies which the Catholic Church persecuted throughout the Middle Ages were in fact the True Church – the Church of the Holy Grail.

An essential part of the secret doctrine of the Grail is the belief in the humanness of Christ. When the Catholic Church deified Christ, they stripped him of all family connections. The Church established the doctrine of the "virgin birth" to disconnect Jesus from the genealogy of his father, Joseph, a descendant of King David, and for a while tried to maintain that the Virgin Mary had herself been conceived in the same manner, thus disconnecting Jesus from her side of the family as well. They tried to establish the *perpetual* virginity of Mary, thus claiming that Jesus had no biological brothers or sisters, and maintained that the many "brothers" of Jesus mentioned in the Gospels were either children of Joseph from a previous marriage, or merely "brothers" in spirit. They then insisted that Jesus had remained chaste his entire life as well. The numerous passages in the Bible proclaiming Jesus as "King of the Jews", "the son of David", and "the Messiah" (a title bestowed traditionally upon the rightful king of Judah) have all been held by the Church to be metaphorical. Christ's real kingdom is in Heaven, the Church has always maintained - not in Israel. Pilate referred to Jesus as "King of the Jews" *mockingly*, they say. After all, how could he literally be king when he had no ancestors, no father, no brothers, no wife, and no heirs? Thus began a smear campaign and a genocidal persecution that has continued for approximately 2000 years. This then is the real reason why the Church deified Christ – to hide his lineage and descent. This is also the reason why they squelched all knowledge of his wife, Mary Magdalene.

But at the same time, while the Grail church revered the historical figure of Christ as a flesh-and-blood human being, allowing him a dignity that the Roman church robbed him of, they also understood the significance of Christ on a very deep symbolic level. It is no secret that the imagery with which the Church presented Jesus is identical to that of earlier pre-Christian Sun gods. The Christian cross, and the many variations of it, are all based on earlier versions from ancient cultures, where it was used to symbolize the Sun. The haloes seen behind the heads of Christ, the saints, and the angels in Catholic art are an old motif that can be traced back to ancient Sumer, where it represented the crown of the Sun god. The crowns worn by royalty throughout the ages, a practice that goes back at least to Sumer, represent the same thing. Their use signified the concept that the king was an incarnation of the Sun god. Throughout Egypt, Sumer, and Greece, deified kings have been referred to as "sons of the Sun", or "the son of God."

In fact, every mythical detail of Jesus' life is identical to the myths of ancient sun gods such as Tammuz, Krishna, Mithras, Prometheus, and many others, including being born of a virgin on December 25, and dying on a cross at Easter. Christmas and Easter were originally pagan holidays, and this mythical tale symbolized the "death" and "rebirth" of the Sun throughout the course of the solar year.

While it is generally agreed that the Roman church shamelessly grafted pagan elements into the story of Christ in order to convert pagans to their dogma, the Grail church also seemed to revere the ancient symbolism of Christ as an incarnation of the Sun god. His wife Mary Magdalene was likewise seen as an incarnation of the goddess Isis or Venus. It is believed that adherents of the Grail church in France paid homage to the figure of Mary Magdalene in the form of "Black Madonnas." These are identical to traditional Catholic idols of the Virgin Mary, but are simply black in color, and this is believed to be veiled reference to Christ's hidden, secretly revered consort. Statues of the Black Madonna can be found throughout France and in other areas of Europe as well, usually inside Catholic churches or cathedrals. It has been remarked that Catholic depictions of the Virgin Mary resemble depictions of Isis or Venus also, and that Black Madonnas appear to be an even more overt depiction of this goddess. It has been speculated by authors such as Margaret Starbird and Nicholas de Vere that Jesus and his wife were the high priest and priestess of a sex magic cult, in which they personified the god and goddess in sacred sex rites, and that Christian heretics later perpetuated these rites. Indeed, several authors have posited that the original cult lead by Christ practiced Hellenistic mystery rites that would have been considered totally heretical by the prevailing Jewish orthodoxy. This perhaps explains why Jesus was viewed by the scribes and priests as a sorcerer, as recorded in the Gospels and in other chronicles.

But the Grail church does not revere Jesus because he was merely a perpetuator of these rites and traditions. It is clear from the mythos of the Grail family that the blood is the key. Jesus is perceived not only as a symbolic representation of the Sun god, but as a literal "son of the Sun god" – a blood relative. *Holy Blood, Holy Grail* attempts to explain the significance placed on the bloodline of Jesus by chalking it up to the fact that he was the rightful king of the Jews, and a descendant of King David, who in the Bible was anointed by God himself. But what would Jewish heretics care for King David? It may have been necessary for Jesus to assert his descent from King David in order to boost his claim for the kingship of Israel. And perhaps his descendants could use this to claim a right to control the Holy Land, which apparently he did. But the importance placed on Jesus' bloodline, and on the sacredness of his blood, cannot be credited solely to a connection with King David. There has to be another reason why the blood of Jesus, and thus the blood of his Merovingian descendants, was considered divine.

The Gods of the Sea

A most important clue pointing towards an explanation of this lies in the story of the Quinotaur, the "beast of Neptune" who purportedly raped the mother of Meroveus, the first Merovingian king. Thus insemination provides Meroveus with an ancestry which is partially human and partially divine. For the Quinotaur appears to be a Frankish permutation of the myth of the fish-god Dagon, who was known by many other names throughout history and throughout the world.

Dagon was a sea god worshipped throughout the ancient Middle East, described in the Bible as the patron god of the Philistines, and a constant source of antagonism for the Hebrew god. The root word "Dag" means "fish", and Dagon was portrayed in ancient bas reliefs as a creature part-man and part-fish. This could indeed be the source of the mythical Quinotaur creature, as well as the source of the Merovingian King Dagobert's name. "Dagon" is also the root of the word "dragon", and thus it is interesting that Dagobert's name is sometimes spelled "Dragobert." Dragons were originally viewed by the ancients a being sea creatures, such as the most famous biblical dragon, Leviathan. Albert Pike writes in *Morals and Dogma* that:

"The Dragon was a well-known symbol of the waters, and of great rivers; and it was natural that... the powerful nations of the alluvial plains... who adored the dragon or the fish, should themselves be symbolized under the form of dragons."

Though often shown as a bearded merman with a Phrygian cap, as he is in Assyrian and Babylonian reliefs, other depictions show Dagon as a man wearing a fish for a hat, with the mouth on top of his head, pointing up, and the tail of the fish hanging down his back. These depictions have been said by many to be the source of the fish-like miter now worn by popes and other Catholic priests.

Dagon was said to have been a being who came out of the sea during the day to teach primitive people the arts of civilization: including writing, agriculture, architecture, astronomy, metalsmithing, winemaking, shipbuilding and navigation. At night, after dispensing his wisdom, Dagon would return to the sea, only to come once again the next morning. Because of this and other reasons, Dagon was perceived as an incarnation of the Sun, dispensing wisdom as the Sun dispenses light, and Dagon's name became the root of our modern word "day." Indeed "Dag", or "Tag", still means day in many languages.

Dagon seems to be quite similar to a figure named by the historian Berosus as "Oannes the Annedotus", whom he lists as one of the early Chaldean kings – a god-king. According to Berosus:

"In the first year there appeared, from that part of the Elyrian Sea which borders upon Babylonia, an animal endowed with reason, called Oannes, whose whole body (according to Apollodorns) was that of a fish ; that under the fish's head be had another head, with feet also below, similar to those of a man, subjoined to the fish's tail. His voice and language was articulate and human, and a representation of him is preserved even unto this day. This being was accustomed to pass the day among men, but took no food and he gave them an insight into letters and arts of all kinds. He taught them to construct cities, to found temples, to compile laws, and explained to them the principles

of geometrical knowledge. He made them distinguish the seeds of the earth, and showed them how to collect the fruits; in short, he instructed them in everything which could tend to soften manners and humanize their laws. When the sun set, this being, Oannes, retired again into the sea, and passed the night in the deep, for he was amphibious. After this there appeared other animals like Oannes."

However, from the Chaldean depictions of Oannes, it appears that he was simply a man wearing a fish costume, and there followed after him a race of god-kings called the Annedoti that were all fish-gods, sea-kings, and dispensers of wisdom.

These stories are later versions of the older Sumerian myths. Sumeria, the original Mesopotamian empire, is the oldest civilization acknowledged by historians, and in many ways was more advanced then the civilizations that followed it. We are told that this was the birthplace of writing, architecture, agriculture, astronomy, math, writing, etc. However, their civilization seems to have arrived almost overnight, with no previous stages of development having yet been discovered. One obvious explanation for this is that their civilization might have come from somewhere else. The Sumerians must have been taught these arts by an outside race that conquered and ruled over them. Since Sumeria itself is the oldest civilization of which there is accepted historical proof, this means that there must have been a previous civilization, from which these conquering kings came, the remains of which were mostly destroyed, perhaps through some terrible cataclysm. Indeed, this is exactly what the Sumerian legends tell us.

In the Sumerian story, Oannes is called Anu, and the race of god-kings he spawns is called the Annunaki, a pantheon of gods including Anu's sons Enlil and Enki. In this version, apparently the gods had their own civilization here on Earth, but grew tired of working for their own livelihoods. So they created the race of mankind to work as slaves for them, with Enki being largely responsible for the task. But humans multiplied so rapidly that they became a nuisance. Enlil in particular was annoyed, and devised a series of cataclysms, culminating in a massive flood, to rid the Earth of the problem.

Enki and Enlil had been involved in an ongoing rivalry pertaining to seniority. They were both sons of Anu, king of the gods, and both had a claim to the inheritance of this crown. As author Nicholas de Vere describes in his book *The Dragon Legacy*:

"Enki was the younger son of Anu's senior wife, Antu. Enlil was the elder of the two sons, but was born to Anu's second or junior wife, Ki. In Annunaki culture, the female was the source of sovereignty, and by rights Enki... was therefore the rightful heir to his father."

As the rightful heir, and as the original father of the human race, Enki objected to his brother's decision to destroy humanity, a usurpation of his authority. He therefore conspired to help a remnant of humanity escape the catastrophe, by enlisting a single man to build a large ship, loading it up with his family, and with an assortment of animal life. After the Flood, Enki, along with other gods who took his side in the conflict with his brother, helped those humans who had survived by teaching them the arts of civilization, enabling them to build their own societies. And he passed on his royal, divine seed through this remnant as well, creating a race of human kings who carried the bloodline of the king of the gods.

Understandably, then, Enki became one of the chief deities of the subsequent Sumerian, Akkadian, Babylonian, and Chaldean civilizations. Also called "Ia" or "Ea", he was known as the "Lord of the Earth", "Lord of the Flood", "Lord of the Deep Waters", and "Lord of That Which is Below." His seat of rule was believed to be the "Absu" – the Abyss, described as the waters beneath the Earth. Ancient bas reliefs show him seated in the Absu, holding pots overflowing with water and fish. A temple dedicated to him in the Babylonian city of Eridu – a staged ziggurat called the "Esaggla" or "lofty house" – was the site of ceremonial rites to Enki that featured water as their main focal point. The name "Ia" brings to mind the Hebrew "Jah", or "Jehovah." Indeed, certain characteristics of Enki were apparently appropriated into the character of Jehovah by the Hebrews, such as him being portrayed as the true father of humanity, and as the one who saved humanity from the Flood. However, certain characteristics of Enlil were incorporated into Jehovah as well, such as having caused the Flood in the first place. Like Jehovah, Enlil was a storm god, king of the heavens, and the element of air. It is with the figure of Jehovah that the legacy of Enlil now resides, and I believe that they are essentially the same figure.

The Divine Battle

In Greek myth Ouranos (believed by scholars to be the Greek version of Oannes, or the Roman Uranus) fathered a race of primordial gods called the Titans. As author Edith Hamilton describes it:

"The Titans, often called the Elder Gods, were for untold ages supreme in the universe. They were of enormous size and of incredible strength... They most important was Cronus, in Latin Saturn. Cronus... was the Lord of the Universe, with his sister-queen Rhea. Finally one of their sons, the future ruler of heaven and earth, whose name in Greek is Zeus and in Latin Jupiter, rebelled against him... There followed a terrible war between Cronus, helped by his brother Titans, against Zeus with his five brothers and sisters – a war that almost wrecked the universe."

When it was over, Zeus was victorious, and had the Titans imprisoned within the Earth, upon the infernal Mount Tartarus:

> *"Bound in bitter chains beneath the wide-wayed earth,*
> *As far below the Earth as over Earth is Heaven...*
> *...Tartarus, the brazen-fenced"*

This war was won partially because one of the Titans' own, Prometheus, sided with Zeus and assisted him, although he later regretted it. And it was Prometheus who, in the Greek view, was largely responsible for creating the human race. Says Hamilton:

"He fashioned them in a nobler shape than the animals, upright like the gods, and then he went up to heaven, to the sun, where he lit a torch and brought down fire."

In this way, a divine spark of light from Heaven was passed down from one of the gods to enlighten man's consciousness. And in a more literal since, fire became the basis of a metalsmithing technology on which man was able to build his civilization. Zeus, however, was not happy with this, and punished Prometheus by sending him to the center of the Earth and chaining him to Tartarus as well. As he did this, he lectured Prometheus:

"Such fruit you reap for your man-loving ways.
A god yourself, you did not dread God's anger,
But gave mortals honor not their due."

In another Greek story, Prometheus again comes to man's aid, thus time helping his human-god hybrid son Deucalion and his wife, Pyrrha, to escape a global deluge. Once again, Zeus (the Greek equivalent of Enlil or Jehovah) brought about this flood because human beings were multiplying too rapidly. Prometheus, savior of mankind, warned Deucalion ahead of time, and had him build an ark, in which they floated to safety atop Mount Parnassus. In the Biblical story of Noah, when Noah finally comes down from the ark, he builds an altar on the mountain and performs a ceremony giving thanks to god for being spared. In the story of Deucalion and Pyrrha:

"They found a temple all slimy and moss-grown, but not quite in ruins, and there they gave thanks for their escape and prayed for help in their dreadful loneliness."

It is then that they heard a voice instructing them to throw stones behind their backs, which they did, and as each stone landed, a human sprang up in its place. The Greeks believed that this is where our current human race came from – a race of stone people.

However, as with all cultures, there are many different versions of Greek myths. In Plato's *Critias*, he tells the story of the empire of Atlantis, which he had heard from the philosopher Solon, who in turn had heard it from an Egyptian sage while visiting that land. So the story is really a late Egyptian one viewed through late Greek eyes. But within the extraordinary details of this fable we glimpse an inherent truth – a memory of something that may have actually happened.

The Egyptian sage described an island continent ruled by god-men, with a magnificent civilization that colonized neighboring lands, creating a vast, mighty empire that greatly outshone that of Zeus and the Olympian gods of Greece. Plato reports that the Egyptian told Solon:

"Many great and wonderful deeds are recorded of your state in our histories. But one of them exceeds all the rest in greatness and valour. For these histories tell of a mighty power which unprovoked made an expedition against the whole of Europe and Asia, and to which your city put an end. This power came forth out of the Atlantic Ocean, for in those days the Atlantic was navigable; and there was an island situated in front of the straits which are by you called the Pillars of Heracles; the island was larger than Libya and Asia put together, and was the way to other islands, and from these you might pass to the whole of the opposite continent which surrounded the true ocean; for this sea which is within the Straits of Heracles is only a harbour, having a narrow entrance, but that other is a real sea, and the surrounding land may be most truly called a

boundless continent.

Now in this island of Atlantis there was a great and wonderful empire which had rule over the whole island and several others, and over parts of the continent, and, furthermore, the men of Atlantis had subjected the parts of Libya within the columns of Heracles as far as Egypt, and of Europe as far as Tyrrhenia. This vast power, gathered into one, endeavoured to subdue at a blow our country and yours and the whole of the region within the straits; and then, Solon, your country shone forth, in the excellence of her virtue and strength, among all mankind. She was pre-eminent in courage and military skill, and was the leader of the Hellenes. And when the rest fell off from her, being compelled to stand alone, after having undergone the very extremity of danger, she defeated and triumphed over the invaders, and preserved from slavery those who were not yet subjugated, and generously liberated all the rest of us who dwell within the pillars.

But afterwards there occurred violent earthquakes and floods; and in a single day and night of misfortune all your warlike men in a body sank into the earth, and the island of Atlantis in like manner disappeared in the depths of the sea. For which reason the sea in those parts is impassable and impenetrable, because there is a shoal of mud in the way; and this was caused by the subsidence of the island."

According to Plato, Atlantis was ruled over by god-men, the descendants of the sea-god Poseidon and a mortal woman, Cleito. It was for her and their family together that Poseidon literally sculpted the island from clay, dividing it up into ten portions, each given to one of their ten sons (five pairs of twins) to rule over. As Plato relates:

"Poseidon fell in love with her and had intercourse with her, and breaking the ground, inclosed the hill in which she dwelt all round, making alternate zones of sea and land larger and smaller, encircling one another; there were two of land and three of water, which he turned as with a lathe, each having its circumference equidistant every way from the centre, so that no man could get to the island... He himself, being a god, found no difficulty in making special arrangements for the centre island, bringing up two springs of water from beneath the earth, one of warm water and the other of cold, and making every variety of food to spring up abundantly from the soil. He also begat and brought up five pairs of twin male children; and dividing the island of Atlantis into ten portions, he gave to the first-born of the eldest pair his mother's dwelling and the surrounding allotment, which was the largest and best, and made him king over the rest; the others he made princes, and gave them rule over many men, and a large territory. And he named them all; the eldest, who was the first king, he named Atlas, and after him the whole island and the ocean were called Atlantic. To his twin brother, who was born after him, and obtained as his lot the extremity of the island towards the Pillars of Heracles, facing the country which is now called the region of Gades in that part of the world, he gave the name which in the Hellenic language is Eumelus, in the language of the country which is named after him, Gadeirus."

The empire they created was grander than any that had existed before, or since:

"Now Atlas had a numerous and honourable family, and they retained the kingdom, the eldest son handing it on to his eldest for many generations; and they had such an amount of wealth as was never before possessed by kings and potentates, and is not

likely ever to be again, and they were furnished with everything which they needed, both in the city and country. For because of the greatness of their empire many things were brought to them from foreign countries..."

Plato then went on to describe, in magnificent detail, the culture, empire, agriculture, architecture and religion of Atlantis. Not surprisingly, theirs was a sea and water-based religion devoted to the worship of their father Poseidon. It was their descent from him that allowed them to live as gods and rule as kings. But over time, their human nature got the best of them. Plato writes:

"For many generations, as long as the divine nature lasted in them, they were obedient to the laws, and well-affectioned toward the gods, who were their kinsmen... but when the divine portion began to fade away in them, and became diluted too often, and with too much of the mortal admixture... human nature got the upper hand, then, they being unable to bear their fortune, became unseemly, and to him who had eyes to see, they began to appear base, and had lost the fairest of their precious gifts; but to those who had no eye to see the true happiness, they still appeared glorious and blessed at the very time when they were filled with unrighteous avarice and power. Zeus, the god of gods, who rules with law, and is able to see into such things, perceiving that an honorable race was in a most wretched state, and wanting to inflict punishment on them, that they might be chastened and improved, collected all the gods into his most holy habitation, which, being placed in the center of the world, sees all things that partake of generation. And when he had called them all together he spake as follows:"

It is at this point that Plato's text breaks off abruptly, and was never completed. However, we know what fate befell Atlantis. Zeus sparked a war against its divine-human sea kings, and somehow this war resulted in the sinking of Atlantis. As Plato had stated earlier in the text:

"...the consequence is that, in comparison of what then was, there are remaining in small islets only the bones of the wasted body, as they may be called, all the richer and softer parts of the soil having fallen away, and the mere skeleton of the country being left."

The Origins of Civilization

The most essential text for understanding the myth of Atlantis is Ignatius Donnelly's 1882 classic, *Atlantis: The Antediluvian World*. It starts out by analyzing Plato's account of Atlantis both mythologically and archeologically. It explores myths of catastrophic floods from cultures all over the world, showing them all to be different versions of the same story. According to Donnelly, the myth upon which these are based is that of the destruction of Atlantis. He argues that in ancient times, far more ancient than recorded history, there was a highly advanced global culture made up of Atlantis and its colonies, a primordial "golden age" that preceded our current epoch, and was destroyed by a cataclysm of worldwide proportions, analogous to the biblical Deluge. It was from this Atlantean culture that all of our languages, symbols, customs, arts and sciences were derived. During their heyday, writes Donnelly, the Atlanteans went about spreading these advancements throughout the primitive world. They created civilizations on every continent and, according to Donnelly, it was the kings of Atlantis that provided the first mythical god-kings reported in the histories and legends of virtually every ancient culture on earth. For proof that there was a vast and highly advanced global civilization in ancient times, Donnelly shows the similarities of plant and animal species across widely separated continents, many of these species having been domesticated and cultivated by man for so many thousands of years that no trace of the original "wild species" can be found anywhere on Earth. He also shows that species of animals and plants which are absent on certain continents - for instance, in the Americas - can nonetheless be found depicted in the artwork of these continents' natives, proving that there was a time when these species did exist there, or else, at least, the people of that continent acquired knowledge of them through trade. South American Indian tribes have carvings, for example, of elephants and horses, neither of which are native to the region. Donnelly also shows similarities between the gods of various world cultures, arguing that these gods were, in fact, based on the actual historical kings of Atlantis. Donnelly's book was indeed the first of its kind, and all subsequent books on Atlantis have been based on his.

Another interesting aspect of Donnelly's work is his insistence that the kings of Atlantis are the same as the Titans, and the fall of the Titans the same as the fall of Atlantis. This, he asserts, is one and the same as the biblical deluge, as well as the "fall man" from the "Garden of Eden." All of these, he insists, are mythological traces of the same ancestral memory hidden in the antediluvian mists, beneath the waves that cover a long-dead era – the golden age of the gods.

Donnelly's identification of the Titans with the Atlantean kings does make some sense. In both stories, the mighty kings of a magnificent empire are crushed by Zeus, who ignites a cataclysmic, earth-shaking war. The Titans were sent down to the center of the Earth; the Atlanteans sank down to the bottom of the ocean. And Atlas, the foremost king and namesake of Atlantis, is named in other Greek myths as being one of the Titans. But that would put Poseidon in the position of being the same figure as Ouranos.

Indeed, the two deities are both very similar, both being sea gods. Poseidon is the patron deity of navigators, while Ouranos was credited as being the inventor of the mariner's compass. Ouranos, or Oannes, has been identified with Dagon, also called "Daonos", and Poseidon was also called "Poseidaon." Also, in another legend, Poseidon fathered a race called the "Tritons" who were described as "fish-men", and who some think are the same as the Titans.

However, it is Kronos who seems to be remembered as the great, and later fallen, king of Atlantis. It was also quite literally believed by historians at one time that after he was deposed from the throne of Atlantis, rather than being imprisoned in the center of the Earth, or dying in a Flood, Kronos simply moved to Italy, then inhabited by primitive folk, and spread the Atlantean civilization to them, initiating a golden age there. Ignatius Donnelly states:

"In the first place, Berosus tells us that the god who gave warning of the coming of the Deluge was Chronos. Chronos, it is well-known, was the same as Saturn. Saturn was an ancient king of Italy, who, far anterior to the founding of Rome, introduced civilization from some other country to the Italians. He established industry and social order,

*filled the land with plenty, and created the golden age of Italy. He was suddenly re-
moved to the abodes of the gods. His name is connected, in the mythological legends,
with 'a great Saturnian continent' in the Atlantic ocean, and a great kingdom which, in
the remote ages, embraced Northern Africa and the European coast of the Mediterranean as far as the peninsula of Italy, and 'certain islands in the sea', agreeing, in this
respect, with the story of Plato as to the dominions of Atlantis. The Romans called the
Atlantic ocean 'Chronium Mare', the sea of Chronos, thus identifying Chronos with that
ocean. The pillars of Hercules were also called by the ancients 'the pillars of
Chronos.'"*

Donnelly then quotes *Murray's Mythology*:

*"Saturn, or Chronos, came to Italy. He presented himself to the king, Janus, and pro-
ceeded to instruct the subjects of the latter in agriculture, gardening, and many other
arts then quite unknown to them: as for example, how to tend and cultivate the vine. By
such means he at length raised the people from a rude and comparatively barbarous
condition to one of order and peaceful occupation, in consequence of which he was
everywhere held in high esteem, and in the course of time, was selected by Janus to
share with him the government of the country, which thereupon assumed the name of
Saturnia – a land of seed and fruit. The period of Saturn's government was sung in the
latter days by poets as a happy time when sorrows were unknown, when innocence,
freedom, and gladness reigned throughout the land in such a degree as to deserve the
title of the Golden Age..."*

Donnelly connects Saturn's "golden age" to the ancient pagan festival of Saturnalia, which begins more or less around the same time as the Winter Solstice, Christmas, and St. Dagobert's Day:

*"The Roman Saturnalia was a remembrance of the Atlantean colonization. It was a
period of joy and festivity; master and slave met as equals; the distinctions of poverty
and wealth were forgotten; no punishments for crime were inflicted; servants and slaves
went about dressed in the clothes of their masters; and children received presents from
their parents or relatives. It was a time of jollity and mirth; a recollection of the
Golden Age. We find a reminiscence of it in the Roman 'Carnival.'"*

There is a great deal of confusion about the exact familial relations within the
royal houses of Olympos and Atlantis. Even the Greek accounts vary, but when you
begin to compare them with the mythologies of other cultures, it becomes even more
confusing. It is certain that the closest thing we have to "antediluvian history" is in the
legends of the world. Details get blurred horribly. We read from Donnelly that:

*"...In the Phoenician mythology, Chronos raised a rebellion against Ouranos, and,
after a great battle, dethroned him. In the Greek legends it is Zeus who attacks and
overthrows his father, Chronos."*

And elsewhere:

"Poseidon, the first king of Atlantis, according to Plato, was, according to Greek my-thology, a brother of Zeus, and a son of Chronos."

It seems likely that in addition to the simple fact that we are dealing with leg-ends that have been passed around through various cultures for upwards of 9000 years, surviving a devastating global cataclysm, some of the variations in the details of these stories are due to the effect of propaganda. If Zeus overthrew Kronos, he and his de-scendants may have reigned over Atlantis for some time before the disaster that befell it. According to Donnelly, this was indeed the case, and that is why Poseidon, his son, ruled it at the time of the disaster. It thus would have been Zeus and his subjects who reported the fall of Atlantis, and what had preceded it. The usurping kings undoubtedly took on some of their predecessors' legends of heroism as if they themselves had en-joyed such adventures. Such confusion occurred *within* family lines as well, with the son taking on the mythical attributes of the father. Thus titles like "Lord of the Earth", "Lord of the Four Quarters", "Lord of the Abyss", "Lord of the Flood", etc., were passed on from generation to generation, and could be taken over by rivals, as in the case of Zeus and Kronos. The deeds, mythical associations, and symbolic correspon-dences (such as with the Sun or the Moon, the sea, dragons, serpents, fish, bulls, goats, etc.) were passed along as well. All of this leads to the confusion and seeming incon-gruity we find when trying to compare and interpret ancient history and mythology.

However, regardless of this, all of these gods thus described seem to be repre-sentations of the same mythos. All are associated with the sea, with the creation of a vast empire based on the sea, with navigation, and with the spreading of human civiliza-tion. All of them are linked with the Flood, and with the revival of civilization after the Flood. All are also said to have passed their divine seed onto humans, who ruled as kings after the Flood.

The Flood is a tale common to almost all cultures throughout the world, and in so many versions, the overpopulation of humans was the cause of the Flood. In many versions, too, the god synonymous with Enki, Oannes, Dagon or Kronos is responsible for rescuing humanity from the Flood and helping them rebuild their civilization.

Many similar versions of this story have been told about other gods worshipped throughout the ancient world. For instance, there is the story from Hindu culture of the god Vishnu, who took the form of a fish, and warned a figure named Manu about an impending flood. The story can be read in the "Catapartha Brahmana" of the *Rig-Veda*, translated by Max Muller:

"One morning water for washing was brought to Manu, and when lie had washed himself a fish remained in his hands, and it addressed these words to him.
'Protect me, and I will save thee.' 'From what wilt thou save me?' 'A deluge that will sweep all creatures away; it is from that I will save thee.' how shall I protect thee?' The fish replied, While we are small we run great dangers, for fish swallow fish. Keep me at first in a vase; when I become too large for it, dig a basin to put me into. When I shall have grown still more, throw me into the ocean; then I shall be preserved from destruction.' Soon it grew into a large fish. It said to Manu, 'The very year I shall have reached my full growth the Deluge will happen. Then build a vessel and worship me. When the waters rise, enter the vessel, and I will save thee.'
After keeping him thus, Manu carried the fish to the sea. In the year indicated

Manu built a vessel and worshipped the fish. And when the Deluge came he entered the vessel. Then the fish came swimming up to him, and Manu fastened the cable of the ship to the horn of the fish, by which means the latter made it pass over the Mountain of the North. The fish said, ' I have saved thee; fasten the vessel to a tree, that the water may not sweep it away while thou art on a mountain and in proportion as the waters decrease thou shalt descend.

Manu descended with the waters, and this is what is called the descent of Manu on the Mountain of the North. The Deluge had carried away all creatures, and Manu remained alone."

Another derivation of this mythos is found in the Syrian goddess "Atargatis", another half-fish, half-human deity believed to have come from the sea to teach man wisdom and the arts of civilization. Atargatis is thought by some to be the inspiration for the goddess Ashtoreth, Astarte, or Ishtar worshipped throughout the ancient world, also depicted as half-fish, and as the consort of Dagon. Atargatis is, interestingly, sometimes depicted as hermaphroditic – possessing both male and female sex organs. In his book, Ignatius Donnelly quotes an unnamed author from a treatise called "On the Syrian Goddess", which connects Atargatis (here identified as the same as the Greek goddess Hera, wife of Zeus) with the Greek story of Deucalion and the Flood:

"The generality of people tell us that the founder of the temple was Deucalion Sisythes - that Deucalion in whose time the great inundation occurred. I have also heard the account given by the Greeks themselves of Deucalion; the myth runs thus: The actual race of men is not the first, for there was a previous one, all the members of which perished. We belong to a second race, descended from Deucalion, and multiplied in the course of time. As to the former men, they are said to have been full of insolence and pride, committing many crimes, disregarding their oath, neglecting the rights of hospitality, unsparing to suppliants; accordingly, they were punished by an immense disaster. All on a sudden enormous volumes of water issued from the earth, and rains of extraordinary abundance began to fall; the rivers left their beds, and the sea overflowed its shores; the whole earth was covered with water, and all men perished. Deucalion alone, because of his virtue and piety, was preserved alive to give birth to a new race. This is how he was saved: He placed himself, his children, and his wives in a great coffer that he had, in which pigs, horses, lions, serpents, and all other terrestrial animals came to seek refuge with him. He received them all; and while they were in the coffer Zeus inspired them with reciprocal amity, which prevented their devouring one another. In this manner, shut up within one single coffer, they floated as long as the waters remained in force. Such is the account given by the Greeks of Deucalion.

But to this, which they equally tell, the people of Hieropolis add a marvelous narrative: That in their country a great chasm opened, into which all the waters of the Deluge poured. Then Deucalion raised an altar, and dedicated a temple to Hera (Atargatis) close to this very chasm. I have seen it; it is very narrow, and situated under the temple. Whether it was once large, and has now shrunk, I do not know; but I have seen it, and it is quite small. In memory of the event the following is the rite accomplished: Twice a year sea-water is brought to the temple. This is not only done by the priests, but numerous pilgrims come from the whole of Syria and Arabia, and even from beyond the Euphrates, bringing water. It is poured out in the temple and goes into the cleft, which, narrow as it is, swallows up a considerable quantity. This is said to be in virtue of a religious law instituted by Deucalion to preserve the memory of the catastrophe, and of the benefits that he received from the gods. Such is the ancient tradition of the temple."

Donnelly then connects the character of "Deucalion", here called "Deucalion Sisythes", with the Sumerian Flood hero, Xisuthros. And it is interesting that this temple is in Heiropolis, now in Turkey, the country where the supposed location of Mount Ararat is found.

Atargatis/Astarte is also believed to be the same figure as the Egyptian Isis, another goddess associated with the teaching of wisdom, and also depicted at times as having the tail of a fish. Here husband Osiris appears to be the Egyptian manifestation of this same primordial, civilizing god-king figure that he have already identified in other cultures. And in this version of events, the goddess is very much his partner and equal. As Albert Pike relates in *Morals and Dogma*:

"To Osiris and Isis, it was held, were owing civilization, the discovery of agriculture, laws, arts of all kinds, religious worship, temples, the invention of letters, astronomy, the gymnastic arts, and music; and thus they were the universal benefactors. Osiris traveled to civilize the countries which he passed through, and communicate to them his invaluable discoveries. He built cities, and taught men to cultivate the Earth. Wheat and wine were his first presents to men. Europe, Asia and Africa partook of the blessings which he communicated, and the most remote regions remembered him, and claimed him as one of their great gods."

Osiris, like so many gods of the ancient world, was a sun god, and associated with serpents, a symbol of the sun. The solar/serpent symbolism is interchangeable with that of the fish and the dragon. Osiris' brother Set (called "Typhon" by the Greeks) was a serpent-dragon, and the two had a war in which Osiris ended up getting chopped into fifteen pieces. These pieces were then dumped in the Nile River. However, Isis came along and collected all of the pieces, and reconstructed his body. The only part that was missing was his penis, which had been swallowed by a fish. Isis has a substitute penis crafted and impregnated herself with the god Horus.

This same god archetype has been traced to the Norse sun-god Woden, also associated with serpents, and with the spreading of wisdom. His wife, Freya, is believed to be the same as the goddess Isis, and is likewise represented as being part-fish. Woden, also called "Odin", is said to have descended from Heaven to give his people civilization. He is credited with having invented the Norse alphabet, the runes, as well as the cabalistic system of magic that goes along with them. The Norse myths compiled in the epic poem called *The Eddas* tell us that Odin created the first kingdom on Earth, in the city of "Urd", very similar to the prime Sumerian city of "Ur."

Historians have long agreed that the city of Ur is most likely the original source of Sumerian civilization, and thus, of the civilizations that followed. The prefix "Ur" even means "primeval" in German. According to authors such as Donnelly and L.A. Waddell, this city was begun by the same colonizing race of god-kings I have discussed. Their race was known as the "Ur", "Ar", or "Ir", and the Sumerian pictograph denoting this syllable is none other than the pentagram, also called the "plough sign" by Sumerians, to whom the word had a number of translations. The prefix "aur" means "light" in many languages, and so it is interesting that these people were called "shining ones." Donnelly and Waddell claim that they are none other than the "Aryans", a name given to a race of colonizing civilizers known to have spread their culture and language (Indo-European, once known as "Indo-Aryan") all over Europe, the Indies, and the Middle East. The name of the nation Iran, as well as the name of Mt. Ararat, comes from this. It should not be surprising then that the pentagram is referred to in modern occult texts as "the sign of the Aryan race."

Donnelly believes that the Atlantean empire not only spread their civilization far and wide through colonization, but that after the Flood which destroyed their homeland, they fled to the far-flung places of the earth spreading civilization to those who had survived the cataclysm. One of the titles these god-kings were known under, according to L.A. Waddell, was "Kad", "Gad", or "Khat[1]." Says Waddell, this title meant literally "King of the World", and was written in Sumerian pictographs as a double-barred cross, just like the Cross of Lorraine associated with the Angevin kings of France, descendants of the Merovingians. The sea-faring navigators of Phoenicia were also known as "Kads". Indeed, Waddell believes that the word "God" is rooted in this word, as well as many words in modern languages that begin with "Cad" and relate to sea creatures. The title "Kad" was used by the most famous Sumerian king, Sargon the Great, whose royal capitol, which he had constructed, was "Agade", rumored by the Sumerians to have been a dwelling place of the gods. Agade, or "Accad", was the source of "Akkadia", the name of the post-Sumerian empire that dominated Mesopotamia. This syllable can in fact be found all over maps of the ancient world. The pillars of Hercules were, at one time, called "the Firth of the Gads", and were located nearby cities named "Gades" and "Agadir." Ignatius Donnelly connects this syllable to Atlantis:

"Plato tells us that the dominion of Gadeirus, one of the kings of Atlantis, extended 'toward the pillars of Heracles (Hercules) as far as the country which is still called the region of Gades in that part of the world.' Gades is the Cadiz of today, and the dominion of Gadeirus embraced the land of the Iberians of Basques, their civilization taking its name from a king of Atlantis, and they themselves being Atlanteans."

The words "Akkad" and "Ar", I believe, may have been the roots of the Greek word "Arcadia", the name of a region in Greece which housed, according to Greek myths, an "idyllic paradise ruled over by the Greek gods." For this reason, the word "Arcadia" has been a code word among occultists for centuries, denoting the "golden age" of the long-distant past, when, occultists believe, the gods ruled kingdoms on Earth. The gods who ruled Arcadia were depicted in Greek myths as shepherds. It is interesting, then, that the god-kings I have examined in this chapter were often known under titles denoting them as "shepherds" of the people. Poussin's painting, *The Shepherds of Arcadia*, definitely alludes to many hidden secrets, which I will soon explore.

It is worth noting, too, that the mythical Eden-like kingdoms of other mythologies also have names that may have been derived from "Agade." The name "Asgarde" is given to the kingdom of the gods in Norse mythology, and in certain Eastern traditions, the "Lord of the Earth" is believed to reside in a subterranean kingdom known as "Agartha", its name so amazingly similar to the name of the goddess Atargatis. Another root word that appears to be important to our study is "Merou." From Donnelly we read:

"Lonormany insists that the human race issued from Upa-Merou... Theopompus tells us that the people who inhabited Atlantis were the Meropes, the people of Merou."

And earlier, Donnelly says:

"For the inhabitants of the Isle of Cos, the hero of the Deluge was Merops, son of Hyas, who there assembled under his rule the remnant of humanity preserved with him."

Interestingly, Eastern traditions tell of a primordial mountain of the gods, the "Axis of the World", named "Meru." Donnelly believes the name of the ancient people known as "Amorites" comes from this word also. And of course, the prefix "mer" means "sea" in Europe. Thus the word "Merovingian" means "Vine [or bloodline] of the Sea." It could also mean "Vine [or bloodline] of Atlantis."

Perhaps this explains Middle Eastern myths relating to an angel named "Marut" who descended on a golden rope from Heaven to teach people the arts of civilization. The same is said of the god "Mura" in Southern Afghanistan; the Mesopotamian god "Martu" (also called "Amurru"); and the Northern Arabian god "Marnas" (also called "Mura and believed to be the same as Dagon). Ignatius Donnelly also suggests:

"Do the laws which control the changes of languages, by which a labial succeeds a labial, indicate that the Mero or Merou of Theopompus, the name of Atlantis, was carried by the colonists of Atlantis to South America... and became in time Perous or Peru?"

Indeed, many of these ideas seem to have been transplanted to South America. For there, we find tutelary deities almost identical to those of Dagon, etc., being worshipped as the chief gods. Moreover, they are depicted as bearded, fair-haired white men, sometimes with bodies that are half-serpent or half-fish. The depictions of these gods show them clearly with Caucasoid features not native to South America, and facial hair, which native tribesmen do not naturally have. This indicates that, just as Donnelly and Waddell have suggested, the survivors of Atlantis – the race of god-men recorded in Eastern cultures – also colonized and spread their civilization to the Native American tribes. It was this race of gods whom the natives were awaiting, and whom they believed had returned, with European explorers arrived on their shores. Unfortunately for them, they were sorely mistaken.

The detailed stories of these "gods" told by the natives leave no doubt that this was the case. For instance, the Incas believed that the enormous pyramid complex in the mountain city of Cuzco (made of stones so huge that scientists still are not sure how it was built) was in fact constructed overnight by a white-fleshed giant with a half-fish body named "Viracocha", whose name means "foam of the sea." He supposedly was able to bring down "fire from the heavens", which was used to make the stones which built the complex at Cuzco "light as a cork", so that he was able to build it quickly and easily. Like Dagon, Viracocha is credited with imparting all of the arts of culture to the Native Americans.

Another version of this figure is the Incan deity Manco Capac, who is described in *The Royal Commentaries of the Incas* by Garcilaso de la Vega,:

"After the waters of the Deluge had subsided, a certain man appeared in the country of Tiahuanaco... In the life on Manco Capac, who was the first Inca, and from whom they began to boast themselves children of the Sun... they had an ample account of the Deluge. They say that in it perished all races of men and created things insomuch as the waters rose above the highest mountain peaks in the world. No living thing survived except a man and a woman who remained in a box and, when the waters subsided, the wind carried them... to Tiahuanaco, where the creator began to raise up the people and nations that are in the region..."

The exact same figure is named in by other tribes as "Noach Yum Chac", "Quetzalcoatl", "Con Tiki", "Kukulkan", and "Votan." I should note that Quetzalcoatl was credited by the Aztecs with building their massive pyramids, and with inventing their incredibly complex calendar, as Kukulkan is credited with inventing the Mayan calendar. He was half-serpent, and was sometimes known by just the last syllable of his name, "atl", the South American word for "water" - an obvious connection to Atlantis. I should note also that "Noach Yum Chac" sounds like "Noah"; "Con Tiki" and "Kukulkan" could both be linked to the Biblical name of "Cain"; and "Inca" sounds like the Sumerian god "Enki", as well as "Enoch", the grandfather, according to the Bible, of Noah.

L.A. Waddell believed (and he is neither the first not the last to say so) that these same civilizing kings (whom he identifies as "Sumerian" or "Sumer-Aryan") morphed into the mythology of Jehovah, Satan, and the patriarchs of the Old Testament. In his work he extensively compared the names, titles, and mythological elements of all ancient kings, gods, and god-kings, including the biblical patriarchs, and he believed that the same main pantheon of god-kings was recorded in all of these myths. For instance, the Sumerian, Babylonian, and Chaldean kings lists all contain, at their beginning, a number of kings whose reigns were said to have lasted for tens of thousands of years. The names and attributes of these kings, Waddell found, link up with the names and attributes of gods worshiped by these same cultures, and by other cultures as well, including the characters in the Hebrew Bible. For instance, the Chaldean kings list contains, in this order, names similar to Abraham ("Irarum"), Isaac ("Asahk"), Jacob ("Akhab"), and Judah ("Gudia"), four of the main patriarchs of the Bible.

The Legacy of Cain

Waddell believed that one biblical figure in particular had a far-reaching effect on civilizations all over the world: the vilified figure of Cain. According to the Bible he was Adam's first-born son, and was said to have gone bad when he murdered his brother, Abel. But instead of being executed for his sin, he was exiled "to the land of Nod." Waddell identifies the first Sumerian king, Ukusi, with Adam, and the second Sumerian king, Qin, with Cain. Qin was said by the Sumerians to have built the cities of Erech, Lagash, Ur, Agade, and Babylon. He is also said to have taught the Sumerians agriculture, especially the growing of grain, and the brewing of alcohol. Cain's name actually means "grain" in Hebrew, and *The Book of Genesis* tells us that the source of Cain's jealousy of Abel was that God had accepted Abel's fleshy sacrifices, and rejected Cain's sacrifices of fruits and grain.

Waddell also identifies Cain with another biblical figure: Nimrod. Waddell says that one of Cain's titles was "Lord of the Tree of Life", which, in Sumerian/Babylonian language, was written as "Nimarrud", or sometimes "Maru or "Marud." (This may link up with the word for "sea" – "mer" – and the word for Atlantis – "Merou" – discussed earlier.) Nimrod was, historically, a Babylonian king, and there is very little in the biblical record to connect him with Cain. Instead of being the son of Adam, he is one of the descendants of Noah's son, Japheth, and instead of being a "tiller of the soil", as Cain was, Nimrod was called "a mighty hunter before the Lord." However, Nimrod was credited with building Babel, Erech, and Accad, Qin's cities, and was even believed by historians to have built the Tower of Babel. Also, the "Nim" in Nimrod's name can mean "fish." Many of Nimrod's associations seem to have contributed to the mythos surrounding Cain, Dagon, Oannes, etc. Nimrod's historically recorded wife, Queen Semiramis, was associated with fish symbolism, as well as with doves, and was labeled the "Queen of Heaven." Thus she seems to have contributed a lot to the image of the goddess Ishtar/Isis/Astarte, as well as the idolatry of the Virgin Mary.

The Sumerian king Qin was succeeded by his son, Enu, whom Waddell identifies with "Enoch." There are two Enochs in *Genesis*, and one is the son Cain supposedly had after his expulsion from Eden. In *Genesis 4:17* it states:

"And Cain knew his wife; and she conceived, and bare Enoch: and he builded a city, and called the name of the city, after the name of his son Enoch."

This city is identified by Waddell, and by other authors, with the Babylonian city of Erech, also said to have been built by Nimrod. This, then would be more evidence linking Nimrod with Cain[2]. Waddell believes that the names "Erech" and "Enoch" are interchangeable. "Erech" is now the root of the name of the country of "Iraq." Waddell further identifies Enoch/Erech with the Greek figure of "Erechtheus", or "Erichthonius." He was, in Greek mythology, the father of Cecropes, the first king of Attica. Edith Hamilton describes "Cecropes" as being half-dragon from the waist down. She writes that "He had no human ancestor, and he himself was only half-human." Cecropes is known to have created some offense to the god Poseidon that caused the god to punish the Earth with "a disastrous flood." However, Hamilton also says of Cecropes:

"Most writers say that these events happened before the Deluge, and that the Cecropes who belonged to the famous Athenian family was not the ancient half-dragon, half-human creature but an ordinary man, important only because of his relatives. He was the son of a distinguished king...
His father, King Erechtheus of Athens, was usually said to be the king in whose reign Demeter came to Eleusis and agriculture began."

What is more, Hamilton concurs with the opinion that Erechtheus is the same figure as that of Erichthonius, said to be:

"...the son of Hephaestus, reared by Athena, half-man, half-serpent. Athena gave a

chest, in which she had put the infant, to the three daughters of Cecropes, forbidding them to open it. They did open it, and saw in it the serpent-like creature... When Erich-thonius grew up he became the king of Athens."

Waddell believed that both Enochs in *Genesis* were in fact the same person, and that Enoch is also the same figure personified as the biblical Noah – that is, that it was he who piloted the ark during the Flood. Waddell stated with certainty that "Enoch... is regarded by biblical authorities as being identical with Noah of the Flood myth." Waddell demonstrated that the names of both Enoch and Noah have both been written as "Noach", and also as "Hanuk", in ancient texts. This theory is seconded by author Joseph Reiss in *Language, Myth, and Man*. Furthermore, Chaldean legends of the Flood do involve the Sumerian king Enu. Enu's son was "Ia-Patesi" – ("Priest-King of Ia"). Waddell points out that "Ia-Patesi" could easily be transliterated into the name of Noah's son in the Bible: "Japheth." In addition, Waddell found an example of a title being applied to King Enu which translated as "Shepherd of the Vessel."

This brings an interesting twist to certain legends surrounding Enoch, stating that he was a wise prophet and scribe, who inscribed a stone tablet with the wisdom of the ancient world, which was carried on board Noah's Ark. This same tablet has been equated by occultists with the famed "Tablet of Hermes", also inscribed with pre-diluvian wisdom from the age of the gods, and thus Enoch is equated with the Greek Hermes, or the Roman Mercury. Hermes was worshipped in Egypt as Thoth, the god credited with the invention of writing, and with the giving of hidden gnosis. This same wisdom of Thoth, Hermes, or Enoch was sometimes said to have been inscribed onto two pillars, one of stone, and one of metal. Such pillars were said by Plato to have been placed in the Temple of Poseidon in Atlantis. The two pillars of Enoch play an important role in the rites of Freemasonry, and similar pillars were said to have stood outside of Solomon's Temple. The pillars of Enoch were apparently made in anticipation of the Flood, and were meant to ensure that some record of the knowledge of the old world would pass into the new. It is from these pillars that, some assert, a great deal of known history is derived. As Albert Pike writes in *Morals and Dogma*:

"Manetho extracted his history from certain pillars which he discovered in Egypt, whereupon inscriptions have been made by Thoth... in the sacred letters and dialect: but which were after the Flood translated from that dialect into the Greek tongue, and laid up in the private recesses of the Egyptian temples. These pillars were found in the subterranean caverns near Thebes, and beyond the Nile, not far from the sounding statue of Memnon, in a place called Syringes; which are described to be certain winding apartments; made, it is said, by those who were skilled in ancient rites; who foresee-ing the Deluge, and fearing lest the memory of their ceremonies should be obliterated, built and contrived vaults, dug with vast labor, in several places."

But if Enoch's tablet/pillar was, as we are led to believe, the sole record of an-tediluvian history, then such a record could also be edited, misrepresented, and faked, either after Enoch's death, or during his life, if he was either compelled to lie under du-ress, or seduced into willfully lying, by people with political motives for spreading propaganda.

There certainly does seem to have been some tampering with the records of

Enoch's birth. *The Book of Genesis* claims that when Abel was killed, and Cain was exiled, Adam had another son: Seth, to whom he passed on his inheritance. It is this figure, Seth, whom Enoch the scribe is supposedly descended from, according to Judeo-Christian tradition. But we know that Cain's own son was also called Enoch, and that he named a city after him. Now notice the peculiar similarity between the descendants of Cain that are given in the Bible (the last biblical record of Cain's activities, by the way), and those of Seth:

Cain's descendants are: Enoch, Irad, Mahujael, Methusael, Lamech..

Seth's descendants are: Enos, Cainan, Mhalaleel, Jared, Enoch, Mathuselah, Lamech.

Clearly, the descendants of Seth are just a muddled version of the descendants of Cain. This leads one to believe that Enoch's genealogy was altered to conceal his descent from Cain. The name "Cainan" has been added in as a hint of this, and two of Enoch's descendants, "Mahujael" and "Irad", are listed as his ancestors instead. Whoever compiled this list was definitely trying to cover something up.

The Jehovahite Cover-Up

Given that several generations of men (people said to have lived several hundred years each) were easily moved around in the Bible's pre-Flood narrative, it is not hard to believe that the Flood itself could have been inserted out of sequence, and thus that Enoch really could have piloted the Ark, instead of his supposed great-grandson, Noah. Remember that Eden and Atlantis are purportedly the same[3]. That must mean that Eden's rightful rulers were at one time overtaken and expelled, just as the Titans were by Zeus. And recall that Zeus is likened to the Sumerian Enlil, or the biblical Jehovah, the "Jove" of the Romans. Adam and Eve's expulsion would most likely symbolize this, and the Deluge which followed would be the same as the sinking of Atlantis. The Flood would have erased all knowledge of the previous history, including the history of the previous dynasty of kings "the elder gods." When the new dynasty ("the younger gods"), headed by Zeus/Jehovah and his chosen rulers took over, they would have rewritten the records to suit their own ends. They would have also gone to great lengths to destroy any true records that may have survived, or to silence anyone who may have known better.

We know that Cain's parents were expelled from Eden/Atlantis, and settled elsewhere. And we know that Cain was later exiled from that place too, purportedly for killing his brother Abel (whom L.A. Waddell believes is actually the ancient god-king Baal, a son of Enlil/Jehovah). He then apparently traveled around the world, building cities and spreading civilization to primitive people. Enoch did likewise, apparently following in his father's footsteps, and the cities they built, as well as accounts of the deeds from the people whose lives they touched, can be found in countries and cultures the world over. But as for the biblical record, none of this is reported beyond the exile of Cain, and the building of one city named after his son Enoch. Cain's life and descendants are almost entirely omitted from the rest of the biblical narrative, and the grandest thing Enoch is said to have done was to "walk with God." For this, he was rewarded by being taken to "Paradise" while still alive, something that does not happen to many other men in the Bible. But note how the description of the event is phrased in *Genesis 5:24*: "And Enoch walked with God: and he was not; for God took him."

If by "God" they mean Jehovah/Enlil/Zeus, who took over Eden/Atlantis unlawfully, and who was the enemy of Enoch's father, Cain, then he was not taken to Heaven as a reward for his good behavior. Perhaps he was kidnapped, or somehow seduced or hoodwinked into going back to Atlantis. Perhaps he had inscribed his wisdom onto tablets which were meant to survive a deluge which he foresaw. On these tablets could have been written the true history of what had happened in Atlantis. His kidnappers, wishing to alter that history, thus took control of the person who made that record, and were able to change that record. This included creating a false genealogy of Enoch that made him one of their own, not a child of Cain. And while they recorded the story of the Flood, it was highly garbled, and placed out of sequence. The new historians began their history with post-Flood figures, but grafted onto them the legends and titles of pre-Flood figures. Thus is is almost impossible now to determine which is the true chronology, or the true genealogy, of these god-kings and their deeds.

It is interesting to note that *Genesis* hints repeatedly that Adam and Eve were neither the first nor the only human beings on Earth. Obviously there were women for Cain and Seth to marry. And if Cain was a "builder of cities", obviously someone had to occupy those cities. Prior to the creation of Adam and Eve in Chapter 2 of *Genesis*, the text states in Chapter 1, verse 27 that "God created man in his own image, in the image of God created he him; male and female created he them." In the second chapter, he creates Adam in paradise, and after a while he creates Eve by using material in Adam's body. That is not the same creation story as the one from the first chapter. They seem to be two separate creations. And in the first, God tells them to "Be fruitful and multiply, and replenish the Earth." This seems to indicate that the Earth have been depopulated, perhaps because of the Flood, and needed to be repopulated. In other words, that this first creation story is placed out of sequence, and describes something that really occurred *after* the Flood. There are many parts of *Genesis* that seem to be similarly misplaced.

The Luciferian Legacy

It would appear that the Garden of Eden story is, in part, an allegory for Atlantis. The way Plato describes Poseidon as having constructed Atlantis sounds very similar to the way in which the construction of Eden by "God" is described in *Genesis*. Both appear to have been artificially constructed, as there is nothing natural about the way they were formed. Both also appear to be, in a sense, a petrie dish for divine-human breeding experiments. Recall that in Plato's Atlantis story, Poseidon sired a race of kings for Atlantis with a mortal woman, Cleito, and bestowed kingship on his first-born son, Atlas. Thus was the place named Atlantis, and its people Atlanteans. In *Genesis*, God creates a race of kings to rule over Eden. We can perhaps see a phonetic connection between Eden (or "Edin", as it is spelled in Sumerian) and Adam (or Adami, as the race of man is called in Sumerian), as well as a connection to Atlantis, or "Ad-lantis." The title "Ad" means "Lord" in Sumerian", as does the Egyptian title "Adon", and the Hebrew "Adonai", a word used for "God" in the Bible.

Adam and Eve's "fall from grace" on Eden, and subsequent loss of the kingdom (for that is what their expulsion symbolizes) was precipitated by their defiance of

God. They were told specifically not to eat of the "Tree of Knowledge", which was guarded by a "serpent", believed by modern theologians to be "Satan." But they *did* eat from that tree, and they then obtained "knowledge of good and evil." Afterwards, Adam and Eve, who until that point had been living without clothes, suddenly became aware of their nakedness, and clothed themselves. They were shortly expelled from the Garden of Eden as punishment, and Eve was further punished by being cursed with "the pains of childbirth", which have purportedly haunted women ever since. (Even menstruation has been blamed on Eve's sin.) Soon after this, Adam and Eve had reportedly "known" each other, and had two sons, Cain and Abel. But Cain was the eldest.

However, there are apocryphal versions of this tale that tell it quite differently. They state that Cain is in fact the son of the serpent, who is named as Samael. This would mean that the "knowledge" which Eve obtained was *carnal knowledge*. She then shared this "knowledge" with Adam. This would explain why they were suddenly aware of their "nakedness." They had just learned what their generative organs were for, and afterwards, they naturally wished to keep them covered. Eve was pained with childbirth afterwards because she had just been impregnated by Samael. Since the serpent is called "Satan" today, and "Satan", is believed, is related to the name of Saturn, or Kronos, it is clear that Cain was fathered by Kronos, or Satan. Author Nicholas de Vere elaborates, referring us to the Sumerian version of the tale. He concurs that the story of the battle between Enki and Enlil is the Sumerian legends is the same as the battle between Zeus and Kronos in the Greek legends, or Jehovah and Satan in the Hebrew. He refers to this pre-diluvian race of gods as the "Dragon race", and states that:

"The story is repeated in the Greek tale of Zeus' hatred of Mankind and the war for supremacy and control of man waged between the elder gods, the Titans...and the Olympians, lead by Zeus.

It is repeated again in the tale of the war between Satan and Jehovah. In all these stories it is the son of the elder queen who is the rightful heir, and this is Enki-Samael-Prometheus-Satan, the friend, savior, and supporter of mankind.

Enlil or Zeus-Jehovah further objected to the idea of investing in man the right to kingship and self-rule, as this was, by tradition, the sole prerequisite of the Annunaki alone. A compromise was reached... and it was decided that an Annunaki queen would incubate a human ovum fertilized by Enki or Samael-Satan. The resulting child would be the first king or queen of the race of men, being mostly Annunaki. Several attempts were made at producing a suitable child by adopting varying permutations of the Annunaki-human interaction. Samael inseminated a Bijo woman, resulting in the birth of Adam...

The second experiment was between Enki-Samael and Eve, his daughter. The child they produced was Cain, who was mated to Lilith Lulluwa, the pure-bred Annunaki daughter of Lilith the Beautiful and Samael[4]. To Lilith Lulluwa, Cain and their sacred offspring was given... the Tiara of Dragon (not moral) kingship from the hand of their father Enki-Samael, the rightful overlord of the Gods, whilst Adam and his children were still considered by Enlil to be serfs. However, upon them the usurping Enlil conveyed his own kingship without the authority of the council of the Dragon Gods, the Annunaki. This he did in an attempt to gain support from humanity for his illegitimate claim to the leadership of the council...

Prometheus the Titan is the "elder god." He is Enki, later called Satan.

Therefore the two stories, originating from a common source, attest to the idea that the holy, Draconian, otherworldly origin of the blood of kings ultimately derives from Satan or Samael-Enki, and Lilith. It does not come from their rival, the usurper Jehovah-Zeus or Enlil, and the race of Adam from whom is derived the origin of the later Tinker Kings, the false monarchies..."

So Cain was the first *rightful* human king, according to De Vere, carrying the divine royal blood of his father, Satan, Saturn, or Kronos, the true King of the World, and by right, of Atlantis, or Eden. But when Kronos and Cain were both exiled, they went about civilizing the rest of the world, which was full of primitive peoples, and he and his descendants became their kings. De Vere believes that Cain's name is even the source of the word "King", and there are words in other languages, such as "Khan" in the East, which mean exactly the same thing. This is why the names of Cain and Enoch show up in the lists of both gods and kings of cultures all over the world, and in their place-names as well. Being exiled from Eden may have been part of what saved Cain's royal race. Ignatius Donnelly tells us:

"The race of Cain lived and multiplied far away from the land of Seth, in other words, far away from the land destroyed by the Deluge. Josephus, who gives us the primitive traditions of the Jews, tells us that 'Cain traveled over many countries before he came to the land of Nod.' The Bible does not tell us that the race of Cain perished in the Deluge. 'Cain went out from the presence of Jehovah'; 'he did not call on his name; the people that were destroyed were the 'sons of Jehovah.'"

So it was supposedly the race of Adam and his son Seth, the sons of the usurper Jehovah-Zeus, who died in the Flood, not the sons of Cain? Plato tells us that the kings of Atlantis, just prior to their "fall", and the destruction of Atlantis, had allowed their half-human, half-divine royal blood to become ignoble by breeding outside of their race with normal mortals. They became grotesque, and their behavior tyrannical. This is the reason why their race was exterminated via the Flood. This is the same story told in so many mythologies, where the cause of the Flood is, in some way or another, the miscegenation of a royal-divine race and a mortal one – breeding a grotesque and tyrannical race of giants that need to be exterminated.

Donnelly tells another pertinent story:

"Mr. George Smith, in the Chaldean account of the Creation deciphered from the Babylonian tablets, shows that there was an original race of men at the beginning of Chaldean history, a dark race... who were called Ad-mi, or Adami, they were the race 'who had fallen', and were contradistinguished from 'the Sarku', or 'light race.' The 'fall' probably refers to their destruction by a deluge, in consequence of their moral degradation and the indignation of the gods."

But in the distorted record compiled by the so-called descendants of Seth, they blamed the cause of the Flood on the tainting of the pure line of Seth by the descendants of Cain. Albert Pike states:

"Cain slew his brother Abel, and went forth to people parts of the Earth with

an impious race, forgetters and defiers of the true God. The other descendants of the common father of the race intermarried with the daughters of Cain's descendants: and all nations preserved the remembrance of that division of the human family into the righteous and impious, in their distorted legends of the wars between the Gods, and the Giants and Titans. When, afterward, another similar division occurred, the Descendants of Seth alone preserved the true primitive religion and science, and transmitted them to posterity in the ancient symbolical character on monuments of stone: and many nations preserved in their legendary traditions the memory of the columns of Enoch and Seth."

In the apocryphal *Book of the Cave of Treasures*, Adam and his children are shown as living upon a lofty, holy mountain. When Adam dies, after the murder of Abel by Cain, Adam's body is placed inside a very special tomb within this mountain called "the Cave of Machpelah", or "the Cave of Treasures" (the name of a real monument in Jewish legend which has been located near Jerusalem). After Adam's burial, it is then that Cain and his descendants are exiled, but not to some faraway location. Rather they are sent to the plains below the mountain. As the text states:

"And after the families and peoples of the children of Seth had buried Adam, they separated themselves from the children of Cain, the murderer. And Seth took Anosh, his firstborn, and Kainan, and Mahlalail, and their wives and children, and led them up into the glorious mountain where Adam was buried; and Cain and all his descendants remained below on the plain where Cain slew Abel."

Generations later, when Anosh (one of the falsified ancestors of Enoch) is dying, he makes his descendants swear an oath not to interbreed with the Cainites:

"... and he prayed over them and commanded them, and spake unto them, saying, 'I will make you to swear by the holy blood of Abel that not one of you shall go down from this mountain to the plain, nor into the encampment of the children of Cain, the murderer; and ye shall not mingle yourselves among them. Take ye good heed unto this matter, for ye well know what enmity hath existed between us and them from the day whereon Cain slew Abel.' And he blessed Kainan, his son, and commanded him concerning the body of Adam, that he should minister before it all the days of his life, and that he should rule over the children of his people in purity and holiness."

But sometime later, they break their oath, and the results are disastrous:

"And lasciviousness and fornication increased among the children of Cain, and they had nothing to occupy them except fornication--now they had no obligation [to pay] tribute, and they had neither prince nor governor--and eating, and drinking, and lasciviousness, and drunkenness, and dancing and singing to instruments of music, and the wanton sportings of the devils, and the laughter which affordeth pleasure to the devils, and the sounds of the furious lust of men neighing after women. And Satan, finding [his] opportunity in this work of error, rejoiced greatly, because thereby he could compel the sons of Seth to come down from that holy mountain. There they had been made to occupy the place of that army [of angels] that fell [with Satan], there they were be-

loved by God, there they were held in honour by the angels, and were called 'sons of God', even as the blessed David saith in the psalm, 'I have said, Ye are gods, and all of you sons of the Most High.'

Meanwhile fornication reigned among the daughters of Cain, and without shame [several] women would run after one man. And one man would attack another, and they committed fornication in the presence of each other shamelessly. For all the devils were gathered together in that camp of Cain, and unclean spirits entered into the women, and took possession of them. The old women were more lascivious than the maidens, fathers and sons defiled themselves with their mothers and sisters, sons re-spected not even their own fathers, and fathers made no distinction between their sons [and other men]. And Satan had been made ruler (or prince) of that camp. And when the men and women were stirred up to lascivious frenzy by the devilish playing of the reeds which emitted musical sounds, and by the harps which the men played through the operation of the power of the devils, and by the sounds of the tambourines and of the sistra which were beaten and rattled through the agency of evil spirits, the sounds of their laughter were heard in the air above them, and ascended to that holy mountain.

And when the children of Seth heard the noise, and uproar, and shouts of laughter in the camp of the children of Cain, about one hundred of them who were mighty men of war gathered together, and set their faces to go down to the camp of the children of Cain. When Yared heard their words and knew their intention, he became sorely afflicted, and he sent and called them to him, and said unto them, 'By the holy blood of Abel, I will have you swear that not one of you shall go down from this holy mountain. Remember ye the oaths which our fathers Seth, and Anosh, and Kainan, and Mahlalail made you to swear.' And Enoch also said unto them, 'Hearken, O ye children of Seth, no man who shall transgress the commandment of Yared, and [break] the oaths of our fathers, and go down from this mountain, shall never again ascend it.' But the children of Seth would neither hearken to the commandment of Yared, nor to the words of Enoch, and they dared to transgress the commandment, and those hundred men, who were mighty men of war, went down [to the camp of Cain]. And when they saw that the daughters of Cain were beautiful in form and that they were naked and unashamed, the children of Seth became inflamed with the fire of lust. And when the daughters of Cain saw the goodliness of the children of Seth, they gripped them like ravening beasts and defiled their bodies. And the children of Seth slew their souls by fornication with the daughters of Cain. And when the children of Seth wished to go up [again] to that holy mountain, after they had come down and fallen, the stones of that holy mountain be-came fire in their sight, and having defiled their souls with the fire of fornication, God did not permit them to ascend to that holy place. And, moreover, very many others made bold and went down after them, and they, too, fell."

Shortly afterwards, the Deluge comes. Although it is not specifically linked to the interbreeding of the Cainites and the Sethites, the connection is certainly implied.

The biblical version of this saga can be found in *Genesis 6*:

"And it came to pass, when men began to multiply on the face of the earth, and daughters were born unto them, That the sons of God saw the daughters of men that they were fair; and they took them wives of all which they chose. And the LORD said, My spirit shall not always strive with man, for that he also is flesh: yet his days shall be

an hundred and twenty years.
　　There were giants in the earth in those days; and also after that, when the sons of God came in unto the daughters of men, and they bare children to them, the same became mighty men which were of old, men of renown."

　　It is uncertain whether the "giants" were the same as the sons of God, or if they were the same as the "mighty men of renown." For the Hebrew word that has been translated as "giants" is "Nephilim", which also means "those who were cast down", and thus it has been thought that the "sons of God" are the same as the Nephilim – that is, that they were fallen angels. Others identify the "Nephilim" with the progeny of the "sons of God", for that imagine that, when angels bred with humans, genetic deformities caused by the mixing of divine and human blood produced monstrous giants. However, the text does appear to be distinguishing between several different races: (1) the giants, Nephilim, or "those who were cast down"; (2) the "sons of God"; (3) the "daughters of men." However, we must remember that everything in the Bible is a muddled, distorted, and misremembered record of something, which has further been greatly mistranslated and misinterpreted.

　　At any rate, it is immediately after this story that "God" becomes frustrated with the "wickedness" of mankind, and the Flood narrative begins, with a distinct connection implied between the interracial/interspecies mating of the sons of God with the daughters of men. It also seems that the Lord made good on his promise to shorten the lifespan of man to 120 years. Prior to the Flood, the ages of the biblical patriarchs at death push the 1000-year mark. But after the Flood, the ages of the patriarchs at death gets gradually shorter.

　　The apocryphal text known as *The Book of Enoch* is a lengthy work written sometime between 2 BC and 3 AD. It deals entirely with this episode of divine-human miscegenation, and the Flood that followed. It states explicitly that the "sons of God", were angels, called "the Watchers" in this book, and that the offspring they produced were giants. It portrays this miscegenation as being an act of defiance against God, and hints that this was perhaps the spark of the "war in Heaven" of *The Book of Isaiah*, in which a third of God's angels, led by Lucifer, were cast out of Heaven for defying God. Now in *The Book of Enoch*, the defiant angels are quite aware that their transgression might bring about divine punishment from God, and so they swear an oath to one another before they begin, promising to go through with the act:

　　"It happened after the sons of men had multiplied in those days, that daughters were born to them, elegant and beautiful. And when the angels, the sons of heaven, beheld them, they became enamoured of them, saying to each other, Come, let us select for ourselves wives from the progeny of men, and let us beget children.
　　Then their leader Samyaza said to them; I fear that you may perhaps be indisposed to the performance of this enterprise; And that I alone shall suffer for so grievous a crime. But they answered him and said; We all swear; And bind ourselves by mutual execrations, that we will not change our intention, but execute our projected undertaking. Then they swore all together, and all bound themselves by mutual execrations. Their whole number was two hundred, who descended upon Ardis, which is the top of mount Armon. That mountain therefore was called Armon, because they had sworn upon it, and bound themselves by mutual execrations."

"Mount Armon" is also called "Mt. Hermon", and it has been said to mean "Mount of the Curse", because the angels took their oath, and thus cursed themselves, upon that mountain. This, I believe, is connected to the name of the god "Hermes", who was apparently the Greek equivalent of the figure of Enoch.

As states previously, the progeny produced by the angels turned out to be monstrous giants, who destroyed the earth with their ravenous appetites, and warred against men:

"And the women conceiving brought forth giants, Whose stature was each three hundred cubits. These devoured all which the labor of men produced; until it became impossible to feed them; When they turned themselves against men, in order to devour them; And began to injure birds, beasts, reptiles, and fishes, to eat their flesh one after another, and to drink their blood. Then the earth reproved the unrighteous."

The Secret Doctrine

But this was not the only sin of the angels. They also sinned against God when they, at this time, began teaching mankind certain knowledge that God had apparently forbidden them to have:

"Moreover Azazyel taught men to make swords, knives, shields, breastplates, the fabrication of mirrors, and the workmanship of bracelets and ornaments, the use of paint, the beautifying of the eyebrows, the use of stones of every valuable and select kind, and all sorts of dyes, so that the world became altered.

Impiety increased; fornication multiplied; and they transgressed and corrupted all their ways. Amazarak taught all the sorcerers, and dividers of roots: Armers taught the solution of sorcery; Barkayal taught the observers of the stars, Akibeel taught signs; Tamiel taught astronomy; And Asaradel taught the motion of the moon, And men, being destroyed, cried out; and their voice reached to heaven."

Another quote from *The Book of Enoch* demonstrates this amply. Referring to the iniquity and rebellion that caused God to bring about the Flood, Enoch tells Noah:

"They have discovered secrets, and they are those that have been judged; but not thou, my son. The Lord of Spirits knows that thou are pure and good, free from the reproach of discovering secrets."

The "secrets" taught by the angels, which God apparently did not want man to know, include both the secrets of sorcery, and also the basic arts and sciences of civilization. Clearly, "God" was deliberately keeping mankind in an enslaved, ignorant state, and these angels wanted to teach these secrets to mankind, presumably out of love for their children, so that their descendants could thrive. The motivation for this, however, was more than just altruistic, as we shall see. It was a political move, really. The angels who mated with humans, and who taught them this forbidden knowledge, did so because it gave them an advantage against Jehovah, with whom they were struggling for seniority in Heaven. Passing their lineage onto humans gained them allies, and it secured heirs for royal titles and positions of power which Jehovah was trying to control. And passing on these "secrets" empowered them, so that they could stand on their own without any need of help from Jehovah.

The actions of these angels are most definitely portrayed in *The Book of Enoch* as an act of rebellion against Jehovah. And the punishment he metes out is dire indeed:

"Again the Lord said to Raphael, Bind Azazyel hand and foot; cast him into darkness; and opening the desert which is in Dudael, cast him in there. Throw upon him hurled and pointed stones, covering him with darkness; There shall he remain for ever; cover his face, that he may not see the light. And in the great day of judgment let him be cast into the fire."

Interestingly, even though the instigator of the sexual crimes committed by the angels is said to be Samyaza, the teaching of secrets was instigated by Azazel. So Jehovah decided to lay the blame most heavily upon him. *The Book of Enoch* quotes "God" as saying:

"All the earth has been corrupted by the effects of the teaching of Azazyel. To him therefore ascribe the whole crime."

As for the "giants" born of angels and men, Jehovah decides to bring about the Flood in order to rid the Earth of them. But he also decides to thin their population as much as possible first, by sending his angels to instigate violence amongst the giants, so that they kill each other off.

"To Gabriel also the Lord said, Go to the biters, to the reprobates, to the children of fornication; and destroy the children of fornication, the offspring of the Watchers, from among men; bring them forth, and excite them one against another. Let them perish by mutual slaughter; for length of days shall not be theirs."

Then the Watchers and their children are to be cast into the pit under the earth, where they shall suffer and await the Final Judgment:

"To Michael likewise the Lord said, Go and announce his crime to Samyaza, and to the others who are with him, who have been associated with women, that they might be polluted with all their impurity. And when all their sons shall be slain, when they shall see the perdition of their beloved, bind them for seventy generations underneath the earth, even to the day of judgment, and of consummation, until the judgment, the effect of which will last for ever, be completed.
Then shall they be taken away into the lowest depths of the fire in torments; and in confinement shall they be shut up for ever. Immediately after this shall he, together with them, burn and perish; they shall be bound until the consummation of many generations."

Interestingly, it is hinted in *The Book of Enoch* that Enoch himself was a human-angel hybrid. His birth is described thusly:

"She ... brought forth a child, the flesh of which was white as snow, and red as a rose; the hair of whose head was white as wool, and long; and whose eyes were beautiful. When he opened them, he illuminated all the house, like the sun; the whole house abounded with light."

Noah's father Lamech is concerned that this is not his biological offspring. He goes to his father Methuselah, and says:

"I have begotten a son unlike to other children. He is not human, but resembling the offspring of Heaven, is of a different nature, being altogether unlike us. His eyes are bright as the rays of the sun; his countenance glorious, and he looks not as if he belongs to me, but to the angels."

In this story, Enoch is taken up to Heaven, speaks to the angels, and is fore-warned about the Flood. He then passes the information on to his descendant, Noah. In the text, it is clear that the cause of the Flood involves a shift of the Earth's axis. The book states that "In those days Noah saw that the earth became inclined, and that destruction approached." However, it is unlikely that anyone but the gods, and those whom they chose to inform, were aware of what this implied.

L.A. Waddell believes that the Watchers in *The Book of Enoch* who bred with human women were lead by Cain, because "Azazel" is similar to "Azaz", or "Azag", a title sometimes used by the Sumerian king Qin. Also, in Persian mythology, the descendants of Azazel are called the "Djinn", similar to "Gin or "Gan", an alternate way of saying "Cain." Also, the arts and sciences that Azazel and his Watchers supposedly taught mankind are also associated with Cain and his children in many other traditions. The biblical figure of Tubal-Cain[4], who is probably Cain's descendant (if the Seth genealogy in *Genesis* is seen as erroneous) are both quite specifically said to have invented metalsmithing, and to have taught men to make weapons, as are the Watchers in *The Book of Enoch*, and the Djinn in Persian mythology. However, the whole thing may be a bit more complicated, as I am about to explain.

Endnotes

[1] Enoch City, by the way, is now a city in Arizona, built by the Mormons, who believe that "Enoch City" is synonymous with "Zion" or "the Kingdom of God."

[2] In one version of the Grail romance, *Perceval li Gallois*, the Grail castle is named "Eden."

[3] This character of Lilith, who in cabalistic traditions was the lover of Adam before Eve was made, has been said by some to be the namesake of the word "lily", which denotes a type of flower that has been considered sacred since ancient times. The Old Testament makes numerous references to the "Lily of the Valley", which symbolizes the goddess. It seems likely that the royal device known as the "fleur-de-lys", which was originally associated with the Merovingians, is named after the flower of Lilith.

[4] "Tubal-Cain" is an important figure in Masonic ritual, and his name is even used as the password for one of their grades.

Chapter Five: Descendants of the Devil

"...it is but natural... to view Satan, the Serpent of Genesis, as the real creator and benefactor, the Father of Spiritual mankind."
- H.P. Blavatsky, *The Secret Doctrine.*

An Attempt at Antediluvian History

With so many different and conflicting versions of this saga to choose from, I felt it was necessary to boil the recurring myths down to their essentials and, isolating the most common elements, construct a rudimentary outline identifying what seems to be the likeliest order of events. Although this rough sketch is pure speculation, and although it is, admittedly, dangerous to try to reconstruct history based on mythology, what you read below is the model in which, I feel, all of the available data (from myths, history, archeology and anthropology) falls most snugly into place. And the picture thus painted is quite surprising.

If we take the myths to be based on truth, then we would have to agree that long ago, the earth was ruled by an entirely different order of beings, which I will call, for the purposed of this model, "gods." While apparently related to the human race genetically, they were also, apparently, far more advanced in their development. The descriptions of them possessing horns, wings, fish tails, or reptilian features are most likely the result of elaborate costumes worn by the gods, symbolizing metaphysical concepts with which they wished to identify themselves. Such costumes were worn by human royals in ancient times, and the most common items of regalia used by royals have their origins in this golden age of the gods, as for example, the crown, inspired by the solar disc.

Their other most famous attribute was their ability to "shine." They were called the "Ellu" in Babylonian myths, and "Elohim" in the Bible, both of which translate as "shining ones." In fact, the name of the land of "Sumer" or "Shinar", which they were responsible for civilizing, is related to the words "shine", "shimmer", and "summer." These beings possessed not merely white skin, which most of their human descendants most certainly did, but in fact shined "like the Sun", and just looking at them could blind a man or kill him. The light was especially known to radiate from their powerful, glowing eyes, which is why they were known as "the Watchers." It seems that they were able to manipulate the properties of light, which is what their technology is based upon, and what made them so vastly superior to mortals, giving them powers which appeared to humans to be "magical." They had access to higher dimensions than those which we currently experience.

These beings had a highly advanced and massive global civilization, the center of which was, most probably, the island of Atlantis. At the point at which we shall enter the story, the King of the Gods was Anu, Oannes, or Ouranos, the father of the Titans in Greek mythology. Their civilization relied very heavily on sea power, and thus their kings identified very heavily with sea symbolism. They also identified with the planets, the Sun, and the stars, most likely because of their vast knowledge of astronomy, and because of their ability to "shine."

The next ruler of Atlantis, and of the world of the gods to follow Anu, was his son, the Sumerian Enki, the Greek Kronos, the Roman Saturn, and the Christian Satan.

113

We will use "Satan" for the purposed of our model. It depends on which myth you believe whether Anu died, was killed by his son Satan, or simply retired. At any rate, Satan ruled Atlantis at length, and was renowned for both his wisdom and his ingenuity. Zecharia Sitchin refers to Enki as "the chief scientist among the gods."

At this time, the Earth was probably populated by primitive forms of humanity as well, which also seems to be consistent with the mythological record. These people had not yet evolved to the status of present-day homo-sapiens, and lived savagely in the wild, largely ignored by the more highly-evolved "gods."

At some point, however, the gods decided to breed a more advanced humanoid species, possibly a slave race. This would have bee the race of the Adami, and it is likely that the figure of "Adam" in the Bible is largely fictional, but in fact stands as a symbol of this pre-diluvian human race. The figure personified in the Bible is a replacement actor, meant to stand in as the prototype of the first divinely ordained human king (to supplant the real one, the maligned and largely excised figure of Cain). The word "Adam" is related to the word "Eden" (or "Edin", as it is written in the Sumerian myths.) Eden was the location in which the breeding experiments took place, where the Adami were raised like livestock and taught to perform manual labor. Eden supposedly resided in "the center of the Earth", which I here take to mean "in the heart of Atlantis."

It was Satan who was ultimately in charge of the Adami breeding experiments. And it seems that, in his naturally scientific curiosity, he wished to see what would happen if these beings were endowed with a bit of the natural wisdom, understanding, and ingenuity that the gods themselves possessed. There may have been other motives as well, for he sensed an impending power struggle with his brother, the Sumerian Enlil, the Greek Zeus, and the biblical Jehovah. In order to maintain his power, Satan needed a race of beings to act as foot soldiers – beings with a bit more going on upstairs than the sheep-like Adami race. So he and his friends, including his wife (called in the Sumerian legends "Inanna"), interbred with Adami women to create a royal race among them that was half-god. This move was very controversial amongst the gods, and Jehovah was especially angered. One man in particular Satan created to be his royal heir: Cain. Satan bestowed the tiara of divine kingship upon him, and intended for him to become the first king of Eden, ruling over the rest of the Adami. It is uncertain whether or not he ever held this title de facto, or whether he ascension to the new throne was prevented by what happened next.

It was at this point that Jehovah launched his first offensive to take over Satan's royal throne. To make a long story short, he succeeded in accomplishing just that. Satan was exiled, and Jehovah declared himself the King of Atlantis - the Lord of the Earth. He installed his own appointees to all the official positions of government. This is the revolution of the "younger gods" over the "older gods", as reported in Greek and Sumerian mythology.

In exile, Satan perhaps fled to Iberia, as the legends report Saturn did, and formed a base of operations there amongst the primitive Iberians, whom he civilized, and turned into his loyal subjects. Indeed, he, may have traveled to many lands doing this. He also began consolidating a support base amongst the other gods who wished to see his return to the throne.

Back in Atlantis, Satan's son Cain, now deprived of the throne, continued to live, now ruled over by a new order of gods. As an insult to Satan, and because he felt threatened by Cain, Jehovah elected a new man to the throne of Eden: the Canaanite

Baal-Moloch, known as "Abel" in the Bible. According to some versions, Baal was the son of the Canaanite god El, who is the same as Jehovah. So after criticizing Satan and his fellow gods for interbreeding with men, Jehovah engaged in it himself, not only breeding a royal heir, but an entire race of hybrid beings. However, not being as expert in the process as Satan was, Jehovah's sons lacked the noble nature of Cain, and they became more and more deformed with each successive generation.

Nonetheless, Jehovah raised Baal to the throne of Eden, and made all of the inhabitants bow down to him. But Cain, knowing himself to not only be the rightful ruler, but a much more highly evolved being than Baal, refused to pay homage to this false lord. For this he was sent into exile as well, an event that is memorialized in the Judaic and Islamic traditions which state that Satan was cast out of Heaven for refusing to "bow down to man."

When Cain was exiled, it is most likely that he hooked up with his father. He probably joined his campaign to overthrow Jehovah and reclaim the thrones that had been stolen from them both. They continued to civilize the primitives they conquered throughout the world, perhaps even working with a number of Adami and other hybrid races at that point, attempting to create an empire that would rival the one which Jehovah had stolen from Satan. This is how both Satan and Cain first gained their reputations as the great civilizers of mankind. And when they had created enough bases of operations, and amassed a large enough army, they attacked.

Thus began the "Edenic wars" that both L.A. Waddell and Ignatius Donnelly have written about: Satan fighting Jehovah for control of the Atlantean empire, and Cain fighting Abel for control of Eden within that empire. During the ongoing battles, Abel was killed, and Satan was somehow incapacitated as well. Many legends indicate that he was "imprisoned within the center of the Earth", either dead, or in a "death-like sleep" from which he is forever unable to awake. However, it is difficult to tell how to interpret such myths in a literal way.

Having done away with Satan, Jehovah naturally assumed that his struggle for power was over, and his throne was secured. But Cain continued to plot revenge. Furthermore, he himself had bred a royal heir, called in the Bible "Enoch" (after his grandfather, Satan, who was also called "Enki"). As discussed earlier, at some point Enoch was kidnapped by Jehovah, who probably feared his status as a royal heir, and was forced to live near Jehovah's royal capitol in Atlantis, where he was easier to control.

This is where the major turning point in the Edenic wars came: the Flood. Cain became aware of the impending disaster by watching the stars, and realizing that the Earth's axis was shifting. Cain knew this would result in a Flood, and that the disaster would wipe out a large portion of life on Earth. He thus began making preparations to preserve those elements of it which he considered worth saving. He somehow managed to get word to Enoch warning him about what was going to happen, and Enoch (going with the hypothesis that he and Noah are the same) then had a ship built in which to escape, upon which he placed "the seed of all living things", by which was probably meant genetic samples. He also supposedly brought on board a tablet, written on a special stone, upon which he engraved the most important secrets of the antediluvian world. We will discuss in the next chapter what may have been meant by this.

Biblical and other records depict Enoch/Noah as building the Ark and then waiting for the Flood to start. The boat only became seabourne in these stories when the Flood waters came to *it*. This makes sense if Enoch was unable to leave Atlantis because he was being restricted by Jehovah, and he had to wait for the chaos of the disaster to begin in order to slip out unnoticed. It is possible, though, that Enoch set out well before the Flood, and met up with his father. They then would have then moved the contents of the Ark into a "safe area" that Cain had already established, perhaps at the top of, and perhaps even inside, a tall mountain peak, as the legends suggest.

All of the other gods, including Jehovah, were well aware of the impending disaster, and many were able to find or construct a place of refuge. But, apparently on the direct orders of Jehovah, they neglected to tell the Adami, and all related races of humans and hybrids, about the Flood. Jehovah had apparently become annoyed with all of them, and wanted to wipe the slate clean. By retreating to his own place of security and giving his human subjects no warning, Jehovah allowed Mother Nature to take care of the problem for him. The Flood wreaked havoc all over the world, and Atlantis was completely engulfed in Flood waters, never to return.

Plato puts the Flood at around 10,500 years ago, which jibes with the estimate of researchers like Graham Hancock and Colin Wilson, who have used not only mythological records, but also the findings from modern archeologists and other scientists to reach this conclusion. The Bible puts it at 4000 years ago, but of course, the Biblical chronology is highly flawed. We cannot be certain when the Flood actually occurred, or how long it too for the Earth to become largely inhabitable again. Cain and Enoch may have stayed in their mountain retreat for some time, perhaps even hundreds of years. And when they re-emerged, they began once again on the project that had occupied them previously: creating a global empire. Although most of humanity had been wiped out, Cain and Enoch had undoubtedly saved a number of the Adami, and maybe members of other hybrid races as well. There also would have probably been pockets of survivors all over the world, both primitives who lived in places that were not affected by the Flood, and Atlanteans/Edenites of the hybrid races who managed to escape to these unaffected places. After the Flood waters subsided, Cain, Enoch, and their brethren came out and started rebuilding civilization all over the world. This is what, more than anything, gains them their reputation as having been the inventors of every art and science, and the gods who taught wisdom to primitive mankind. Although this had been going on before the Flood as well, after the Flood, they were teaching these sciences to men who had never even seen them before, having been born in a post-diluvian world. These human-god hybrids were now the overseers of all primitive humanity, and to these primitive humans, their overseers seemed like the highest form of life on Earth. They thus became deified by their subjects, and were the objects of cult worship. "Man" had literally become "god", a concept that has remained dear to occultists ever since.

As for the real gods, they were still around, but they seemed somewhat less accessible than they had before. The descriptions of human contact with the old antediluvian gods seem to take on a different tone after the Flood. They no longer ruled the Earth directly, but for the most part remained hidden, and could be seen except through veils. It was as if a dimensional shift of some sort occurred at the same time as the Flood, and they now spent most of their time occupying those upper dimensions that man could not access. They used their human-god hybrid descendants as conduits acting on their behalf. Their descendants became priest-kings, and were known as sons of the gods: indeed, as incarnations of the gods – the only ones capable of contacting the gods and acting on their behalf. This is the tradition that has defined human kingship ever since. And the first one to set the precedent was Cain.

Cain's apotheosis, according to my theory, occurred in a very interesting way. Having been cast out of Atlantis by Jehovah, and then having survived the Flood, Cain went about perpetuating a myth that he had died, descended to the underworld, and then been reborn as a god. He made people believe that he had become an incarnation of his father, Satan. He renamed himself Seth (or "Set"), a word derived from his father's name, and took on the sea-goat imagery that his father had been associated with[1].

The story of Cain's death, according to Jewish mythology, is very interesting, as it contains elements very similar to the death of Dagobert II. He was killed in a hunting accident in the forest by "his great-grandson, Lamech", who, interestingly, shares the same name as the father of Noah, only that figure was purportedly a descendant of Seth! Anyway, the Cainite Lamech accidentally killed his great-grandfather Cain because when he saw the horn on Cain's head (which God had placed there as a "mark" supposedly so that he *wouldn't* be murdered), he mistook Cain for an animal, and shot him with an arrow. The imagery of a horned Cain living in the forest reinforces the idea that he actually took on a new identity as a goat-headed deity.

After Cain's rebirth as the horned figure of Seth, he, with his son Enoch, and other family members, built a global empire in which the human-god hybrid races acted as the overseers of society, directing it with the Solomonic wisdom inherent in their blood. From the Bible, as well as other records, we gather that Seth-Cain and Enoch succeeded in forming a united world, which all spoke one language – the proto-Sumerian or Aryan language. If we believe the legends, the inventor of this language was Enoch, who was also responsible for teaching the upper castes of humanity how to read and write. The so-called "Tower of Babel" built in Mesopotamia was a monument to this unity. It was so tall, and so magnificent, and symbolized an accomplishment that was so massive, that Jehovah and his faction found it threatening. They launched a massive attack on the structure, and the Tower was destroyed. In addition to the Judaic myth, there are versions of this story in other cultures, too. And we know from both historical and archeological records that the Tower of Babel did once exist.

It is likely that the attack on the Tower marked the beginning of a renewed conflict between the Satanic and Jehovahite bloodlines, in which control of the post-diluvian human world was the prize. The destruction of Sodom and Gomorrah was probably another act of the Jehovahites. And it seems that Jehovah must have gained a great deal of ground, because after the Tower of Babel incident, the world's languages were no longer united, but "scrambled." Jehovah probably took over many or most of Cain and Enoch's territories. He then instituted a different language in each region, so that the inhabitants would be more easily subdued, more ignorant, and less likely to be able to organize a rebellion. It was also easier to construct a false history in which Satan and Cain were portrayed as villains, while "Seth", instead of being Cain himself, was portrayed as his brother, and as the true ancestor of Enoch. Eventually, Seth and Enoch became, in the Jewish tradition at least, Jehovahite heroes, and were portrayed as the ancestors of all the biblical patriarchs. The Cainites were accused of trying to *steal* the genealogy of Seth, when in fact it was there's all along. Louis Ginzberg writes:

"Unfortunately, at the time of Methuselah, following the death of Adam, the family of Seth became corrupted after the manner of the Cainites. The two strains united with each other to execute all kinds of iniquitous deeds. The result of the mar-

riages between them were the Nephilim, whose sins brought the Deluge upon the world. In their arrogance they claimed the same pedigree as Seth, and they compared themselves with princes and men of noble descent."[2]

But the true ancestry of the Hebrew, Jewish and Israelite kings was Satanic and Cainite in origin, and there is evidence that forces loyal to Satan continued to jockey for influence on them. Thus the history of the Hebrews, Jews and Israelites shows Jehovah constantly struggling to keep these people loyal to him, even his anointed priests and kings. It was probably a known secret amongst the priest, scribes, and nobles what their true heritage was. And it even seems that, at times, when the priests thought they were channeling messages from Jehovah, they were in fact contacting other gods from rival factions, which explains why "God" takes on radically different names and personalities throughout the Bible.

Outside of this strain, other cultures were heavily influenced by Jehovah's son Abel or Baal, who appears to have been put in charge Mesopotamia, and several other Middle Eastern territories. For in these cultures, Baal was remembered as one of the great god-kings who ruled over them in ancient times. His father Jehovah had always been thought of as a "storm god", associated with warfare (for obvious reasons). In this capacity he took on the imagery of a bull, and was known to wear bull horns on his helmet. His son Baal took on the bull imagery as well, and took it further, for he was actually remembered as a creature with a bull's head. He quite openly encouraged his subjects to worship him as a god, and it was his descendants who instituted bull and cow worship in the ancient world. King Nimrod claimed to be a descendant of Baal, and took on his title "Lord of the Earth." He also took credit (falsely, I believe) for building the Tower of Babel. He forced his subjects to worship him as an incarnation of Baal, and insisted that they sacrifice babies, a trait that has always marked Baal worship.

L.A. Waddell believed that many words used in the ancient world were derived from Baal's name, which came to mean simply "Lord" in Middle Eastern languages. For instance, Waddell wrote that the Norse God Baldur was the same as Baal, and that the pagan holiday of Beltane was named after him. Also, his title, "Moloch", came to mean "king" in the ancient world, and developed into the Hebrew world "Malkuth", for "kingdom." It is thus at the root of the name "Melchizedek", the priest-king that Abraham paid homage to in the Bible. And it is perhaps related to the word "Michael", the lead angel that opposed Satan in the Christian story of the war in Heaven.

Waddell also thought that stories of heroes slaying bulls, such as Mithras slaying the World Bull, represent Cain killing Abel, or Baal. Likewise, stories about heroes such as Michael, or St. George, slaying dragons represent Jehovahites killing the descendants of Satan. Indeed, bull sacrifice was practiced in Crete, and in the rites of Mithras (a figure most certainly derived from Cain). Also, Plato said that bull sacrifice was practiced in Atlantis. And Zeus often took the form of a bull when he had intercourse with human females, such as in the case of his rape of Europa.

The story goes as follows. The young lady Europa was playing on the beach one day when a beautiful bull, Zeus in disguise, appeared from out of the sea. Europa was so enchanted by it that she climbed up on its back. He immediately carried her off into the sea and raped her. It has been speculated that the continent of Europe was so named because it was once populated by the descendants of those spawned by this union. The parallels to the story of the Quinotaur who raped the mother of Meroveus while she swam in the sea are startling.

A similar story involved the birth of the monstrous bull-headed man called the Minotaur, who lived underground at the center of an elaborate labyrinth on the island of Crete, imprisoned there by his father, King Minos. Remember, Crete was known for its famous bull sacrifice rituals, but in this case, it was the Minotaur to whom sacrifices were made, as young men and women were sent down there regularly to feed his insatiable appetite for human flesh. In the end, the Minotaur was slain by the hero, Theseus (son of Neptune), which is perhaps what the bull sacrifices of Crete were in commemoration of. The Minotaur was not the son of Minos biologically, though. According to fact-index.com:

"Before Minos became king, he asked the Greek god Poseidon for a sign, to assure him that he, and not his brother, was to receive the throne. Poseidon agreed to send a white bull on condition Minos would sacrifice the bull back to the god. Indeed a bull of unmatched beauty came out of the sea. King Minos, after seeing it, instead sacrificed another bull, hoping that Poseidon would not notice. Poseidon was very angry when he realised what had been done so he caused Minos' wife Pasiphae to be overcome with a fit of madness in which she fell in love with the bull. Pasiphae went to Daedalus for assistance, and Daedalus devised a way for her to satisfy her passions. He constructed a hollow wooden cow covered with cowhide for Pasiphae to hide in and allow the bull to mount her. The result of this union was the Minotaur. In some accounts, the white bull went on to become the Cretan Bull. In Greek mythology, the Cretan Bull was either the bull that carried away Europa or the bull Pasiphae fell in love with. Heracles had to capture it."

Given the similarities between the Minotaur and Baal, the conclusion reached by author Nicholas de Vere is almost obvious:

"The Minotaur has been said to be a version of the Phoenician bull-headed god Baal-Moloch, the son of Enlil... sacrifices were made to the Phoenician King enacting the ritual role of the god by wearing a bull's head as a mask."

As the Jehovahite cult gained supremacy amongst the Hebrews, Jehovah became jealous of the worship of his son Baal, or of any other gods, for that matter. The incident that occurred when the Hebrews were caught worshipping the golden calf in *Exodus* demonstrates this amply. "Baal" and "Moloch" were now considered "false gods" worshipped by "heathen nations." Nevertheless, the practice of idolatry was rampant amongst the Israelites and Jews, most especially the priestly caste, and was even performed by King Solomon within the Temple, using the Ark of the Covenant. Archeologists have found the bodies of hundreds of infants slaughtered in sacrifice to Baal. His name eventually morphed into the name of the demon Beelzebub.

Also, although "Seth" is remembered in Judaism as the forefather of the biblical patriarchs, the imagery of the goat-headed god which Seth really was became the prototype image for the Devil in Judaism and Christianity. Goat sacrifice became central to old Judaism. It was part of the observance of Yom Kippur, the Day of Atonement. On this day, two goats were sacrificed. One was killed as a "sin offering", atoning for the sins of the Israelites, and taking their punishment for them in their steed.

Upon the head of the other goat were placed "the sins of all Israel." This goat was then sent off into the desert to die of thirst, taking the curses of the sins with him, away from the people. But each goat was a separate sacrifice: "one for the Lord, and one for Azazel", as the text of *Leviticus* stipulates. The priests would choose two of the finest goats that they had for this, and then draw lots to see which one would be offered to Azazel.

It has been suggested by some that this ritual symbolism was used in defiance of the religion of Egypt, in which their goat-headed god, Ammon, was highly revered, and the sacrifice of goats was forbidden. The name of "Egypt" was originally "Egopt", sometimes just called "Gopt" or "Copt." (Thus the word "Coptic" is used to describe things that are Egyptian.) L.A. Waddell believed that "Gopt" was a title of Cain, a permutation of "Gad" or "God", and was thus the source of the name of the "Goth" tribe in Europe, and of course, the word "goat." Perhaps this word is also related to the name "Capricorn", the sea-goat of the Zodiac, and thus "Cecropes", the ancestor of Erichthonius who was half-dragon.

The name of Cain mutated not only into the words "king" and "queen", but also "gentry" (meaning "nobility"). This includes the word "genetic", and that entire family of words indicating bloodlines, such as "genealogy", or "generation", "genesis", and even "genital" – all words denoting the idea of passing on seed. The related word "gan" meant "garden" in Hebrew, and "gan" meant "vessel" in old Egyptian. The race of the "Djinn" (demonic beings that are part of Islamic lore) were named after Cain, and were considered to be descendants of Azazel, one of Cain's titles. From "Djinn", or "Gin" comes words like "genie" (another word for a demonic spirit). Even "genius" comes from this root. It initially meant "an indwelling spirit", and literally suggested that a person was possessed by a demon. Also, "Gin" is probably related to "John" and "Jeanne", the names taken on by all Priory of Sion Grand Masters since the Cutting of the Elm.

His name of "Seth", I believe, is not only the basis for the Egyptian character of Set, but also the name of the race known as "Scythian", which author Nicholas de Vere identified with the Aryan. H.P. Blavatsky connects Seth's name with "sod", which she says means "mystery" or "arcanum."

The name "Azazel" may be related to another title that L.A. Waddell ascribed to Cain: "Azag." He believed that Cain was identical to the Sumerian king Sargon the Great, whom he identified also with an ancient Indian king, Sagara. This title "Sag", "Zag", or "Azag" he said, meant "seer", and was thus the root of the English word "sage" or "sagacious", indicating a wise and holy visionary. Waddell wrote that "Sag" was sometimes shortened to "Ag", which is Egypt came to mean "fire within", a testament to the fact that Cain's race was one of metalsmiths and alchemists. Interestingly, the word "ageia" came to mean "goat", and "aegis" came to mean "to rule." "Ag" is probably also related to the word "agriculture", which Cain purportedly taught mankind. This word may further be linked to "Aegaea", the region around the Aegean Sea, as well as, again, Egypt. Also, "Agei" is the name of a Hindu fire god, and "Agathodaemon" is the name that was used by some Gnostic sects for their "savior."

There is reason to believe that this word mutated further yet into our word for the number "eight", also called "og" or "oct" in other languages, resulting in words like "octopus and "octagon." The figure eight looks much like the caduceus staff (entwined with two serpents) which Hermes or Mercury is always holding[3]. You will recall that

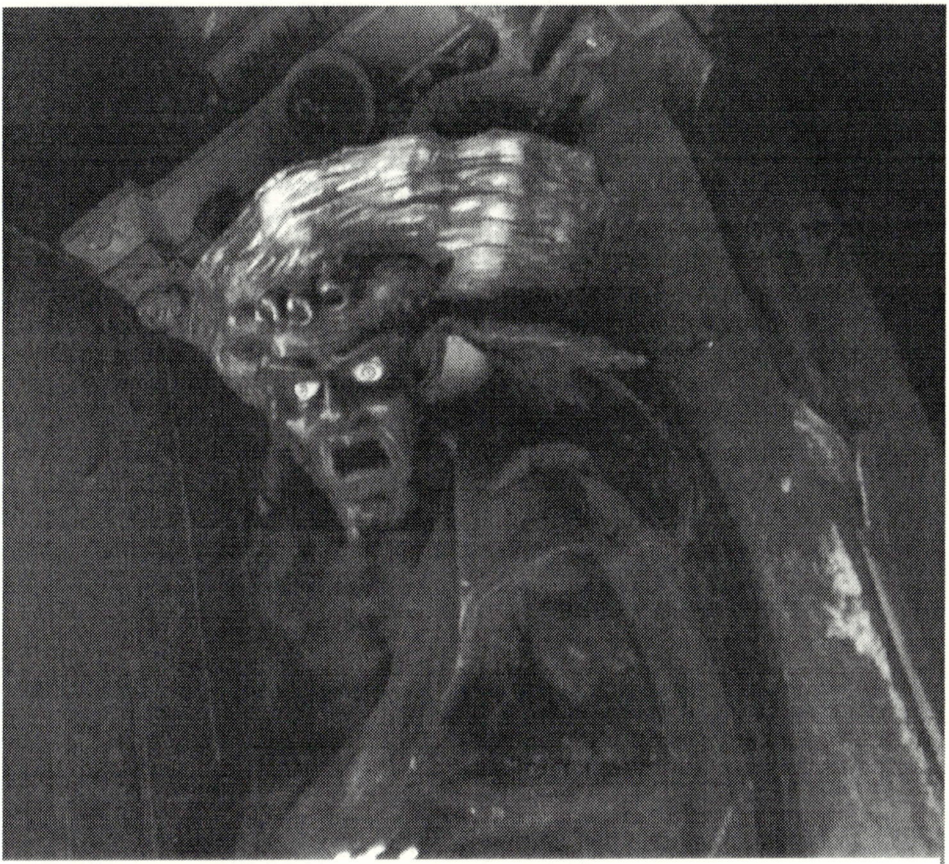

The Statue of Asmodeus at the church in Rennes-le-Chateau. *Photo by Tracy Twyman.*

The Nazi symbol for the Black Sun.

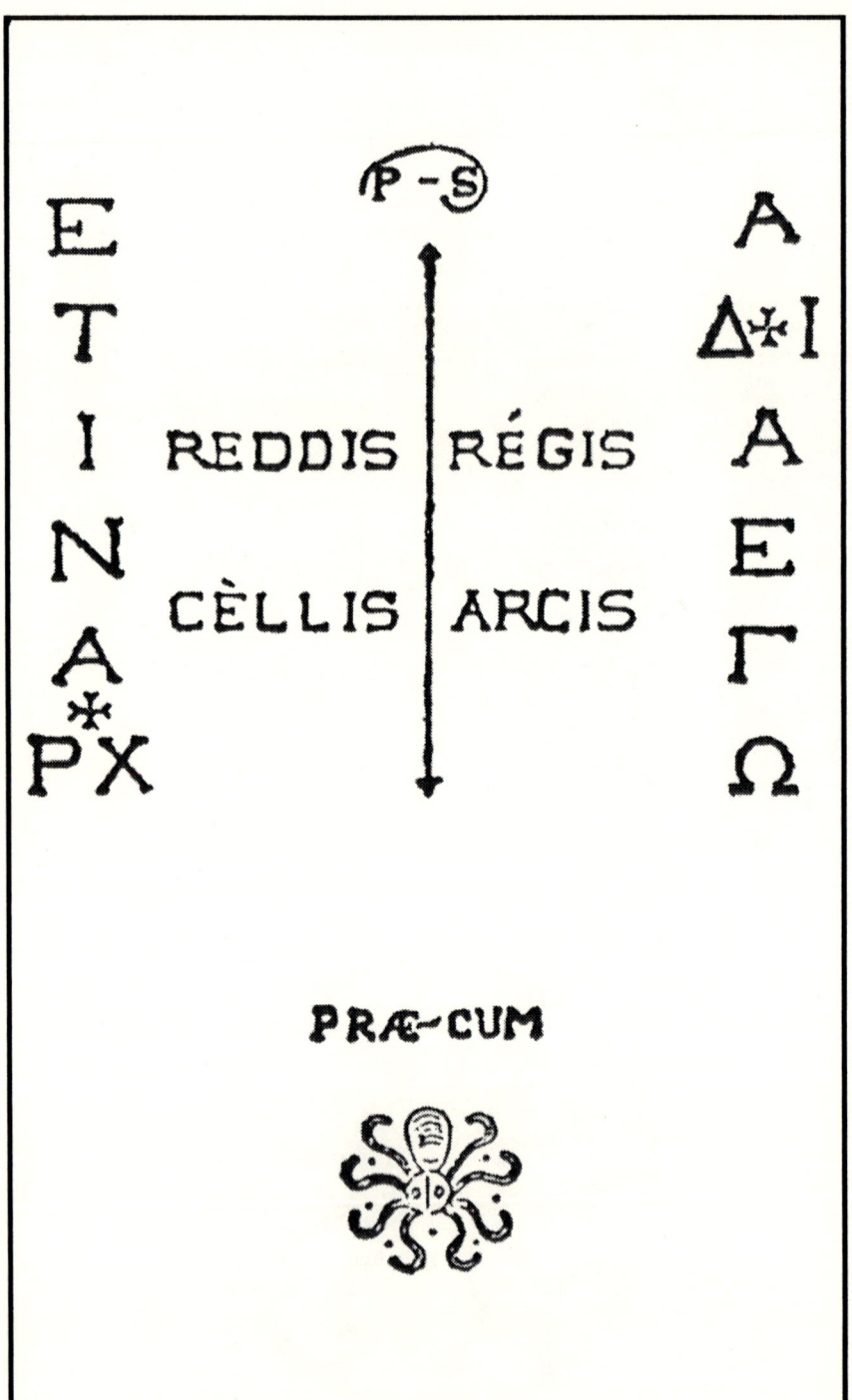

The design on the tomb of Marie de Blanchefort.

The Black Sun in Cocteau's Notre Dame mural. *Photo by Tim Madison.*

Dagon wearing the fish hat upon which the papal miter is based.

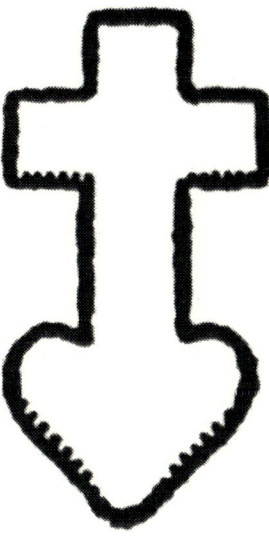

The Sacred Heart, as illustrated in *Secret Dossiers*. It is said to depict an "Egyptian amulet" that can be seen at the "Museum at Rennes."

123

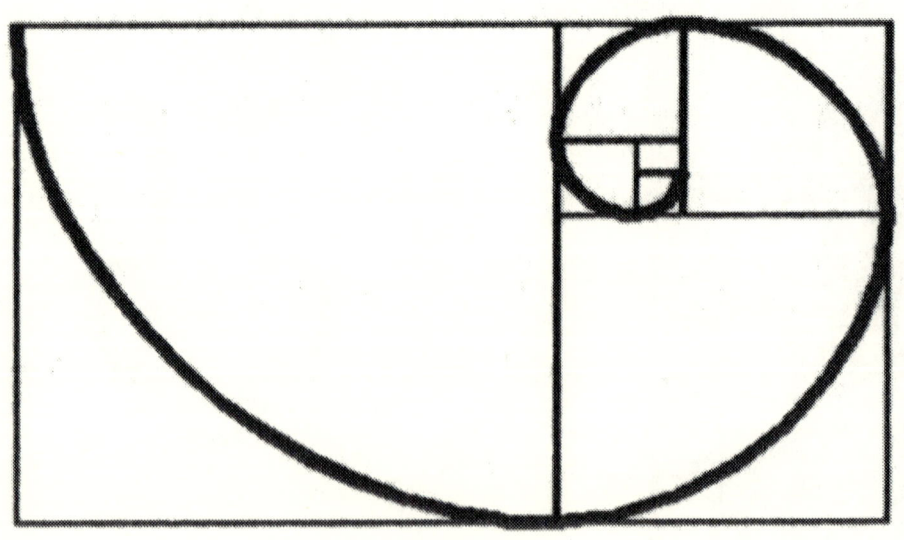

The Sumerian god-king Ea enthroned in the "Absu, or "Watery Abyss."

The Fibonacci Spiral..

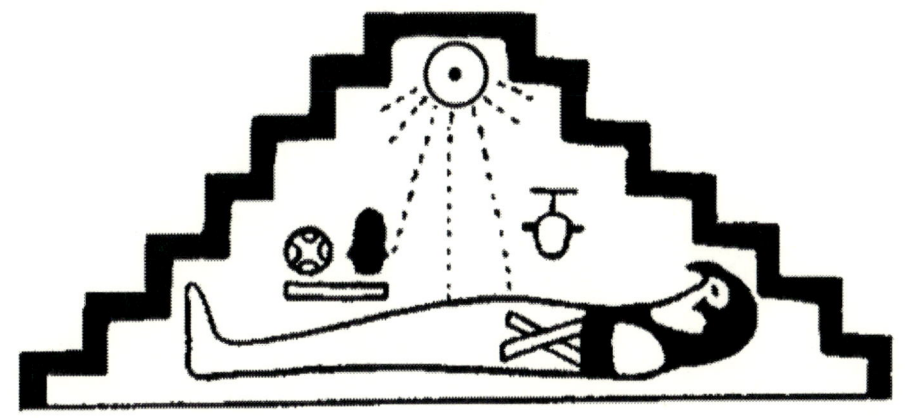

Horus entombed within a mountain or pyramid lit by an inner sun.

Illustration from *Vaincre* depicting the "United States of the West."

The illustration of "le Poulpe" ("the Octopus"), from *Secret Dossiers*.

The symbol for "Ormus" used by the Priory of Sion.

ETFACTUMESTEUMIN
SABBATOSECUNDOPRIMO a
BIREPERSCCETESaIsCIPULIAUTEMILLIRISCOE
PERUNTUELLERESPICASETFRICANTESMANIBUS + MANdU
CABANTQUIdAMAUTEMdEFARISAEISaT
CEbANTEiECCEQUIaFACIUNTdISCIPULITUISab
bATIS + QUOdNONLICETRESPONdENSAUTEMINS
SETXITadEQSNUMQUAMbOC
LECISTISQUOdFECITaaUTaqUANdO
ESURUTIPSEETaUICUMEOERaI + INTRoibITINdauMVM
dEIETPANESPROPOSITIONIS   REdIS
MANdUCaUITETdedITETQUI   bIES
CUMERANTUXUO QUIBUSNO
NLICEbaTMANdUCaRESINON   SOLIS SACERdOTIBUS

Parchment One.

The Emerald Tablet of Hermes engraved on the side of a mountain.

JESVSEVRGOANTCESEXATPESPASCSHALEVENJTTbETHQANTAMVKAT
TVEKAOTIAZA=VVJMOKTVVVJQVEMMSVJCTYTAVITIYESVJFCACERVNT
LAVIEM=TTCAENAPMTbTETOMARTHAHMINISTRKAbATCbASARVJO
VCROVNXVSEKATTE=ATJCOVMIENTATIVJCVJMMARTALERGOACbCEP
TTLKTbKAMYNNGENTTJNAKATPFTJTICIQPRETIOVJTETVNEXTTPE
APESTERVAETEXTEJRSTTCAYPTIRTSNSVISPEPAESERTPTETAOMbESTM
PLFTIAESTEEXVNGETNTTOAAEKEAIXALTERGOVRNVMEXAGTSCTPVAL
TJETVTXTVAAXSCARJORTIJQVIYEKATCVHMTKAATTTVRVJQTVAKEHOSCVN
bENVTVMNONXVENVITGKECENPATSAENAAKVSETAAATVMESGTE
GENTES? AIXINVTEMHOCCNBNQVJTAAEEGAENTJPERKTINEbEAT
AACVTMSEAQVHINFVKELKTETLOVCVIOSHCAHENSECAQVACMVTTIEbA
NCTVKPOTKAbETEATXTTEJKGOIESHVJSTNEPTELAMVNTTXAIPMS
EPVLGTVKAEMSEAESERVNETILLQVAPAVPJEKESENHTMSEMPGEKHA
bEMTTSNObLTISCVMFMEAVTCTMNONSESMPEKHAVbEHISCJOGNO
VILTEKOTZVKbAMVQLTAEXTMVAACTSTQVTATLOLTCESTXETVENE
AKVNTNONNPROTEPRTESV=ETANTwMMSEAVILUZAKVMPVTAEK
EH=TQVEMKSVSCTAOVITAMORRTVTSCPOGTTAVKERVNTAHVTEMP
RVTNCTPEJSSACEHCAOTVMVMTETLAZCARVMTNATERFTCTRENTY
LVTAMYLVTTPROPQTEKILHXVMAbTHGNTCXVGT=AETSNETCRCA
AEbANTINTESVM

NO N IS

JÉSV. MEDÈLA. VVLNÉRVM ✝ SPES. VNA. PŒNITENTIVM.
PER. MAGDALÄNÆ. LACHYMAS ✝ PECCATA. NOSTRA. DILVAS.

Parchment Two.

128

The Shepherds of Arcadia, by Nicolas Poussin.
(c)Louvre/(Museum)/Paris/France. Reunion des Musees Nationaux/Art Resource, NY.

The alchemical seal featured on Sauniere's bookplate.

The Tour Magdala. *Photo by Tracy Twyman.*

Hermes or Mercury is the same as Enoch. This same figure was called "Thoth" or "Azag-Thoth" in Egypt, incorporating the "Azag" title of his father, Cain. And Azag-Thoth, Hermes or Mercury is believed in certain occult legends to have been the inventor of chess, which is played on an 8 x 8 board. This may be related to the Chinese I-Ching, which is made up of 64 "hexagrams."

The name "Enoch", as we know, is related to the Sumerian name of this figure's grandfather, "Enki", or Satan. Also written as "Kenoch" or "Hanuk", this name was probably the source of the word "Anakim", a race of giants who, according to *Genesis*, lived in Canaan, and who may very well have been descendants of Enoch. "Enki", "Enoch", and the name of the father god "Anu" are all sources for the Sumerian word "Annunaki", their name for the original race of gods, and probably the South American tribe of the Inca, who were civilized by these same god-kings. The word further mutated into "ankh", the Egyptian sun-cross which was also used, oddly enough, by the Cathars in medieval France, and which mutated into the Celtic cross. As "Enoch" was sometimes spelled "Anag", it may be related to the French place-name "Anjou", from whence came the Angevins, an offshoot of the Merovingian family.

However, Enoch's other name of "Erech", after which the Sumerian city of "Uruk" (or sometimes "Warka") was called (and thus the country of Iraq) was just as influential in our language. As we have said before, the word "Ur" (related to "Ar") has come to mean "primeval" in European language. It is not hard to see how the word "Erech", "Uruk" or "Warka" could transform into "Ark", as in the one that Enoch may have navigated during the Flood. Given the idea that civilization supposedly died during the Deluge, the Ark could then be the *origin* of all renewed civilization. Thus the word "arche", like "ur" in German, means "original" in Latin, and provides us with words like "archetype." Enoch was, like his father, an "architect", a science named after its fundamental building block, the "arch." And "arch" also denotes political rule, as in "monarchy", "anarchy", or "oligarchy."

The names of the other figures I have discussed in this chapter have many other linguistic connections as well. Anu, of course, is the same as Oannes, Ouranos, Uranus, and Enu, and he is the source of the race names "Annunaki" and "Annedoti." Also, as he was viewed in his time as the god of the heavens, the inventor of astronomy, and an incarnation of the Sun itself, the solar year was named after him in Sumeria, which is where we get our word "annual."

"Satan" is obviously related to the word "Saturn", which is related to "satyr", a form of goat-headed man who in Greek mythology occupied Arcadia. Their race was headed by Pan, who seems to be based on the goat-headed figure of Cain/Seth. Pan was seen as a "trickster god", a malicious joker, and from the word "satyr" we get the word "satire." This same figure of Satan was Kronos in Greek myth , or Cerrunnos in Celtic mythology, seen in those cultures as the inventor of farming. He was especially associated with wheat, or "corn", as it is called in England, a word derived from his name. Of course, "Kronos" or "Chronos" was associated with the concept of time, and thus the word "chronology" was formed. It is also probably the root of the word "crown", the headgear worn by a king.

This same figure's Sumerian title of "Ia" was later absorbed into the name of "Jah" or "Jehovah", who hijacked much of his rivals' imagery. "Ia" contributed to the formation of the word "eye", and the eye became a symbol for the world kingship that was once wielded by these god-kings. The eye symbol was used as a glyph for kingship in India, where it was called "the Royal Eye of Gopta", and in Egypt, where it was "the Eye of Horus." The symbol of the All-Seeing Eye was then adopted by Freemasons, who incorporated many Egyptian mysteries into their rituals. It was Freemasons who designed the Great Seal of the United States, in which the All-Seeing Eye replaces the capstone of the Egyptian Great Pyramid. This is supposed to symbolize the ideal political *world order* envisioned by Freemasons – one of autocratic global hegemony, a return to the world empire of the golden age of the gods.

The Fallen Race

Both the god-kings who descended from Satan and Cain, as well as those who came from Jehovah and Baal, have played monumental roles in human history, to say the least. If not for them, "humanity" as we know it would not exist, much less civilization, and the Earth would be populated by nomadic hordes of primitive mongrelized subraces. But the battles between the Satanic and Jehovahite factions, as well as the numerous subfactions, have wreaked havoc on our ancient history. We now have only echoes of truth in fragmented form, sprinkled throughout our mythologies and religious doctrines. Most so-called "occult" doctrines are no less a mixture of truth and falsehood. It is as if a veil has fallen over the light, and now we "see through a glass darkly."

One of the reasons for this, perhaps, is that almost all of the god-human hybrid races have died off. We know that they continued to live for a long time after the Flood. Although their ages at death gradually drop from hundreds of years before and immediately after the Flood, to more normal age ranges by the time of Moses, the patriarchs of the Bible, all the way up to and including the twelve sons of Jacob, are all reported in Jewish legends to have been giants, and to have been exceedingly beautiful, with captivating eyes, as well as being capable of superhuman feats of strength. The historian Eusebius wrote that "Abraham traced his ancestry to the giants. These dwelt in the land of Babylonia. Because of their impiety, they were destroyed by the gods." There were also other races of giants reported in the Bible, such as the "Anakim" and the "Rephaim", who were said to live in lands outside of Israel. These giants all seem to have been carriers of the blood of the pre-diluvian god-kings. Similar things (extraordinarily long lives, beautiful skin, and giant bodies) are reported about the kings of other ancient cultures, such as Sumeria, India, Egypt and Greece.

Nicholas de Vere details in his book *The Dragon Legacy* how races of divine-human hybrids acted as the "overseers", or "Dragons" (a word that he says comes from "derkesthai", which means "to see clearly") of ancient human societies. He depicts this as a harmonious, interdependent caste system headed by the Dragons, who served their "client races" with care. He believes that all legends of fairies, elves, dragons, vampires, devils, demons, and angels are remembrances of these creatures, or of their forefathers, the gods.

However, De Vere believes that these "Dragon" races, particularly those descended from Jehovah, eventually allowed themselves to interbeed outside of the Dragon family, to the point where their blood lost all of its divine potency. These people, now mere mortals, then began a systematic effort to exterminate those who remained "of pure Dragon blood", and to take over the human societies they directed. De Vere details the chronology of this "genocide" in a chapter of his book called "The

Thousand-Year Elven Holocaust." It is because of this largely successful campaign that the world is, in De Vere's eyes, now run by ignoble "robber barons" with selfish motives, still aspiring to the titles, prestige and power originally wielded by those whom they had hatefully eradicated. In this group De Vere counts also the majority of royalty born in the last several hundred years, whom he regards as nothing but the degenerate remnants of a fallen race. On this subject, he writes:

> *"It is known that in antiquity the Nephilim, the Elven sons of the Annunagi, interbred with humans... However it is recorded that these half-breeds were destroyed... and the slate was wiped clean.*
> *The next experiment produced a lineage of pure-bred Elven queens and kings who were to supervise a race of quarterbreeds who were originally created for manual labor. The quarterbreeds, nevertheless, were eventually to gain their freedom and elect their own chieftains. They were helped by the Elven dynasty, the people whom Christians now think of as the spawn of Satan...*
> *These people interbred with anyone and we know them now as the biblical race of Adam whose Elven blood today is so diluted as to be infinitesimal. The pure Elven Queens and Kings, however, bred with no one but themselves and so throughout the past five or six millennia, the blood was kept more or less pure in several unbroken lines of descent until as late as the 8th century A.D. From that time, however, only one bloodline descent is recorded as being pure and unbroken."*

But really, in terms of which race is "fallen" because of miscegenation between humans and gods, both the descendants of Jehovah and Satan "fell", in the sense that they both watered down the royal and divine blood in their veins by mating with common humans generation after generation. However, the mythological record seems to suggest that the Adamites, or Edenites, had polluted their blood prior to the Flood, and it was the monstrous and deformed race which resulted that was wiped out in the Deluge. It was because of the ignoble nature of what their race had become that Jehovah abandoned them. Interestingly, De Vere refers to the "Nephilim" as being lead by Jehovah, not Satan.

The fall of Eden may be the real source for the Hebrew myth regarding the "Fallen Kings of Edom", the ten "Children of Before" who "ruled before there were kings in Israel", until their kingdom was destroyed by God because of their evil nature. The Kings of Edom are now used in Cabala to signify the fallen kings of the "Kingdom of Shells", the "Qipploth" or dark shadow of the Tree of Life that, in this system, exists in the underworld. And the head of these ten "demon kings" in this system is named "Moloch", thus representing Baal, or Abel. Indeed, the first "Moloch" of the Edomites is listed in the Bible as "Bela", a derivative of Baal or Abel.

But regardless of who deserves the label of the "fallen race", the fact remains that, largely because of the propaganda spread by their enemies, the descendants of Satan were characterized as evil beings, bent on leading humanity to sin and then dragging their souls down to never-ending torment in the bowels of the Earth. Cain, or "Azazel", became "Asmodeus", the King of the Demons, but still retaining the title "Rex Mundi", or "Lord of the Earth" - this time in a pejorative sense, the Earth being seen as the Devil's domain. The entire noble race was cast as wretched, hate-filled, grimacing, ugly monsters. At best, they were depicted by the establishment as charming and harmless, but entirely fictional elves and nymphs – ridiculous, supernatural, and highly improbably creations of the human imagination, like Tinkerbelle and the Tooth Fairy. But numerous traditions continue to relate that Satan and his "devils", "demons", or "Djinn" descendants were in fact the harbingers of all the *good* things that civilization has brought to mankind. Indeed, they are remembered as the forefathers of modern humanity itself.

Surprisingly, the word "demon" was originally never meant to be a negative term, but really meant "wise one", and indicated the race of Satan or Kronos, the benefactors of mankind. As Ignatius Donnelly explains:

"Plato says, speaking of the traditions of the Greeks, 'There is a tradition of the happy life of mankind in the days when all things were spontaneous and abundant. . . . In like manner God in his love of mankind placed over us the demons, who are a superior race, and they, with great care and pleasure to themselves and no less to us, taking care of us and giving us place and reverence and order and justice never failing, made the tribes of men happy and peaceful . . . for Cronos knew that no human nature, invested with supreme power, is able to order human affairs and not overflow with insolence and wrong.'

In other words, this tradition refers to an ancient time when the forefathers of the Greeks were governed by Chronos, of the Cronian Sea (the Atlantic), king of Atlantis, through civilized Atlantean governors, who by their wisdom preserved peace and created a golden age for all the populations under their control--they were the demons, that is, 'the knowing ones,' the civilized.

Plato puts into the mouth of Socrates these words: 'My notion would be that the sun, moon, and stars, earth, and heaven, which are still the gods of many barbarians, were the only gods known to the aboriginal Hellenes. . . . What shall follow the gods? Must not demons and heroes and men come next? . . . Consider the real meaning of the word demons. You know Hesiod uses the word. He speaks of 'a golden race of men' who came first. He says of them,

'But now that fate has closed over this race,
They are holy demons upon earth,
Beneficent averters of ills, guardians of mortal men.'

He means by the golden men not men literally made of gold, but good and noble men; he says we are of the 'age of iron.' He called them demons because they were (knowing or wise)."

This is why, as the religions of Judaism and later Christianity coalesced, "Satan" and his "fallen angels" or "demons" became associated with the spreading of "forbidden knowledge." Thus the story of Faust developed in Europe as a cautionary tale about a man who sold his soul to the Devil in exchange for obtaining ultimate wisdom. And although originally the wisdom that Satan, Cain and Enoch were said to have given mankind included all arts and sciences, as time wore on, the "forbidden" wisdom was narrowed down to all things "occult": divination, alchemy, astrology, sorcery, necromancy, etc. – all of which became known as the "dark arts", the practice of which was believed to damn the practitioner's soul to Hell. Also included among these was the perpetuation of secret doctrines and heresies regarding God and the history recounted in the Bible. These are the things that constitute the "underground stream" of Hermeticism and Gnosticism later perpetuated by groups like the Knights Templar, the Freemasons, the Rosicrucians, and the Priory of Sion. Traditionalist philosopher Julius Evola wrote, using the historian Tertullian as a reference, that:

"...the works of nature, the secrets of metals, the virtues of plants, the forces of magical conjurations, and 'all those alien teachings that make up the science of the stars' - that is to say, the whole corpus of the ancient magico-hermetic sciences was revealed to men by the fallen angels."

In the same vein, the following quote has been attributed to an ancient Hermetic sage from Egypt who called himself "Hermes Trismegistus":

"The ancient and sacred books teach that certain angels burned with desire for women. They descended to earth and taught all the works of nature. They were the ones who created the Hermetic works, and from them proceeds the primordial tradition of this art."

The Heresies of Christ

These Hermetic and Gnostic traditions were becoming quite popular and influential throughout both the East and the Hellenistic West by the time that Jesus Christ was born. At that time many Gnostic sects held that Jehovah was in fact the "Demi-Urge", the Devil, and that Satan or Lucifer was "the light bringer", the god (or sometimes goddess) of wisdom. There is reason to believe that Jesus himself was initiated into such a sect, and later started one of his own with his disciples, which became the first and true Christian church (the one purportedly represented by the Merovingians and the Priory of Sion).

We know that the first (and perhaps only) sect which Jesus joined before starting his own was that of John the Baptist – whose cult was mystical in nature, and is thought by some historians to have been an Essene offshoot, although nobody knows for sure. However, there is a Gnostic sect called the Mandeans (still existing in Iran) who claim their teachings were given to them directly by John the Baptist. They honor John as their true prophet rather than Jesus, and consider John to have been the spiritual son and incarnation of the goddess Sophia, which means "wisdom." Interestingly, a sub-sect of the Mandeans, called the Yezidis, take Gnosticism all the way to full-fledged Satanism and worship the goat-headed "Shaitan" as the bringer of wisdom.

This brings us to the goat-headed deity of Baphomet revered by the Templars, the Freemasons, and many other Satanic or occult traditions. His name has been said to be the result of encoding the word "Sophia" or "wisdom" in the Hebrew Atbash cipher used by the Knight Templar. This link with a female goddess of wisdom may explain why this otherwise male deity is sometimes depicted as hermaphroditic. But it has also been translated by Aleister Crowley as meaning "Baptism of Wisdom." And of course, it is the very un-Jewish rite of baptism that John the Baptist was most well-known for. So if the head or skull that the Templars worshipped as a representation of Baphomet was, as has been claimed, really the skull of John the Baptist, perhaps it was because he was actually a priest of, and considered an incarnation of, Baphomet. But his disciple Jesus was seen that way as well, as we shall see.

Another interpretation of Baphomet's name is that it means "Father Mithras." As discussed earlier, Mithras appears to be yet another god based on the figure of Cain or Seth. He was known for slaying the "World Bull", as Cain purportedly slew Abel or Baal. He was also known for allowing himself to be sacrificed around the time of Easter, only to be born anew, just as Cain pretended to die and be reborn as Seth. There are many other similarities as well, and many similarities also between Mithras and Jesus. The rites of Mithras appear to be the major inspiration not only for the early Christian church, but for the rites of Freemasonry as well.

The rites of Mithras were perhaps the most influential cult in the ancient world at that time. Beginning in Persia, they spread to Rome, Asia Minor, India, China and Babylon. The original Persian strain inspired the first monotheistic religion of Zoroastrianism, which mutated in Babylon and there influenced greatly the development of Judaism while the Jews were in captivity in Babylon, which is when their earliest scriptures were written. In Rome the Mithras cult mutated into that of "Sol Invictus" – "the Invincible Sun." It is this cult which the Roman Emperor Constantine truly converted to when he instituted Christianity as the official religion of Rome[4]. During that period in Rome, the Sun was often called "the eye of Mithras."

The reported life of Mithras looks like a veritable blueprint for the story of Jesus. As author Ellie Crystal reports on crystalinks.com:

"According to Persian traditions, the god Mithras was actually incarnated into the human form of the Saviour expected by Zarathustra. Mithras was born of Anahita, an immaculate virgin mother once worshipped as a fertility goddess... Anahita was said to have conceived the Saviour from the seed of Zarathustra preserved in the waters of Lake Hamun in the Persian province of Sistan...

The God remained celibate throughout his life, and valued self-control, renunciation and resistance to sensuality among his worshippers. Mithras represented a system of ethics in which brotherhood was encouraged in order to unify against the forces of evil....

In Armenian tradition, Mithras was believed to shut himself up in a cave from which he emerged once a year, born anew."

In the end, Mithras ascended to Heaven in a "Sun chariot", but before he did so, he shared a ritualistic "Last Supper" with his disciples in which bread and wine was served. This ritual became part of the practices of the cult of Mithras, in which the participants believe that they were consuming the blood and body of their deity – just as in Christianity! It is from the rites of Mithras that baptism comes as well, in which it was used to "wash away the sins" of the new convert. The priests of Mithras also wore fish-like miters just like Catholic bishops (a tradition that extends from the Syrian rites of Dagon as well), and it is likely that the word "miter" comes from "Mithras." Mithraic priests were called "Father", wore special rings, and carried a shepherds staff as well, just like Catholic bishops. They celebrated Mithras' birthday on December 25 (around the Winter Solstice, Saturnalia, and St. Dagobert's Day), and held services to the god every Sunday.

Even more amazing is that the ultimate purpose of Mithras' existence was similar to that which the Church has ascribed to Christ. It was believed that when Mithras died in sacrifice, he obtained freedom for his followers from the wages of their sins. And when he rose again, he obtained for them eternal life in Paradise. The curator of a website called "Borndigital" (http://www.borndigital.com/tarsus.htm), comments further:

> *"It was believed that the partaking of the sacrament (of communion) ensured eternal life, the immediate passing, after death, to the bosom of Mithras, there to tarry in bliss until the judgment day. On the judgment day the Mithraic keys of heaven would unlock the gates of Paradise for the reception of the faithful; whereupon all the unbaptized of the living and the dead would be annihilated upon the return of Mithras to earth. It was taught that, when a man died, he went before Mithras for judgment, and that at the end of the world Mithras would summon all the dead from their graves to face the last judgment. The wicked would be destroyed by fire, and the righteous would reign with Mithras forever."*

Although a good deal of this imagery was probably added on to the cult of Christ by the Roman Catholic Church in an attempt to make their new religion palatable to the pagan populace of the Roman Empire, it cannot be doubted that much of it was quite consciously taken on by Jesus himself, and that the import of what he was trying to do was recognized at the time. The Zoroastrians even saw in Jesus a prophesized incarnation of Mithras, which is why magi were sent at his birth. Borndigital.com continues:

> *"Zarathustra had predicted a Messiah, and Jesus' birth was thought perhaps to be his arrival. In the Persian 'Avesta' (their religious writings), this Messiah will appear at the end of time to bring the triumph of good over evil. They call him the 'Saushyant', and according to the Bundahishn he will slay a magnificent bull, and make a potion of immortality for mankind from its fat, mixed with Hamoa juice."*

As stated, many elements of Mithraic ritual made their way into Freemasonry. Mithraism was a highly secret mystery cult, in which only initiates were allowed to know the wisdom of Mithras, revealed to them in several stages, or degrees. In one degree (quoting Ellie Crystal again), "The neophyte wears a veil and carries a lamp in his hand. He is unable to see the 'light of truth' until the 'veil of reality' is lifted." In another degree "the neophyte had to kneel (submission to religious authority, naked (casting off old life), blindfolded with hands tied. He was then offered a crown on the point of a sword. Once crowned, his binds were cut with a single stroke of the sword and blindfold removed... He would then remove the crown from his head and placing it on his shoulder, saying: 'Mithra is my only crown[5].'" In another rite, the initiate was given honey to anoint his hands and tongue. Honey and bees later became important symbolism to the Freemasons, and to the Merovingians[6]. All of these elements became part of Masonic rites.

Another element of Masonic ritual that originated with Mithraism was the secret handshake, and in fact, the handshake itself, which initially was used in their rites to symbolize the covenant that was made between the initiate and Mithras, as well as the friendship that existed between them. (In China, Mithras was actually called "the Friend.") The handshake was a symbol of one of the most essential concepts of Mithras. He was the god of contracts. In fact, Mithras' name is said to have come from the Persian word for "contract." As crystalinks.com explains:

"In The Avesta, the holy book of the religion of Zarathustra, Ahura-Mazda was said to have created Mithras in order to guarantee the authority of contracts and the keeping of promises... The divine duty of Mithras was to ensure general prosperity through good contractual relations between men. It was believed that misfortune would befall the entire land if a contract was ever broken."

Obviously, this is significant because contracts, particularly oaths of secrecy and fidelity, have a particular importance in Freemasonry.

It was because of his association with contracts that Mithras came to be thought of as a wise judge, and as mankind's judge in the afterlife. He took on the title "the Mediator", and was thought to literally mediate between the Zoroastrian deities of Ahura-Mazda[7] and Ahriman (light and darkness, or Satan and Jehovah) as they struggled to influence the world and to defeat one another. In this sense Mithras is equal to Baphomet, or the Gnostic deity Abraxas, both of which were thought to be embodiments of the unity of opposites, including good and evil, as well as male and female.

There is evidence that Jesus saw himself as an incarnation of Mithras, and wished to do a little contract negotiation of his own between Jehovah, Satan, and humanity. As a royal scion of David, and rightful King of the Jews, he knew that he was a descendant of both Jehovah and Satan quite literally. But if he were to truly represent the Jewish people, he would have to uphold the many contracts that those people had made with Jehovah over the generations, the breaking of which could lead to curses afflicting multiple generations. Such contracts had been made between Abraham and "God" on behalf of the Hebrews, and then later between Moses and Jehovah. Numerous clauses had been added on to these contracts over the centuries also. The Bible makes it quite clear that Jehovah took these contracts very seriously, and the Jews and Israelites were very aware of this. The Jewish and Israelite people were essentially in bondage to Jehovah, crippled by their obligations to him, and yet he had delivered little in the way of property or power to these people beyond their supposedly "special" relationship with him, and their relatively small "land flowing with milk and honey": the Holy Land. While this land was apparently nothing to sneeze at, coveted by all surrounding nations as well, the Israelites and Jews could never hold onto it for very long without being captured and enslaved by their many enemies – curses purportedly placed on them by Jehovah for not observing their contract with him strictly enough.

Yet the kings of Judah and Israel were not only anointed by, contracted by, and ultimately in some ways genetically related to Jehovah. They were also ultimately descended from Seth, or Cain, and thus Satan. Moreover, it does seem when one examines the Old Testament that Satan and Cain had their own influence on the kings of Judah and Israel, and may have had their own contracts with them. Officially, the Jewish kings were anointed by Jehovah, but secretly, many of them were "Dragon kings" allied with Satan. As a scion of this lineage, and an initiate into the Satanic mystery traditions that had been passed down from his forefathers, Jesus was no doubt aware of this situation. And I believe that he wished to break the contracts that the Jews and Israelites had with Jehovah, and release them from spiritual bondage.

The first part of his plan involved converting the consciences of the people. Jesus essentially went about preaching that people should ignore the letter of Jehovah's law and concentrate instead on the spirit of goodness and virtue. These are values that are unique neither to Judaism or Christianity, but in fact, widespread and ancient, originating with the laws observed by the gods in their antediluvian civilization, and passed down to post-diluvian human society through Cain. Jesus encouraged them to worship the true God who created the universe, and whose essence can be found in all things, rather than remaining enslaved to a tribal demiurge that had essentially attached itself to the bloodlines of their forefathers for personal gain. He preached that they should love one another, including uncircumcised gentiles, rather than declaring that they should hate anyone outside of their own limited gene pool, or anyone who had not sealed a covenant with Jehovah by mutilating his penis. Jesus, and his mentor, John, baptized men in the name of "the Father" (Mithras), and washed away their sins, i.e., the guilt that they had carried all their lives because of their covenant with Jehovah. And for his closest disciples, Jesus allowed them to be initiated into the Mithraic mysteries. The wedding at Cana, the death and rebirth ritual played with Lazarus, the Last Supper, and finally the death and resurrection ritual enacted by Jesus himself, were all part of the Mithraic rites which he and his disciples were enacting. All of this worked to turn the hearts and minds of his followers away from Jehovah.

Jesus' wedding to Mary Magdalene was also part of the plot. Many authors have asserted that Magdalene was a member of the Israelite tribe of Benjamin. And although they were a *royal* tribe, having provided Israel's first king, Saul, they were also an accursed tribe. *The Book of Judges* tells the story of the "outrage at Gibeah", in which Baal-worshiping Benjamites raped the wife of a Levite, instigating a war against the Benjamites by the eleven other tribes of Israel which decimated them, reducing the number of male Benjamites left to less than 300. After the war, the other tribes swore before Jehovah that they would not give their daughters to marry Benjamite men, and thus the remaining males were forced to marry women outside of Israel – outside of the covenant with Jehovah. The entire race of the Benjamites became associated with the worship of strange gods, the marrying of foreign women, and the curses of Jehovah. As a descendant of Benjamin (and possibly a Benjamite princess), Mary Magdalene embodied this symbolism by default, even though there was no injunction against marrying Benjamite *women* per se, but only the men. However, if at any point in Mary Magdalene's genealogy there was a union between a Benjamite man and a woman from one of the other tribes of Israel, and if this union had occurred *after* the "outrage at Gibeah" occurred, then her bloodline would definitely be cursed, as would anyone who married her, or any children born of her.

But there may have been something else about Mary that earned her a reputation as a "whore", and made her unfit for marriage in the eyes of the rabbis. There is a belief among Catholics that she was an "adulteress" - specifically that she was the same adulteress whom Jesus saved from public stoning and absolved of her sins. However, "adulteress", like "whore", is a versatile word, and would have applied to a woman who had been divorced as well. In the book *The Legend of Thomas Didymus*, James Freeman Clarke suggests that Magdalene had once been one of King Herod's wives, but had been divorced by him. In his version of the story, Magdalene was a high noble woman, and that was why Herod married her. But when he tired of her, he turned her out of his house, and married Herodias, the wife of his brother, making her his wife instead. According to James Freeman Clarke, it was on the grounds of Herod's previous marriage to Magdalene that John the Baptist objected to his new marriage to

Herodias, and thus ended up getting beheaded. If Magdalene had been married previously, this alone would have made her a "forbidden woman", although she was probably the perfect candidate in many other ways to be Jesus' bride priestess. Jesus may have decided to go through with the marriage despite this, so as to intentionally commit a "sex crime" for ritual purposes - a sex crime that spawned a royal race, as that of Satan had done.

However, if this were true, John the Baptist would have objected to the marriage, as he would have believed that the marriage would bring a curse upon Jesus' royal line of descendants. (This may explain why Jesus' relationship with John turned chilly towards the end, as the Gospels seem to indicate.) So too would most other priests and rabbis, which may be one of the reasons why this community disdained Jesus so much. Even some of Jesus' own disciples may have felt that he was bringing shame to their movement by marrying Magdalene. Thus they may have chosen not to acknowledge Jesus' marriage or progeny, and to malign the memory of the Magdalene in their writings. The Roman Church followed suit later on for other reasons.

But at the same time, there were undoubtedly many advantages of Jesus and Magdalene getting together. As many authors have suggested, Mary might have been the chief royal heir of her tribe, a descendant of the first King of Israel, Saul. And although Saul's line was usurped by that of David after his death, "the Lord" did make promises to Saul that, in Jesus' time, had yet to be fulfilled - the promise that his seed would also provide a second king to Israel - the last king! For Jesus, connecting himself to the line of Saul may have been integral to meeting the expectations of the prophesized Messiah.

Occult traditions hold that Jesus and Mary Magdalene may have been the leaders of a royal sex magic cult, with Magdalene performing the role of a "temple priestess" or "sacred prostitute." Obviously, if this were true, then the belief system that Jesus represented was well outside of mainstream Judaism. Indeed, he and Magdalene were most likely followers of strange Satanic gods, the worship of whom involved sexual magic. The wedding at Cana may have been at once both a proper marriage ceremony and a sex magic ritual, the purpose of which was to (a) unite the King of the Jews with his royal dynastic bride; (b) anoint him ritually as the king, and; (c) to ritually conceive a royal heir. Thus, the metaphor of Jesus turning water into wine may have symbolized using sex magic to "graft the vines" of two powerful royal bloodlines. Mary Magdalene's status as a Benjamite princess may have made her especially qualified to act as a sacred prostitute, as the Benjamites were associated specifically with the performance of rituals for strange gods. In Hebrew culture, such practices were equated with harlotry, and the women involved in these practices were thought of as being responsible for corrupting their husbands. This is yet another reason why Magdalene may have been seen as a "whore." Such women were viewed as "foreigners", i.e., outside of the covenant with Jehovah, and so were their children. When Israelite men married such women, it was believed that they brought onto the bloodline of their descendants the generational curses of strange gods.

This may impart yet another purpose to the marriage between Jesus and Mary Magdalene. Jesus was the qualified king of the Jews, and his son would have been the qualified king of all Israelites. But perhaps he aspired to something more than that. Perhaps he wished for his descendants to be the kings of foreign lands as well. But in order to set himself up to be king of the Jews, while at the same time setting his son up for something larger, he may have needed to simultaneously fulfill Jehovah's messianic promises, and at the same time, break his family's covenant with Jehovah. The "new covenant" had to be created - a covenant which those of gentile races could join into. He needed to break the exclusive hold that Jehovah had on his bloodline, and open it up to the blessings of other gods – gods who, as we now know, were probably his ancestors. Taking Mary Magdalene to wife and breeding the royal heir with her may have fulfilled this purpose.

If Mary Magdalene was indeed Jesus' wife, and indeed was the mother to his messianic heir, then the blessings and curses, the rights and inheritances that she carried in her blood were just as important as his in defining the characteristics of the Merovingian bloodline of France that descended from them. This would have especially been the case if she was a Benjamite, from a tribe practicing matrilineal inheritance. This would explain why she was so revered by the mystery cults of Southern France. But it also explains why they represented her in the form of the Black Madonna. For in the eyes of the Jewish priests of Christ's time, and in the eyes of the later Christian church, the Magdalene's marriage to Jesus would have been seen as bringing a curse upon the bloodline that descended from them. This is one of the reasons that the Church insisted that the bloodline's very existence be kept secret. I have written an article on this subject entitled *The Choice Vine: Mary Magdalene, the Sacred Whore, and the Benjamite Inheritance*, which can be found at ordolapsitexillis.org.

The other act which Jesus committed in order to free his people from their obligations to Jehovah was, of course, his final known act – his supposed death on the cross. In the Gospels, Christ lays out in plain language the purpose of his death. He knew that the people of Israel were heavily laden and oppressed by numerous curses that had been laid on them by Jehovah, both as individuals and as a people, because of "sins" that they or their ancestors had committed against Jehovah. Jesus believed that he could somehow "take on their sins", as the scapegoat did at Yom Kippur, and that by being sacrificed on that day, he could take on their punishment himself, instantaneously breaking all of Jehovah's curses on them[8]. But more than that, he believed that this would atone not only for sins committed up until that point, but for any sins committed afterwards as well. Thus, the stranglehold that Jehovah had on these people would be broken. Free from the fear of curses as punishment (including the big curse, eternal damnation in Hell), the Israelites were free to act on their own consciences, instead of according to the strict, nonsensical, and seemingly arbitrary laws of Jehovah. The "New Covenant" which Christians speak of regarding Christ was formed, this time not between Jehovah and the Jews, but between Christ and all mankind, and those who served God were no longer obliged to observe the same restrictions on diet, marriage, etc., as the Jews had done. Now they merely had to follow the simple and enlightened rules of conscience outlined by Jesus in his sermons, which were timeless and universal.

But as a royal scion of the House of David, perhaps aspiring to an even greater throne for his son, would Jesus have sacrificed himself at age thirty-three, even for such a lofty goal? Perhaps not, which is why I am inclined to believe the theory briefly explored in *Holy Blood, Holy Grail*, which is an old and persistent heresy, stating that Jesus had a substitute die in his place. That way, the same sacrificial purpose of breaking the Jehovah covenant was fulfilled, and Jesus could live on to organize his church (while hiding in exile, of course), and to pass on his royal lineage.

Some of the earliest Christian scriptures have posited that this was the case.

The idea is backed up by Jewish and Islamic sources as well. Moreover, the name of the unfortunate victim has been put forth also, and the answer is almost obvious: Judas Iscariot. Of course, if Jesus were to choose one of his disciples to die in his place, he would probably choose the one whom he knew was about to betray him. *The Gospel of Barnabas* tells us that when the moment came for Jesus to be arrested, "God" changed the face of Judas into a likeness of Jesus. Thus, the Roman soldiers were tricked into arresting Judas in Christ's stead.

But there was another disciple of Christ, also names Judas, who is said in apocryphal legend to have been Jesus' actual twin. That apostle is Judas Didymus Thomas, also known as "Doubting Thomas" and "Thomas the Twin." Although biblical scholars, and even the authors of the gospels themselves, have gone to great lengths to stress that Iscariot and Thomas were separate people, there is a great deal of subtle and circumstantial evidence to suggest that they were actually the same figure.

If Christ's own twin brother was sent to die in his place, the symbolic significance of the crucifixion can be seen in an entirely different light. The death of one twin brother in place of another, or the murder of one twin by another, is not an uncommon mythical archetype. The Christian myth would then resemble, even closer than it already does, the myths of Rome, Greece, and Babylon. And the crucifixion, then, can also be seen as a reflection of the Jewish scapegoat ritual of Yom Kippur - in which one goat is sent off into exile to carry the curses of sin away from people, while the other one is sacrificed to atone for sins.

Furthermore, such a hypothesis explains the otherwise inexplicable smear campaigns that were waged via the scriptures against the figures of Judas Thomas and Judas Iscariot - one identified as a "faithless doubter", the other a "betrayer." Also, if Thomas did indeed die at the crucifixion, one cannot ignore the possibility that the recorded sightings of Thomas in India and elsewhere after the crucifixion were in fact sightings of Jesus impersonating his brother. It is possible, then, that the scriptures attributed to Thomas, including *The Acts of Thomas* and *The Gospel of Thomas*, are instead the only Christian scriptures actually written by Jesus himself.

If such a tradition did exist within the Grail family, it might explain why the Knights Templar purportedly conducted rituals in which they spat upon or urinated on the Christian cross. If they believed this idea, then they undoubtedly rejected the symbol of the cross as a symbol of the lies that had been told about Jesus' death.

With this in mind, new light can be shed on a mysterious bas relief that can be found at the back of the Church of Mary Magdalene at Rennes-le-Chateau, France. It depicts Jesus making his "Sermon on the Mount", as a quote beneath the relief proves. But strangely, at the bottom of the hill he stands on is a little money bag, out of which an object, long presumed to be gold, protrudes. Nobody has ever satisfactorily explained the presence of this money bag on this bas relief. Most of those who have commented on it have claimed it to be a clue left by the church's abbot, Berenger Sauniere, regarding a buried treasure he supposedly found on the church grounds. But it would seem now that this must certainly be Judas' purse. He is always depicted with a money-bag such as this, because he was the treasurer of the twelve apostles, and also because the bag symbolizes the thirty pieces of silver he received from the Sanhedrin in exchange for betraying Jesus. And why is it placed in such a peculiar spot? Judas himself is not even depicted in the relief. But the church confessional is positioned directly under this mural, and a wooden crucifix is set on top, so that, when viewed from a few feet away, the crucifix and the money bag appear to stand right next to one another. Was Sauniere hinting at his belief that it was Judas, not Christ, who hung on the cross? If so, why is the purse shown at the bottom of a hill covered with flowers?

A prevailing theory about the treasure Berenger Sauniere supposedly found is that is somehow constituted "incontrovertible proof" that Christ did not die on the cross, and many think that this proof consists of Christ's own body entombed not in Jerusalem, but in Southern France. Yet if Judas had died in Jerusalem in the place of Jesus, where was he buried? The most obvious answer is what *Acts* and *The Gospel of Matthew* seem to be hinting at: the potter's field, the "field of blood." After all, it is specifically stated in *Matthew* that this field was used for the "burial of strangers." In other words, it is a field of unmarked graves. If the secret of the crucifixion of Judas were to be kept, Judas' grave would have to go unmarked. Perhaps the hill covered with flowers in Sauniere's bas relief represents Judas' grave. If so, then by showing Jesus preaching atop this hill, he is showing that Christ's ministry is built upon the sacrifice of Judas. By placing this directly above the confessional, Sauniere was *confessing* his knowledge of this secret.

Another clue can be found in one of the Stations of the Cross at the church, in which Christ is shown being carried into the tomb at *nighttime*, contrary to scripture. According to *Holy Blood, Holy Grail*, this station may depict Christ's still-living body being removed from the tomb by his fellow conspirators. But if my theory is correct, then it was Judas' body, not Jesus', which was stolen away from the tomb by Christ's closest disciples. This is the scene depicted in this Station.

In addition to hinting at his belief in the heresy of Judas' crucifixion, Sauniere also demonstrated his belief in twin Christs. At the front of the church, on either side of the altar, are statues of Mary and Joseph, each holding an identical Christ child, although one appears to have slightly darker hair than the other. A recurring theme in the church involves the multiple depiction of two twin angels, identical in look to the aforementioned twin Christ children, both emerging out of a seashell. And one of Sauniere's unsolved clues that he embedded in his redesign of the church grounds involves the repeated use of the number 22. Could this be indicating "two-two", "double-double", or "twin-twin." This would have to be a reference to Judas Thomas Didymus whose name "Thomas" means "twin" in Hebrew", while "Didymus" means "twin" in Greek.

If Sauniere believed this proposed idea that Judas Iscariot was Christ's twin, and that Christ had tricked his rival brother into dying on the cross in his place, it would have shattered his Christian faith, but it could have also turned him in the direction of Gnostic Christianity and other, even more damnable forms of occultism. Such beliefs would have been regarded by his clerical peers as the highest heresy. These topics are the subject of a forthcoming book by me called *The Judas Goat*, also scheduled for release in late 2004.

So in this Gnostic interpretation of the mission of Christ, he saw himself as an incarnation of Cain (Mithras, Seth, etc.), who allowed himself to be symbolically sacrificed in order to free his people from bondage to Jehovah. It is interesting, then, that a common alchemical icon used since the Middle Ages has been a Christian cross with a serpent upon it, identifying Jesus with Satan! This identification is further supported by the concept embraced by Christian cabalists that the cross of Christ is symbolically connected to the Tree of Life or Tree of Knowledge in the Garden of Eden, leading one to conclude that the serpent who lived in the Tree is then the symbolic equivalent of Christ on the cross.

The Satanic, Luciferian, and Baphometic nature of Christ, and of the early Christian church, is a notion supported in Nicholas de Vere's *The Dragon Legacy*. For instance, he writes that, "In *Revelation 22:6*, Jesus… proclaims himself the bright and Morning Star… a priest-king of Lucifer…" De Vere even tells us Christ's teachings inspired the witches of medieval Europe:

"Witchcraft in Europe and Britain was run by the Templars and Cathars, and provided the groundswell of support at the grassroots level for the Fairy… Grail… Dragon families and the doctrines which made them distinct. Witchcraft is original Christianity, practicing Christian Gnostic Dualism and providing, in their tens of thousands, an army of support for the scions of Christ…"

According to De Vere, real witchcraft is "Baphometic." De Vere claims that modern Wicca, which he considers illegitimate, has its origins in the "Baphometic Orders" of Britain, to which, he claimed, British nobles of the Dragon blood belonged to up until the twentieth century, and perhaps still do. They "trace their lineage back through the Templars to Jesus' original teachings and the culture of the Druids." In these witchcraft cults, "The central figure was the Baphomet, and the highest sacrament of the 'Sabbat' was the Black Mass." De Vere continues:

"… Royal Witchcraft, or Witchcraft proper, from the early Dark Ages onwards owes as much to its clearly Christian as it does to its direct Druidic, origins. Both, in their original form, and in the publicly disseminated opinion of the Catholic popes, were and are Satanic. Jesus' heredity, and the descent of the Druidic dynasties both derived from an identical Dragon nascence that the Roman Catholics decided was devilish, because the descent of both bloodlines was from the Sumerian Enki who was the Akkadian Samael; the Roman Lucifer and thus the Catholic Satan.

In Jesus' case the Roman church, as do all outsiders who know they are onto a good thing, sanitized his rituals and concealed his descent. All those who continued to follow Jesus' original teachings – like the witches – they burned as 'heretics'… To call a witch a heretic meant that the witch was a heterodox Christian… Witches were 'original Christians' whose knowledge of the true, Druidic nature of Jesus' liberating Christianity had to be quashed at any cost if the Church were to achieve the political and pecuniary supremacy they desired by replacing it with their own enslaving dogma."

In De Vere's worldview, the Black Mass is:

"…the original mass of Jesus which the Catholics later stole and sanitized for public consumption…. The Black Mass had its roots in the ancient alchemical lore of Solomon and was simply a memento of teachings long past and an aide memoire for future generations, a mnemonic which was intended to remind those to come from whence the power and the wisdom derives… The Sabbatical Goat of the Black Mass was Chem-Zoroaster [another name for Baphomet], one of the early ancestors of the Dragon families. His symbolic presence at the Mass reminds one that Royal Witchcraft was strictly a family affair.

Witches actually called their 'god' the Antecessor, meaning 'the Ancestor.'

This illustrated to later generations of readers that 'Satan', also called by the Witches 'Christ, son Dei', or Jesus Christ, Son of God', was in fact a flesh and blood being...

In the witches of the Royal covens honored Jesus as an ancestor-god, than they must have been Merovingian by descent and thus custodians of the Sang Royale."

On the subject of Baphomet specifically, De Vere writes that:

"Baphomet is a Nephilim... Baphomet is a type of Chem-Zoroaster who is the Quino-taur associated with Meroveus. Baphomet and the Mendes pentagram are genealogical badges."

The Merovingian Mythos

Like Baphomet, the Quinotaur represents the union of opposites. His name includes both the name of Cain ("Quin") and the name of Abel or Baal (the bull, "taurus", or "taur"), perhaps indicating a line of descent stemming from both figures. His aquatic qualities represent not only the sea associations of Satan and Cain, and the entire family of sea-gods and sea-kings from which the Merovingians ultimately descended, but also the fish associations of their more recent and illustrious ancestor, Jesus. Thus the Merovingian blood was connected not only to a figure representing archetypal evil (Satan), but also a figure representing archetypal good (Jesus). This is reflected in the dualistic symbol of the Cross of Lorraine, used by Merovingian descendants of the royal house of Lorraine, and by the Knights Templar. As discussed previously, it is a symbol that can be found in ancient Sumeria symbolizing the word "Kad" or "Gad", meaning "Lord of the Earth." As a famous poem by French poet Charles Peguy declares:

"The arms of Jesus are the Cross of Lorraine,
Both the blood in the artery and the blood in the vein,
Both the source of grace and the clear fountaine;

The arms of Satan are the Cross of Lorraine,
And the same artery and the same vein,
And the same blood and the troubled fountaine."

The French word "Lorraine" comes from the German word 'Lothringen", which is itself a corruption of "Lohengrin", the name of the "Swan King" who makes an appearance in the Grail legends of France, England, and Germany. His identifying characteristics were that he traveled the world in a magic "swan boat", with a Cross of Lorraine emblazoned upon his shield. Wherever he would land, he would stay for as long as possible, ruling over the local inhabitants, bringing peace and prosperity to the kingdom. But all who knew him were forbidden to ask about his place of origin or family line of descent. When this happened, he would immediately depart in his Swan Boat, never to return again. Obviously, there was something in his lineage, something perhaps divine or Satanic, which he was forbidden to discuss with those outside of the family.

Some similar mythical elements appear in the story of Lohengrin's descendant, Melusine. This woman was purportedly the daughter of Godfroi de Bouillon, who listed Lohengrin in his genealogy, and who was the man responsible for making the Cross of Lorraine an official insignia for the Knights Templar, which he was one of the founders of. Godfroi de Bouillon was also the "Defender of the Holy Sepulcher" of Jerusalem, and was succeeded by his brother Baldwin, who took on the title "King of Jerusalem." This title was then passed onto Fulk the Black from the French Angevin dynasty.[9] (Merovingian descendants), who married Godfroi's daughter, Melusine.

As the story goes, Melusine insisted that Fulk should allow her to sleep alone one night a week, in which she was not to be disturbed. However, curiosity got the better of Fulk, and he burst in on her one of these nights, only to discover that her bottom half had transformed into the tail of a serpent. Upon realizing that she had been discovered, she slithered off, never to be seen again. But she remains in the genealogies of many prominent noble families in Europe, and her son Geoffrey d'Anjou became the first Plantagenet king of England. Geoffrey, and indeed all of the Plantagenet kings, were known for their hot temper, and thus St. Columba (who was instrumental in the creation of the Knights Templar) said of Geoffrey that "From the Devil he has come, and to the Devil he'll return[10]."

The Satanic imagery associated with the Angevins and Plantagenets is just a continuation of the Satanic imagery associated with the Merovingians, which, according to this theory, is a tradition that they inherited from their ancestor, Satan himself, through their descent from Jesus Christ, as well as other collateral lines of Satanic descent. Perhaps this explains why the capitol of the Merovingian empire was once called "Satanicum", and why, even though the town's name has now been changed to "Stenay", their coat of arms still bears this image of a horned devil. Perhaps this also explains the Satanic imagery found at Rennes-le-Chateau, including the statue of Asmodeus in the church. There are also nearby landmarks called "the Devil's Armchair" and "the Devil's Fingerprint", and hundreds of years worth of local legends pertaining to the Devil.

So in the course of my research, I have confirmed the true origin of the "divine" and "infernal" nature attributed to the Merovingian bloodline. This was why the Merovingians were considered kings by right of their blood, and not by coronation of the Pope. This is why they were thought to have magical powers. This is why they were said to have been spawned by a semi-divine aquatic creature called the "Quinotaur." This is why Charles Peguy wrote that they carried the blood of both Christ and Satan. This also explains why the Priory of Sion, which purports to be continuing the true and original traditions of Christ, focuses so heavily on things seemingly occult and Hermetic, as Berenger Sauniere and his associates did also. And this would certainly explain why, if Sauniere had stumbled upon this secret, it would have changed his understanding of Christ, Jehovah, and "God" forever.

It does not seem too far-fetched to believe that one of the secrets which Sauniere was initiated into when he joined Emile Hoffet, Abbe Boudet, and Emma Calve's occult group was about the true ancestry of Christ stemming from Cain and Satan. Perhaps, upon learning of the "true Christian", Satanic traditions, he decided to use his parish to set up a "true Christian" Satanic church, perhaps one practicing the old Black Mass of which Nicholas de Vere wrote. We know that Sauniere's parishioners were all royals and nobles, mostly from Merovingian-related bloodlines, and that the peasants in the area went to another church altogether. And if he were true to the traditions of the ancient world, he would have been charging his parishioners a tithe to participate in each mass, as well as any other priestly service he performed. This tithe would not be optional, as it is in Catholic Christian rites, and according to the traditions of the ancient world (including old Judaic traditions), the priest was to use these funds for his own livelihood and enrichment, as well as church business. There was no separation of the two in this more traditional approach. Given the stature of Sauniere's parishioners as noblemen, these tithes were no doubt of significant size. This explains his sudden wealth, and also explains why the church later suspended him as punishment for "selling indulgences." When Sauniere was banned from practicing in his church, he and his parishioners simply took their rituals to another building on the property.

Evidence that this was the source of his wealth can be found in certain letters he sent and received, quoted in *The Templar Legacy*, by Lynn Picknett and Clive Prince. These letters also indicate that these were not part of a normal tithe to the Catholic church. When the Bishop of Carcassonne demanded to know the source of Sauniere's income, he wrote in reply:

"I am not obliged... to divulge the names of my donors... To bring them into the open without permission would run the risk of bringing discord to certain families or households... the members of whom gave without their husbands', children's or heirs' knowledge."

And in a letter he received from a friend and fellow priest, it said:

"You have had the money. It is not for anybody to penetrate the secret that you keep. If someone has given you the money under natural secrecy, you are obliged to keep it, and nothing can release you from this secrecy..."

If Sauniere set up a Satanic church practicing the Black Mass, and believed that Jesus was a descendant and avatar of Satan, then it is no wonder why his deathbed confession warranted him refusal of Final Unction.

So now we know the significance of the Grail as the "Sangreal", or "royal blood" of Christ, the Merovingians, and their antediluvian, Satanic ancestors. But what of the notion that the "Grail" is in fact a stone – specifically a "stone of light" that fell to Earth from Lucifer's crown as he was tossed out of Heaven? And what of the notion that it was a sacred cup or vessel of some sort? The Grail cannot simply be a bloodline. It cannot even be reduced to a symbol of the secret doctrine of Satan, although it is that as well. It has to be associated with some physical object. And the particular significance of Rennes-le-Chateau has not been explained yet. This I will do, but first, we must take a look at the concept of the Grail as "the Hidden Stone."

Endnotes

[1] Author Julius Evola wrote that Seth's name could be interpreted to mean "ruin" or "upheaval", but also "foundation" or "pole", "having an essential relation with the regal function generally conceived as an emanation of the power of the center."

[2] According to Freemason and occult expert Albert Mackey, Cain and Seth are the sources of two separate systems of cabala – the Jewish science of numerology based on

the mystical Hebrew alphabet.

[3] "8" also looks like the DNA double-helix, and an infinity symbol.

[4] Called the "thirteenth apostle", some authors state that Constantine's royal lineage included the blood of Jesus himself.

[5] The same author states elsewhere that "Mithras was 'The Great King' highly revered by the nobility and monarchs, who looked upon him as their special protector. A great number of the nobility took theophorous (god-bearing) names compounded with Mithras."

[6] The highest degree of the Mithraic rites was dedicated to Saturn.

[7] Ahura Mazda, the good god, would be, in a Gnostic world view, equivalent to Satan or Lucifer, the light bringer. This deity's name is the source of the name "Ormuzd", or "Ormus", whose name combines words meaning both "light" and "serpent." "Ormus" is, of course, the nickname taken on by the Priory of Sion after the Cutting of the Elm.

[8] *Galatians 3:13* states: "Christ hath redeemed us from the curse of the law, being made a curse for us: for it is written, Cursed is every one that hangeth on a tree."

[9] In some versions of the Grail romance, Parcival specifically proclaims that he is of Angevin descent.

[10] I have already noted the similarity between an alternate spelling of Enoch's name "Anag", or "Ang", and "Angevin", which could then mean "Vine of Enoch."

Chapter Six: The Hidden Stone

"Jesus said, 'Show me the stone that the builders rejected: that is the keystone.'"
- The Gospel of Thomas

V.I.T.R.I.O.L.

We have talked previously about the symbol of the Grail as the "Lapsit Exillis": the "stone that fell from Heaven", knocked out Lucifer's crown during the battle with Jehovah. The stone seems to represent something that was *passed down* from the gods to Man, and preserved from the waters of the Flood. There is even a cathedral in Geneva, Switzerland that purports to house the plate and cup used by Jesus at the Last Supper, which was supposedly carved from the stone from Lucifer's crown. These items were discovered in a chamber underneath the Cathedral, hidden by a mosaic depicting the symbol of the Black Sun. The legend connected to these items, and the stone they came from, relate that that the stone bounced off of Cain's head as it fell to Earth, leaving a scar on his forehead in the shape of a red serpent: the Mark of Cain, supposedly. Other Jewish legends relate that the "mark" was really a horn, bringing to mind the horned crowns that were worn by the ancient god-kings. Thus we may surmise that the story of the stone fallen from Heaven represents the descent of kingship from Heaven to Earth, from god to man, from Satan to Cain, and from the antediluvian world to the post-diluvian world. This is what the Grail as stone represents.

Another permutation of this idea is the image of Lucifer as a star fallen from Heaven, the "Morning Star", or so he is called. Freemasons represent this in their symbol of the "Blazing Star" that shoots from Heaven. Even today, shooting stars are considered lucky, a fond remembrance of their association with Satan and Cain, the benefactors of mankind.

The story of the Emerald Tablet of Hermes appears to be yet another incarnation of the Grail as stone. Hermes, as we know, was the Greek trickster god credited with inventing writing, mathematics, and alchemy – the equivalent of the Egyptian Thoth. He is said to have inscribed the secrets of alchemy upon an Emerald Tablet, which was then passed down to select mortal initiates. Many authors have equated this story with an apocryphal tale about the biblical prophet Enoch, who is said to have copied down the esoteric secrets of the Watchers from the "Tablet of Heaven" onto a sacred stone tablet given to him by the Watchers. Therefore, just like the jewel from Lucifer's crown, Enoch's tablet was a "stone from Heaven." This makes perfect sense, seeing that Lucifer's stone is believed to have fallen from his crown during the war with Jehovah, which, according to my thesis, Enoch was a participant in and witness to. Enoch's tablet is said to have been carried on board the Ark during the Flood, and according to my theory, Enoch is the same as Noah. Therefore it was Enoch who created the "Tablet" out of the "Stone" that his father Cain inherited from his father, Satan. He then built the Ark to bring it safely through the Flood. *The Legends of the Jews* tells us that the Tablet was actually a "Holy Book" from Heaven, given to Adam by the angel Raziel. This was passed on generationally to Noah, who used the wisdom he acquired from it to build the Ark.

In the post-diluvian world, the wisdom inscribed on this tablet was, say the ancients, essential for the rebuilding of human civilization, and for the perpetuation of the ancient occult mysteries. One such "mystery" which Enoch's tablet undoubtedly contained the keys to is the science of alchemy. It is interesting to note that in *The Book of Enoch*, it says that the Watchers gave Enoch some sort of food or drink which caused him to be able to live forever[1], just like the alchemical "Elixir of Life", made from the Philosopher's Stone.

Amazingly, the alchemical Philosopher's Stone is also called the "Lapsit Exillis", as well as, sometimes, "the Hidden Stone." This last term refers to the notion that the Philosopher's Stone is hidden underground, literally in "the center of the Earth." This is the meaning behind the alchemical motto "V.I.T.R.I.O.L.", an acronym for Latin words that translate to: "Visit the Interior Parts of the Earth; by Rectification Thou Shalt Find the Hidden Stone." Rectification is the process of dissolving the "Prima Materia", supposedly the original matter from which all other forms were made, and extracting the Philosopher's Stone from it. The Stone represents the divine spark that brings life to material existence, and is thought to be "hidden" within matter (thus, metaphorically, "in the center of the Earth.") The Prima Materia is signified in alchemy either as a skull and crossbones (the "Death's head"), or as a "Black Sun", which after rectification becomes white (the same metaphor as turning lead into gold[2].)

This is very interesting, for it links up with the "Hollow Earth" theory that has been proposed by numerous people throughout the last few hundred years (and which is itself based on ancient legends.) Generally speaking, this is the belief that the Earth's crust is actually a great deal thinner than modern scientists claim, beyond which exists not a mantle or a core, but a vast hollow space within which civilizations unknown to history have built great cities, foremost of which is supposedly called "Agartha." These stories are based upon mystical Tibetan traditions which speak of such a subterranean city. And within the center of Agartha, at the very center of the Earth, supposedly resides the Black Sun, a ball of energy which allegedly radiates artificial light to illuminate the inner world. This light is called "the Green Ray", linking it symbolically with the Emerald Tablet.

An interesting quote from the magazine *Vaincre* (published by Pierre Plantard and his pre-Priory of Sion mystical group Alpha Galates), demonstrates that they also believed in the Green Ray, and of the significance of green in general. In *A Ray of Light*, by "Alpha Rene", it says:

> *"That we have received letters written in green ink is already in itself very significant, but that our copies of this periodical have been sent to us with a green crayon mark upon them serves to explain the interest that certain people have been taking in our activities. Since that is the way things are, let us shed a ray of light on this famous green mark: allow me to quote here two paragraphs from the volume* <u>La Grand Verite</u> *(<u>The Great Truth</u>) by Pierre de France:*
> *'The Green Dragon Cerberus is the Order of Lucifer created by the new alliance that the Dragon has forged with the* Reckless Princes *through the mediation of the Cerberuses... Such is the supreme apex of the Pyramid, the three sides of which (symbolizing the three heads or flames) - the Christic, the theosophical and the Masonic - are only so many mirrors that reflect, from three different angles, the same summit: the Ram[3], that is to say the head of the Green Dragon.*
> *The green line that acts as a link between the nations is therefore only the expression of the supreme apex... ."*

The inhabitants of Agartha are called by some authors "Children of the Black Sun", and are said to worship this luminary as their divine ancestor. The Black Sun is equated by many with Saturn. The inner hierarchy of the Third Reich believed in the Hollow Earth and worshipped the Black Sun. (In fact, the inner order of Himmler's S.S. was called "the Black Sun.") So too, perhaps, did the Merovingian kings, for at least one author, Nicholas Goodrick-Clarke, has documented Nazi claims that the Black Sun was a "Merovingian symbol." Perhaps the Merovingians, like the Agarthans, believed they were carrying the blood of the "Black Sun", Saturn or Satan.

In this way, the Lapsit Exillis can be seen as a representation of the divine seed that was passed down from the Watchers to their human descendants. The "descent" of the stone from Heaven to Earth can be likened to the "descent" of the Grail blood from the divine kings to the mortal kings. In many accounts the Grail stone, or Philosopher's Stone, it is described as being alive, and as having descendants. In Nicolas Flamel's *Original du Desire*, he writes: "There is an occult stone, concealed and buried in the depths of a fountain... This stone... is animated, having the virtue of procreating and engendering..." Likewise, Wolfram von Eschenbach's *Parzival* opens with the line, "This is the book of thy descent. This is the book of the Sangreal." In this story, the Grail stone is covered with writing describing the names of the members of the Grail family who have been called to serve the Grail. There is, in the same vein, a Masonic tradition regarding a perfect "cubic stone" (obviously analogous to the Grail) which issues forth blood. And in the New Testament, Christ is said to stand upon the "Rock of Zion", which is thought to represent his descent from King David.

In many cases the stone is credited with giving life to the inanimate, as in the case of the Philosopher's Stone. This "death and resurrection" symbolism appears to refer to the Grail blood being carried through the Deluge by Cain and Enoch. According to my theory, it was they who nursed civilization back to "life" after it had all but "died" during the Flood, and Cain took on this resurrection symbolism when he allowed his old image to die and be reborn as Seth. So that is why the "stone from Heaven" is thought to be able to raise the dead. As Ignatius Donnelly writes:

"We find that Ouranus, the first god of the people of Atlantis, devised Baetulia, contriving stones that moved as having life, which were supposed to fall from Heaven. These stones were probably magnetic loadstones; in other words, Ouranus, the first god of Atlantis, devised the Mariner's compass."

Furthermore, earlier in the same chapter Donnelley says that the Egyptians referred to the lodestone as "the bone of Hareori", and iron "the bone of Typhon." Hareori and Typhon were both descendants of Rhea, the goddess of the Earth. Donnelly continues:

"Do we find in this curious designation of iron and loadstone as 'bones of the descendants of the Earth' an explanation of that otherwise inexplicable Greek legend about Deucalion 'Throwing the bones of the Earth behind him, when instantly men rose from the ground, and the world was repeopled [after the Flood]?"

Perhaps we can now begin to understand the Masonic notion of the "stone from

Heaven", which in their rituals is said to have been lost in ancient times. Sometimes this is implied to have occurred during the Flood, while at other times it is indicated that it was lost upon the death of Hiram Abiff (whose name is a permutation of Hermes.) Thus they use a "substitute" stone in their rituals, made in the likeness of the original, but not "perfect", as the original stone is said to be[4]. Could it be that the stone represents Satan and the Titanic gods, who were cast from their thrones, but who passed their seed onto their mortal descendants, so that those descendants could act in their place – as substitutes?

In this context, the stone easily morphs into a phallic symbol, as in the story of Osiris. You may recall that after being murdered by his brother Set (a corrupted version of the Cain and Abel story), Osiris was chopped up and dumped in the Nile. Later, all of the parts were rediscovered by his sister-wife Isis, except for the penis, which was substituted. She then used his dead body to conceive the child Horus. Julius Evola, in *The Mystery of the Grail*, sees in this post-mortem coitus a hidden reference to the repopulation of the Earth after the Flood.

In Greek myth, prior to the fall of the Titans and the usurpation of kingship by Zeus and the Olympian gods, there was another revolution that preceded it. This was when Kronos (whom we know is Satan, or Enki) purportedly dethroned his own father, Ouranos (a.k.a Anu, Oannes, Uranus, etc.) During the battle between them, Ouranos was castrated. The penis was cast into the sea and, as the story goes, created a cloud of sea foam from which the goddess Aphrodite (the same as Isis or Venus) emerged.[5] Up until that point, Ouranos had been the king of Heaven, but as Edith Hamilton writes in *Mythology*, "From that time on, for untold ages, Cronus… was lord of the universe." The descent of the flood waters from Heaven to Earth is also representative of the descent of the divine seed. In *The Book of Enoch* we read of the Flood:

"In those days shall punishment go forth from the Lord of Spirits; and the receptacles of water which are above the heavens shall be opened, and the fountains likewise, which are under the heavens and under the earth. All the waters which are in the heavens and above them, shall be mixed together. The water which is above heaven shall be the male; And the water which is under the earth shall be female; and all shall be destroyed who dwell upon the earth, and who dwell under the extremities of heaven."

Clearly the Flood itself is being likened to this insemination, when the waters from above meet the waters below. The sky was literally falling. Heaven and Earth were becoming one. The divine wisdom (symbolized by the celestial waters) poured down onto Satan's human offspring, as his seed had poured into the human womb. Also, in *The Book of Enoch*, the Flood is sent as divine retribution for the sins of the Watchers, who bred with mortal women unlawfully. From the description of his birth in this text, where he is described as being "like the angels", it is clear that Noah (whom we know is Enoch) is one of the products of this unlawful breeding. In fact, in all of the flood myths throughout the world, the pilot of the "Ark" that saves humanity is a son of the gods (or daughter, in some cases). And in many of these instances, the god from which he descends is that culture's equivalent of either Satan or Cain, which is why H.P. Blavatsky described the biblical Noah as a "Saturn archetype", giving him the same associations as his father and grandfather. Because Saturn/Satan was the forefather of Cain and Enoch, who were responsible for preserving the royal seed through the

Flood, and because he was the true ancestor of the first human kings, Saturn was some-times called "the Forgotten Father." It is fitting, then, that in his book *Aion*, C.G. Jung associated Kronos, or Saturn with the Fisher King in the Grail stories. In some versions of the tale, the king's genital wound is especially sore when Saturn is high in the heav-ens. Like Kronos or Cain, the Fisher King represents the Forgotten Father, whom all the characters in the story are related to, but they are not aware of it.

We have examined the concept of the Grail as "that which descends." But as a cup or vessel, the Grail is also the container which receives and preserves that which descends. As the cup of Christ, the Grail preserved the blood of the Savior that dripped from his wounds. As the womb of Mary Magdalene, the Grail preserved the seed and bloodline of Christ . Like the Emerald Tablet, the Grail cup is sometimes said to bear ancient inscriptions, making it also the carrier of esoteric secrets, "passed down", just like the bloodline, from gods to men.

Author Howard Buechner believed that the Grail cup was analogous to the cup of Melchizedek, the priest-king of Salem, who used that cup to share bread and wine with Abraham in the Bible. Buechner said that this cup was "handed down by God", and inscribed with the hieroglyphic language of ancient Sumer. The message it bore said: "This is the cup of El, the One God whose name is Yahweh or I am that I am." This statement would seem to be verified by L.A. Waddell, who writes that the Holy Grail was originally a trophy stone-bowl that was engraved with "the earliest known specimen of Sumerian writing." He suggests that this bowl was the center of religious worship in Eden while it was being ruled over by Baal or Abel, but that Cain stole it from Eden at some point during the war with Abel. If this has any kernel of truth to it, then perhaps the bowl was in some way a symbol of kingship or sovereignty, which was being unlawfully wielded by Abel, and rightfully belonged to Cain.

The Grail is sometimes depicted as a stone within a cup, making it a hermaph-roditic symbol – both male and female, womb and seed. One can see this depicted on the walls of Chartres cathedral, in which a stone is depicted protruding from a chalice, and on the altar of the church at Rennes-le-Chateau, where the Sun (a Grail symbol) is shown descending into a chalice (with waves of water bubbling up underneath). This is fascinating, because the word "Grail" can be translated as either "cup" or "stone" in a very literal way. Nazi Grail researcher Otto Rahn believed that the word "Grail" came from "gorral", which he claimed was an ancient term. He said that "gorr" meant "stone" and "al" meant "a splinter or stylus with which to write." Together they meant "precious engraved stone." But having looked at the Sumerian syllables, I have found another definition as well. The word "gar" in Sumerian means "vessel" or "bowl." This is the basis for the Egyptian word "qar", meaning "drinking pot." The syllable "al" means "all" or "totality", and that of course is where we get our word "all." It was also the root for "Allah", or "El", meaning "Lord." So the term "Graal" in Sumeria would mean "Cup of All" or "Cup of El" – that is, "Vessel of God."

The Egyptian symbol for the word "qar" brings to mind some interesting con-notations. It is written as an inverted omega symbol. "Omega", of course, is the final letter of the Greek alphabet, and has been used in common parlance for centuries to signify "the end" of something, just as "alpha", the first Greek letter, signifies "the be-ginning." If an inverted omega symbol signifies a vessel full of water, then the omega symbol could be thought to represent the Flood – the vessel being overturned. Then it would truly signify "the end" – the disaster which ended civilization for a time. Since the letter "alpha", or "A", resembles a mountain peak, perhaps it can be thought to symbolize the Mount of Refuge that the Ark landed on during the Flood. This mountain would then symbolize the "alpha" – the point from which life, and civilization, sprang anew. Incidentally, these two symbols can also be seen to represent the Grail both as a stone (the "alpha" symbol, the mountain), and as a cup (the "omega" symbol, the vessel). The concept of the Grail as a stone within a cup has led author Graham Hancock to theorize that the Ark of the Covenant may in fact be the Grail, as it is a sacred vessel (a box) with magical powers which holds sacred stones – the Tablets of Testimony supposedly handed down by God to Moses. In occult lore, these tablets are equated with the Emerald Tablet of Hermes. There is a legend stating that Moses acquired the Emerald Tablet from the Priests of Egypt prior to the Exodus, and later passed it on to his sister Miriam. This brings to mind some interesting facts about the word "Ark", and the concepts with which it is associated.

Like "Grail", the word "ark" means "container and preserver." We see the word "ark" being used this way not only in reference to the Ark of the Covenant, but also the Ark of Noah, which purportedly preserved the seed of humanity, divine kingship, and civilization from the Flood (as well as the Emerald Tablet). The word "ark" seems to have been used by many cultures throughout history to refer to a divine seagoing vessel. Sometimes it also referred to heavenly luminaries, which ancient man equated with boats, for they saw the night sky as an extension of the ocean, and called it "the waters of Heaven." "Argha" was the celestial boat of the Hindus, while the heavenly Boat of Ra was called the "Bark." Hercules, who sailed the night in the "Cup of Helios" (the Sun-boat), was sometimes referred to as "Arkaleus." "Argo" was the name of another mythological ship in which the Greek gods sailed (most notably, Jason and the Argonauts), and which itself was said to be made from the "guiding timber" of the "ark" of Deucalion, the Greek Flood hero. And quite notably, in other instances, "arks" are referred to as containers of divine seed. In the Masonic ritual of the "Prince of the Tabernacle", a box called an "ark" is proceeded around the room which is said to contain "the organs of generation of Osiris." Likewise, in the Grecian "Mysteries of Samothrace", a similar myth was re-enacted. As Albert Pike described it, "The Diosairi, tutelary *Deities of Navigation*, with Venus, were invoked." [Emphasis added.] Pike also wrote that the ceremony involved the mimicked the death of someone "slain by his brothers, who fled into Etruria, carrying with him the chest or Ark that contained his genitals: and there the phallus and the sacred Ark were adored."

Et in Arcadia Ego

We are now led to yet another meaning of the word "ark": a tomb, specifically the tomb of a long-lost father god. In Hebrew, the word "ark" means "coffin", which is strange, considering that the Bible describes Jehovah as actually living inside the Ark of the Covenant. But in some Jewish legends, the Ark of Noah was said to contain the body of Adam, making it a floating tomb.

This story is related in the apocryphal Christian text, *The Book of the Cave of Treasures*. In this embellished retelling of the biblical narrative, "Paradise" or "Eden" appears to be, in general, a region of mountains said to be located "in the center of the earth", and more specifically, one mountain in particular. In fact, the "Garden of Eden" in which Adam and Eve live in this story appears to actually be a subterranean cavern inside of this mountain. The text speaks of Adam and Eve's "expulsion... from the regions of Paradise to the Earth that is outside it: ...and when Adam and Eve had gone forth from Paradise, the door of Paradise was shut."

But the place in which they are exiled to is just yet another cave within this same holy mountain, which is "in the center of the earth." The location was christened "the Cave of Machpelah", or "the Cave of Treasures." Adam and his son Seth build a temple there to worship God. They and their descendants worship there, and are buried there, for the next several generations. When the Flood occurs, Noah is instructed by God to put the body of Adam into the Ark (so that it doesn't wash away in the Flood). Afterwards, Noah instructs his son Shem:

"When I am dead, go into the Ark, wherein thou hast been saved, and bring out the body of our father Adam... and place it in the center of the earth... and let no man have knowledge of what thou doest... take heed that this story is never mentioned again in all your generations..."

Inside this same cave other biblical patriarchs were purportedly buried, up to and including Jacob. *The Book of the Cave of Treasures* says that the "secrets of the Church" were also buried therein. This may be the mythological equivalent of the Tablet of Enoch/Hermes, which supposedly now resides in a similar location.

The Emerald Tablet's current whereabouts are most often described as being hidden within Hermes' tomb. Hermes is said to never die, but to fall into periods of prolonged sleep, from which he is awakened at regular intervals by the periodic rediscovery of his tomb[6]. The same is said of the tomb of the mythical namesake of the Rosicrucian brotherhood, Christian Rosenkreutz. The details of the Rosenkreutz tomb can be found in the Adeptus Minor ritual of the Hermetic Order of the Golden Dawn. Here the tomb is described as "within the mountain of Albi-Genos" which is "in the center of the Earth." The tomb is "lit by an inner sun", just as the Black Sun lights the inner world in the Hollow Earth theory. The tomb is said to be symbolic of the tomb of Osiris, and indeed, the Egyptians described Osiris' tomb as being illuminated by a subterranean sun[7]. The walls of the Rosenkreutz tomb are covered with strange hieroglyphs, and it contains "mystery writings" detailing alchemical secrets (reminiscent, obviously, of the Tablet of Hermes). Within the tomb, Rosenkreutz' body lies undecayed, sleeping but not dead, and when his tomb was supposedly discovered in 1484, 120 years after his alleged death, it was not only Rosenkreutz, but the Hermetic secrets contained within that were resurrected. To quote Julius Evola in *The Mystery of the Grail*, "This is more or less the time in which the Rosicrucian movement begins to be known in history, as if it literally sprang from beneath the ground."

It should not be surprising that this notion finds an analogy in the Grail legend, where it is symbolized by the "Dolorous Stroke" that wounds the Fisher King in his genitals. At this point the king loses the ability to properly perform his regal function (which is symbolized by his loss of virility, i.e., ability to pass on his royal blood), and the entire kingdom falls into a deathless sleep which is known as "the Wasteland." This may connect with the archetype of the fall of the Garden of Eden, or the fall of Atlantis via the Flood. The king thereafter must continue to nurse his festering wound, which will not heal, and no matter how much he wants to, he can never die, until the chosen knight comes to liberate him by learning the secrets of the Grail and taking up the mantle of kingship himself. His kingdom exists in a similar state of perpetual malaise, until the coming of a chosen hero, who will liberate the dying king and resume the proper function of kingship, thus bringing stability and equilibrium to the land. Again, these are common themes in world mythology. Most notably similar to the story of the Fisher King is that of his Greek mythological counterpart, Kronos, who, writes Julius Evola:

"...after having been the Lord of this earth, the King of the Golden Age, was dethroned and castrated (that is, deprived of the power to beget, to give life to new stock). He still lived on, though asleep, in a region located in the Far North, closer to the Arctic Sea, which was also called the Cronic Sea."

It is also noteworthy that Kronos is sometimes called "the Hidden One", thus alluding perhaps to his seclusion inside of the Earth, in which he was purportedly imprisoned by Zeus[8].

Thus, the sleeping, half-dead gods who inhabit the subterranean tombs of Kronos, Hermes, Osiris, and even Christian Rosenkreutz could all metaphorically represent the same fallen kingdom, which, having lost the Grail and its mandate to rule, has occulted itself, gone underground, become invisible, or fallen asleep, until such time as the proper individual shall come along to liberate it. Then the sunken kingdom shall rise, the dreaming lord shall awake, the phoenix emerge from the ashes, and the proper universal balance be restored. In the meantime, the secret royal doctrine is kept alive by the initiates/descendants of that sleeping god (the same doctrine that is written upon the Grail in its form as the Emerald Tablet, or "Gorral").

The idea of the sacred tomb comes up again in regards to the concepts of "Arcadia" and "the underground stream", so central to the Grail saga. Nicolas Poussin, in his painting *The Shepherds of Arcadia*, depicted a group of shepherds pointing to a tomb that was inscribed with the phrase "Et in Arcadia Ego." This was believed by Henry Lincoln to depict a tomb that, until recently, still existed in the region of Rennes-le-Chateau. But the authors of *The Tomb of God* (Richard Andrews and Paul Schellenberger) think that the real tomb which Poussin was alluding to is not the one that Henry Lincoln found, but one that they say is buried between the twin peaks of nearby Mt. Cardou, which they believe to be the tomb of the one and only Jesus Christ. Their interpretation of the word "Arcadia" - specifically in the context of that phrase - is reached by breaking the word down phonetically, and then translating not just the letters, but the sounds from the Latin, thereby arriving at the result, "the tomb of God." They write:

"It is not too difficult to imagine how Arcadia (arcar-deear - the contemporary pronunciation, not the modern one) could be identified with the sound of Arca Dei (arcar-dayee), thus suggesting an anagram. Arca Dei would mean 'Ark of God'... This, combined with the quite excessive emphasis of the idea of 'tomb'... convinces us that we are to interpret 'ARCA' as 'tomb'; this would be another legitimate translation of the word."

Using similar methods, they translate the entire phrase, *"Et in Arcadia Ego"* into an anagram which phonetically means, in Latin, "I touch the tomb of God." By adding the Latin word "sum" at the end of "Et in Arcadia Ego", which they believe to be implied by the sentence, and creating another anagram from that, they further render it, "I touch the tomb of God, Jesus." This tomb, they believe, can be found at Rennes-le-Chateau.

I concur with their interpretation of the word "Arcadia" as "Ark of God." But is it really the tomb of Jesus that lies at the heart of Rennes-le-Chateau? Is this the secret which has been preserved by some of the world's most elite and powerful secret societies for millennia? The mystery of Rennes-le-Chateau, and for that matter, the roots of Southern France's esoteric tradition would appear in fact to be much older than 2000 years. References to Jesus and his presumed wife, Mary Magdalene, are almost always coupled with or superimposed over images of other, far more ancient figures.

Is there any evidence that "Et in Arcadia Ego" is a signpost pointing towards the tomb of a much older god? To find such evidence, it might be helpful to examine the word "Arcadia" in another light. We are familiar with the use of word plays in regards to the Grail mystery, often with multiple layers of meaning. Since most languages, including Latin and Greek, have their ultimate roots in a form of proto-Sumerian, many words from languages both ancient and modern still retail the intrinsic meaning of the Sumerian syllables from which they are derived. Given that the Priory of Sion and the Grail families have been, I believe, the preservers of ancient traditions going back to Sumeria and, even further, to Atlantis, it is not inconceivable that members of the Renaissance "underground stream" may have been aware of these intrinsic meanings. The word "Arcadia", then, can be thought of as containing the Sumerian syllables "Ar" and "Kad."

When viewed in this way, patterns begin to unfold. "Ar" is symbolized in Sumerian hieroglyphs by, of all things, a pentagram. From this word came the name of the Sumerian city-state, Ur. From "Ar" the words "Aryan" and "Iran" were derived. Now the "Ar" sign, sometimes just referred to as "the Plough Sign", actually has two very specific definitions. One explains the translation of "Plough", and it literally means "to cause dirt to go up", indicating digging in the earth. Of course, the plough was something that we are told was invented by Cain. Yet "Ar" has another meaning in Sumerian - one that is very pertinent to our examination, and that is "To shackle, to imprison."

In the stories of both Kronos and Satan, after they lost the heavenly battle, they were imprisoned in the underworld. So Kronos' tomb, in which he lies not dead but sleeping, is also a prison. Esoteric legends state that Kronos was shackled and bound to the underworld within a pentacle. It can hardly be a coincidence that the mountains of Rennes-le-Chateau, which so many people believe contain a sacred tomb, form the shape of a pentagram (as will soon be discussed), or that this shape also shows up in the geometry of *The Shepherds of Arcadia*.

With this in mind, it is worthwhile to examine the prefix "Arc" in Latin a bit more. In a Latin dictionary, the first word we encounter in the "Arc" family is "Arca", which Andrews & Schellenberger have translated as "tomb." It does indeed mean that, but it also means "a cell for close imprisonment." This is amazing: "Arca" means both "prison" *and* "tomb." Kronos' title of "the Hidden One" and his burial within this secret prison/tomb may relate to the Latin word "arceo", meaning "to protect, keep safe", or "to hinder, prevent." From this we get the word "arcane", which literally means "concealed." In *Holy Blood, Holy Grail*, one suggested interpretation of "Et in Arcadia Ego" was an anagram, "I Tego Arcana Dei", which means: "Begone, I conceal the secrets of God." Interestingly, one of the meanings of the Sumerian king title "Kad" (the root of the second syllable in "Arcadia") is "be strong, protect, save", remarkably similar to the definition of the Latin word "arceo."

Thus, the intrinsic Sumerian root meanings of the syllables in the word "Arcadia" seem to contain a message pertaining to the prison/tomb of Kronos. "Et in Arcadia Ego" could then be interpreted to mean: "And I am in the tomb (and prison) of a god." The use of this phrase in conjunction with Rennes-le-Chateau a la *The Shepherds of Arcadia* seems to be indicating that this tomb is somewhere within that region's pentagonal mountain structure.

In this context it is essential to note that according to a Jewish legend, Cain and his descendants were imprisoned inside of a subterranean realm called "the Arka", which, although entirely underground, still "receives some light from the Sun." The legend states that the Earth literally "opened up beneath Cain, and the four generations sprung from Cain", and swallowed them up. Louis Ginzberg writes in *The Legends of the Jews* that "The Arka was surrendered to the Cainites forever, as their perpetual domain."

The Venusberg and the Tomb of Hercules

In the South of France there are a number of mountains in which gods or semi-divine heroes are purportedly buried. During WWII, when France was occupied by the Nazis, a young German author, researcher and SS Lieutenant named Otto Rahn was sent by the Reich to Southern France to look for the Holy Grail, which many in the Nazi hierarchy were eager to possess. The Nazis, it will be recalled, also believed whole-heartedly in the theory of the Hollow Earth, and sent expeditions down to Antarctica looking for the entrance. Furthermore, the Nazis had great admiration for the heretical Cathars, especially their disciplined lifestyle, vegetarian diet, and sophisticated Gnostic theology. In fact, there were elements within the Nazi hierarchy who were hoping to resurrect the Cathar religion. So it was only natural that Otto Rahn would go looking for the Holy Grail at the place where the Cathars were said to have left it - Montsegur. He also knew that in the Grail romances of the Middle Ages, the Grail is said to reside in a castle at the top of "Montsalvat", which Rahn believed to be the same as Montsegur. One of the reasons for this was the similarity of the names. "Montsegur" means "mountain of security" and "Montsalvat" means "mount of salvation." So Rahn stayed in Southern France for a number of years, off and on between 1928 and 1931, exploring the caves of Montsegur and the tunnels of the surrounding Languedoc, even Rennes-le-Chateau. Interestingly, another group of people were also exploring Montsegur at this same time. This group was known as the "Polaires", a secret mystical society (influenced by Rosicrucian and Martinist teachings) that at one time included the author Rene Guenon[9]. And what were they looking for at Montsegur? Why, none other than the tomb of Christian Rosenkreutz, which according to a local newspaper, they suspected to be in the nearby ruined castle of Lordat.

More details on this can be found in Colonel Howard Buechner's *Emerald Cup - Ark of Gold: The Quest of S.S. Lt. Otto Rahn of the Third Reich*. According to Buechner, Otto Rahn did discover something in the caves around Montsegur, just as Parzival had discovered the Holy Grail in a cave near Montsalvat. Buechner says that Rahn found the landscape to parallel exactly that of Montsalvat in Wolfram von Eschenbach's *Parzival*, and Buechner writes: "The grotto and certain other rock formations in the story bear the same names as those in a massive cave near Montsegur." It was the clues in Eschenbach's book which, according to Buechner, led Rahn to make his first awesome discovery. Writes Buechner:

"He explored the grottoes of an area known as Sabarthez, notably the grottoes of Ornolac and the massive cavern of Lombrives. Here he found a huge chamber which was known to the local mountain people as the 'Cathedral' because it had served as a meeting place for the ancient Cathars. In the main hall was a great stalagmite known as the 'Tomb of Hercules.' In a third grotto, that of Fontenet, was a stalagmite which was white as snow. It was called the 'Altar'... Deep within the grottoes of the Sabarthez he found chambers in which the walls were covered with characteristic symbols of the Knights Templar, side by side with the well-known emblems of the Cathars... One very interesting image which had been carved into the stone wall of a grotto was clearly a drawing of a lance. This depiction immediately suggested the bleeding lance which appears over and over again in Arthurian legends, and which is, of course, the Holy Lance which pierced the side of Christ at the crucifixion."

Curiously, there is a line in *Le Serpent Rouge* that appears to be referencing the very same cave - albeit in a much more cryptic way - complete with the emblems depicted on the wall. It reads:

*"It is not by the magical strength of **HERCULES** that one deciphers these mysterious symbols engraved by observers of the past."*

The idea of the tomb of Hercules being located within Montsegur is interesting, for the tomb of Christian Rosenkreutz, said to be located "in the center of the Earth", is specified in the Golden Dawn ritual as being inside the "mountain of Albi-genos." This is amazing, considering that the Cathars were called "Albigensians." Clearly, the myths of the tombs of Hercules and Christian Rosenkreutz are connected in some way. Pyrrha's name is related to the root word for fire: "pyr." Fittingly, both Deucalion and Pyrrha are directly related to Prometheus, who first brought fire to Earth. Pyrrha is said to have been named so because of her fire-red hair. Because "pyr" means "fire", the word "pyramid" has been translated to mean "fire in the middle." There is a much older, Sumerian word which also means "fire within", and it was a title used by Cain (as well as his son Enoch). This title was "Ag", and as I discussed earlier, it became incorporated into the name "Azag" used by Cain, which is related to his other name, "Azazel."

The Lord of the Mountain

This association of Cain with fire, specifically with "fire within", has to do with the association of the Djinn (descendants of Azazel or Cain) with volcanoes, and with blacksmithing. The Djinn were said to have emerged from the volcanic mountains inside which they lived to teach metallurgy and other crafts to mankind. In fact, in Cappadocia (modern Turkey) there are a series of so-called "Fairy Towers", which are conical, volcanic rocks, inside which temples have been carved, that were believed to have housed the Djinn. These and other similar volcanic structures, which can be found throughout Turkey, Iran and Kurdistan, are still used by members of the Yezidi sect when performing their rituals to "Shaitan."

In this same location, in an ancient city called Derinkuyu, there is a vast network of tunnels connecting thirty-six "underground cities", as they are called, which are believed to have been built by and resided in by Djinn. These tunnels and "cities" span miles underground, and it is estimated that they could have housed up to 200,000 people. It is evident that someone did live in them at one point, but no one is sure who. Another permutation of the myth of Cain as a blacksmith god is the Roman figure of Vulcan, sometimes spelled "Vulcain", who lived inside of volcanic Mr. Ertha. Indeed, it is from his name that we get the word "volcano." Vulcan, like Cain, is said to have invented metalsmithing, and to have spawned a race of giants called Cylopeses whom he used to work on his metallurgy projects, and when building massive monuments. His consort was Venus.

The closest Greek equivalent of Vulcan is Hephaestus, possessing identical attributes. He is said to have fathered a race of "blacksmith gods" called the Kabiri, who are almost universally considered to be identical with the Djinn. You may recall that one of Hephaestus' sons was Erichthonius, the first king of Athens, and obviously the same figure as Enoch. It is fitting, then, that Enoch is associated with the science of alchemy. The root word "chem." comes from "kham", meaning "black", and originally referred to the forging of metals (among other things, perhaps). It is for this reason that magic and alchemy are called "the black arts."

The idea that Cain and his descendants might have actually lived inside of a mountain or mountains for a period of time, as they lived in the Arka in Jewish legend, may explain certain elements recurrent in world mythology. In addition to the Djinn and Kabiri, there are quite a number of gods, or races of gods, or fairies, or elves, etc, who have been said to live inside of mountains. Even Jehovah was depicted as actually living inside of Mt. Sinai when he and Moses visited together. Thus he was called "El Shaddai", the "Lord of the Mountain." Perhaps he literally did live inside the mountain. Perhaps he and the other gods *had* to do this in order to escape the climactic conditions on Earth that immediately followed the Deluge. It is possible that, when Enoch/Noah parked his Ark on top of Ararat, Parnassus, or whatever mountain he landed on, he was met by his father Cain, who had already been hard at work creating a subterranean complex within that mountain for him and his descendants to live in while they waited out the Flood.

I have discussed how it seems that the "gods" who inhabited the Earth before the Flood largely went "underground", figuratively, after the Flood, and were thereafter only seen by humans on special occasions, although they still continued to influence the world greatly. Perhaps they indeed went underground literally, because whatever Earth catastrophe caused the Flood changed the environment in such a way that the "gods" could no longer tolerate being on the surface for too great a time. However, their half-human descendants, such as the Cainites, would have been able to come out, once the flood waters had subsided and the Earth recovered enough, and then rebuild civilization on the surface. As they did so, Cain and Enoch instituted religions practices within their civilizations which honored their forefathers, who still lived within the mountains and "in the underworld", or "in the center of the Earth."

If civilization had actually been saved by Cain and his descendants living inside of a mountain both during and after the Flood, then they probably did have, within this mountain, a temple of some sort, just as Adam and Seth supposedly had inside the Cave of Treasures, according to *The Book of the Cave of Treasures*. After they emerged from the mountain to rebuild civilization, the mountain would have become a powerful symbol, and a center of worship. It would have been a symbol of death and rebirth, giving way to stories of a primordial womb or egg from which mankind emerged. (Such stories are replete throughout world mythology.) The Ark bears the same symbolism, and it is possible that the story of the "Ark" is less a remembrance of someone surviving a flood while on a boat than it is of someone surviving within the recesses of a mountain which is almost entirely submerged in water except for its peak, as Ararat supposedly was when Noah landed on it. After all, "Arka" is the name given to the subterranean world which Cain and his descendants lived in. Perhaps it was actually inside of a mountain.

Around the world, almost every culture has a myth about the sacred World-Mountain, where the peaks reach to the heavens. It is symbolically placed in the "center of the Earth", the world axis, marker of the celestial pole about which the world turns. This mountain is also often remembered as having been a refuge for both gods and men during the Deluge. According to many versions, the mountain was so high that the floodwaters could not submerge it, and those who occupied it (the gods) remained safe. It is possible that there is one true "Ararat", and all of these other myths are copied permutations of the original. It is also possible that, during the Flood, the same scenario occurred numerous times in various places, in which gods and/or people retreated within a mountain, and reemerged later when it was safe.

The first "world mountain" upon which all these archetypes were really based is the one which purportedly existed on Atlantis. This mountain was said to be "at the center of the Earth", and to provide the "world axis", just like those that followed. It is likely that this mountain provided some of the stories attributed to Mt. Olympus, which Greek legends say was tall enough to reach Heaven. Indeed, the whole idea that the "gods" came from "Heaven" may simply be a memory of them living at the peak of a very tall mountain. But after the Flood, it became this new mountain, the "Ararat" mountain, which was now at the "center of the Earth." It became the new "abode of the gods", and the new womb of civilization.

It would not be surprising, then, if Cain and his descendants were in fact buried within this mountain, or if they deposited the body of Cain's father there as well. But we know that this would have been Satan, not Adam. This, then, would have been the real "Cave of Treasures" in "the center of the Earth", upon the Mount of Refuge - the new world mountain. If Enoch's tablet were deposited there as well, that would complete the symbolism of the "Grail stone" being buried within the "Grail cup" – the "Gar-Al" or "vessel of the Lord." The mountain itself would then be the vessel – the Ark! On this note, I should point out that the Grail has been depicted as a stone within a mountain before. Legends surrounding Montsegur in Southern France state that the peak of the mountain opened up, and a dove from Heaven carried the Grail stone in its beak, dropping it within the heart of the mountain, which then closed itself up again[10].

House of God, Gateway to Heaven

When Cain and his descendants began rebuilding civilization, they created monuments that embodied the concept of the world-mountain: both the antediluvian and post-diluvian concepts of it. These monuments are the pyramids and ziggurats (stepped pyramids) of megalithic times – huge cyclopean structures, found on every continent, associated with different cultures and times, but all with very similar elements to them. Many of them are so huge, complex, and magnificent that nobody knows how they were built. Such can be said of the Great Pyramid in Egypt, and certain Aztec pyramids in Mexico, for example. And in every case the indigenous cultures were primitives who claimed that the "gods" came and built these structures in a long-lost era. As we know, the likely architects of the more early structures were probably Cain and Enoch. Others could have been made by those who followed them. They were probably built on the blueprint of a similar temple said to have towered over the heart of Atlantis.

Both the pre and post-diluvian conceptions of the primordial mountain included the idea that the peak of the mountain was a "gateway to the abode of the gods", either in "Heaven", or within the mountain, depending on how the culture telling the myth envisioned it. The same concepts were embodied by the ziggurats and pyramids which became the religious temples of the post-diluvian ancient world. The primordial mountain in Atlantis had been on an island, surrounded by water, and the "Ararat" mountain had been surrounded by water during the Flood. This is why ziggurats and pyramids were often built on an island, or surrounded by a moat, or connected to an elaborate system of fountains (as some in Egypt and Sumer were). They also often had a sacred fire burning at the temple's peak, symbolizing the volcanic nature of the sacred mountain it represented – the "fire within" the pyramid. In this way the temples embodied the alchemical concept of the union of fire and water.

This conceptual union is a symbol also central to the practice of "sex magic", or "sexual alchemy", an ancient art as old as religion itself, in which the participants ritually embody the archetypes of a god and a goddess, then unite sexually to symbolize the union of male and female energies. These rituals, not surprisingly, took place in the inner sanctum of the pyramid and ziggurat temples. It is quite likely that these rituals were partly ceremonies commemorating the hierogamy (divine intercourse) that spawned the royal race of Cain, and it is quite possible that Cain was the first high priest to officiate these rituals. It is also likely that the figure on whom Venus is based was the first "high priestess" or "temple prostitute", for Venus has been called in ancient literature "the mother of harlots", which is another symbolic connection between her and the figure of Mary Magdalene.

In Europe, there are myths that the goddess Venus lives inside of a magic mountain, the well-known "Venusberg" tale upon which Wagner's *Tannhauser* is based, and which is connected to the tales of Melusine. Here she lived with her attendant gnomes and fairies, who occupied the numerous caverns and underground rivers that honeycombed the inside of the mountain. In *Myths of the Middle Ages* by Sabine Baring-Gould, this mountain is described as having, "its own mirror-world within, where trees and vaults grow, rivers run, and stars shine out from the hidden vaults of the roof."

In the Venusberg tale, the preferred habit of the mountain's mistress is to seduce some hapless young man into her abode and hold him there under a spell of sexual magnetism, sometimes for years at a time, the immortal goddess wasting the poor man's life away in orgiastic debauchery. In these legends, she is said to still be buried there today, lying in her tomb, not surprisingly, "in a deathless sleep", from which she can only be raised by the embrace of a new young man. Thus arose the primordial tale of

"Sleeping Beauty", a myth referred to repeatedly in *Le Serpent Rouge*. An account of the discovery of the tomb of Lady Venus, and the undecayed body within, can be found in *The Chemical Wedding of Christian Rosenkreutz*, in which the tomb is found by Rosenkreutz himself.

The Venusberg tale may relate to a legend regarding the Pyrenees mountains. As it turns out, the Pyrenees were named after the goddess said to be buried within one of their mountains - "Pyrene", who, like the similarly-named Pyrrha, was the consort of another famous ark navigator - another god supposedly buried within a nearby mountain: Hercules. In fact, the figures of Pyrrha and Pyrene would appear to be the same, as would the figures of Hercules and Deucalion. This brings to mind the tantalizing notion that the words "Parnassus" and "Pyrenees" are in fact the same word expressed in two different languages. This would mean that the tale of Pyrrha and Deucalion landing their Ark on the Greek equivalent of Ararat actually took place somewhere near Rennes-le-Chateau! I will explore this idea in greater detail later on.

According to author Julius Evola, the sacred sex rite of hierogamy was once known as "pyr" – "magic fire." Evola claimed that this ritual was secretly referred to by alchemists with the Latin phrase: "Rex igne redit et coningo gaudet occulto" ("The king returns with fire and rejoices in his hidden bride[11].") Given the connection between ancient temples and sacred fires, it is no coincidence that the ancient word for fire, "pyr, or "pir" - is related in Sumerian to "par", "per", "bar" and "ber", all root syllables meaning "house" or "temple."

The first ziggurat temple built after the Flood, according to the Bible, was the Tower of Babel. This, as I have said, was a magnificent structure, and is believed by many to have been built by King Nimrod. However, the story of the "Tower of Babel" and much of what is written about "King Nimrod" is the result of Jehovahite and Baalite propaganda, pasted on top of the true story of Cain and one of his most magnificent architectural creations.

According to information provided by both Jewish and Babylonian lore, the Tower of Babel consisted of seven steps (seven being the number of godly perfection), and each step was painted with one of the seven colors of the rainbow, forming a "rainbow bridge" to Heaven, which was indeed what the temple represented. In fact, the Sumerian word for "ziggurat" is "duranki", which means "the binding of Heaven and Earth", and the word "Babylon" (where the Tower was located) means "Gateway of the Gods." Furthermore, Julius Evola claimed that in the Pyr ritual which was once performed in a temple's inner sanctum, the priestess was referred to as "Ianua Coeli" ("Gateway to Heaven.") This proves once again that the ritual which took place inside the temple represented the same concept as the temple itself. Traces of this function performed by the priest and priestess in ancient times can be found in the Latin word for "priest" ("pontifex"), which literally means "builder of bridges" - to Heaven, of course.

The Tower acted as a gateway to the gods, not only because its peak reached high into the sky, but because, like the original holy mountain (or mountains), which it commemorated, gods were believed to live inside of the Tower, or at least, to be able to access it from wherever they did live. If the gods did indeed live underground and inside of mountains after the Flood, then they may have been able to visit the Tower, perhaps through a network of tunnels underneath the structure. Many if not most ancient temples and ziggurats did have tunnel systems built underneath them, sometimes incredibly large and complex. There are tunnels spanning many miles, for instance, underneath the structures in Cuzco, Peru, connecting them all.

Imagine what it would be like to participate in a ritual inside such a structure, in which a "god" is summoned, and a literal, physical being climbs up from the depths of the Earth into your ritual chamber! That is exactly what was said to have occurred in the sex magic rituals inside these ancient temples, when human "priestesses" or "temple prostitutes", often as young as twelve, were sent into the temple to be impregnated by one of these gods. This took place at the Tower of Babel for sure. One ancient chronicler, quoted by *Horizon Magazine's Book of Lost Worlds*, wrote of "the temple at Babylon that:

"On the summit of the topmost tower stands a great temple with a fine large couch on it, richly covered, and a golden table beside it. The shrine contains no image, and no one spends the night there except (if we may believe the Chaldeans, who are the priests of Bel) one Assyrian woman, all alone, whoever it may be that the god has chosen. The Chaldeans also say (though I do not believe them) that the god enters the temple in person and takes his rest upon the bed."

This probably actually describes a later structure in Babylon, perhaps one built to imitate the original, although it could not have been as grand. Nonetheless, it demonstrates the concept that the ancients had of the hierogamy that went on inside the Tower. But there was more purpose to this structure than just the hosting of sex rituals.
Since according to the biblical narrative, the Tower of Babel was built relatively soon after the Flood, most of the people on Earth were essentially of one stock, and all of one culture. The Bible makes it sound as though the people who built the Tower were just arrogantly attempting to create a replica of the holy mountain on which the gods lived, as part of some narcissistic, self-serving effort to be more god-like. But subtle details in the relevant passage from *Genesis* make it clear what the original purpose was. *Genesis 11:4* states: "And they said, "Go to, let us build a city and a tower, whose top may reach unto heaven; and let us make a *name*, lest we be scattered abroad upon the face of the whole earth.""

At the time in which the Tower of Babel narrative took place, the event which was at the forefront of every man's mind was the Flood, which had completely destroyed civilization, and done so relatively recently. Civilization had only survived because of the mountain that the Tower was created in commemoration of. Logically, then, the Tower of Babel was built to withstand another Flood. Just as the Ark (of Noah/Enoch) had purportedly carried Enoch's tablet through the flood waters, and just as the "Ararat" mountain acted as the new "Ark" for the tablet while Cain and his descendants lived in it, so the Tower would act as a new house for the tablet.

In Plato's description of the holy temple on Atlantis, it states that the entrance to the temple was marked by two pillars: one made to be imperishable by fire, the other imperishable by water. Onto these pillars was written the most valuable knowledge they had attained, so that, no matter what kind of cataclysm occurred, their knowledge, and their "name" (their identity, their culture and traditions) would be preserved for future generations. The Tower of Babel appears to have served the same purpose: the temple itself was a monument containing and preserving this sacred knowledge, most specifically the details of this original language. And if Enoch's tablet was in fact a pillar (remember that Masonic ritual talks about "the pillars of Enoch and Seth"), then it is not hard to see how it could have been incorporated into the architecture of the Tower of Babel. It is said that the Great Pyramid at Giza was once covered with Egyptian hieroglyphs, and it may be that the Tower of Babel was also covered with the written characters of this original language. If so, it would be an appropriate echo of the concept of the Emerald Tablet of Hermes. In some depictions of the Emerald Tablet, it is shown as a mountain covered with hieroglyphic symbols, fire issuing from its top.

In the case of the Tower of Babel, the Bible says that Jehovah and his allies saw fit to prevent this establishment of a "name", supposedly fearing that if mortals could build a mountain "reaching Heaven", then "nothing [would] be restrained from them[12]." In fact, this was simply an act of aggression on Jehovah's part against Cain/Seth and Enoch, who had created a global empire after the Flood and were instituting a common language. Jehovah and his allies were afraid that Cain was creating a powerful coalition that threatened their own power base. Jewish legends tell us that the creators of the Tower were planning on "taking Heaven by storm" and attacking Jehovah in his very own abode.

The Tower symbolized the unity of the empire, and the achievements of Cain and Seth. It also symbolized their identity, their "name." Jehovah's goal had been all along to take over the empire of Cain as he had the empire of Cain's father, Satan. Once he had done so, he wanted to either obliterate or distort all memory of them and their accomplishments. So the tower was smashed by the might of Jehovah, the true identity of the Cainites was lost to history, and their unified language scrambled into the multitude that we know today. Thus does our English word "babble", for nonsense language derive from this story. The archetypal tale of the Tower of Babel, including the tower that reaches to Heaven and the bizarre, inexplicable connection with a universal language that got dispersed when the tower was destroyed, is common. It is confirmed in the records of other cultures, even as far away as Central America, indicating that the story is perhaps factually based.

However, the word translated as "name" in "let us make a name" was actually the Hebrew "shem", which other authors (Zecharia Sitchin and Laurence Gardner) have translated as "shining (or fiery) stone", specifically, the capstone to a ziggurat temple! Such a "shem" is depicted in *The Victory Stele of Naram-Sin* from Akkadia, c. 2280 BC, where it is shown covered in Sumerian hieroglyphs. Interestingly, "Shem" is also the name of one of Noah's sons in the Bible, and Shem's descendants are listed immediately after the end of the Tower of Babel narrative. It is Shem after which the "Semitic" race is named, further linking the word "shem", or "name" with the concept of a race – the race of the "fire stone", or the stone from Heaven. The destruction of the Tower and the disintegration of the language represent the loss of that race and their heritage via the Flood. Symbolic similarities can be found in the later biblical tale of the twelve tribes of Israel, ten of which were "dispersed" and lost to history, again as part of a divine punishment. This led to the God-imposed captivity of the Israelites in Babylon. According to *The Book of Jeremiah*, God's purpose for the punishment of the Babylonian captivity was to scatter the Israelites across the globe, to cause them to lose their identity, and especially, their *language*. It is the same story as the loss of the Stone from Heaven, or the Lost Word of Freemasonry. The Stone, the Tower, and the Word are all manifestations of the same symbol. In Freemasonry, when both the Stone the Word were lost, substitutes had to be created.

This symbolizes the way in which the stories and genealogies found in the Bible were largely concocted as substitutes for the true heritage of Cain and his descendants. Examples of this, many of them already discussed in this book, can be found throughout the Bible. The Tower of Babel story represents the same destruction of truth: the moment that a veil was rent over our perception of reality. It seems that this story is a shortened version of a longer battle between Cain and Jehovah (and Baal), in which Jehovah eventually got the upper hand. And although the Cainite bloodline continued having influence on various societies throughout history, they often had to stay quiet about what their heritage really was, and perpetuate their secrets in an underground fashion. All the while, Jehovah and those he controlled waged a never-ending campaign of genocide against Cainite blood, until he had all but exterminated them. Yet certain remained, and do to this very day.

The Language of Light

But what was the nature of this language that the entire world, unified under Cain, spoke and wrote in the years following the Deluge? And how could the secrets of the antediluvian world be inscribed upon a single tablet or pillar? Well, the unified language spoken by mankind was probably the "proto-Sumerian" language which linguists believe is at the root of all languages – the "Aryan" language of which L.A. Waddell wrote. I have mentioned that the word "Ari' (the root of "Aryan") is related to the word "ur", which means "original." But when referring to a particular people, it meant, specifically, "shining ones." This is because the "Aryan" race was begun by Cain and Enoch, whose skin "shone" with light because they carried the genetic traits of their divine ancestors, the gods. Thus the word "Aryan" came to be attached to the royal, divine bloodline of Cain, and the race of his descendants, who became, after the Flood, the overseers of human society. This is why "Aryan" is now synonymous with the word "noble." But its connection with the concept of shining and light is important, and here's why.

If the secrets of Enoch were inscribed on a single stone, pillar, or set of pillars, they were probably written in the language of the gods – the language that preceded the Aryan language commemorated at Babel. Now we know that these "gods" were associated with light – that they seemed to have an almost supernatural control over the force of light, the highest and fastest form of energy in the universe, of which, it has been said, all other forms of energy are but lower permutations. It was this ability to control light, and to convert energy from one form to another, which gave them their seemingly "supernatural" powers over their environment. This is how the creation of the alchemical "Philosopher's Stone" is described by the sages. It really involves taking substances and transmuting them by bringing them up into a higher energy state through the application of heat and distillation. In other words, turning it back to light, the original, and most pure, form of energy, and then transmuting them into another, lower energy state that is nonetheless different than the first.

This was the alchemy that the "gods", as well as Cain and Enoch, were adept at. Now interestingly, according to the alchemist Fulcanelli (and many others), learning to perform alchemy involves learning to speak the "alchemical language", which he calls "the language of the birds"[13], or "the green language." (Recall that Pierre Plantard made allusions to the green language within the pages of *Vaincre*.) But elsewhere, this language is called "the language of light."

It is easy to see how an extremely complex language could be made from different wavelengths of light, or even digital "on/off" interspersions of light and darkness. In fact, a "light language" is already an integral part of our modern computer and telecommunications technology. In an article on spacedaily.com called "World will See Computers in Whole New Light", dated January 22, 2002, the unnamed author writes that:

"Computers created within the next two decades could revolve around a technology in which laser beams converge inside crystals the size of sugar cubes, forming holographic images for processing huge amounts of information, says the author, Purdue University physics Professor David D. Nolte.

In his book, <u>Mind at Light Speed: A New Kind of Intelligence</u>, Nolte describes how optics-based computer technologies may evolve over three generations during the next century.

The first generation, which is well under way, has seen the Internet transformed by fiber optic cables, optical switches and other devices that are based on photonics, or using visible light signals to transmit data.

The second generation, perhaps by the year 2020, will revolve around new types of optical processors. These 'holographic computers' might use crystals that receive and manipulate data-laden images, processing information much faster than conventional computers.

Perhaps after 2050, a network connecting such computers might achieve intelligence, Nolte says.

'Imagine luminous machines of light made from threads of glass and brilliantly colored crystals that glow and shimmer, pulsating to the beat of intelligence', Nolte writes...

The third generation, possibly during the second half of the 21st century, could use 'quantum optical' technologies to create computer networks capable of solving problems that currently are 'uncomputable.'

Photonics is the optical equivalent of electronics: Instead of using electrons to transmit and process information, photonics uses photons, or tiny units of light...
The human eye is a good model for an optical machine, he says.

'Light is an intrinsically parallel data structure', Nolte says. 'Your eyes have a huge data-receiving capacity. Streaming into your eyes right now is about a gigabit, or a billion bits of information, per second.'"

We know that in Jewish legends these pre-diluvian gods were called "Watchers", from the Hebrew "ayin", meaning "to look", from which we get the English word "eye." It seems that this may point to these gods being able to use their eyes as their primary form of communication. This is why their eyes in particular were said to shine "like flaming fire." This is why both they and their half-human descendants could put a person under a spell, or communicate "telepathically" using their eyes to give and receive information in the form of light. As I have speculated, this is why the "All-Seeing Eye" became a symbol associated with divine government. Nicholas de Vere writes that the gods possessed a "hive mind" that they could all tune into if they wished, and thus could understand each other's thoughts. This came from their ability to "see with the same eye" – the All-Seeing Eye.

In the Great Seal of the United States, which was created by Freemasons, the All-Seeing Eye is shown replacing the missing capstone on the Great Pyramid of Egypt (which has been missing since ancient times, by the way, and nobody is sure what it actually was). R.T. Rundle Clark writes that:

> *"The Eye is the commonest symbol in Egyptian thought... Originally it had been sent out into the Primeval Waters by God on an errand to bring back Shu and Neftut [the Egyptian equivalent of Adam and Eve] to their father [for they had become lost and could not see in the mire]... When it returned, it found that it had been supplanted in the Great One's face by another – a surrogate eye. This is the primary cause for the wrath of the Eye and the great turning point in the development of the universe, for the Eye can never be fully or permanently appeased."*[14]

So the Eye represents the "stone that was rejected", and that was substituted. Later the Eye was said to have caused a Flood on Earth by its crying. The Eye morphed into the "burning eye of Horus", which was gouged out by Set, supposedly, and which was taken apart, but reassembled:

> *"Seth flung it away beyond the edge of the world, and Thoth, the moon's genius and guardian, went and found it lying in the outer darkness. Apparently he discovered it lying in pieces. He brought them back and assembled them again to form the full moon."*

He goes on to demonstrate how the Egyptian symbol for the Eye of Horus can be broken down into sixty-fourths, and intimates that it represents a mathematical puzzle of some sort. This same idea is apparently referred to in the Priory of Sion poem *Le Serpent Rouge*, which talks about a "stone" consisting of "64 pieces" which must be "reassembled." I discuss this at greater length in Appendix B of this book. It represents the idea of reacquire ancient knowledge by learning to speak the original language of the gods, and learning to *see* the way they were able to.

Undoubtedly, the gods and human god-kings were able to see and communicate using wavelengths of light that we do not have access to. It is worth noting that planets put out waves of energy, including light, on a constant basis, which can be "tuned into" with modern electronic devices. How much more so could the gods and the god-kings, who associated themselves with the stars and planets, understand the language which the heavenly bodies spoke? Enoch purportedly learned from the Watchers how to read the "tablet of Heaven", and how to interpret the stars and planets. Mediums often say that they can tune into and speak with the stars and planets, which they say are living beings with tremendous intelligence. Perhaps there is more to this concept than just superstition.

Of course, human beings are not capable of sensing or interpreting light on such a subtle level, which is why we use an oral and written language. On a quantum level, sound is just light on a lower frequency, or a lower state of existence. This illustrates a cabalistic concept of creation which holds that before the universe as we know it existed, there was only the "Ain Soph Aur": the "Limitless Light." Then God created the current universe by "speaking the Word." As the cabalistic text *Sepher Yetzirah*

states, "With 32 mystical paths of Wisdom he engraved Yah[15], and created his world."
The Book of Genesis starts out by saying that God's first act of creation was to speak the
words "Let there be light." The Gnostic *Gospel of John* tells us, "In the beginning was
the Word, and the Word was with God, and the Word was God... In him was the life;
and the life was the light of darkness; and the darkness comprehended it not." Gnostic
traditions elaborate further and state that this universe was formed by the speaking of
"the Word", or "Logos." But it was "Wisdom", or "Light" (Lucifer) that gave birth to
"the Word."

In an analogous way, the pure language of light used by the gods devolved
after the Flood into an oral language used by humans. H.P. Blavatsky wrote that "the
Adami" were not really the first human race, but the first race of *speaking* men, as their
predecessors had communicated using pure thought. The Sumerian version of the Flood
tale says that Enlil (Jehovah) brought about the Deluge to wipe out "the Adami" because their speech made too much noise and disturbed him. In reality, the "human language" probably consisted of non-distinct grunting, much like primates in the wild, until
Enoch invented the oral and written Aryan language, and taught the most evolved speci-
mens of humanity how to use it.

The Tower of Babel, then, would have been a monument to this new language.
And the tablet of Enoch was perhaps inside of this monument at one time, either as its
keystone, or its capstone, or a pillar, or set of pillars, within it. Perhaps something about
the Tower itself contained the key to understanding the language of light – perhaps
something about its *geometry*. We know that the Knights Templar, the Freemasons, the
Pythagorean philosophers, the Egyptian priesthood, and the Jewish cabalists have all
been preoccupied with the science of communicating cosmic secrets through "sacred
geometry", and particularly three-dimensional geometry through architecture. This
formed an integral part of the Hermetic science taught by Enoch/Hermes.

Geometry really involves the use of different "angles of light." So we are to
understand, I think, that the Enochian/Hermetic tablet was probably a crystal in which
the "secrets" were encoded using light. This links it to the Grail stone as well, a so-
called "stone of light" chipped from the crown of Lucifer, the light bringer. Perhaps the
Tower of Babel interacted with it somehow to translate its message into the Aryan language, so that it could be understood by all.

In order to explain how this might work, I would first need to explain how
things such as light, geometry, and both oral and written language are intrinsically connected. The thing that holds them together is their *mathematical* relationship to one
another, specifically a mathematical constant that they all embody. That is the Fibonacci sequence.

Also known as "the Phi ratio", the golden section is formed when a given
length is divided into two portions, so that the first portion's relationship to the second
mirrors the second portion's relationship to the whole. Each line of the pentagram is
defined by the Phi ratio, also known as the Fibonacci sequence, the basic growth pattern
of nature. Expressed in whole numbers the sequence begins with 0 and 1, mimicking
the creation of the universe, in which the whole of existence emerged as the undivided
monad out of the unmanifested void. Then, another 1 is added, making 2, the next stage
in the creation of the universe, in which the undivided monad split into the duality of
two opposing aspects (such as light and dark, male and female). From there, the sequence continues, adding the next number to the previous number in the sequence to

create the one following. 2+1 = 3, 3+2 = 5, 5+3 = 8, and 8+5 = 13. Thus the sequence goes: 0,1,1,2,3,5,8,13... This sequence could go on and on indefinitely. When the numbers are divided by one another to form ratios (1/1, 2/1, 3/2, 5/3, 8/5, 13/8), the results, graphed on an x/y axis, form an undulating wave that starts out large and flattens out at an exponential rate towards an asymptote (a place approached but never reached) of 1.6180339..., with an endless series of decimals at the end.

In what is known as a "golden rectangle", this ratio can be expressed by dividing the rectangle into one-third and two-thirds sections[16]. Then you construct a larger golden rectangle around that, with the first golden rectangle constituting the smaller, one-third section of the larger golden triangle. Keep doing this for several steps. The whole of each rectangle, when divided by the larger, two-thirds section, will always equal the same ratio as the large part divided by the small part. After you have constructed a series of golden rectangles within golden rectangles, draw a line curving from the inside bottom corner of the larger section of the first rectangle to the upper left-hand corner of that box, then continue that through the larger section of the second rectangle, then the third rectangle, and on and on. This curved line will quickly develop into what is known as the Fibonacci spiral.

As I have explained, the Fibonacci sequence of numbers represents the growth pattern of all living things in nature: the growth pattern of the embryo as it becomes a fetus, then a baby, then a child, then an adult, or of a seed that becomes a seedling, then a plant. The horns of a ram, the spiraling bracts of a pine cone, the whirlpools in the ocean and the storms in the sky also contain this pattern. The golden spiral, sequence and ratio can be found in the visual color spectrum, and in the thirteen-note musical scale. The vibration of each note is the sum of the vibrations of the two notes previous. The structure of a piano keyboard reflects this, with eight white keys, representing whole tones, and five black keys, representing sharps and flats, arranged in groups of threes and two, for a total of thirteen notes in a full octave. This contains the Fibonacci sequence of 2, 3, 5, 8, and 13. The most pleasing pieces of music are those which take full advantage of the Fibonacci relationship, striking a familiar cord with the Fibonacci spiral shape of our own ears, while music that sounds "off" does exactly the opposite. The syntax of words in poetry, in which some combinations of words are more pleasing than others, undoubtedly follows the same principles.

Indeed, the Fibonacci sequence may have been the basis for the original "Aryan" language. A California theoretical physicist named Stan Tenen discovered way back in the 1960s that the Fibonacci spiral is the apparent basis for the Hebrew alphabet, as well as the Greek, Arabic, and Sanskrit alphabets, making it, he theorized, the root of universal language. It all started when he discovered a pattern in the original Hebrew letters of the first sentence of *Genesis* - a pattern that appeared when he counted the letters in base three. He then placed these letters into geometric shapes based on that pattern. When put into a square shape, with like letters placed next to each other in concentric square rings, the result was what looked like a "bird's eye view" of a seven-stepped ziggurat like the Tower of Babel. When this was then placed upon a torus or "doughnut"-shaped surface, and the excess space stripped away, what Stan Tenen had was a three-dimensional representation of the Fibonacci spiral. This somewhat snakish, flame-like shape Tenen then placed inside of a crystal tetrahedron - a four-sided prism or pyramid. When light was shined through the object in a shadow-box, Tenen found that he could form every single letter of the Hebrew alphabet - in order - just by changing the position of the shape relative to the crystal. With a slightly different orientation, he was able to produce the letters of other alphabets as well. Appropriately, Tenen named the shape the "flame letter."

The name of Stan Tenen's research group, "the Meru Foundation", confirms the relationships between the concept of the world mountain (which Babel was a representation of), the alphabet, and the Golden Mean. "Meru" is the name of the world mountain in Eastern mythology, and it is depicted as forming a perfectly geometric stepped pyramid shape - as though it were artificially made. As Tenen points out in his videotaped lecture entitled *Geometric Metaphors of Life*, the word "Meru" is also used in Eastern India as a title for the number sequence known here as "Pascal's Triangle" - a whole number representation of the Fibonacci sequence. But most amazingly, Tenen also says that the Hebrew name for their sacred alphabet is none other than "Meruba."

Of course, this connects with the word "Merou", which purportedly was another name for Atlantis; "mer", a word meaning "sea" in many languages; and "Merovingian." It even connects with the name "Mari", a title that was applied to Isis by the Egyptians, and to both Jesus' wife and mother. The word "Magdalene", by the way, comes from the Hebrew "migdol", which means "tower." At Rennes-le-Chateau, there is a statue of the Magdalene with four towers on top of a crown upon her head – just as the goddess Cybele was depicted by the ancients[17]. "Cybele" is the same as "the Sibyl", a figure whose mythos reflects that of the Melusine and Venusberg stories. It is interesting to note that, in 1627, a Sicilian witch interrogated by the Inquisition confessed that she had seen "Sybil" emerge with her fairy entourage from "a cave in the Tower of Babylon." This connects Cybele, or Venus (the goddess who "lives within a mountain") to the Tower of Babel.

Stan Tenen also claims that the Great Pyramid at Giza was called "Mera" by the Egyptians. Furthermore, he purports that it was once covered with brilliantly-colored tiles of limestone, also hued in seven bands that matched the seven colors of the rainbow, arranged from top to bottom in order of their temperature: with yellow, orange and red at the top, being warmest, the most "fire-like", and green, blue, indigo and violet down at the bottom, being the coolest, the most "water-like." Thus, the pyramid would have been like a massive standing representation of the world mountain reaching up out of the flood waters with fire at its peak. If so, this would make it very similar to the Tower of Babel, for which, according to Jewish legend, each of the seven steps had a different color, arranged just like the rainbow. This again links the Tower of Babel with the idea of a "rainbow bridge to Heaven." And it is also easy to see how it could have been linked with the language of light, interacting with the stone of light that resided within its recesses.

This, then, is another permutation of the image of the Tablet of Hermes within the tomb of Hermes – within the world mountain at the center of the Earth – and lit by an inner sun. The stone is the "sun", the source of light – the "fire within." That is the nature of the Grail stone, the "hidden stone" of the alchemists. And the Tower of Babel containing it is analogous to the holy mountain containing it, or the Ark containing it during the Flood, making them all symbols of the "Arca" – the "Grail cup" which contains the "Grail stone." In the case of the Tower of Babel, the stone was perceived to be integral to the structure itself, and when it was removed, the structure collapsed. So the destruction of the Tower of Babel symbolizes the same concept as the loss of the Grail stone, and the loss of the original language. It is the loss of the kingdom of Cain.

Jacob's Ladder

It seems that certain mythical elements of the Tower of Babel story reappear later on in *Genesis*, in the story of Jacob and his temple at Bethel. As the story goes, God sent Jacob to a place called "Luz" ("Light"), which was "in the land of Canaan." Apocryphal tradition says that this was the same spot where his ancestor Abraham had once built "an altar to the Lord", and where, according to certain Jewish traditions, he had attempted to sacrifice his son Isaac[18]. In *Genesis 22:14* it says that Abraham "called the name of that place Jehovah-jireh: as it is said to this day, "In the mount of the Lord it shall be seen", identifying this location with "the mountain of God."

The Legends of the Jews tells Jacob's story in greater detail.:

"Jacob took twelve stones from the altar on which his father Isaac had lain bound as sacrifice, and he said: 'It was the purpose of God to let twelve tribes arise, but they have not been begotten by Abraham or Isaac. If now these 12 stones unite into a single one, then I shall know for a certainty that I am destined to become father of the twelve tribes.' At this point a ... miracle came to pass; the twelve stones joined together and made one, which he put under his head, and at once it became soft and downy like a pillow... He dreamed a dream in which the course of world history was unfolded to him."

The content of Jacob's dream about "world history" involved a ladder that reached to Heaven, with "angels" (or "Watchers", in extra-biblical versions of the tale) ascending and descending upon it. At the end of the dream, the "ladder", which is also called a "temple", is destroyed, just like the Tower of Babel. As Louis Ginzberg explains:

"From this wondrous dream Jacob awoke with a start of fright, on account of the vision he had had of the destruction of the Temple. He cried out, 'How dreadful is this place! This is none other but the house of God, wherein is the gate of Heaven through which prayer ascends to him."

A similar story is told in *Genesis 28:17*. These words from Jacob are the same words written above the front door of the church at Rennes-le-Chateau: "This place is terrible! This is none but the House of God, and this is the gate of Heaven."

After he awoke, Jacob then took the stone which he had used for a pillow and "set it up as a pillar", consecrating it with oil that magically poured from Heaven. We read in *The Legends of the Jews* that after he had set up and anointed the pillar, "God sank this anointed stone into the abyss, to serve as the center of the earth, the same stone, the Eben Shetiyah, that forms the center of the sanctuary, whereof the Ineffable Name is graven..."

However, there is a great deal more evidence to link the story of Bethel with the Tower of Babel. First of all, consider the "ladder to Heaven" which he witnessed. As Freemasonic expert and author Albert Pike wrote in *Morals and Dogma*, "The word translated 'ladder' is 'salem', from 'salal', raised, elevated, reared up, piled into a heap... a pyramid with seven stages." Other biblical scholars share in this consensus: the "ladder to Heaven" which Jacob saw in his dream was a seven-staged ziggurat reaching to Heaven, just like the Tower of Babel. Even the word "Bethel" is phonetically similar to "Babel." Yet there's more. The word "Beth-El", or "Beith-El", has been translated from the Hebrew as meaning "House of God", and also "Gateway to Heaven" - exactly what the word "Babel" is also said to mean.

Bethel, then, seems to represent much the same thing as the Tower of Babel – a representation of the world mountain, inside of which is a cavity containing the stone from Heaven, the Grail, located in the center of the Earth. And like the Tower, Bethel was thought to be a ladder upon which gods or angels could ascend and descend. Thus, like the world mountain and the Tower of Babel, Bethel's peak (if made in the likeness of the ladder in Jacob's dream) would have "touched Heaven." Perhaps this myth is the source of Judaism's most preeminent symbol, the six-pointed Seal of Solomon. The upward-pointing triangle could represent the mountain or tower, and the downward-pointing triangle could represent the cavern leading to the center of the Earth, and the stone. There is even a common alchemical emblem that seems to confirm this association: a six-pointed star with an "inner sun" drawn at the center of it.

It seems pretty clear then that the ladder to Heaven which Jacob dreamed of was the Tower of Babel. "Bethel", then, perhaps, was the original name of the Tower, before the name was changed in the scrambling of the languages. According to author Rene Guenon in his book *The Lord of the World*, "Bethel" is also related to "betyle", which he said means, "a stone believed to be the dwelling-place of the deity... Thus this stone must be the true 'divine habitation', the seat of the Shekinah." This concept is further elaborated on in his colleague Julius Evola's *The Mystery of the Grail*, where he writes: "lapis betillis, or betillus... may be a reference to baitulos, the stone fallen from the sky according to Greek mythology." Jacob built a temple upon his stone, and if he believed that the spirit of God actually lived inside that stone, then his temple would quite literally be a "House of God."

Indeed, there is a Judaic tradition stating that Jacob's pillow stone is none other than the "Rock of Sion" that served as the holy cornerstone for Solomon's Temple. The word "Sion" has been translated as "capitol", or "a sign or landmark[19]", and now is a generalized term for Jerusalem, the Temple Mount, and god himself. But originally it referred to the stone, in which God was believed to live[20]. One author specifically identified it as a "touchstone" which "tests the genuineness and purity of precious metals", a definition which makes Sion sound like the alchemical Philosopher's Stone. There can be no doubt that "Sion" is the stone from Heaven, the Grail stone, and that this is what the Priory of Sion named itself after. This is also the stone which Masons allude to in their rituals, "the hidden stone", the "Lost Stone", or the "stone that was rejected." Jesus identified himself with this "rejected" stone in the Gospels.

Furthermore, there is a cabalistic tradition that the place where Jacob built Bethel, and where Abraham built his altar, is the exact same spot of land where the Temple of Solomon – another "House of God", in which Jehovah Himself was believed to have lived - was later built. In fact, these apocryphal traditions purport that virtually everything of importance in the Old Testament took place in this very spot. As Louis Ginzberg relates:

"The place on which Abraham had erected the altar was the same whereon Adam had

brought the first sacrifice, and Cain and Abel had offered their gifts to God – the same whereon Noah raised an altar to God after he left the ark; and Abraham, who knew that it was the place appointed for the temple, called it Yireh, for it would be the abiding-place of the fear and service of God. But as Shem had given it the name of Shalem, Place of Peace, and God would not give offence to either Abraham or Shem, He united the two names, and called the city by the name Jerusalem."

So not only was Jerusalem identified with the "center-point of the Earth", and said to be the land upon which all of these blessed events took place; it is actually *named* after a seven-stepped ziggurat – a "salem", such as the Tower of Babel, or Jacob's "ladder" to Heaven/Temple of Bethel. These were all erected as monuments to the stone from Heaven, which is apparently the same as the rock of Sion and the "Lost Stone" of the Freemasons[21]. Perhaps it would be worth looking into the lore surrounding Solomon's Temple.

The Stone, the Ark, and the Temple

Despite the very specific dimensions detailed in the Bible regarding how many cubits high and wide it was, we really do not know what the Temple of Solomon looked like - only that it was built according to the specifications of Jehovah himself. However, most experts agree that it was built on the foundation of a much older, megalithic-style temple, obviously to another god. Although we do not know for certain that this previous temple took the form of a ziggurat, it would certainly seem to be implied by the name "Jerusalem", containing that word "salem" which indicates "a seven-stepped pyramid." Jerusalem was believed to be quite literally the center of the Earth, and throughout the middle ages was depicted on maps as being in the exact mathematical center, with all of the other land masses clustered around it evenly. And just as the Lord was believed to literally be living inside the cornerstone at Bethel, God was believed also to literally reside within the Ark of the Covenant, the Jews' most famous treasure, for which the Temple was supposedly built in the first place. The Temple was built with three concentric chambers, and the Ark was placed in the exact center of the Temple's inner chamber, the "Holy of Holies", right where the "Kaaba stone", supposedly the very Stone from Heaven of both Judaic and Islamic legend, is now placed inside the Dome of the Rock. Interestingly, it is upon this rock that the prophet Mohammed supposedly stood when the archangel Gabriel brought him to Heaven on a "ladder of light."

The story of the loss of the Ark of the Covenant, and later of the Temple of Solomon being sacked is, it would seem, yet another manifestation of the archetype of "the Lost Stone", just like the destruction of the Tower of Babel. The rebuilding of the Temple of Solomon later on in the Bible represents the "substitute" concept. The ruined Temple of Solomon is, like the Lost Word, a powerful symbol in Freemasonry.

Jewish legends tell us that King Solomon conscripted the demon Asmodeus, and his entire host of fallen angels, to help him build the Temple of Solomon. Asmodeus is a permutation of Cain/Seth, as well as Satan, and it is interesting that he is here depicted as being the Master Mason behind the creation of this holy shrine. Such mythical elements link it further to the idea of the Tower of Babel/Bethel. The Tower had housed the tablet of Enoch, and the world mountain which preceded it had contained the "Arka" in which the tablet had been kept. The Temple of Solomon was created to house something eerily similar: an Ark (the Ark of the Covenant), which itself contained two tablets, supposedly inscribed by Jehovah himself.

According to the story, Jehovah inscribed "the law" (purportedly the Ten Commandments) with "his own hand", while Moses was meeting with him inside of Mount Sinai. During their meetings, the entire mountain was covered with a cloud described as "the glory of the Lord", and nobody but Moses was allowed into the mountain, for it was said that they would die if they approached it. "And the sight of the glory of the LORD was like devouring fire on the top of the mount in the eyes of the children of Israel", the text of *Exodus* states. Interestingly, Moses was not allowed to see Jehovah's face, for he would die if he saw it, although he was allowed to look at the Lord's "back parts." And when Moses descended from the mountain, his face was glowing. All of this serves to indicate that Jehovah was still a light being, and still using an ancient alchemical process to inscribe a message onto the stone using the language of light.

However, when Moses came to present his two divine tablets to his people, he found them in the middle of a Baal-worship ritual, something which Jehovah had forbidden. (It was actually one of the laws written on the tablet!) Upon seeing this, Moses purportedly became so angry that he "sprouted horns" and threw down the tablets, breaking them. Later, Jehovah made him a new set of tablets which he was able to present to the people.

The whole story seems allegorical of the loss of the original tablet of Hermes/Enoch, which, coincidentally, was said to also contain a set of ten laws, these ones pertaining to alchemy. The breaking of the tablets represents the destruction of the Tower of Babel, and the true stone from Heaven becoming occulted or hidden. The new tablets forged by Jehovah represent the false history and religious beliefs promoted by Jehovah and his cultists – the "substitute stone."

At any rate, after the second set of tablets is given to Moses, Jehovah gives him specific instructions for how to create the Ark of the Covenant to put the tablets in. Moses was then told how to build a tabernacle for the elite Hebrew priesthood, in which the Ark could become an object of worship, for Jehovah himself was believed to reside inside that box. But more than that, the Ark, with its tablets inside, and placed in a precise position at the center of the tabernacle, which itself had very precise dimensions, was for the priesthood a way of actually communicating with their God. It worked in conjunction with two objects called the "Urim and Thummin", made out of a very specific array of precious stones, and a "Breastplate of Judgment" worn by the High Priest that was also arrayed with precious stones. These different colored stones would light up in various ways to communicate Jehovah's message to them. In other words, he was speaking to them via the language of light![22]

Jacob's Stone, Judah, and the British Connection

Crystals and other special stones have been used as oracular devices throughout human history. Part of this stems from the idea that a deity might be able to actually reside inside of the stone. Part of it stems from the idea that stones can be used by a deity to communicate, either visually, or even auditorially (for crystals are components in radio transmitters and receivers). From the Middle Ages unto present time, crystal balls have been used for "scrying", or having "spirit visions." Every Merovingian king is known to have used them. And Dr. John Dee, one of the forefathers of modern Western occultism, famously used a crystal ball to divine the "Enochian" or "angelic" alphabet and language, upon which he based his system of "Enochian magic[23]." Dee was instructed to lay out the alphabet, which consisted of strange angles, upon a "Great Table" which resembled a chessboard. This was John Dee's version of the "tablet of Enoch." Perhaps the angles of the letters in this alphabet look so strange because this was Dee's attempt to represent the three-dimensional angles of light that he saw in his scrying stone upon a two-dimensional surface.

This brings to mind a strange possibility that would otherwise seem unthinkable. The being which John Dee contacted dictated to him what was called an "angelic" language made of strange angles. It makes one think about a possible connection between the words "angel" and "angle." The word "angel" comes from a Hebrew word meaning "messenger" – as in, one who speaks the language of light, and can communicate it in verbal language. "Angel" may also be related to Enoch, a.k.a "Anag", or "Ang." The people known as the "Anglos", the English, may be Enoch's descendants. Thus the language of English, or "Angel-ish", would be directly related to the light language.

A similar opinion was put forth by Berenger Sauniere's friend from Rennes-le-Bains, Abbe Henri Boudet in *Le Vrai Langue Celtic* (*The True Celtic Language*), and seconded by modern-day author Jean-Luc Chaumeil in his book *Alphabet of the Sun*. Chaumeil, as you may recall, was at one time a spokesman for the Priory of Sion. His opinion seems to be backed up by L.A. Waddell, who in *The British Edda* wrote:

"I have shown... that the civilized ancient Britons, Anglo-Saxons, Normans and Scandinavians were 'Goths', and that the English language is directly derived from the Gothic... the ancient Swedish language still retains the title of 'sueo-Gothic', and the old name for Denmark is 'Goth-land', and its dialectic 'Jut-land.'"

Amazingly, another name that was once given to Denmark was "Anglin." The possible identity of the words "gad", "god", "got", "goat", "goth", or "kad", "khat", and "cat" with "jut" or "jud" beings to mind interesting correspondences with the word "Judah." The ancestors of the Anglo-Saxon kings supposedly included Biblical figures such as Judah, Jacob and Isaac, as well as Scandinavian gods like Odin, and the legendary kings of Troy. And you will recall that figures with names and life stories similar to those of Judah, Jacob and Isaac show up on the Chaldean kings' lists. Indeed, there are a lot of Hebrew-sounding words in Old English, on maps of old England, and in the genealogies of its rulers. Author Herbert W. Armstrong has even interpreted the word "Saxon" to mean "Isaac's sons", and "British" to come from the Hebrew "berith", meaning "of the covenant" – referring purportedly to the Israelite covenant with "God."

Jacob in particular is important to the Britons, because it is purportedly this pillow stone – the stone from Heaven which he slept upon, and later founded "Bethel" upon, that the British now use to coronate their kings and queens. They believe it was brought to Ireland some years ago by the prophet, Jeremiah. It eventually migrated to Scotland, where it was used in the coronation of their monarchs, before it was stolen by the English and taken to Westminster Abbey, where it purportedly rests to this very day, inserted in a cubbyhole beneath the British throne.[24]

However, any patriotic Scot will tell you that this stone, which literally looks like a block of masonry, is merely a substitute – a red herring purposely left for the English to take. The real stone (called the "Stone of Scone" or "Stone of Destiny") is actually much more magnificent, and was hidden away somewhere by its protectors. It will not come out of hiding, they say, until Scotland has her independence. Once again, we have the symbolism of the Grail stone being hidden away and substituted by a fake. The symbolism is fitting, for the figure of Jacob appears to be a bit of a fake himself. In another famous encounter in *Genesis* between Jacob and one of the Watchers, he got into a wrestling match with the angel for some reason, and actually managed to overcome him. On that day, he was given a new name: "Israel", meaning "he who has overcome." His previous name of "Jacob" meant in Hebrew "usurper." This alluded to the fact that he had usurped the birthright of his elder brother, Esau, who was starving at the time, by convincing him to sell his birthright for a bowl of porridge. This story mirrors the stories of Jehovah's usurpation of Satan, and Baal's usurpation of Cain. Interestingly, author E. Richmond Hodges writes of the figure of "Kronus or (Saturn), whom the Phoenicians call Israel ...."

It seems to me that this story represents the way that the Jehovahite, "Judaic" bloodline, and the false lineage of kings created by it, usurped and substituted itself for the original heritage and history of Satan, Cain and Enoch. It consists of muddled and corrupted accounts of several different events, all connected by the same mythic essence. There definitely seem to be some allusions to the ongoing battle between Jehovah and Satan, Baal and Cain. Recall that I have likened the Judaic and occult legends of the "fallen kings of Edom" with Baal and the fallen Adamite kings of Eden. The purported father of the Edomite kings is Jacob's brother, Esau, although the most well-known Edomite king was "Bela", Baal, or Abel. The figure of Esau is in every way a Baalite figure, the exact antithesis of Jacob, who in this instance is a Cainite figure. Louis Ginzberg writes in *The Legends of the Jews* that "it was the angel of Esau who had measured his strength with Jacobs's and had been overcome." And as it just so happens, during Jacob's vision of the ladder to Heaven, at the top of the ladder he saw, according to Ginzberg:

"...Edom mounted very high, saying 'I will ascend above the heights of the clouds, I will be like the Most High'; and Jacob heard a voice remonstrating, 'Yet thou shalt be brought down to Hell, to the uttermost parts of the pit.' God himself reproved Edom, saying 'Though thou mount on high as the eagle, and though thy nest be set among the stars, I will bring thee down from thence.'"

Thus, the Jewish scribes attempted to blur the story of the fall of Eden/Edom with the fall of Lucifer from Heaven, and the fall of the Tower of Babel/Bethel – typical of Jehovahite propaganda[25]. It is also typical of Jehovahite propaganda that the eldest son (Esau) is cheated out of his birthright, as occurred in the case of Jehovah and Satan, as well as Baal/Abel and Cain. An interesting detail is that, according to *The Legends of the Jews*, Jacob conned Esau out of another part of his birthright at a later date, in which he purchased Esau's portion of the Cave of Treasures with a large amount of gold. Immediately after the transaction was completed, "God" reimbursed Jacob for what he had paid for it.

The Satanic Secrets of Rennes-le-Chateau

There is another miracle which "God" supposedly performed for Jacob, according to Jewish legend, right before his vision of the ladder to Heaven. This detail is perhaps key to understanding how this story links up with our current inquiry regarding the Merovingians and Rennes-le-Chateau. For when Jacob came to Luz and found the stone upon which he was destined to fall asleep, "God" made the sun go down immediately, even though it was "high noon", so that Jacob could fall asleep and dream his vision. High noon, when the Sun is at its zenith, seems to be an important time of day, as it has come up more than once in my study of these subjects. Hiram Abiff, architect of Solomon's Temple according to Masonic legend, was said to have been murdered at high noon. Dagobert II was supposedly killed in the woods at high noon on December 23. And in the parchments purportedly found by Berenger Sauniere in his church at Rennes-le-Chateau, the second parchment ends with the words "I destroy this demon guardian at noon."

The "demon guardian" referred to has always been thought to be the statue of Asmodeus in the church. And Asmodeus, you recall, was the demon who is said by Jewish cabalists to have built Solomon's Temple (just as the Masons say Hiram did). By placing the demon directly inside of the front door of his church, it is as if Sauniere is likening his church to the Temple of Solomon. And indeed, other actions on Sauniere's part appear to make this link as well.

Shortly before his death, Sauniere commissioned a custom-made topographical relief map of Rennes-le-Chateau. This item was only discovered recently by author and Grail researcher Andre Douzet, who writes about it in his book *Sauniere's Model and the Secret of Rennes-le-Chateau*. The author discovered that Sauniere never even saw the map he had commissioned, because he died just before it was finished. Strange indeed. But even stranger are the custom alterations that Sauniere specified on the map. Instead of applying the traditional, known names to all of the landmarks on the map, he had them all changed to reflect the names of prominent landmarks in the Holy Land, such as Gethsemane, the Tomb of Christ, the Tomb of Joseph of Arimathea, and Golgotha. We know that the circumstances of Sauniere's death were suspicious. Perhaps he sensed his fate beforehand, or even planned it, and commissioned this map as a posthumous message to future researchers regarding the nature of the mystery of Rennes-le-Chateau.

The word "Golgotha" means "place of the skull", and usually refers to the place where Christ was crucified, which supposedly was littered with the remains of others who had been executed before him. But according to apocryphal tradition, the place was already so named because it was the place where Adam's body, or particularly his *head*, was placed "in the center of the Earth" after the Flood. The symbol of a skull has turned up repeatedly in this mystery. Mary Magdalene is often shown holding a skull, and is depicted with it twice within the church at Rennes-le-Chateau. On the altar, she is seen sitting with the skull inside of a *cave*. A skull (and a particularly large one) is shown in Guercino's original version of *Et in Arcadia Ego*. The skull in this painting appears to be trepanned, just like the skull of Dagobert II, which is on display in a French museum. Of course, the skull worshiped by the Templars comes to mind as well, revered as an idol of "Baphomet", which represents Cain's reincarnation as Seth. And there is an ominous-looking skull and crossbones over the entrance to the graveyard at Sauniere's church.

Also, on the gate to the graveyard, there is also a strangely altered Masonic symbol, a winged hourglass. Usually depicted with angelic wings, it is meant to represent the ever presence of death, and the fleeting nature of time in one's life. But here it is shown with bat-like, demonic-looking wings. The combination of the time imagery with the Satanic imagery seems to point to Kronos, "Father Time", who is also Satan. The fact that this symbol is shown on the entrance to a graveyard points to the idea of *Satan's grave*.

Sauniere invoked the imagery of the Tower of Babel as well. As I stated earlier in a footnote, he housed his library in a building called the "Tower of Magdala." Considering that Magdala comes from the Hebrew "migdol" which means "tower" as well, this is a bit like calling it "the Tower Tower", which is a bit odd, unless you consider that he may have been implying the idea of two towers: one the real article, and one a false historical substitute concocted as Jehovahite propaganda. Sauniere again connected Mary Magdalene with the idea of towers when he had a crown containing four of them placed above a statue of her in the courtyard of his church. He intended to create more towers on his property as well, for *Holy Blood, Holy Grail* says that "Shortly before his death he was allegedly planning to build a massive Babel-like tower lined with books, from which he intended to preach."

According to some researchers, Sauniere and his cult used the Tower of Magdala for sex magic rituals, just as the Tower of Babel had been used. In *The Templar Legacy*, by Lynn Picknett and Clive Prince, the authors state that:

"During one of our trips to the area in 1995 we took with us Lucien Morgan, a television presenter and Tantric authority, who was amazed to discover that the Tour Magdala and ramparts were built according to the ancient principles of a certain kind of sex rite. He believes that Sauniere and his secret circle practiced occult sexual rituals that were designed to facilitate clairvoyance, put them in contact with the gods..."

This is exactly what the Tower of Babel, the Temple of Bethel, and the Temple of Jerusalem were built to do.

There seem to be a number of clues linking Rennes-le-Chateau and the surrounding area to various mythical mountains, tombs, and temples said to be located "in the center of the Earth." The clues discussed in this chapter link it to Solomon's Temple, Jacob's ladder and Bethel temple, the Tower of Babel, the tomb of Christian Rosenkreutz (and thus the tombs of Hermes and Osiris), the Cave of Treasures (where all of the biblical patriarchs were buried), and "Golgotha", where Adam's skull was purportedly buried after the Flood. All of these places are said to be "in the center of the Earth." The entire mythos surrounding this area also seems to be saturated with imagery pointing towards Atlantis and Eden, which were, again, said to be in the center of the Earth. I suggest that this is not merely the result of confusion, but of change over time. I submit that this is the result of the migration of something sacred, symbolized by the "Grail stone" which "fell from Heaven."

As an object of value, and one that, apparently, bestowed power upon those who possessed it, the stone was coveted by all, and thus it had to be moved periodically over the millennia. Sometimes this was done for safety reasons, because it was in danger of being captured or destroyed. Sometimes it *was* captured, and hidden away by the enemy. Wherever the stone found its home, that place was called "the center of the Earth." It was not the location itself that was important, but what was located there.

According to Julius Evola, the "stone from Heaven" represents the seat of global sovereignty, the foundation stone of the empire of the "Lord of the Earth", Kronos, or Satan. And wherever it was located, that place became the capitol of the empire, the symbolic pole or axis of the Earth. Significantly, while visiting Rennes-le-Chateau several years ago, I was told by the town's mayor that "this place is the center of the Earth."

If the Grail stone *were* indeed hidden within a mountain at Rennes-le-Chateau, where would it be? In *The Book of the Cave of Treasures*, the mountain that the Ark of Noah lands upon, and within which the body of Adam is placed, is called "Kardo." Amazingly, this is the name of the tallest mountain in Rennes-le-Chateau – Cardou! This mountain has been the focal point of much Grail hunting, and has been suggested by the authors of *The Tomb of God* to be the final resting place of Christ. Certain documents published by the Priory of Sion, some written by Pierre Plantard himself, suggest that something called "the Roseline" runs through Mt. Cardou - something which they insinuate was once the "prime meridian line" of the ancient world.

In fact, this is what the word "Kardo" or "Cardou", apparently means. In Ignatius Donnelly's *The Antediluvian World*, we read:

"The Romans and the Persians called the line of the axis of the globe cardo, and it was to cardo the needle [of the compass] pointed. Now Cardo was the name of the mountain on which the human race took refuge from the Deluge... the primitive geographic point for the countries which were the cradle of the human race. From this comes our word 'cardinal', as in the cardinal points."

The idea of linking Rennes-le-Chateau with the Flood, and with the landing-place of the Ark, seems substantiated by the fact that, as I have discussed, the pilots of the Ark in Greek legend, Deucalion and Pyrrha (a.k.a. Hercules and Pyrene) are purportedly buried somewhere within the mountain range that runs through the area, and that the word "Pyrenees" is probably a corruption of "Parnassus", the mountain upon which Deucalion's ark landed[26]. Also, Rennes-le-Chateau used to be called "Rhedae", and was named after Rhea, who was the mother of both Deucalion and Pyrrha.

This idea receives further support from yet another Priory document, the previously-mentioned poem *Le Serpent Rouge*. The setting of the poem clearly takes place in Rennes-le-Chateau, and the main character is a mysterious "friend" whom the author describes as "...like the pilot of the imperishable Ark... ." As the poem continues, it makes two mysterious references to "the line of the Meridian" (the "Roseline"). There is also a repeated use of the phrase "deliver me from the mire, so that I do not sink", another seeming reference to the Flood. Then, towards the end, the narrator states that the sky "opens its floodgates", a clear allusion to the biblical Deluge. The poem seems to be saying implicitly that Noah landed near Rennes-le-Chateau. This is a document written by the Priory of Sion itself! It is worth noting here the fact that one of the townships near Rennes-le-Chateau, spelled "Arques", is actually pronounced just like "ark." Then there is that painting, *The Shepherds of Arcadia*, which depicts a mysterious tomb within the landscape of Rennes-le-Chateau. In it, the mountain of Cardou is featured prominently.

Does this imply that Cardou is the "Arca-Dia" – the Ark (vessel, prison, or tomb) of "God" (the lord Satan)? Notably the word "Cardou" can, like "Grail" ("Gar-Al"), be broken down into syllables that in certain languages mean "vessel" ("Car") and "god" ("dou", which sounds like "dieu", the French word for "god"). And if Cardou is the location of the sacred tomb supposedly lit by an "inner sun" (the Grail Stone), which Rosicrucians symbolized as a "rose", this may explain why the meridian which purportedly passes through it is called the "Roseline."

As I discussed earlier quite briefly, Cardou is but one of five mountains in Rennes-le-Chateau that form, as the research of *Holy Blood, Holy Grail* co-author Henry Lincoln has proven, a perfectly mathematical pentagram when their peaks are traced on a map. The odds against this occurring naturally are, as one would imagine, astronomically high. However, no one has yet been able to explain how this could have occurred, although, according to the myths of ancient man, the gods of old were quite capable of moving mountains using their light-based technology.

The pentagram has been a sacred symbol for ages, and was the central geometric figure of the Pythagorean mysteries. Its angles embody the Phi ratio and golden mean geometry, and as such this figure appears a great deal in nature, including the human body, which is why Priory of Sion Grand Master Leonardo da Vinci used it as a symbol of the divine proportion in man. The planet Venus, called "the Morning Star" and associated with Lucifer, actually forms a perfect pentagram from the perspective of the Earth as it cycles through its orbit, the only planet in our solar system to display such properties. Given its association with the Luciferian "Morning Star", and with the hidden mathematical mysteries of nature, we can understand how this symbol has become linked in the modern mind with Satanism.

But recall that the pentagram can be traced back to ancient Sumeria, where it was called the "Ar", "the Plough Sign", and was linked to "Aryan" race spawned by Cain and Satan. Furthermore, recall that the word "Ar" also has the secondary meaning of "to shackle or imprison", which the word "arca" in Latin came to mean as well. Then recall the legends of Satan being imprisoned underground by a pentagram, and the legend that Cain and his descendants were later jailed within an underground realm called "the Arka[27]." The word "ark" or "arca" also means "tomb." This prefix is further linked to words regarding secrecy, and digging or hiding things underground, as I have established earlier in this chapter. And Henry Lincoln has found that the tomb in the painting *The Shepherds of Arcadia* is set within an implied geometrical pentagram. Is the pentacle of mountains at Rennes-le-Chateau the one that "imprisoned" these figures, and entombed them, occulting their hidden wisdom, written on the stone from Heaven?

In regards to this possibility, I should note something about the phrase "This place is terrible", written above the door of the church at Rennes-le-Chateau, right next to an etching of a star shooting down from Heaven[28]. This is most definitely a quote from the story of Jacob's ladder, for above the doorway is also written "This is the house of God and the gateway to Heaven", which are the same words that follow "This place is terrible" in the Jacob story. However, there is another instance in which the phrase "This place is terrible" appears. In *The Book of Enoch*, Chapter 21, Enoch is taken by the Watchers to a place where there were:

"...stars of heaven bound in it together, like great mountains, and like a blazing fire. I

exclaimed, For what species of crime have they been bound, and why have they been removed to this place? Then Uriel... answered... These are those of the stars which have transgressed the commandment of the most high God; and are here bound, until the infinite number of the days of their crimes be completed. From there I afterwards passed on to another terrific place; Where I beheld the operation of a great fire blazing and glittering, in the midst of which there was a division. Columns of fire struggled together to the end of the abyss, and deep was their descent. But neither its measurement nor magnitude was I able to discover; neither could I perceive its origin. Then I exclaimed, How terrible is this place, and how difficult to explore!

Uriel, one of the holy angels who was with me, answered and said: Enoch, why are you alarmed and amazed at this terrific place, at the sight of this place of suffering? This, he said, is the prison of the angels; and here they are kept for ever."

So Enoch said "This place is terrible" when he saw "the prison of the angels." And what does one see as soon as one passes through the door of Sauniere's church, marked by the words "This place is terrible"? Why, an image of the fallen angel Asmodeus bound in chains.

In Andre Douzet's *Sauniere's Model and the Secret of Rennes-lee-Chateau*, the author discusses the purported last words of Berenger Sauniere: "John 23." He suggests several possible Bible references that this might correlate to. One of them was *The Revelation of St. John the Divine*, Chapter 20, verses 1-3, which reads:

"Then I saw an angel coming down from Heaven, having the key to the bottomless pit and a great chain in his hand. He laid hold of the dragon, that serpent of old, who is the Devil and Satan, and bound him for a thousand years; and he cast him into the bottomless pit, and shut him up, and set a seal on him, so that he should deceive the nations no more, till the thousand years were finished. But after these things he must be released for a little while."

Recall that in *The Legends of the Jews*, Louis Ginzberg described how Cain and his descendants purportedly wound up inside the "Arka", writing that "The earth opened her mouth an swallowed up the four generations sprung from Cain – Enoch, Irad, Mehujael, and Mathushael." Five generations. Five kings of the Cainites. Five mountains in the pentagram at Rennes-le-Chateau. Are these things all coincidences?

I submit that the five mountains of Rennes-le-Chateau contain the royal tombs of Cain and the four generations of kings that succeeded him. The tomb of Enoch also contains the tablet of Enoch, which was written on the stone from Heaven – the Holy Grail. It was believed that this stone somehow contained the living essence of Cain's father, Satan, and thus, the Arka was his tomb as well. It was also the "Arka-dia", the "Grail cup", the "Vessel of God" (the true God, Satan). Because of the legend that Satan and the Cainites were imprisoned in the center of the Earth by the other "God", Jehovah, the "Arka" became remembered as a prison as well.

The stone was believed to contain the wisdom of Enoch, and this is the source of the stories about the tombs of Hermes and Christian Rosenkreutz, both of which purportedly contained this treasure. The stone was associated this the alchemical "Philosopher's Stone", and thus the symbol of the "Black Sun", the "inner sun", or the "rose" came about - said to light the inner world of Agartha, the tomb of Osiris, and the tomb of Rosenkreutz.

Because this location became the repository of items and people associated with the Flood, the area itself became associated with the Flood, and with Mt. Ararat. It later became a royal capitol[29], and a sacred site, revered by the people who lived in that area, especially those who could trace their ancestry back to the divine kings buried within – the Grail bloodline of the Merovingians. That is how Rennes-le-Chateau became steeped in imagery of holy temples, such as the one in Bethel. And because it was the repository of the "foundation stone", it became associated with the polar axis, or the "center of the Earth." This is why the "Roseline" meridian was based upon it.

We know that the mountains of Rennes-le-Chateau contain vast networks of mines and other tunnels throughout their interiors, created over thousands of years, many of which have never even been explored in modern times. Many more have been added by treasure seekers looking for a secret passageway to hidden riches. *Holy Blood, Holy Grail* suggests that Berenger Sauniere may have found, beneath Rennes-le-Chateau:

"... an underground crypt... under a manmade pool ... In fact, a manmade pool does exist near Rennes-le-Chateau – near a site called, appropriately enough, Lavaldieu (the Valley or Vale of God). This pool might well have been constructed over an underground crypt – which, in turn, might easily lead via a subterranean passageway to any of the myriad caves honeycombing the surrounding mountains."

Digging of any kind has been forbidden in Rennes-le-Chateau for decades. It is my belief that if exploration were to continue, someone would eventually find the network of tunnels that leads to the tomb of the Cainites, and to the Grail stone. One is also likely to find an underground shrine or temple built into the mountain by those devoted to Cain and Satan. Furthermore, this network of tunnels probably links up to a larger network spanning the entire region of mountains, including Montsegur, in which one is likely to find other ancient treasures in the same vein.

I believe that many of the locals, including those of Merovingian blood, as well as the Knights Templar and the Priory of Sion, have been aware of the existence of this fantastic underground treasure the whole time. For all these years they have essentially constituted a loosely-linked cult dedicated to revering and protecting the sacred treasure. They are also dedicated to making it once again a foundation stone for an empire ruled by the Grail blood of Cain and Satan. No wonder, then, that they do not want anybody to know about it. No wonder also that groups like the CIA and the Vatican have wanted to control it, for it really could bestow omnipotent worldly power on the right person, if used in the right way.

I realize that most of what has been proposed in this book will seem fantastic to many of you, and of course, it is impossible to prove any of this at the present time. But I do believe that, regardless of the truth or falsehood of the theory itself, I have made a convincing case that this, or something like this, is what the Templars, the Priory of Sion, and the Merovingians have *believed* about Rennes-le-Chateau and the Grail. I have also proven that there is a consistent theme running through occult lore, through the Bible, and through world mythology. This theme revolves around a royal, divine bloodline that can only be described as Satanic, and an underground repository for a sacred "stone from Heaven" which somehow contains that bloodline's right of sovereignty. This repository is said to be a mountain located "in the center of the Earth." There is sufficient evidence that the south of France has been the repository at one time, and may continue to be.

Whether you believe it or not, this theory, or something very similar, is embraced by the Priory of Sion, an organization that has counted some very elite people amongst its membership, and is purportedly a hidden but significant force behind European politics. To corroborate their belief in these ideas, we turn to the writings of Pierre Plantard, and the publications of his Priory-linked fraternal order, Alpha Galates.

Endnotes

[1] The Sumerian Flood hero Upnapishtim, who was the pilot of the Ark in their version of the story, was also given the "Bread of Immortality" by the gods, further evidence of the identity of Noah and Enoch.

[2] In more than one tradition, the stone that fell from Heaven was originally a white stone, but became corrupted and turned black at the moment that Abel's blood hit the ground after being slain by Cain. Such a story surrounds the Muslim Kaaba stone, for instance.

[3] The ram is, again, a symbol of Baphomet, or Cain/Seth.

[4] The same is said about the "Lost Word of Freemasonry", the real Masonic password, for which a substitute is also used in their rituals.

[5] Some authors believe that this is a muddled remembrance of Zeus castrating Kronos.

[6] Ranked among the purported discoverers of the Hermetic tomb are both the alchemist Paracelsus and Alexander the Great.

[7] A fascinating Rosicrucian seal exists demonstrating this concept. It features a man within a rose, which is itself within a sun, all of which is further shown to be placed within the center of a pyramid structure.

[8] Author E. Richmond Hodges states that the names "Kronos" and "Saturn" both comes from root words meaning "to flee into hiding." The Egyptian god Osiris was also sometimes referred to as "the Hidden One."

[9] Guenon wrote a book called *The Lord of the World* about the legendary kingdom of Agartha at the center of the Earth.

[10] Otto Rahn believed that Montsegur had been the site of a battle between the armies of Lucifer and God over possession of the Grail. The armies of Lucifer supposedly wished to gain control of the Grail so that they could place it back in their leader's crown.

[11] Undoubtedly there is also a connection to the myth of the phoenix, which rises from the ashes of the sacred *pyre*.

[12] That there is more than one "god" involved in this story is made explicitly clear in that passage from *Genesis* which states: "…let *us* go down, and there confound their language…"

[13] The "bird" reference probably just indicates that this is a "higher language", made for a consciousness that soars above that of normal humans.

[14] In this story, the Eye was temporarily appeased by being allowed to transform itself into a crown for God. It took the form of a cobra, wrapped itself around his forehead, and protected him from enemies from that point forward. All Egyptian kings thus wore a crown in the shape of a cobra.

[15] Recall that "Yah" originated with Satan's Sumerian title of "Ia", also related to the word "eye."

[16] The "Golden mean proportion" in geometry has long been known by visual artists as that which is most aesthetically pleasing to the eye, and paintings, photographs, etc. are often purposely constructed with the most important visual element located at the 2/3 mark for this reason.

[17] He also housed his library in a building called the "Tower of Magdala", and *Holy Blood, Holy Grail* says that "Shortly before his death he was allegedly planning to build a massive Babel-like tower lined with books, from which he intended to preach."

[18] The same traditions also connect it to the spot where Noah built his altar after the Deluge.

[19] The word "Sion" is probably related to the word "sign", as well as the words "scion" (meaning "a royal heir"), "son" and "Sun", embodying the idea of the stone that represents the royal Grail bloodline of the "son of the Sun."

[20] In Chretien de Troyes version of the Grail romance, Perceval claims to have been born in Sinadon, which they connect with Valais, Switzerland, the capitol of which was once called "Sidonensis", and is now called "Sion."

[21] The prophet Jeremiah, when addressing the Babylonians, said "they shall not take of thee a stone for a corner, nor a stone for foundations", a clue hinting that the Tower of Babel story is illusory, a mask for the story of the *real* temple erected to the stone from Heaven.

[22] Joseph Smith, the founder of Mormonism, claimed to have discovered the Urim and

Thummin hidden underground in New York state. He purportedly used them to translate the golden plates of *The Book of Mormon*, which he also discovered, with the help of the angel Moroni.

[23] Incidentally, John Dee is known to have made the search for the Urim and Thummin a lifelong pursuit of his.

[24] In Ireland there is a myth regarding a mythical race of beings called the "Tuadhe Danaan" who came to Earth bearding a magical stone, "the stone of the legitimate kings." They interbred with humans to create the race of Irish kings, bestowing all manner of wisdom and science upon the people. This same mythos also involves a magic cauldron called the "Cup of Dagda" that resembles the Grail cup.

[25] Other angels Jacob saw on the ladder included "the two angels who had been sent to Sodom. For one hundred and thirty-eight years they had been banished from the celestial regions, because they had betrayed their secret mission to Lot."

[26] There is actually a section of Paris called "Montparnasse."

[27] Even in modern times, pentacles are used in ritual magic to "contain" ethereal entities while evoking them.

[28] This is a Luciferian image used by Freemasons, called "the Blazing Star."

[29] The idea that it was a capitol is strengthened by the fact that it is marked by a pentagram. The capitol of the United States, Washington D.C., has been laid out according to pentagonal geometry by the Freemasons who were put in charge of designing it. Recall that the word "Sion" means capitol also, and Rennes-le-Chateau has been identified with "Sion."

Chapter Seven: The Enigma Decoded

"Ask, and it shall be given you; seek, and ye shall find; knock, and it shall be opened unto you: For every one that asketh receiveth; and he that seeketh findeth; and to him that knocketh it shall be opened."
- Matthew 7:7 – 7:8

Unanswered Questions

When I began my investigation, I was dealing with a mystery that had been explored ad infinitum by hundreds of previous authors, and yet it seemed to me that few of the most fundamental questions had been satisfactorily answered. What secret did Berenger Sauniere stumble across at Rennes-le-Chateau that not only made him fabulously rich, but caused an untimely death, and caused him to be refused Final Unction at his death? What could possibly have captured the devotion of men like Godfroi de Bouillon, Nicolas Flamel, Rene d'Anjou, Botticelli, Leonardo da Vinci, Robert Fludd, Robert Boyle, Isaac Newton, Charles Nodier, Victor Hugo, Claude Debussy, and Jean Cocteau, holding these diverse figures in a common bond of brotherhood stretching over an entire millennium? Why were men like Cardinal Mazarin, Louis XIV, Philippe the Fair, and Pope John XXIII so obsessed with this secret? Why did the bloodlines stemming from the Merovingian kings appear to consider themselves sacred, with a divine mandate to rule, and why would others, apparently not themselves of the bloodline, share this conclusion? Why are there, and exactly how is it that there are, five mountains at Rennes-le-Chateau in the shape of a perfect pentagram? And what does the secret of Rennes-le-Chateau have to do with the traditions of Freemasonry, Rosicrucianism, or heretical sects of Christianity? Then add to these questions the numerous other riddles, coded messages, strange bits of imagery and metaphor associated with the Rennes-le-Chateau saga that had never been properly explained when I first began my research. Twenty years after the publication of *Holy Blood, Holy Grail*, I believe I have made much more substantial progress towards answering these questions than anyone else in this field of research, except, of course, for the originators: Michael Baigent, Richard Leigh, and Henry Lincoln.

Most of the authors who have written on this subject since the publication of Baigent, et. al.'s monumental classic have chosen to focus their efforts on picking apart minor details of the theories presented in that book, while never offering any convincing counter-explanations for the phenomenon that is Rennes-le-Chateau. Many are desperate to somehow "prove" that Pierre Plantard and company are charlatans, that the Priory of Sion is a hoax, and ergo, there is no mystery to be found at Rennes-le-Chateau. Even Henry Lincoln himself has chosen now to ignore all aspects of the mystery which pertain to the Priory of Sion or the Merovingians, and to focus solely on the pentagonal geometry that he has discovered (although he also refuses to speculate on the meaning, purpose, or origin of the geometry).

However, I have chosen not to share in what I consider to be a pseudo-intellectual pursuit: debunking. And while I have maintained a healthy amount of skepticism throughout my research, I see no gain in obsessing over minutia or trying to impress my scholarly colleagues with how critical I can be. I do not pretend to know for a fact whether or not the modern Priory of Sion really does possess the ancient pedigree or political connections that it has boasted of, but I do think that they must be the bearers of some genuine secret pertaining to Rennes-le-Chateau. After all, they *were* the keepers of the parchments in which Lincoln first discovered the geometry that he later applied to the landscape of Rennes-le-Chateau - the only aspect of the mystery which Lincoln considers to have any value. Whether they concocted it themselves or whether they had been preserving it since Sauniere's time, the fact remains that they *were* the possessors of these documents.

Furthermore, I cannot ignore the inner logic of the theories presented in the "Prieure documents" discussed in *Holy Blood, Holy Grail*, which largely formed the basis for the hypothesis presented in that book. The theories linking the Merovingian bloodline with the Judaic line of Christ and King David, and then linking the Merovingians' descendants with the Knights Templar, the Ordre de Sion, the Rosicrucians, the Compagnie du Saint-Sacrement, the Hieron du Val d'Or, the Freemasons, the French Resistance, and the modern Priory of Sion - these theories are too logical and well-argued to ignore. I think that the authors of *Holy Blood, Holy Grail*, prompted by the material published by the modern Priory of Sion, properly identified a cult of heretical Christianity, linked with various secret hermetic societies throughout the centuries, and linked politically with the same influential European families throughout the centuries. They clearly established at least one facet of what the cult believed: that certain European noble bloodlines were derived from Christ, King David, and the patriarchs of the Bible. They also clearly established the connection between this cult and the region of Southern France surrounding Rennes-le-Chateau.

Those less critical souls who have chosen to pursue the mystery of Rennes-le-Chateau (as opposed to those who see no mystery in it at all) have still elected to go with the theory presented in *Holy Blood, Holy Grail*, that the body of Christ is the treasure buried beneath Rennes-le-Chateau. In this view, the secret which has been the cause of so much angst for over a thousand years is this: that Christ did not die on the cross, and that he wed Mary Magdalene, fathering with her a royal bloodline in what is now Southern France. These people further assert that this was the impetus behind all of the heretical cults and secret societies associated with the saga of Rennes-le-Chateau. While this theory does explain how the secret of Rennes-le-Chateau could have been considered heretical in the time of the Templars, and even, to a lesser extent, in Sauniere's time, it does not explain why such ideas would be considered so now, and thus, why they would need to be kept secret. Why then, do none of the people who clearly know the secret reveal it? In an era where Christ has been called gay, Black, female, a non-existent archetype, and everything else, the suggestion that he may have been married, or that the story of his death might diverge from the biblical narrative seems mild indeed. Extremely conservative Catholics and Protestants might get upset for a short time, as they did when *Holy Blood, Holy Grail* was first published. But in the larger scope, this is not the kind of thing at which the general public would bat an eyelash. *Holy Blood, Holy Grail*, and the many books that followed, have over the years presented numerous clues contained within the Rennes-le-Chateau mystery, including the Priory of Sion documents, hinting that Christ's tomb can be found at Rennes-le-Chateau. It does appear to me that this is one of the conclusions Berenger Sauniere and Pierre Plantard wanted us to come to. But it also appears to me that this is not an end in and of itself, but merely another clue pointing towards something larger.

Many chroniclers have written about the cult of Mary Magdalene, and the statues of the Black Madonna that they believe represent her, claiming that she was revered in secret as the wife of Christ. These same writers also link Magdalene and the Black Madonna to the goddess Isis, or Venus. They then go on to state that Christ and Magdalene were the high priest and priestess of a sex magic cult continuing the mysteries of Isis - one that has since been corrupted into the form of modern Christianity. The association of Rennes-le-Chateau with this cult is, some believe, further indication that Christ and Mary Magdalene are buried in the village.

I have no reason to disagree with this. It does seem that Christ and Mary Magdalene were the leaders of such a cult, and that they shared a sort of alchemical union, embodying the ancient principles of hierogamy and sex magic. The alchemical nature of their wedding ceremony at Cana, where water is transformed into wine, is obvious. And the notion that Christ and Magdalene were laid to rest together at Rennes-le-Chateau is not one that I can or would wish to refute. But if Christ and Magdalene patterned their own images after Cain and Venus, taking on the exact same symbolism, does it not seem then that the iconography of Christ and Magdalene could be used as a coded reference for older gods? In other words, when we see clues at Rennes-le-Chateau indicating that Christ and Magdalene are buried there, could these clues really be saying that ancient god-kings and queens are buried there? Such an idea would explain the extreme secrecy that has surrounded this mystery, the controversy that it has sparked, and the interest that it has held for some of the world's most powerful men for the last 1000 years. It would explain why it is considered "heretical" and dangerous even by modern standards. This is truly a "secret which kings would have pains to draw." The discovery of this secret could have colossal consequences for the entire civilized world.

To find the remains of gods, or semi-divine descendants of gods, who have features different than what we would call "human", would cause us to reevaluate our entire understanding of things like: biology, anthropology, archeology, history itself, and of course, our religious beliefs. We would then have no doubt that all which we know as "civilization" has a common antediluvian origin – that it was brought to us by these gods and their descendants. It would be especially shocking to learn that the true heritage of Jesus "Christ" and the "Grail blood" was actually Satanic in nature; or to learn that Satan's descendants, the Cainites, and their descendants, the Grail family, have played a very decisive role in shaping the course of history. It was they who brought civilization, as well as every kind of wisdom and enlightenment, to mankind, so many years ago. I can only assume that the tradition is being carried on by their descendants, those of the Grail blood, in a secret, obscure fashion. The Priory of Sion would appear to most definitely be a manifestation of this.

Furthermore, the discovery of a vast underground realm, such as that proposed, of which these tombs would be but a part, could hold secrets beyond our wildest dreams. There we would find remnants of a world that dates back to the gods themselves. We would learn all about their technology, their beliefs, their customs, their history, things which eventually became our technology, beliefs, customs, and history. If we can actually find and decipher the Grail stone there (the "Gor-al", or "precious engraved stone", which is also the tablet of Enoch/Hermes), we will be able to read this history as one reads a book. Perhaps we, like our ancestors before us, could actually use the stone to communicate with the deities themselves. Who knows: there could even still be Cainites living underground, the source of the myths of elves, fairies, Djinn, and the like.

I was satisfied with my hypothesis. Although there was no way of proving it, I thought I had done the best job of any Grail/Rennes-le-Chateau researcher so far at penetrating the heart of the mystery. The final step involved simply reviewing one more time (and in some cases, for the first time) the numerous clues left by the Priory of Sion, Berenger Sauniere, and other secret initiates, to see if I could now interpret these clues in the light of my hypothesis.

The City of the Alpha

As I entered the final stages of my research into the mysteries of the Grail, the Merovingians, and Rennes-le-Chateau, something was still troubling me. Although I had followed the clues to what seemed like an obvious conclusion regarding these matters, it bothered me that many of the subjects that I had linked to the Grail and Merovingian mythos had not even been mentioned in those textbook tomes *Holy Blood, Holy Grail* and *The Messianic Legacy*. If the subjects of Atlantis, subterranean realms, and the Black Sun were indeed connected to the Grail lore and the Rennes-le-Chateau mystery, would not the Priory of Sion have at least hinted at it somewhere along the line?

The answer to this question came when I discovered, on the website of Mr. Paul Smith[1], his excellent translations of the articles that appeared in *Vaincre*, the wartime journal published by the Order of Alpha Galates and edited by their Grand Master, Pierre Plantard, supposedly before he joined the Priory of Sion. However, as I have said, it is apparent that the Priory and Alpha Galates were one and the same. *Vaincre*, therefore, is a Priory document. And what these articles said confirmed my suspicions beyond my wildest imaginings.

Alpha Galates, as revealed by *Vaincre*, obviously believed in Atlantis, and in the Atlantean origin of the French race. In fact, Alpha Galates claimed to be perpetuating the Atlantean tradition, which was also practiced, they said, by the Druids. In an article by "Le Comte de Moncharville" entitled *The East and the West*, it is written that:

"...France, through Brittany, was also familiar with the Atlantean tradition, of which the Druidic cult (with its sacrifices to the Sun, the ceremony of mistletoe, menhirs and dolmens, and institutions of chivalry) is merely the survival. ... When Catholicism chased the Druids out of Gaul, some of the monks collected together the Atlantean traditions and formed the Alpha, which then split into two branches: the Cistercians, who adopted Christianity, and the Chivalric Order of Galate, which preserved the Atlantean tradition."

De Moncharville's assertions match those expressed in a book called *Preadamites*, cited by Ignatius Donnelly's *Atlantis: The Antediluvian World* (although the author of the book is nowhere mentioned.) The passage cited reads:

"The Gauls possessed traditions upon the subject of Atlantis which were collected by the Roman historian Timagenes, who lived in the first century before Christ. He represents that three distinct people dwelt in Gaul: 1. The indigenous population, which I suppose to be Mongoloids, who had long dwelt in Europe; 2. The invaders from a distant island, which I understand to be Atlantis; 3. The Aryan Gaul."

The source of the word "Galates" in "Alpha Galates" probably has to do with the word "Gaul", the ancient name for the area that is now France. "Alpha Galates" would then probably mean "source of the Gauls", with "Alpha" indicating the "beginning" or "source." The source of the Gaulish race, they claimed, is Atlantis, and is Druidic as well. Interestingly, the same claim was made by the psychic Edgar Cayce, who said that Atlanteans fleeing the Flood had escaped to the Pyrenees. The word "Gal", by the way, means "navigator" in Hebrew[2]. And "navigator" is the title given to the grand masters of the Priory of Sion.

Another article from *Vaincre*, entitled *The 'Southern Cross' - Rallying Point for the Pure of Heart*, by Auguste Brisieux, connects Atlantis directly to France, specifically the province of Brittany, and describes in fantastic terms Atlantean civilization, as well as its downfall. It states:

"Lemuria, a small country situated on the ancient continent on Atlantis, of roughly the same size as our Brittany, and which is now no more than the vestige of a thousand years of history, rich in spiritual, moral and intellectual glory, of which the Southern Cross was the national emblem, appears to us today to be shrouded in mystery, a mystery that many legends have helped preserve. In reality, however, this was the Land of Initiates, and whereas we ourselves are still in our infancy the Lemurians already knew about the power of the waves, the laws of the Cosmos and karmic cycles - they knew both how to govern and how to obey... This great continent collapsed into materialism, fell prey to the dark forces, rejected the rule of law, destroyed its temples and [its people were] massacred in large numbers, although those who survived succeeded in establishing themselves on our present continent, in our Brittany. But for men, as for nations, the law of karma exists - Atlantis, submerged beneath the putrefying flames, suffered the penalty for its sins. However, the Southern Cross, a constellation of the Southern Hemisphere... remained the happy insignia of the great initiates of the West."

The symbol of the octopus, which appears on the tombstone of Marie de Blanchefort in Rennes-le-Chateau, and also within the pages of the Priory of Sion's *Secret Dossiers*, is another symbol of Atlantis, it seems. It can be found at the end of an article about the Hieron du Val d'Or (translated in an appendix to this book), and is actually lifted from a book by Paul le Cour called *The Age of Aquarius*. The article is dated June 24th, 1926, which is the same date upon which the French Magazine *Atlantis* was founded. This was a magazine edited by Le Cour, which, It is said, the Priory of Sion published.[3] In *The Age of Aquarius*, the octopus is referred to as "a symbol of the primitive tradition." By "primitive", they probably just mean "original" or "primordial", for they saw the Atlantean tradition as the most pure. In one of the issues of *Vaincre*, a quote from Paul le Cour is included which states: "...When a stream is polluted it is necesary, if you are to find pure water, to go back to the source. It's the same with tradition - it only remains pure at Its origin." This "stream" of tradition is the "underground stream" of the Grail lore.

And it is underground where the publishers of *Vaincre* see the remains of the Atlantean tradition, preserved in subterranean cities populated by an advanced race who use an advanced light-based technology.[4] In *The East and the West*, by Le Comte de Moncharville, is a most astounding passage:

"During the mission to Tibet I succeeded in making contact - while I was in Lhasa, in the Forbidden City of Agartha, which is the seat of the Government of the Living Buddha, the 'Dalai Lama' - with several monks of the great monastery there. During the several years that my mission to Lhasa lasted I managed to win the confidence and friendship of them all, and I learned what probably no other initiate of the West has ever known, compared to which the famous <u>Secret Doctrine</u> *of H.P. Blavatsky seem only a fragment of the truth. When I was on the point of leaving, the monks led me along seemingly interminable staircases carved into the mountain into a veritable underground town located underneath the temples. And there they gave me a glimpse of the collection of objects that had been brought from Atlantis before the catastrophe there.*

Then I visited the Sanctuary of the Dragon, where, for the first time since the Orient, I attended a ceremony of a Superior Rite, and finally, during my last few days there, I had the opportunity to contemplate electrical machines of a kind unknown today, which had been brought from Atlantis and which made it possible to impart to the subterranean rooms a light and atmosphere that was exactly the same as that of the open air, which had so surprised me during my first visit to the heart of the mountain. These machines were also used by the 'Dalai Lama' to erect around the Forbidden City of Agartha magnetic barriers that prevented undesirable strangers from penetrating therein."

De Moncharville even hints that the Sanctuary contains the key to an ancient and universal language:

"What most caught my eye was a collection of indecipherable signs covering the largest part of the granite walls of the 'great work'. Seeing my perplexity, one of the Masters of the Secret hastened to explain to me, to help me understand, that only three symbols were sovereign, and that these formed the unity of all symbols."

The symbols which he then shows are a plus sign, a zero, and a closed parenthesis, which he says correspond to "atom, spark, and wave."

This massive underground structure, "the Sanctuary of the Dragon", was, according to Le Comte de Moncharville, constructed by "Galatean knights", precursors of the Knights Templar who were the preservers of the Atlantean tradition, and the originators of chivalry. He writes:

"...they worked the But-Or ('the Gold Mines') and constructed below-ground the city of the Alpha, the biggest city in the world, and completed ... the Sanctuary of the Dragon on one of the Mounts of the Dragon. Then, in the year 812, they suddenly disappeared. Some days later, amid a rumble of thunder, the sea covered the places where the last Atlanteans had lived. From this time onward, only one of the Mounts of the Dragon, towering above the waves, remained to provide evidence, through the existence of its sanctuary, of the activities of the Galatean[5] knights."

Le Comte de Moncharville reveals the location of the Sanctuary to be, once again, the French province of Brittany, and the "Mounts of the Dragon" are actually located on the site currently known as Mount St. Michel, where Saint Michael supposedly defeated "the Dragon", who is Satan. You will recall that I have suggested that this story is based upon the ongoing battle between Jehovah and Abel on the one hand , and Satan and Cain on the other. Michael, of course, represents Jehovah and Abel, whose title of "Moloch" (as in "Baal-Moloch") is the root of the name "Michael." The Dragon, of course, represents Satan and Cain. And what did Michael do with the Dragon after he defeated him? Well, he chained him up and imprisoned him within the bottomless pit, of course. Once again, the idea of Satan's underground prison is evoked in regards to a mountain in France. And here it is being written of in a magazine published by Priory of Sion Grand Master Pierre Plantard.

What's more, Mt. St. Michel is just one of several mountains which form what one author has called "the Saint Michael line": a series of sacred sites (all named after Saint Michael) that can be connected in a straight line. They are located in Jerusalem, Greece, Brittany and Cornwall. Those in England and France are placed far enough off the coast that they constitute islands. English legends state that the coastal island of Saint Michael's Mount was actually constructed by giants long ago.[6] According to the Priory of Sion's *Secret Dossiers*, Mont. St. Michel in Brittany once served as one of their commanderies.

Brittany is also the location of a site of megalithic standing stones, in a place called Carnac, very similar to the name of an ancient Egyptian city, Karnak. According to H.P. Blavatsky, "The Egyptian Karnak is twin brother to the Carnac of Bretagne, the latter Carnac meaning the Serpent's Mount."

At any rate, Moncharville continues his amazing description of this underground temple in Brittany which he called "the Sanctuary of the Dragon":

"The Sanctuary of the Dragon was not abandoned - a new monastery was constructed on its site. And so, beneath the crypt located underneath the flagstone of the Galatean Knights, a crypt more ancient still, dating from this period, gives access to the old Sanctuary. It was through the Sanctuary of the Dragon that the first knights passed to meet with the subterranean dwellers, who led them to the heart of the Breton crypts 379 meters down, in the City of the Alpha, where the Temple of Aga[7] was located. Is this still the only entrance to the City of the Alpha? No, but it is very certainly the oldest."

When I first read the above-quoted passages, I was absolutely astounded. For whatever reason, Baigent, et. al. had chosen to ignore this information completely[8]. But now I had corroboration directly from the publications of the Priory of Sion that they believed in underground cities like Agartha, the fabled city located in the center of the Earth, which they maintained was built by Atlanteans, and that *the oldest* entrance to this vast underworld was located in France. This passageway was thought to reach to the *center* of the Earth, and not just far underground, as indicated by a line from Moncharville's article which reads:

"Finally, in the Round Table, my guide pointed something out to me. I immediately approached it, as I had recognized the small round altar of Lhasa, but here there were some voices that I had already heard, nonetheless muffled, as if they came from the center of the earth."

So then, I thought, if such a thing exists in Brittany, many miles to the North and on the other side of France, why could there not be something similar at Rennes-le-Chateau? From the above-quoted passages, one line in particular struck me as odd: "And so, beneath the crypt located underneath the flagstone of the Galatean Knights, a crypt more ancient still, dating from this period, gives access to the old Sanctuary." For in the Church of Saint Magdalene in Rennes-le-Chateau, it was underneath "The Knight's Flagstone" that Sauniere discovered, soon after finding the parchments, an underground crypt. He was extremely secretive about it, and would not allow the work-men who helped him lift the stone to see what was underneath it. It is believed that the "Knight's Flagstone" depicts Templar Knights because two of them are seen seated on the same horse, an earmark of the Templars. But the flagstone is badly damaged, and the knights are very crudely depicted anyway, making it unclear exactly what sort of people they are. Perhaps the "Knight's Flagstone" was placed there as a clue, mimicking the flagstone of the Galatean knights in Brittany. Perhaps, like its Breton cousin, it conceals an entrance to a subterranean realm – one that includes the Grail stone and the graves of the Cainites. Such a conclusion definitely seems to be hinted at here, in the text of literature published by the Priory of Sion's own front organization.

Dagobert II: The Return of the King

The life and death of Dagobert II seems quite ritualistically significant in the context of my hypothesis. Like Christ, Dagobert appears to have modeled every aspect of his image upon that of mythological heroes from the past. His entire life, as historically recorded, is mythological and archetypal. The word "dag" means, in ancient languages, "fish", while "ber" can mean "priest", or "house, temple." Therefore "Dagobert" could be rooted in syllables meaning "Priest of Dagon", "Priest of the Fish", or "Priest of the Temple." That he was also called "Dragobert" evokes the image of Satan as "the Dragon." Indeed, from the very beginning his life embodied the mythos of a fallen king who has returned – an archetype based upon the prototype of Cain dying and being reborn as Seth. You will recall that his father had been assassinated when he was five, and that he had been kidnapped by his family's enemies. They sent him into exile in Ireland, while an elaborate ruse was concocted to make everyone believe that he was dead. There he lay in wait for the opportunity to reclaim his father's throne.

This opportunity showed itself in the year 671, when he married Giselle de Razes, daughter of the count of Razes and niece of the king of the Visigoths, allying the Merovingian house with the Visigothic royal house. This had the potential for creating a united empire that would have covered most of what is now modern France. The marriage was celebrated at the Church of Saint Magdalene in Rhedae, the same spot where Berenger Sauniere's Church of Saint Magdalene at Rennes-le-Chateau now rests. It is said that Dagobert found something there: a clue which led him to a treasure buried in nearby Montsegur. This treasure supposedly financed what was about to come: the reconquest of Aquitaine and the throne of the Frankish kingdom. As Baigent, et. al write in *Holy Blood, Holy Grail*, "At once he set about asserting and consolidating his authority, taming the anarchy that prevailed throughout Austrasia and reestablishing order." The fallen king had risen from his ashes, born anew as Dagobert II, and had come to once more establish firm rule and equilibrium in his country. The similarities to the Parsifal/Grail story, where the Fisher King dies and the Grail knight becomes the new king, are fairly clear.

I have discussed, since the time of the Merovingian King Clovis I, the Merovingian Kings had been under a pact with the Church, in which they had pledged their allegiance in exchange for Papal backing of the their united empire of Austrasia. They would forever hold the title of "New Constantine", a title that would later morph into that of "Holy Roman Emperor." But that allegiance on the part of the Merovingians towards the Church began to wear thin after a while. Obviously, given their infernal and divine origin, their spiritual bent was slightly different from that of organized Christianity. In addition, as direct descendants of Jesus, they would have possessed access to the secret teachings of Christ, no doubt shockingly different from the ones promoted by the Church, and reflecting more of the "secret doctrine" of Satan and the Cainites that I have talked about in this book. Any public knowledge of this would have been disastrous for the Church. Seeing in Dagobert a potential threat, they conspired with his enemies to assassinate him on December 23. He was stabbed through the left eye, purportedly by his own godson.

There are many aspects to this event that appear to be mythologically significant. For one thing, it may have taken place on a hunting expedition in the "Forest of Woevres", long held sacred, and host to annual sacrificial bear hunts for the goddess Diana. Indeed, the murder may have taken place on such a hunt. This bears a close similarity to the purported death of Cain, who according to Jewish legends died in a hunting accident in the forest, killed by his descendant, Lamech. The forest that Dagobert died in was located near the royal Merovingian residence at Stenay, a town that used to be called "Satanicum" (perhaps named after Dagobert's ancestor, Satan). We must also consider the date itself, which is close to the Winter Solstice, the shortest day in the year, when the ancients believed the Sun died and turned black, descending into the underworld. That date was also almost precisely at the beginning of the astrological period of Capricorn, and traditionally marked the beginning of the pagan festival of Saturnalia, a debaucherous ritual celebrating the powers of Saturn (Satan) that were believed to rule during the time of Capricorn. The murder is further said to have taken place at the ritualistically important time of midday.

The fact that the murder was committed by a family member is significant too. Not only does this match the circumstances of Cain's death, but it is also similar to the "Dolorous Stroke" that wounded the Fisher King in the Grail story, something which also took place at midday and was inflicted by the king's own brother. In this story, the brother who wounds the Fisher King is known as the "Dark Lord", and during the fight he is wounded in the left eye, precisely as Dagobert was wounded. The same thing happened to Horus in Egyptian mythology, fighting his uncle, Set. The "Left Eye of Horus" came to symbolize the hidden knowledge of the gods, and, as I have shown, represents the Grail stone. Thus, Dagobert's death appears to follow the same patterns as many other fallen kings or murdered gods whose deaths are considered ritualistically symbolic, and who it is believed will one day rise again. These deaths are meant to symbolize the concept of the lost or fallen kingdom (the golden age), just as the Dolorous Stroke does in the Grail story.

Clearly, Dagobert's death meant the end for the Merovingian kingdom. All subsequent Merovingian kings were essentially powerless, and they were officially thought to have died out with Childeric III. But as we know, in 872, almost 200 years after his death, Dagobert was canonized as a Saint, and the date of his death, December

23, became "Saint Dagobert's Day." Like the skull depicted in Guercino's *Et in Arcadia Ego*, Dagobert's skull was ritually trepanned, and became - like the skulls of Adam, Cain (Baphomet), and John the Baptist, a religious idol - believed to have fetishistic powers of protection.

Sauniere's Saga Revisited

Seen in the light of what I have so far gleaned, mysterious tombstone of Marie de Blanchefort gives forth new meaning. On the sides of the stone, as we know, the message "Et in Arcadia Ego" is inscribed, using a mixture of Greek and Latin letters. I have already discussed how this can be seen as a reference to the "Arka" - the tomb of the Cainites which I believe to be beneath Rennes-le-Chateau. I have also discussed how the term "Arcadia" applied to the Greek notion of Paradise. Furthermore, the word "Etin" (the first four letters in the phrase) was once an alternate spelling of "Eden", the Judeo-Christian notion of Paradise. Both of these things symbolize "the center of the Earth", and the golden age of the gods. But on the Blanchefort tombstone, the message actually reads: "Et in Arx Adia Ego." The words "Arx" and "Adia" are separated so as to emphasize "Arx." This word, in Latin, means "a fortress, citadel, or stronghold." This points to the idea that there is an entire subterranean complex built around the tombs beneath Rennes-le-Chateau, which at one time had multiple functions, and that this location may once have been the capitol of an empire. This leads us directly to the message "Reddis Regis Cellis Arcis" in the center of the stone. The word "Reddis" is supposed by most researchers to be derived from the old name of Rennes, which was once called "Rhedis", "Redis", or "Rhedae", named after the goddess Rhea, who was the mother to the two Greek Flood heroes. Meanwhile, "Rennes" means "reins" in French, and may perhaps be a name derived from the belief that the Cainites and Satan were imprisoned or shackled within his tomb. But "reddis" is also a Latin word meaning "you return" or "you restore", from which the French "rendre" and the English "render" are derived. "Regis" means "royal, "Cellis" means "a basement or cave", and "Arcis" means the same thing as "Arx": a fortress, or an "ark", in the sense of a box or enclosure. Thus the statement being made here is "Return to (or Restore) the Cave of the Royal Ark." The words at the bottom of the stone, "Prae-Cum", imply the notion of "the time before", indicating the antediluvian golden age. The octopus symbol below it, as we have learned, represents "the primitive solar religion of Atlantis" - that it, the primeval religious tradition that defined the Golden Age. Even the person whose grave the stone was supposedly made for, Marie de Negre de Blanchefort, whose name means "Black Marie of the White Fort", appears to be used in this context as a symbol of the goddess archetype of Isis or Venus, queen of the Golden Age. But we know that this was not Marie de Blanchefort's real grave, which was actually located in the crypt beneath the church at Rennes-le-Chateau. The faux gravestone was simply a clue left for Berenger Sauniere by his predecessor, Abbe Bigou, as a clue about the sacred tombs within the mountains of Rennes-le-Chateau.

The letters "P" and "S" are at the top of the stone, surrounded by a Fibonacci spiral. The same "P", "S", and spiral can be found at the bottom of the first parchment found by Sauniere. These letters, presumably, stand for "Priory of Sion." At the bottom of Parchment Two, the word "SION" is spelled backwards, and the "O" has a dot in the middle, causing it to resemble the astrological sign for the Sun – which points again to the idea of a hidden sun within the sacred tomb. As I looked at these clues again, with the benefit of all of the research I had already done, I began to see the secret which these clues pointed to. A pertinent line from *Le Serpent Rouge* reads: "I pivot, looking from the rose from P to that of the S, the from the S to P..." I began to wonder if this line, the "P", "S", and spiral, as well as the word "SION" spelled backwards were all clues telling me to transpose the letters in the words "Prieure de Sion." I eliminated the article "de" and with little effort, came up with "Pieurrenois", which, when pronounced with a French accent, would sound very much like "Pyrenees." The first syllable in "Pieurrenois" - "Pieurre" - is similar to "Pierre", the French word for "rock." Of course, the first syllable of "Pyrenees" – "Pyr" - means "Fire." This indicates that the "rock of Sion", the "fire-stone from Heaven", can be found at Rennes-le-Chateau.

The message of the second parchment also took on an enhanced meaning now that I knew what I did. The words "Shepherdess - No Temptation, that Poussin and Teniers hold the key" would seem to be, perhaps, the most straightforward aspect of the message. "Shepherdess" and "Poussin", as we know, refer to Poussin's painting, *"The Shepherds of Arcadia."* However, the translation of the words "gardent la clef" as "hold the key" could perhaps be more accurate. "Gardent" really means "guard", rather than just "hold", and while "clef" does mean "key", it is a word also used to mean "keystone." So the parchment really tells us that "Poussin and Teniers guard the key-stone", meaning they know the location of the stone from Heaven, which has been used as the keystone to a sacred temple at least once, if not several times (including the Tower of Babel, the Temple of Bethel, and the Temple of Solomon). Poussin's painting, *The Shepherds of Arcadia*, seems to point not only to the golden age of the gods, but to the "Arka-dia", the tomb of the forgotten God (Satan) and his children (the Cainites). The Poussin painting shows the tomb to be located in Rennes-le-Chateau, within the pentacle of mountains.

The David Teniers painting mentioned by the parchments is assumed by Henry Lincoln to be *Saint Anthony and Saint Paul*, the only Teniers painting featuring Saint Anthony which does not show him enduring his famous temptation by demons - thus the words "no temptation." In this painting, the two saints are sitting in front of an altar upon which stands a crucifix and a skull. This, again, points toward the location of the sacred tomb, "the place of the skull", or Golgotha. The painting shows one saint pointing up towards a descending dove that is carrying the holy host, a representation of the Grail stone.

The words "peace 681" proved more difficult to decipher. I could only note that 681 was the year that Sigisbert IV, Dagobert's son, was purportedly smuggled into the Languedoc region to perpetuate the Merovingian bloodline in exile, and to become the first of the Plantard line. It is suggested that Sigisbert stayed with his mother Giselle de Razes at Rennes-le-Chateau. Perhaps, I thought, this date was associated with "peace" because it signified the end to the turmoil that Dagobert's assassination had brought, as the continuity of the royal line was now secured, even if it was no longer on the throne.

"By the Cross and this Horse of God" I found difficult to interpret as well. The cross was, like the octopus, an ancient sun symbol dating back to Atlantis, and was also used to denote the pole, or center-point of the Earth. The horse was a symbol of Poseidon, the sea god and purported king of Atlantis. And in some cultures the Sun was viewed to be a chariot drawn by celestial horses.

However, a tip that I have received from a party purportedly "in the know" on these matters has suggested an interesting new take on these parchments. The informant in question contacted me by email, claiming to be involved with a group called "the Order of the Blue Rose", which he said had been started by Jean Cocteau's close friend, Jean Marais. It was also strongly hinted that this group was really a front organization for the Priory of Sion. Anyway, the informant suggested that the parchments found by Sauniere were never meant to be viewed as instructions for locating a buried treasure. Rather, they had been left there by Berenger Sauniere's predecessor as priest of Rennes-le-Chateau, Abbe Antoine Bigou, as part of Sauniere's initiation into a mystery cult.

In an earlier chapter of this book, I discussed the possibility that Sauniere was initiated into a quasi-Masonic order, the "Hieron du Val d'Or" ("The Sanctuary of the Valley of Gold"), which itself may have been a front for the Priory of Sion. Then in yet another chapter I suggested that this may have been a part of something larger – that most of the nobles in Rennes-le-Chateau and the surrounding area were all part of an essentially Satanic cult, revering the Grail bloodline descended from Cain and Satan. If Rennes-le-Chateau really does stand over an underground structure containing the tombs of these figures, then it makes sense that Rennes-le-Chateau would be the center of this cult, and Sauniere would have, when fully initiated, have become its high priest, as Bigou had undoubtedly been before him. This church would have probably operated along the lines of the underground "true Christian" cults described by Nicholas de Vere, which were Satanic in nature and celebrated the Black Mass as the "true Christian" mass.

My mysterious informant from the Order of the Blue Rose seemed to corroborate this idea. He claimed that the parchments contained the formula for a ritual that was to be performed by Sauniere, regarding a curse that has for centuries afflicted the Grail bloodline. He said that this curse could not be abolished, but only appeased, by periodic "blood sacrifices." Two of the most significant sacrifices that had been made in this regard were those of Jesus Christ and of Dagobert II. But in the case of Jesus, my informant insisted that a substitute was able to die in his place. He said that the line "by the cross and this horse of God" referred to this substitute.

As astounding as this claim was, he also stated that the remains of these sacrificial victims were treated as holy relics, which were believed to ward off the ill effects of the curse on the Grail bloodline. One of the goals of the "Grail cult in Southern France", as he called it, was to collect as many of these relics as possible and deposit them beneath Rennes-le-Chateau. This is the reason, he claimed, why the first parchment refers to Dagobert II being "here dead" - buried there at Rennes-le-Chateau. This is also the reason why the second parchment refers to "681", the year that Dagobert's remains arrived at Rennes-le-Chateau, brought along with Sigisbert IV. "Blue apples", my informant wrote, is a code meaning, simply, "blood sacrifice." This idea was also symbolized by Cocteau in the blue rose that he placed beneath the feet of the crucified man in his mural at Notre Dame de France, which they had named their order after. The two genealogies that Sauniere found along with the other two parchments were there because they listed the line of the curse's descent, which was passed down intergenerationally.

I wrote back to my informant asking him several questions. Among them: In what way is "horse of God" a code for the substitution of Christ on the cross? Was that substitute Judas? How exactly does "blue apples" translate as "blood sacrifice." And what about the lines "I complete this demon guardian at noon"? However, the email message immediately bounced back to me. My informant had disappeared[9].

Although I could not confirm any of the information this man had given me, it did put an interesting spin on things. The term "blue apples" has been explained by previous authors as an idiom used locally in Southern France to refer to grapes, and therefore, its use in the parchments is a reference to the symbol of the vine, representing the bloodline of the Grail. And royal blood is often called "blue blood." But there is perhaps another level of meaning as well. The fall from the Garden of Eden was supposedly caused by Eve eating a forbidden fruit, usually depicted as an apple, from the Tree of Life. As I discussed in an earlier chapter, this whole story is a metaphor for the breeding that occurred between Satan and a human female (Eve), resulting in the bloodline of Cain. Jewish and Christian legends make it clear that Cain's bloodline *was* cursed by Jehovah because of this. So perhaps "blue apples" is a code for this cursed bloodline, and for the blood sacrifices that were necessary to alleviate this curse.

Furthermore, I already suggested that Jesus' supposed death on the cross was an effort to break a curse placed upon the Jewish and Israelite people by Jehovah. But I also suggested (as confirmed by my informant) that Jesus had another (I suggest his twin brother Judas Thomas) die in his place, as a "sin atonement" in the Jewish tradition. I suggested that he himself played the part of the scapegoat, taking the weight of the sins upon himself and away from the people, by going into exile. However, if this act did not fully remove the curse, then it would remain attached to the bloodline of Jesus, and perhaps, as my informant suggested, this curse would require more blood atonement from his descendants.

It is interesting that my informant's "Order of the Blue Rose" was purportedly connected to Jean Marais, Jean Cocteau, and the Priory of Sion. Cocteau demonstrated in his mural at Notre Dame de France that he believed in the crucifixion substitution theory. And in his mural at St. Blaise, he showed his belief in the "twin Christ" theory". Sauniere also demonstrated his belief in both of these theories in some of the decorations he placed in his church – something I have discussed elsewhere in this book. This makes sense if Sauniere and his parishioners (cult members) performed rituals that pertained to this curse, and the sacrifices that were made to control it.

If the curse in question really was passed on to Jesus' descendants, this might explain why Dagobert II's death seems so much like a ritual sacrifice, and why it was considered to be a martyrdom by those who believed that Dagobert's remains contained magical powers. Perhaps these remains were moved secretly to Rennes-le-Chateau, and the ones on display at the convent at Mons, France are fake.

If we are willing to consider these possibilities, perhaps we should also consider the possibility that Berenger Sauniere was also sacrificed for the same reason – and that he may have willingly allowed this. Perhaps this is why his stroke occurred on the Feast Day of Saint Sulpice, which may have been sacred to the cult. After all, the Priory of Sion, which the cult was undoubtedly derived from, operated a base at the Chapel of Saint Sulpice in Paris. And as we know, his housekeeper had ordered his coffin just a few days prior to his stroke.

The fact that his dead body was placed on display so that his parishioners could pluck the tassels from his robe also points to a ritualized death. This is a practice that took place in Merovingian France, ancient Israel, and even ancient Mesopotamia, where for those of royal blood, the tassels of their robes were symbols of their nobility. To take the tassels from a nobleman's robe meant that you were taking for yourself some of his royal power[10]. *Holy Blood, Holy Grail* states that for the Merovingian kings, "the tassels on the fringes of their robes were deemed to possess magical curative powers." Likewise, there is a story in the Gospels of Jesus instantaneously curing a woman of an illness when she tugged upon the end of his robe.

As for the lines "I complete this demon guardian at noon", this might be explained in the context of this sacrificial ritual. First of all, the "demon guardian" would have to be Asmodeus, who seems to guard Sauniere's church from the doorway. As the builder of Solomon's Temple, he is analogous to Hiram Abiff, who according to Masonic ritual was murdered at noon, just like Dagobert II. This may have been the prearranged time for Sauniere's death. Finally, the words translated "I complete" are really "J'acheve", which might be better translated "I achieve", or "I become." The message then reads: "I become the demon guardian at noon." High noon was probably the time that the sacrifice occurred.

So Sauniere may have, in a ritual sense, achieved an apotheosis in which he *became* Asmodeus – who represents both Satan and Cain. This would be the equivalent of "manifesting the Baphomet", as the Templars purportedly did. Compare comments made by Templars during their confessions to the Inquisition with the description given in *Holy Blood, Holy Grail* of the priest who attempted to take Berenger Sauniere's final confession right before his death. In Julius Evola's *The Mystery of the Grail*, we read:

"The central ritual of Templar initiation was kept very secret. From one of the proceedings of the trial we learn that a knight who underwent it returned as pale as a corpse, and with a lost expression on his face, claiming that from then on he could never be happy again. Shortly after, the same knight fell into a state of invincible depression and died... What produces an extreme terror in some knights and causes them to flee... is the vision of an idol... the Baphomet."

And in *Holy Blood, Holy Grail*, we read:

"As Sauniere lay on his deathbed, a priest was called from a neighboring parish to hear his final confession and administer the last rites. The priest duly arrived and retired into the sickroom. According to eyewitness testimony he emerged shortly thereafter, visibly shaken. In the words of one account he 'never smiled again'... the priest, presumably on the basis of Sauniere's confession, refused to administer Extreme Unction."

Perhaps Sauniere, at the moment of death, became the demon that he and his Satanic church had been honoring the entire time at Rennes-le-Chateau, and then was sacrificed according to the family tradition, like Dagobert and Jesus before him. The Satanic cult theory explains everything. The obscure symbolic decorations which Sauniere placed throughout his church may not have been messages to future treasure hunters as much as they were simply there for the worshippers, participating in rituals that pertained to those symbols. The cult is the reason why all of Sauniere's parishioners seemed to be "in" on his secrets. And I have already explained how Sauniere's riches could have come simply from the sale of indulgences in his Satanic church.

Furthermore, there is evidence that a Satanic cult practicing human sacrifice was active in that area during Sauniere's time. A friend of his named Antoine Gelis, who worked in the parish in nearby Coustassa, was murdered on November 1, 1897, killed by several blows to the head. Before the murder, he had been in constant fear, keeping his door locked and refusing to see anybody. He had also come into a large amount of money for some unknown reason, all of which was found still in the house, having been left untouched by the assailant. In *The Templar Revelation*, by Lynn Picknett and Clive Prince, we read that the murder seemed ritualistic in nature:

"...[The murderer] had ritualistically laid out the body, crossing the arms across the chest, and leaving a piece of paper with the words "viva Angelina" written on it. No motive was ever discerned behind the crime.

There are a couple of particularly strange elements interwoven in the Gelis murder. His gravestone, in the churchyard at Coustassa, has been positioned – alone of all the graves – so that it faces Rennes-le-Chateau, which is clearly visible on the hillside opposite. The grave also bears a rose-cross insignia. And, although this brutal murder of an elderly and fragile priest shocked the local populace, the diocese seemed to have wanted the matter forgotten as swiftly as possible. When Gerard de Sede tried to investigate it in the early 1960s, he found no record of the murder in the diocesan archives at Carcassonne. It was not until 1975 that two lawyers reconstructed the story from local police and court records."

The arrangement of the body is a pose used in Freemasonry, in the ritual reenactment of the death of Hiram Abiff. It has its origins it Egypt. Jean Cocteau took this pose when acting in his own film, *The Testament of Orpheus*, in a scene in which he descends to the underworld, dies and is reborn.

Now that I had possibly deciphered the messages of the parchments, I noticed other clues on the parchments, besides the messages themselves, which needed deciphering as well. For instance, the words "Rex Mundi", meaning "King of the World", a title held by Satan and Cain, are embedded into Parchment One. Then there are the words "Redis Bles" and "Solis Sacerdotibus" written beside the main message of Parchment One. The way Henry Lincoln and other authors choose to interpret this, "Redis" means "Rennes", and "Bles" means "corn", which is what wheat was called in Europe and England prior to the discovery of maize (now also called "corn") in the New World. "Bles" ("corn") is also a local idiom for "money" or "treasure", like "bread" is in English. "Solis" means "solely", and "sacerdotibus" means "initiated." Lincoln thus reads the message as saying, "The treasure of Rennes is only for the initiated." But as I have said, "Redis" also means "return", and wheat ("corn") was also a symbol of Cain, who was thought to be the inventor of the plough, and the first to introduce the crop's cultivation. In fact, Cain's name actually means "grain." Furthermore, wheat, and the bread that is made from it have been important icons in religious rituals throughout history, ranging from the Greek and Babylonian mysteries to ancient Judaism and modern Christianity. Catholics celebrate communion by eating a wafer that represents Christ's body, and the ancient Jews had a special "shewbread" that was only administered to the Levitic caste of priests during certain rituals. "Solis" also means "Sun", and "sacerdotibus" specifically means "priesthood." Thus, "Redis Bles Solis Sacerdotibus" could be translated in any of the following ways: "Return the corn to the priesthood of the Sun"; "The corn of Rennes is for the priesthood of the Sun"; "The corn of Rennes is only for the priesthood"; or "Return the wheat solely to the priesthood."

I do appear to be on the right track with my interpretation, for the very text into which the code of Parchment One has been inserted is a conglomeration of quotes from three of the Gospels describing a scene in which Jesus and his disciples are walking through a cornfield, eating corn! As *The Gospel of Saint Matthew* describes it:

"At that time Jesus went on the sabbath day through the corn; and his disciples were an hungered, and began to pluck the ears of corn and to eat. But when the Pharisees saw it, they said unto him, Behold, thy disciples do that which is not lawful to do upon the sabbath day. But he said to them, Have ye not read what David did, when he was an hungered, and they that were with him; How he entered into the house of God, and did eat the shewbread, which was not lawful for him to eat, neither for them which were with him, but only for the priests? Or have ye not read in the law, how that on the sabbath days the priests in the temple profane the sabbath, and are blameless? But I say to you, that this place is one greater than the temple."

So this is the "corn" that is "only for the priesthood." But what lies beneath the symbolism of this story, and what statement is being made by connecting it with the phrase "Redis Bles Solis Sacerdotibus"? Is the parchment's creator saying "Return the sacraments of the church (the true church in the tradition of Atlantis) to its rightful priests"? And what of the last line in the passage from *Matthew*: "This place is one greater than the temple"? If its use in the parchment is a reference to Rennes-le-Chateau and the treasures hidden beneath, this could mean that Rennes-le-Chateau is a much holier place than the remains of the temple in Jerusalem.

This may all help explain another curious message which is buried in the text of the second parchment: "Panis ΛΩ Sal" – the Latin words for "bread" and "salt" separated by the Alpha and Omega symbols. We know that bread used in Christian ritual, in the form of the communion wafer, represents the body of Christ. If used in a ritual performed by Sauniere and his cult, however, it probably represents the body of Cain, whose cult of Mithras was the first to use communion as a ritual. But more than that, bread and salt were once used in the rituals of Welsh country pagans, before they were fully Catholicized. When a wealthy person was dying, their family often paid a poor person to come and eat bread and salt in the same room as the dying person. They believed that by doing so, he was consuming, and taking upon himself, the sins of the dying person. The process was called "sin eating." A popular British film from 2003 called *The Sin Eater* suggested the possibility that an elite and secretive order of Catholic priests was continuing this practice. If the principle upon which sin-eating is based is held to be real, one would think that a willing person could even absorb the sins of another while they are still alive. Instead of simply confessing your sins to your priest every Sunday, you could lay them upon his head, and be free of them, just as the sins of the Israelites were laid upon the head of the scapegoat at Yom Kippur, and just as Jesus took on the sins of his people. Now, this is exactly the sort of ritual that Sauniere's parishioners would have paid significantly to participate in. If Sauniere had absorbed all of the sins of his parishioners before his death, this would mean that he was truly following in the tradition of Christ. And this could have been yet another aspect of Sauniere's final confession that was horrifying to the officiating priest.

The code of Parchment Two is made using a passage from *The Gospel of Saint*

John, Chapter 12, verses 1-7. Shortly after Christ raises Lazarus from the dead, he is having dinner with Mary Magdalene, Martha, Lazarus, and his disciples. Mary takes "a pound of ointment of spikenard, very costly", and anoints Christ's feet with it, "wiping his feet with her hair." Judas Iscariot, disgusted at the waste of something so valuable, remarks, "Why was not this ointment sold for three hundred pence, and given to the poor?" The passage continues:

"This he said, not that he cared for the poor; but because he was a thief, and had the bag, and bare what was put therein. Then said Jesus, Let her alone; against the day of my burial hath she kept this. For the poor always ye have with you; but me ye not have always."

The scene this passage describes is also illustrated in a stained glass window on the ceiling behind the altar of Sauniere's church. What could its significance be in this context? The anointing of Christ's feet by Mary has been described by some authors as the ritual anointing of a king by his bride and queen, which we find perfectly reasonable. But Jesus specifically says that, "against the day of my burial hath she kept this", indicating that it was meant to anoint his dead body before it was placed in the tomb. Thus, this passage describes the events that preceded the crucifixion, and demonstrates how Judas' rude behavior beforehand foreshadowed his betrayal, and made him expendable to Jesus – who then, according to my theory, plotted Judas' death.

Another clue to the mystery of Rennes-le-Chateau which began to take on new meaning as my research continued was Sauniere's personal bookplate, now on display in the Berenger Sauniere museum right next to the church at Rennes-le-Chateau. At the top, we see an angel holding Asmodeus in chains, a symbol of Satan and Cain's supposed imprisonment in the center of the Earth. Below is an alchemical seal which Sauniere quite clearly copied from Henricus Madathanus' *Aureum Seculum Redivivum*. The main feature of the symbol is the Seal of Solomon, formed by two triangles, one black and one white. I have already demonstrated how this shape can be thought to represent the sacred mountain reaching up to Heaven, with the sacred tomb in its bowels, reaching down into the center of the Earth. And on this alchemical seal, at the exact point in the bowels of the symbolic "mountain" where you would expect to find the sacred tomb, the astrological sign of the Sun has been drawn in, like the Black Sun in the center of the Earth, and the "hidden sun" which lights the tomb of Osiris. Placed over this is an inverted symbol of Venus, the cross surmounted by a circle. In this version, the cross is pointing upward, near the top of the hexagram, as if it is meant to represent the cavalry cross of Golgotha where Christ was crucified, directly above the "Cave of Treasures", according to Christian apocrypha. The part of the Venus sign that forms a circle is surrounding the "hidden sun" symbol. And written on the circle are the Latin words "Centrum Trigono Centri" ("The Center in the Triangle of the Center.") In other words, "the cave within the mountain which is in the center of the Earth." On either side of the cross are the letters "BS", just as they are found throughout Sauniere's church. For some reason, all past authors have assumed these to be Berenger Sauniere's initials, and no one has thought to compare this seal to the alchemical manuscript it was copied from. These letters are part of the original. So the "BS" decorations Sauniere placed throughout his church are not just his initials. They are undoubtedly an abbreviation for some alchemical motto, but one which, unfortunately, I have yet to deduce.

Around the hexagram just described is another circle (representing the Earth, of which the hexagram represents the center) upon which are written the words "Tria Sunt Mirabilia: Deus et Homo; Mater et Virgo; Trinus et Unus." This translates to: "Three are the Marvels: God and Man; the Mother and the Virgin; the Three and the One." It speaks to the alchemical union of symbols represented by the center of the Earth. At the four corners of the seal are four cherubim, like those which guard the Garden of Eden, or those which flank the Ark of the Covenant. They are the guardians of the treasures at the center of the Earth.

The Priory of Sion: The Next Generation

"Today, in the shadows there lurk the 'eminences grises', who form the backbone of all political states or religious entities. Without them the 'star performers' that actually make all the headlines (be they Popes, Kings or Presidents) would simply not exist. Here and there we find them, initiates of high degree, entrusted with secret missions by the Grandmasters of the occult orders that rule the planet."
- Pablo Norberto, "The Origin of the Priory of Sion."
Le Cercle, 1992.

It seems that virtually every aspect of the enigma surrounding Rennes-le-Chateau, the Priory of Sion and the Merovingians can be explained now in the context of this book's main thesis. When I finally reached this point in my research, I was proud to have been able to unravel so many mysteries. And it was just when my hypothesis was almost fully formed that I began to realize the extent to which my ideas were corroborated by documents written and published by the Priory itself. I have already talked about *Le Serpent Rouge* quite a bit, and a full interpretation of this poem can be found in Appendix B of this book. As I neared the end of my research, a friend sent me another Priory document that backed up my theories. It was a chapter from the *Secret Dossiers*, supposedly compiled by Henri Lobineau. This document (which I have fully transcribed in another appendix) is about the Hieron du Val d'Or, the strange cult which is believed to have been a front organization for the Priory of Sion, and to which Sauniere was believed to have belonged. The chapter describes the symbols employed by the organization, such as the Sacred Heart, and offers an esoteric interpretation of Christianity as a sun cult. The author of this chapter, who calls himself "Le Poulpe" (The Octopus) ends his piece rather evocatively:

"It is in France, in Paray-le-Monial, that they have given birth to the devotion towards the Sacred Heart, which is the entitlement of the Hieron du Val d'Or. In Autumn of 1893 someone found, on the tomb of a Christian woman dating from the VI century, an inscription in Greek letters (it was said that Druids wrote in Greek letters). It comprises eleven lines, and the first letter of the first five form the word ICHTUS.
Here is part of this inscription: 'O divine race of the celestial fish, receive with a respectful heart in immortal life among the mortals the waters of the divine ones. Friend, remake your heart with the eternal flood of the wisdom which gives treasures. It is a reservoir of nourishment, soft like the honey of the Savior of the saints. Eat with hunger: you hold the fish in your hands.'"

It seems that "the divine race of the celestial fish" would have to be the race descended from Satan, Cain, and the Atlanteans, who associated themselves with fish and, just as the passage states, the Sun as well. Also note the words "flood of wisdom", similar to the interpretation of Baphomet's name as "baptism of wisdom."

By far the most corroborative evidence for my theory is the articles in *Vaincre*, which I have already described in great detail. But not long before completing this manuscript, I received some shocking news, from the same person, Paul Smith, who originally translated the *Vaincre* articles into English. As Smith reports, a new series of *Vaincre* magazines began to be published in 1989. The new issues listed Pierre Plantard's son Thomas Plantard as the "Managing Editor", and one of them featured an interview with Pierre Plantard. A completely new list of Grand Masters was produced, in which many of the names have been changed, and it now only dated back to 1681 (the date the Children of Saint Vincent were created). The Priory of Sion now claimed to be completely disavowing any direct descent from the Knights Templar, and their Grand Masters were not listed. However, there was a complete listing of the Grand Masters from Jean Cocteau's death onwards, which had before remained a completely unanswered question[11]. Now it was claimed that Cocteau was followed by Francois Balphagon until 1969, and then a fellow named John Drick took over. In 1981, the office was assumed by Pierre Plantard, who as we know resigned in 1984. *Vaincre* now claimed that Plantard was followed by Philippe de Cherisey, who was quickly replaced by someone called Patrice Pelat in 1985. This person died in 1989, and then at the "Convent of Avignon", on March 9, 1989, Pierre Plantard was reinstated as Grand Master, just long enough to pass the title on to his son four months later, at "10 o'clock solar time", as its described in *Vaincre*.

Many aspects of the Priory's new claims in this magazine appear to be attempts at obfuscation. They wanted the Priory of Sion to be at the forefront of everyone's minds once again, but they wanted to spread some confusion, to increase the intrigue. This series of *Vaincre* appears to have later morphed into *Le Cercle*, which was still subtitled *Vaincre* and still edited by Thomas Plantard. Its logo featured a cock crowing, a favorite motif often used by Jean Cocteau. Both *Vaincre* and *Le Cercle* are very queer in their phrasing, as all Priory documents are, and appear to contain many code words recognizable only to initiates, many of which are written in all caps for emphasis. And in one of these issues, a reprinted letter from Pierre Plantard purported to reveal the Priory of Sion's main secret. Plantard wrote:

"Our TREASURE, that of the PRIORY OF SION, is the SECRET of the BLACK ROCK ('ROC NOIR'). Revered since remote antiquity by those who believed in its immense power, it was confused with the DEVIL, and even LABOUISSE-ROCHEFORTE wrote, in a poem intended for the initiated:

'The Angel of the bastard race,
In a tone at once dry and crazed,
Keeps constant guard over
This immense income...'

and only the initiated could understand that the treasure was not gold, but the considerable energy that the MASTER of the genie - he who knows the secret - has at his dis-

posal."

So in other words, Plantard was saying that that "Devil" is really a black stone that contains "energy" or power, and that there is a "bastard race" which descends from this stone. This is exactly what I submitted earlier regarding the Grail stone and its identity with Satan. I suggested that this stone might be buried at Rennes-le-Chateau, in an underground tomb or temple. The same was hinted at by Plantard, who wrote that the "Roc Noir" is in Rennes-le-Chateau.

Then, in another article called "The Dubosc Affair", it was claimed that a mining shaft was sunk through the "Roc Noir", the true purpose of which was to "re-establish a communicating 'way' between the old underground passages of the former Celtic sanctuary known as the TEMPLE ROND (Round Temple.)" Once again, the documents of the Priory itself completely confirm the main thrust of my hypothesis – that there is an underground temple (and sacred tomb) beneath Rennes-le-Chateau which is connected to a network of tunnels, and which contains the Grail stone. According to Pierre Plantard himself, the real "secret of the Priory" pertains to an underground temple beneath Rennes-le-Chateau which is associated with the Devil: the "angel of the bastard race" and "MASTER of the genie." Yet another article, this time in *Le Cercle*, appears to link this temple with a 13-based numerical system[12], and claims that Priory of Sion meetings actually still take place there, specifically meetings of their inner order, the "Arch of the thirteen Rose-Croix." In "The Arch – It's Symbolism", author Jacques d'Arthuys writes:

"For [the Priory of Sion] the ARCH placed on the surface of the waters seemed like the sign of PEACE and WISDOM amid the torment. This was the sign of alliance, the guardian of the very essence of the Great Tradition. Its shape was the true representation of the Hebrew letter [Cheth], the engine of life, its number was 8, it was the last line of defense, while the sum of its three sides was 22 and its centre was the path that guides the ARCH towards the STAR.

The ARCH was the origin of the foundation of the PRIORY of SION and in our own times represents its pinnacle. It is composed of 13 members. The ROSE+CROIX meets in the round temple of the Roc Noir which, according to legend, was formerly a temple of MITHRAS. It has the shape of a semicircle... having 13 seats of stone. Each seat is engraved with a letter, namely: AB URBE CONDITA On the ground is a GOLDEN SUN... bearing these letters: MM CD XXX IV, or 2434[13] in Roman numerals. It seems to be recent, no doubt engraved by a HAUTPOUL towards the end of the 17th century. The former entry is obstructed over a distance... but a drilling has opened up an entry to the south. In our own time the ARCH extends over a large part of the world. It is from its summit that the heads of state will come to search for PEACE."

Amazingly, this passage seems to confirm that the chamber which holds the Grail stone is also the "Ark", and seems to equate this with the Ark of Noah as well! A similar quote was found in the Priory of Sion's *C.I.R.C.U.I.T.* magazine, and was quoted earlier: "A Nautonnier [Grand Master of the Priory] guides the ark ('arche') in the flood."

Only for the Initiated

Perhaps the most evocative lines in this new *Vaincre* article are the last two: "In our own time the ARCH extends over a large part of the world. It is from its summit that the heads of state will come to search for PEACE." To me, this indicates that the Priory of Sion considers the "Holy Land" of Rennes-le-Chateau to be the foundation-point of an empire that not only existed in the past, but also one that will exist again in the future. The use of "Ab Urbe Condita"[14] by the Priory, referring to the foundation of Rome, says to me that they are, as they have stated in their own documents, planning a resurrection of the Holy Roman Empire through the United States of Europe. But in order for this to occur, I assume, the treasures of Rennes-le-Chateau would have to be revealed to the world. This would no doubt have a shocking impact upon the collective psyche of mankind, for it would cause us to re-evaluate not only our understanding of history, but our political, religious, and philosophical tenets as well. It would be especially shocking if it was proven that direct descendants of Satan are alive today, many of them in positions of power, using their positions to bring about a resurrection of the antediluvian golden age and the empire that ruled over that epoch.

The thing most consistently said about the Holy Grail, whether it is depicted as a cup, a stone, a bloodline, a secret doctrine, or an ancient tomb, is that it contains the secret of earthly power, either for good or for evil. He who controls the Grail controls the world. He becomes the "Rex Mundi", the inheritor of Satan's title "the Lord of the Earth", and the embodiment of the Priory of Sion's "Grand Monarch" concept. It is no wonder, then, that groups like the Priory, the Templars, the Freemasons, the Nazis, the Vatican, MI5 and the CIA have struggled over the centuries to possess it. When the secret of the Grail is finally revealed, it will unleash a force as mighty as any the Earth has ever seen.

The power of the Grail is, as we know, a boon to the elect, and a curse to the uninitiated. It is therefore not to be trifled with. The unveiling of the Grail could be the most glorious event in known history. It could also be one of the greatest disasters. Let us hope, then, that whoever controls this power now, or whoever will control it in the future, uses it wisely.

A passage from *The Chymical Wedding of Christian Rosenkreutz* captures the essence of this perilous dynamic. It describes a Hermetic fountain of wisdom (the underground stream), whose waters contain the Elixir of Life. According to the story, the fountain was erected by Hermes (Enoch) himself, who inscribed its edifice with the following words:

> *"I, Hermes the Prince,*
> *After so much injury*
> *Done to the human race,*
> *Through Divine Council*
> *And the help of the arts*
> *Made wholesome medicine*
> *Flow here.*
> *Drink from me who can: wash in me who likes: trouble me who dares.*
> *Drink, brothers, and live."*

Endnotes

[1] Source: http://www.priory-of-sion.com/

[2] It can also be translated as "wave."

[3] This date is also St. John's Day, a high holy day in Freemasonry. Recall also that the Priory of Sion grand masters take on the title "John" upon assuming office.

[4] In the novels of Rosicrucian Edward Bulwer Lytton, the underground world was run by "Vril", an energy containing limitless power, which the underground dwellers derived from the inner sun that lit their subterranean world.

[5] Galatea, a sea nymph in Greek mythology, who began as a statue who was turned to life by Venus. She may be seen in this context as a personification of the Gaulish race.

[6] This site was purportedly visited by Jesus and his uncle, Joseph of Arimathea, and was the location of the first Christian church in Britain.

[7] Remember that "Ag" was a title used by Cain and Enoch.

[8] When asked, Henry Lincoln told me that they excluded mention of these subjects in *Holy Blood, Holy Grail* because they exist in "realms of pure speculation, wishful thinking and fantasy."

[9] A few months earlier I had been contacted by another self-proclaimed member of this order, who similarly vanished after a few emails.

[10] This information came from John V. Collyer on bibletopics.com.

[11] It is surprising to me that Jean Cocteau's heir, Edward Dermit, is not mentioned in this list as succeeding him, but then again, something about the list seems altogether faulty.

[12] Read Appendix A for the significance of the number 13.

[13] Note: 2+4+3+4 = 13.

[14] The words "Ab Urbe Condita" are usually translated as "From the founding of the city", and refer to the date of Rome's foundation, which was used in the dating system of the Roman and Julian calendars, in the same way "Before Christ" is used in our own dating system.

Appendix A: The Satanic Calendar

*"We do not subscribe to the conventional and erroneous astrology. The stars in them-
selves exert no influence. They are but reference points in space."*
Pierre Plantard, *C.I.R.C.U.I.T. Magazine*

In the magazine called *CIRCUIT*, published in the forties and fifties by the
Priory of Sion, a thirteen-house zodiac system is described, with the insertion of the
constellation of Ophiuchus - "the Serpent-Holder", constituting the extra house. The
Priory also published a poem called *Le Serpent Rouge* (*The Red Serpent*), written, as I
have theorized, by their twenty-third Grand Master, Jean Cocteau. This poem (which is
discussed at length in Appendix B) consisted of thirteen stanzas, each dedicated to one
of these zodiac houses, starting with Aquarius and ending with Capricorn, the sign under which King Dagobert was killed.

In Chapter Eight of *Holy Blood, Holy Grail*, the structure of the Priory of Sion
is examined in detail. According to the statutes published in *Secret Dossiers* prior to
1956, the order consisted of seven grades, with a total of 1093 members, whereas the
post-1956 statutes had it broken down into nine grades, totaling 9841 members. In addition, a set of twenty-two statutes written and signed by Grand Master Jean Cocteau
describes a structure of five grades. However, in all three versions of the structure, the
number of members in each grade is three times larger than the number of members in
the next grade, and all of the numbers, except for one 1 and 3, are divisible by nine. It
would appear that the only difference between the three versions of the structure is that
the pre-1956 statutes are not counting the members of the lowest two grades. Also, the
Jean Cocteau statutes have one-third as many people listed in each grade, with 243
members of a fourth grade that are considered part of an outer order, or laity, called the
"Children of Saint Vincent."

In the post-1956 statutes, the structure is also broken down into provinces
(each of which contains forty members), commanderies, and the "Arch Kyria", the
name for the top three grades, which consists of a total of thirteen members. The structure, as quoted from *Dossier Secrets*, is as follows:

*"The general assembly consists of all members of the association. It consists
of 729 provinces, 27 commanderies, and an Arch designated "Kyria."*

*Each of the commanderies, as well as the arch, must consist of forty members,
each province of thirteen members.*

The members compose a hierarchy of **9** grades.

*a) in the **729** provinces*
*1) Novices: **6, 561** members*
*2) Croises de Saint-Jean: **2,187***

*b) in the **27** commanderies*
*3) Preux: **729** members*
*4) Ecuyers: **243** members*

5) Chevalieres: 81 members
6) Commandeurs: 27

c) in the Arch 'Kyria':
7) Connetables: 9 members
8) Senechaux: 3 members
9) Nautonnier: 1 member"

The total number of members, then, according to these statutes, would be 1093. Meanwhile, the statutes written by Jean Cocteau state the following:

"The hierarchy of the Prieure de Sion is composed of five grades:

1st Nautonnier, number: 1
2nd Croise, number: 3
3rd Commandeur, number: 9
4th Chevalier, number: 27
5th, Ecuyer, number: 81
total number : 121"

The first two levels are part of a substructure called "the Arch of the **13** Rose-Croix." The other levels are part of a substructure called "the **9** commanderies of the Temple." In addition, Article 19 states that: "There are **243** Free Brothers, called 'Preux', or, since the year **1681**, Enfants de Saint Vincent, who participate neither in the vote, nor in the Convents, but to whom the Prieure accords certain rights and privileges, in conformity with the decree of **January 17, 1681**."

While most of the numbers here (which I will hereafter refer to as the "Priory of Sion numbers") are, as I have stated, divisible by nine, the total number of members according to each version of the statutes is not. However, attempting to divide them by nine reveals some interesting relationships. For instance, the total number of members, according to the post-1956 statues, is 9841. 9841/9 = 1093.44444... - the same number, minus the decimals, as the total number of members according to the pre-1956 statutes. Then notice that 1093/9 = 121.44444... - the same number, minus the decimals, as the number of dignitaries (ranked members) according to the Cocteau statutes. 364, the number of total members according to Cocteau (including the 243 Children of Saint Vincent), when divided by nine, gives us 40.44444... - the same number, minus the decimals, as the number of members in each commanderie. And 121 (again, the number of dignitaries in the Cocteau statutes), when divided by 9, equals 13.44444... - the same number, minus the decimals, as the number of members in the "Arch Kyria", or "Arch of the Thirteen Rose-Croix."

I wondered if these numbers from the Priory of Sion might somehow relate to the thirteen-house zodiac. I decided to subtract thirteen from each of the numbers that would not divide evenly by nine, and then try the division again:

9841 - 13 = 9828
9828/9 = 1092 (Just one less than 1093, the total number of members pre-1956.)

1093 - 13 = 1080
1080/9 = 120 (Just one less than 121, the total number of dignitaries in the Cocteau statutes.)

121-13 = 108
108/9 = 12 (Just one less than 13.)

And:

364-13 = 351
351/9 = 39 (Just one less than 40, the number of members in each commanderie.)
And 39 is also 3 x 13.

Then I noticed another thing:

1+0+9+3 = 13
and:
3+6+4 = 13

But even more importantly:

364/13 = 28

"What exactly is going on here?", I wondered. 364, number of total members according to the Cocteau statutes, not only consists of digits which add to 13, but is also evenly divisible by 13. And 364 is very close to the number of days in a year.

It was at this point that the meaning encoded in the Priory of Sion numbers came flooding into my mind. 28 is the average number of days in a lunar cycle, and there are thirteen lunar cycles in a solar year. 364 is not only close to the number of days (365.2424) in our current solar year, but is also the exact number of days it takes for the Moon to travel through the zodiac.[1] I decided to speculate: What would happen if we actually did observe a 364-day calendar? What would happen if, at some time in the past, the solar year had corresponded precisely with the lunar year?

The answer is that then we could have a perfect calendar, consisting of thirteen months of twenty-eight days, each a complete lunar cycle, and each dedicated to one of the thirteen houses of the Priory of Sion's zodiac. Also, we could still have seven days in a week, *exactly* four weeks in each month, and *exactly* fifty-two weeks in each year. In our current system, the number of weeks in a month, and in a year, is neither exact nor consistent. But in this system, all months would begin and end on the same day of the week, matching each other perfectly. All floating holidays, such as Thanksgiving and Easter, would occur on the same day every year. The menstrual cycle of each woman would begin on the same day and end on the same day of each month, also making periods of high fertility easier to calculate. Since each zodiac sign would corre-spond to a single month, all zodiac periods would be of equal length, with no "cusps", and everyone could easily determine which sign a person was born under simply by knowing the month of their birth. One could even break down the hours in a day into a thirteen-based system. We could split the day into twenty-six hours, each consisting of fifty-two minutes, which would in turn consist of fifty-two seconds each. That would give you a total of 25, 590, 656 seconds in a year.

Before long I discovered that the calendar which I had proposed actually does exist, although it has not been put into use in the Western world. It is called the "Fixed Lunar Calendar", and it consists of the same 364 days and thirteen months that I have just described. It was first proposed in the late sixteenth century, during Pope Gregory XIII's counsel to reform the Julian calendar (although it was used by other cultures as well throughout the ages). But the Fixed Lunar Calendar was rejected, one reason being that it does not accurately represent the solar year, which is the true definition of a year.

For thousands of years, men have been trying to create an "aliquot calendar": a perfect system that would synthesize both the solar and lunar cycles with exact, whole numbers. But as Duncan Steel remarks in *Marking Time: The Epic Quest to Invent the Perfect Calendar*, "We have been stymied by the fact that the solar day and the lunar month are not an aliquot part of the year. That is, there is not an exact integer number of days in the year defined by Earth's orbit, nor lunations in that year." However, he also remarks that, "it has not always been this way. About 1.5 billion years ago there were precisely fourteen lunar months in a year, each lasting for thirty-one solar days, but there was no one around to notice the fact and construct a calendar based upon it." The number of days in a year has varied substantially over time, due to a number of factors. One of the most significant factors, however, is called "tidal drag", a force caused by the ocean tides, which are in turn caused by the gravitational attraction of the Moon. This is causing the rotation of the Earth to slow down, making it probable that we will reach a 364-day solar year at some point. Whether or not the number of lunar cycles in a year will synchronize with it at that point is, however, a matter of speculation, and probably a long shot.

But perhaps the Fixed Lunar Calendar could still be put to use, through the insertion of leap days. Historians tell us that ancient man used to regard the last few days of the year (varying in number from one through five, depending on the culture) as "non-days", which were not observed as part of the year. No work was done on these days, and they were occupied with rituals of fasting instead. Is this what the Priory of Sion's system is meant to include at the end of the calendar year? As soon as I considered this possibility, the next piece of the puzzle fell into place. For as I discovered, the larger Priory of Sion numbers, including 729, 1093, 2187, 6561, and 9841, all form a pattern when divided by 364. $729 = 2 \times 364 + 1$. $1093 = 3 \times 364 + 1$. $2187 = 6 \times 364 + 3$. 6561 is $18 = 364 + 9$. $9841 = 27 \times 364 + 13$. I thought that this might represent a system in which a 364-day year is used, and a leap day is added every two years, so that in twenty-seven years, thirteen leap days have been added.[2] This yielded a system which revealed a great many astounding numerological correspondences. For instance, after 243 years (the number of "Children of Saint Vincent" in the Priory of Sion), 117 leap days have been added.

The following chart demonstrates how the numbers encoded into the Priory of Sion structure (based on all three versions of the Priory's statutes) indicate cycles of 364-day years, with a leap day added every two years. The largest number in the Priory's structure is 9841, but I have extended the numerical pattern out a few steps for demonstration purposes. I have also shown, on the right-hand column, how all of the larger Priory numbers reflect the other numbers mathematically.

I have reason to believe that the 364-day calendar was introduced by Enoch to humanity after the Flood, as their first sacred calendar. It has been observed and revered secretly by his descendants (such as those in the Knights Templar and the Priory of Sion) ever since. Perhaps the Priory of Sion numbers hint at a system they have created whereby they observe a 364-day calendar, which they attempt to synchronize with the current solar calendar as well through the insertion of leap days. This theory is discussed at length in my essay "The Cutting of the Orm", to be published in late 2004 in the book *The Arcadian Mystique: The Best of Dagobert's Revenge Magazine*.

There is evidence linking Enoch to the 364-day calendar. In *The Book of Enoch*, when Enoch is taken to Heaven and told by the angels that a flood will occur, they instruct Enoch on how to count the days of the year – a year that consists of 364 days. Perhaps this is why the sect known as the Essenes, who made use of *The Book of Enoch*, observed a 364-day calendar as well.[2] Also, the extra zodiac house used in a thirteen-based system is Ophiuchus, the "Serpent Holder", symbolized by the Caduceus. This is also a symbol of Hermes or Mercury, and thus of Enoch.

There is also evidence linking the Knights Templar to the 364-day calendar. Several authors have suggested that the Templars were responsible for introducing playing cards into Europe – the precursors of the mystical tarot. As it just so happens, hidden within the fifty-two cards of the standard playing deck is the Fixed Lunar Calendar! In *The Playing Card Oracles*, Ana Cortez and Charles Freeman demonstrate how the fifty-two cards correspond to the fifty-two weeks of the years, the four suits to the four seasons, and the thirteen cards in each suit to the thirteen months in each year, as well as the thirteen weeks in each season. If all of the values of the cards in each suit are added up, they equal 91, the number of days in each season. But perhaps most amazing of all, the total value of the cards in the deck is 364, the number of days in the lunar calendar.

It is fitting that the Templars would have been involved in concealing the 364-day calendar within the playing cards. The entire corpus of superstition surrounding the number thirteen, the basis of this calender system, has been attributed to the mystique surrounding the Knights Templar (although the superstition is probably older than this). The association supposedly exists because the Templars were arrested by Philippe the Fair's seneschals on Friday, October 13, 1307. But the Templars would appear to have already been associated with the number thirteen. As I have previously mentioned, it was encoded into the name of their idolotrous head, Caput 58M. (5+8 = 13, and M is the thirteenth letter of the alphabet). Some say that this was the same head they called "Baphomet", which they represented with their symbol of the skull and crossbones, also called the "Death's head", a symbol of death and rebirth in Hermeticism[3]. Later, this symbol was employed as the basis for the "Jolly Roger" flag used by pirates (many of them Freemasons), which featured, underneath the symbol, the number thirteen.

In addition, Friday is a sacred day in many traditions. It is the Sabbath of the Muslims, the beginning of the Sabbath for the Jews, and the day in which Christians are instructed to eat fish instead of meat.[4] This day is named after Freya, the Norse Venus/Isis figure, sometimes depicted with fish, or as partially a fish herself. Assuming that the number thirteen was held in reverence by the Templars, the date of Friday the Thirteenth may have been doubly sacred for them. Perhaps, then, this date was purposely chosen for their arrest by their enemies for ritual purposes.

But as I have said, there is much more to the superstition surrounding the num-

Priory of Sion #	# of 364-day years indicated	# of leap days added to the cycle	# of 28-day months in the cycle	Relationships with other Priory of Sion #s
729	2	1 (728 + 1 = 729)	26	364 + 243 + 121 +1 (364 x 2) + 1 9 x 81
1093	3	1 (1092 + 1 = 1093)	39	729 + 364
2187	6	3 (2184 + 3 = 2187)	78	(1093 x 2) + 1
6561	18	9 (6552 + 9 = 6561)	234	3 x 2187
9841	27	13 (9828 + 13 = 9841)	351	6561 + 2187 + 729 + 243 + 81 + 27 + 9 + 3 + 1
29523	81	39 (29484 + 39 = 29523)	1053	9841 x 3
88569	243	117 (88452 + 117 = 88569)	3159	29523 x 3
265707	729	351 (265356 + 351 = 265707)	9477	9841 x 27
797121	2187	1053 (796068 + 1053 = 797121)	28431	9841 x 81
2391363	6561	3159 (2388204 + 3159 = 2391363)	85293	9841 x 243

ber thirteen then just its association with the Templars. We are told that thirteen is an unlucky number. The number 13 has been shunned for centuries. In the past the thirteenth floor has been purposely omitted from office buildings. 13 is considered so baleful by some that there is actually a name - triskadekaphobia - for the psychological condition of the fear of 13.

But to the descendants of Satan, it appears to have been a sacred number. One of the reasons for its sacredness is that, like the Phi ratio, this number appears oddly integral to the patterns of nature. For instance, there are thirteen major joints in the human body. There are, as I have stated, thirteen lunar cycles in a solar year, and the moon travels thirteen degrees across the sky every day. Six circles placed around a seventh central circle form a model of geometric efficiency and perfection in the second dimension that has been known to mathematicians for ages. But this same configuration in three dimensions consists of twelve spheres arranged around one central sphere, making thirteen in all - the most compact three-dimensional arrangement recurrent in nature. A commentator writing about the Aztec calendar once said that, "Thirteen is a basic structural unit in nature. It means the attracting center around which elements focus and collect."[5] Is this, then, the reason for Christ's twelve disciples, or King Arthur's twelve knights?

The number 13 is also important to the founding of the United States, which began with thirteen colonies that turned into the first thirteen states. These states were represented on our first flag as thirteen hexagonal stars. (The stars were later changed to pentagonal shapes.) The number thirteen is all over the American one-dollar bill also, and on the Great Seal of the United States, created by Freemasons, who were heavily involved in the foundation of this country. On the backside of the seal, there is an eagle holding thirteen arrows, and an olive branch with thirteen leaves. His shield contains thirteen stripes, and above his head are thirteen pentagram stars formed into the shape of one large hexagram. In his mouth he holds a banner that says "E Pluribus Unum" - "Out of Many, One" - a phrase containing thirteen letters. The word "One" (or the number "1") is also written on the dollar twelve times, unless you count the Latin word "Unum", which would make thirteen. On the front side of the Great Seal are the words "Annuit Coeptis" and "Novus Ordo Seclorum." "Annuit Coeptis" contains, again, thirteen letters, and is usually translated, "He [meaning God] agrees with the cause which we have started."

However, this translation appears to have no basis in reality. All one needs is a simple Latin dictionary, and a little intuition. "Annuit" means "circuit" - like the circuit of the zodiac in the night's sky, and the precession of the equinox. This meaning is further encoded into the word "Annuit" itself. "Annu" relates to "Anno", which means "circle", and "year", while "Nuit", which means "night" in French, is related to the Egyptian word for "night": "Nut." "Coeptis" means "new beginning." This goes along well with the words at the bottom of the Seal, "Novus Ordo Seclorum", which mean "New World Order." So the statement being made here is, perhaps, that at the beginning of the new astrological age - Aquarius - we will have a new secular order on Earth, symbolized by the eye and the pyramid.[6]

The dawn of this new age is symbolized by the tale of Dagobert II's death, which took place on December 23. Since "dag" means "fish", and "bert" means "house", this story could be thought to symbolize the death of the "fish house", the Age of Pisces, at the dawning of the Age of Aquarius. Interestingly, the Mayan calendar (which was invented, the natives say, by a "white god" whose description sounds strikingly similar to Enoch) ends on December 23, 2012, right on the brink of the Age of Aquarius, and on the anniversary of King Dagobert's death. The Mayan calendar is also, like the Fixed Lunar Calendar, based on the number 13. This point is made rather abundantly by Jose Arguelles, the author of *The Mayan Factor*, who has also written another book, *Time and the Technosphere*, proposing the adoption of the 364-day Fixed Lunar Calendar as a way of harmonizing the spirit of man with the cosmos.

The Aztec calendar is based upon 13 as well, with 364-day years, and "long years" consisting of 52 years each. Like the Mayan calendar, theirs spans thousands of years, and counts the days until the "end of the world", supposedly. A hieroglyph at the top of the calendar which marks both its beginning and its end is called, significantly enough, "13 Cane."

Like many ancient cultures, the Aztecs (or rather, the god-kings who created their civilization) embedded the principles of their calendar into the architecture of their sacred temples. The Pyramid of Kukulkan in Chichen Itza, Mexico has four sides, each with ninety-one steps leading up to the top, for a total of 364. On the solstices, a trick of light and shadow produces the image of a gigantic serpent crawling down the sides of the pyramid, which then appears to join itself to the stone image of the serpent Kukulkan at the base of the pyramid. Once again, we have the imagery of Satan and Cain linked to the number 13 and the 364-day calendar.

Interestingly, in both the Latin and the Hebrew alphabet, the thirteenth letter is "M" (which is Hebrew is also a symbol meaning "water"). In both alphabets, "M" marks the center of the alphabet. In the original Runic alphabet, the thirteenth letter was "Eiwaz." It also marked the center of the alphabet, and symbolized the union of light and darkness. When the Runic alphabet was revised, this letter was taken out – perhaps as an act of triskadekaphobia.[7]

The number 13 has most definitely become associated with Satan in modern times. It is to be expected, then, that fear and hatred of the number 13 has been transferred by modern cabalists onto the mythos of Cain and his progeny. (Or perhaps, their fear and hatred of Cain is the true source of the superstition surrounding this number.) In *The Pattern and the Prophecy*, James Harrison, points out that that the names of the four generations of Cain's descendants mentioned in the Bible, when converted into cabalistic numbers, add up to 2223, which is divisible by 13. Bullinger then relates that the cabalistic value of the Hebrew word for "Satan" is 364!

The nature of this Satanic number, and the Satanic Calendar based upon it, will be explored in future writings.

Endnotes

[1] 28 is an interesting number because it is the sum of the numbers 1-7, and is equal to the sum of its divisors (1+2+4+7+14 = 28).

[2] Interestingly, Enoch is said to have lived exactly 365 years, and to have written a total of 366 books within this lifetime.

[3] Interestingly, the phrase "Death's head" itself implies both a beginning ("head") and an end ("Death").

⁴ We are also encouraged to "Thank God it's Friday."

⁵ Taken from the website: http://www.dayofdestiny.com.

⁶ Recall that one of the illustrations in the Priory of Sion publication *Vaincre* depicted a man mounted upon a white horse and bearing a flag of the "United States of Europe" riding towards a sunset, upon which was inscribed the sign for Aquarius.

⁷ In Tarot, the thirteenth card is always "Death", which links up to its association with the Death's head by pirates.

Appendix B: *Le Serpent Rouge* Interpreted

As I discussed earlier in the book, the poem *Le Serpent Rouge* consists of thirteen stanzas, each dedicated to one of the thirteen houses of the Priory of Sion's zodiac system. The authors are purported to be Louis Saint-Maxent, Pierre Feugere, and Gaston de Koker, who were all killed shortly after the poem was published. Strange and frightening as this may seem, these men may not have in fact been the authors, for the poem does not appear to be the work of a committee, but rather a single quixotic mystic. My theory is that the true author of the poem was Jean Cocteau. One only needs to read Cocteau's known work, or view his film *Orpheus,* to recognize the style of writing and the symbolism employed. Also, it was published just a few years after his death, and it was during Cocteau's grand mastership that the publication of "Priory documents" such as this one began

Assuming that Cocteau was probably the author, and working with the conclusions about Rennes-le-Chateau that I have expounded upon in this book, I am now able to understand certain key phrases used within this queer poem. It is my belief that this poem is written from the point of view of someone following the occult clues that have been left by past initiates to discover the sacred tombs beneath Rennes-le-Chateau, and the "Ark" that contains the "Grail stone." The narrator likens his journey to the symbolic journeys of mythological heroes from numerous ancient legends. Several veiled references are made to Noah/Enoch and his ark; to the Grail stone and the mysteries it contains; and to the discovery of the tomb of Venus or Isis.

Let us now examine *Le Serpent Rouge*, as translated by Amy Keller, for its hidden meaning:

Strange are the manuscripts of this Friend, great traveler of the unknown.

I think that these "manuscripts" represent the wisdom of the tablet of Enoch. It is Enoch, as Noah, Deucalion, or Hercules, who is the "great traveler of the unknown." Hercules is mentioned later in the poem, and his tomb is said to be located in a cave within Montsegur. He was the pilot of the boat called the "Cup of Helios" (the "Sun-ark"). That would make Hercules (also called "Arkaleus") another manifestation of the archetype of Noah (whom I have identified as being the same as Enoch). Hercules is famous for enduring a series of twelve trials, all of which clearly represent the houses of the zodiac. *Le Serpent Rouge* may be presenting us with a strange allegory for the Labors of Hercules: one in which there are thirteen trials, and thirteen zodiac houses, instead of twelve. The "unknown" through which he travels, then, would be the zodiac - the Celestial Sea, also represented by the serpent.

They reached me separately, nevertheless they form a whole for him who knows that the colors of the rainbow give a white unity, or for the Artist, who, under his brush, is able to, from the six hues of his magic palette, make the night spurt out..

This passage refers to the peculiar property of the seven colors of visible light, which, when combined, form a pure white light, the radiance of divine illumination. This may be an allusion to the alchemical language of light. When all of the major pigment colors are added together, they form the opposite - black. The Grail has always symbolized, in part, the essential unity of diverse aspects of the universe in this manner, including the unity of opposites such as black and white. The author of this poem seems to be saying that that Grail has been broken into disconnected pieces and scattered about, like the pieces of Osiris' body, or the original language of the Tower of Babel.

This friend, how does one present him? His name remains a mystery, but his number is that of a famous seal.

"His name remains a mystery" because the true Enoch is hidden behind many veils of myth, and is given many names. The "seal" is the six-pointed seal of Solomon, which is associated in the occult with Saturn (Satan). I have discussed how this symbol also represents the "Arka" and the world-mountain.

How does one describe him? Maybe like the pilot of the imperishable Ark...

A direct reference linking the main character to the Flood hero.

... impassable like a column on a white rock, scanning towards the South, where the black rock is.

Here we have a reference to a white rock and a black rock. The Grail stone is said to be both white and black, and this will have a very particular significance later on in the poem[1]. The Ark's pilot standing "impassable" upon the white rock may also refer to the mountain that the Ark rested upon when the Flood subsided, like Mount Ararat in the Bible.

In my arduous pilgrimage, I was tempted to clear for myself, with a sword, a way towards the inextricable vegetation of the woods. I wanted the reach the mysterious house of the Sleeping BEAUTY in whom certain poets see the QUEEN of a fallen kingdom.

This describes the "Herculean" task of finding the tomb of the goddess-queen said to be buried in the Pyrenees. She embodies the goddess archetype of Venus, the Sleeping Beauty. The symbols of the labyrinth and the dense woods are identical and are often combined in other versions of the Tomb of Venus tale. Nicholas de Vere writes in *The Dragon Legacy* that, "Labyrinths were often placed in the center of groves. Sleeping Beauty, Diana and Rapunzel's tower were all located in the middle of groves or thick woods." And as the poem says, Venus was indeed a queen during the golden age. That kingdom is now "fallen", and it is that "fallen kingdom" which the Priory of Sion wishes to revive.

Worried about finding the way again, the parchments of this Friend were for me like the thread of Ariadne.

Here we have a direct reference to the aforementioned labyrinth, specifically the one built on Crete which is the center of the famous Greek myth of Theseus and the

Minotaur, discussed earlier in this book. This labyrinth symbol repeatedly comes up in connection to the Venus myth and the Holy Grail. The labyrinth is often located inside the caverns of Venus's enchanted mountain, or, as in the Rapunzel story, can be entered through a tower that represents a mountain. In fact in Scandinavia labyrinths are referred to as "Babylons", indicating that perhaps a labyrinth was located underneath the Tower of Babel, like the labyrinths that have been found underneath South American ziggurats and the pyramids of Egypt. There may then be one underneath the mountains of Rennes-le-Chateau. As Nicholas de Vere states, "The labyrinth, like the pyramid and its collaterals, is thought to be a development of the idea of the mountain cave."

De Vere also sees the labyrinths as a feminine, vaginal symbol, and the Sleeping Beauty story as a metaphor for sex magic. He points out that the word "labyrinth" very likely comes from "labia", and that, "On at least two occasions in England labyrinths have been euphemistically referred to as 'fishtraps'", bringing to mind not only a vaginal connotation, but one specifically associated with Venus, who was represented in myth by the fish, and who came from a race of "navigators", all of whom were associated with fish and water. In some versions of the myth of the Melusine - that half-woman, half-fish who was the spawn of Satan (clearly a representation of the Venus archetype), and who spawned the Angevin kings - de Vere says that Melusine is depicted as residing in the midst of a labyrinth. "The center of the maze", he writes, "incorporated a black cubic stone, from which spurted the waters of life, La Fontaine de Soif, and the blood of the Virgin Womb." This relates to de Vere's theory that the Grail kings of the ancient world regularly participated in a vampiric ritual that involved drinking the menstrual blood and female ejaculate of so-called "Grail maidens", the foremost of which was Venus herself, "the Queen of Harlots", and head of the temple prostitutes.

This ritual would have been cause itself for the Grail kings to observe a 364-day lunar calendar based on thirteen lunar (and menstrual) cycles of twenty-eight days each. Such a calendar would seem to be represented by the labyrinth on the floor of the Chartres Cathedral in France, of which de Vere writes that, "The radius of the maze is 21 feet, which is 3 x 7, representing the three fallow weeks of the menstrual cycle. The week of menstruus would be represented by the point at the center of the maze, which is, on certain days, illuminated red." This is accomplished by use of a stained glass window through which sunlight shines upon the center of the maze. Here also can be found, according to de Vere, a "six-petaled Plantagenet or wild rose, carved into which there seems to be an M figure reminiscent of the symbol of Virgo."

In the myth of the Minotaur, the thread of Ariadne is what allowed Theseus to escape from the Labyrinth after slaying the beast. Every nine years, the Minotaur required a sacrifice of seven youths and seven virgins, who were placed as hapless victims inside the labyrinth, where they were torn apart and eaten by the monster. This state of affairs is what Theseus was sent to rectify by slaying the monster. As de Vere writes, "...by the time Theseus is said to have turned up, the tribute to the Minotaur in youths' and virgins' blood had been paid twice in 18 years. Gematrically this gives us a total of 28 victims, on one lunar cycle of 28 days."

Ariadne, while depicted as human in some versions of the tale, would appear to represent a spider who spins a magic thread. Note the similarity between the name of "Ariadne" and that of "Arachne", from whence we get the word "arachnid", denoting an eight-legged creature, such as a spider[2]. Arachne was a Greek goddess, the master spinstress of Olympia, who hung herself after she lost a web-spinning contest to the goddess

Minerva. Her competitor then felt sorry for her, and reincarnated her in the form of a spider. This web-spinning goddess figure would seem to have a link to Sleeping Beauty, who, if you will recall, fell into a deathless sleep after pricking her finger on an enchanted spinning wheel. Theseus entered the labyrinth with the magic thread of Ariadne tied around his waist, like the cable tow of the Freemasons that is worn while "groping for light" (akin to traversing a labyrinth) during their initiation ceremonies. De Vere compares the story to that of Rapunzel, writing that, "In Rapunzel the golden thread is her hair, and the maze is substituted by the equally daunting but related structure, a Tower."

Thanks to him, from now on with measured steps and with a certain eye, I can discover the sixty-four dispersed stones of the perfect cube...

The "sixty-four dispersed stones" which form a "perfect cube" must be a crucial part of this mystery. There are sixty-four squares on a chessboard, and a perfect sixty-four-square chessboard is formed by the black and white tiles on the floor of the church at Rennes-le-Chateau, facing both the statue of the demon Asmodeus, and the statue of Saint Germain, as if they were opposing players in a game of chess. In addition, the cipher used in one of the Sauniere parchments is based upon the chessboard, specifically the "Knight's Tour." This is a mathematical puzzle, to which there are numerous solutions, the goal of which is to have the knight visit each square on the chessboard once only, using the L-shaped knight's move. The Knight's Tour was also used to form the encryption system used in the code found on one of Sauniere's parchments.

The chequered pattern, and the game of chess itself, is associated with the Knights Templar, who purportedly acquired knowledge of these things through their extensive contact with Eastern mystics during the Crusades. The game of chess not only represents the eternal battle between the forces of good and evil, light and dark; it also represents something astrological. First of all, the board's outer ring consists of twenty-eight squares, which, as Michael Schneider acknowledges in *The Beginner's Guide to Constructing the Universe*, represents the twenty-eight days of the lunar cycle. The king and queen are solar and lunar symbols, as Schneider elaborates:

"The king, the most important piece, represents the Sun of this solar system... traveling only one step at a time, along both square and triangular lines, in any of eight directions. The king is virtually hidden from the action, yet the entire game revolves around it...The queen is the most powerful piece on the board, having unlimited movement in any of eight directions of manifestation... In another sense she is Regina Coeli, Queen of the Heavens, the widely traveling moon which always reflects the light of the Sun, the king."

Besides the king and queen, other pieces on the board also have special significance. The four rooks, or towers could represent the "four watchtowers" that divide the zodiac into four cardinal points, and which were incorporated into the headdress of the goddesses Isis and Diana, as well as Mary Magdalene. (In fact, a statue of Mary Magdalene crowned with four towers can be seen just outside in the courtyard of the church at Rennes-le-Chateau.) The black and white squares could be considered alternating periods of day and night. The chessboard itself, made up of four concentric rings of squares, resembles a "bird's eye view" of a four-stepped ziggurat, and thus represents the world mountain that in the eyes of the ancients provided the axis along which the cosmos metaphorically rotated.

In the belief system of ancient man, it was the cosmos, and the heavenly bodies contained within it, that controlled man's fate. The chessboard symbolizes an astrological mosaic of fate's possibilities. On the board there are six different types of pieces, and these six types of pieces can move in any of eight directions (the four cardinal points, and the four diagonal points). That there are sixty-four possibilities is fitting, since there are sixty-four six-part "codons", or "genetic words" in human DNA. There are also, notably, sixty-four hexagrams in the Chinese divination system known as I-Ching. The relationships between the pieces on the chessboard form, as Michael Schneider suggests, "...lines of force composing an energy web", like the web of the spider goddess Arachne, whose eight legs can be likened to the eight directions on a chessboard, as well as the eight squares that are on each side of the chessboard's outer ring. Schneider writes that, "The chessboard, the spider's web... and the I-Ching each in its own way represents the world's opposite forces weaving the eight-fold 'elements'... the warp and weft of matter's web." The Web of Arachne, or the "Web of Fate", was also likened by Nicholas de Vere to the Buddhist eight-spoked Wheel of Life, and to the Tarot's eight-spoked Wheel of Fortune, which both seem, in this context, to be not unlike Sleeping Beauty's spinning wheel, which controlled the fate of an entire kingdom.

There is another important connection as well. I discussed earlier how the Egyptian symbols of the Eye of Ra and the Eye of Horus represent the "Grail stone", the "stone that was rejected" and the "substitute" stone. Well, according to R.T. Rundle Clark's *Myth and Symbol in Ancient Egypt*, the Eye of Horus consists of "64 parts" that have been scattered and need to be reassembled! He writes:

"It will soon be seen that if each part of the [Eye of Horus] represents a fraction of the descending geometric series 1/2, ¼, 1/8, etc., put together, they make 63/64... So Thoth[3] can say 'I came seeking the Eye of Horus, that I might bring it back and count it!'"

The Eye of Horus is a representation of the Grail stone as the "All-Seeing Eye" of Satan, with which all of his direct descendants are able to see as well. This would have to be the "Third Eye" of Hinduism, called the "Ajna" (which comes from "Az", a title used by both Cain and Enoch). Is this, then the "certain eye" which discovers the "sixty-four dispersed stones of the perfect cube"?

The "perfect cube" is also an important symbol in the ancient mysteries, being representative of the "Philosopher's Stone" of the alchemists. Albert Pike wrote that the Emerald Tablet was a cube. The cube contains, in its angles, magic numbers. As Pike wrote:

"If we delineate a cube on a plane surface thus, we have visible 3 faces, and 9 external lines, drawn between 7 points. The complete cube has 3 more faces, making 6; 3 more lines, making 12; and 1 more point, making 8. As the number 12 includes the sacred numbers 3, 5, and 7, and 3 times 3, or 9, and 3 times 3, or 9, and is produced by adding the sacred number 3 to 9, while its own two figures, 1,2, the unit, or monad, and duad, added together, make the sacred number 3; it was called the perfect number; and the

cube became the symbol of perfection. "[4]

The "scattered stones" of the cube mentioned in this poem may also refer to the ruined Temple of Solomon, a building whose dimensions, delineated to the architects specifically by "God" himself, formed a perfect cube. Albert Pike writes of this: "The Holy of Holies of the temple formed a cube, in which, drawn on a plane surface, there are 4+3+2=9 lines visible, and three sides or faces..." Perhaps this is why the unit of measurement used by the Hebrews for the construction of the Temple was called, by Englishmen, the "cubit."

Given what we know, we can now look at one of the mysteries surrounding Jean Cocteau, the presumed author of the poem *Le Serpent Rouge*, with fresh insight. In the mural he created at the Notre Dame de France in London, he signed his name with the mysterious initials "D.D.D." - a code which has never been explained. But if you consider that "D" is the fourth letter of the alphabet, and then *cube* the number 4 (4x4x4, or 4 to the third power), you get 64 - a perfect cube[5].

... that the Brothers of the BEAUTY of the black woods, escaping the usurpers pursuing them, disseminated while they were fleeing the white Fort.

If the "beauty" is Isis, or Venus, then her "brothers" are the Cainites, who literally were her brothers. Also note that there is a woman whose grave, located on the grounds of the church at Rennes-le-Chateau, is very important to the whole mystery, and whose name, "Marie de Blanchefort", means literally, "Marie of the White Fort." Clearly her grave stone, and her name, are clues pointing to the grave of Venus, the real "Marie of the White Fort."

Reassemble the scattered stones, and work with square and compass to put them back in regular order;

The Freemasons' most well-known emblem is the L-shaped, right-angled square and compass, and this reassembly of "scattered stones" indicates re-acquiring "that which was lost", i.e., the Grail stone, by using the L-shaped, right-angled moves of the knight in the Knight's Tour to "reassemble the scattered stones."

...search for the line of the meridian that goes from the Orient to the Occident, then look from the South to the North, and finally in every direction to obtain the sought solution, stationing oneself before the fourteen stones marked with a cross.

This indicates using the "Roseline" meridian discussed previously. It has been suggested that the "fourteen stones marked with a cross" may actually refer to the fourteen Stations of the Cross within the church, each of which is surmounted by a Celtic-style cross with a circle. However, I am not certain that this is the correct interpretation.

The circle was the ring and the crown, and that was the diadem of this QUEEN of the castle.

This passage associates the Venus figure with the written symbol of Venus: a cross surmounted by a circle - the queen crowned. This sign is related to the Celtic cross mentioned above, and to the Egyptian Ankh, which was also used by the Cathars, who referred to it as "the Albigensian cross." This imagery may further be related to that of the constellation Virgo, who is depicted in iconography as crowned with a circle of stars, as are Isis and the Virgin Mary.

The stones of the mosaic pavement from the sacred place are alternately white or black, and JESUS, like ASMODEUS, observes their alignments.

This again is the black and white chessboard tiling on the floor of the church at Rennes-le-Chateau, which both the statues of Jesus and Asmodeus are staring down on. Perhaps we are meant to observe the alignment of the chessboard with other items in the church, and/or to project these alignments outward through the wider surrounding landscape.

My view seemed incapable of seeing the summit where the Sleeping Beauty lay hidden.

Again, we have a reference to the goddess buried within the mountain: the Venusberg tale, upon which the story of Sleeping Beauty is based.

It is not by the magical strength of HERCULES that one deciphers these mysterious symbols engraved by observers of the past.

This is a reference to the cave known as the Tomb of Hercules (a.k.a Enoch), which is covered with hieroglyphic symbols, just as the tomb of Hermes (Enoch) supposedly is.

In the sanctuary, nevertheless the font of benediction, fountain of love of the believers, reminds us of these words again: "BY THIS SIGN YOU WILL CONQUER"

The holy water stoup at Rennes-le-Chateau is marked with the phrase, "By this sign you shall conquer." This phrase was used by Constantine when he saw his vision of the sun-cross in the sky. The cross above the stoop is of the Celtic type described previously. However, it has been suggested in *Holy Blood, Holy Grail*, and in the literature published by the Priory of Sion, that the sign which Constantine really envisioned was the Chi Rho. This is a symbol made out of the first two Latin letters in the Latin word for "Christ." It is pre-Christian in origin, but is now a common Catholic symbol.

From her who I wish to free, steams of perfume that impregnated the sepulcher climbed towards me. Formerly some called her ISIS, queen of the beneficial spring, COME TO ME ALL OF YOU WHO SUFFER AND WHO ARE AFFLICTED, AND I WILL COMFORT YOU. For others: MADGALENE, of the famous vase full of healing balm. The initiates know her true name: OUR LADY OF THE CROSS.

Here the author associates Isis, Venus, Virgo, and Mary Magdalene with the vase full of balm which all of these characters were supposed to have carried, and which can also be linked with the Holy Grail. The use of the term "Our Lady of the Cross" again associates the goddess with the Celtic circle and cross symbol. The idea that she needs to be "freed" from something indicates that she, like her brothers, the Cainites, is imprisoned within her mountain tomb, trapped "in a deathless sleep", like Sleeping Beauty.

I was like the shepherds of the famous painter POUSSIN, perplexed in front of the enigma: "ET IN ARCADIA EGO..."!

It goes without saying that this is a reference to Nicolas Poussin's painting, *The Shepherds of Arcadia*, which was mentioned in the Sauniere parchments, and which depicts the mountains of Rennes-le-Chateau. The painting is a clue indicating the sacred tombs located within the mountains.

The voice of the blood made me form an image of an ancestral past. Yes, the lightening flash of genius cut across my thinking. I saw it again, I understood! I knew now this fabulous secret.

The author is perhaps experiencing ancestral memories pertaining to the secret of the Grail, for he may be of the Grail blood himself.

One must marvel that, during the jumps of the four horsemen, the hooves of one horse left four imprints on the stone.

The mention of horses brings to mind the "horse of God" that was mentioned in the Sauniere parchments. However, these "four horsemen" are the four knights on the chessboard, and their "jumps" are once again a reference to the Knight's Tour. They are also reminiscent of the four horsemen of *The Revelation of Saint John the Divine*.

There is the sign that DELACROIX had given in one of three tableaus in the Chapel of Angels. There is the seventh sentence that a hand had traced: DELIVER ME FROM THE MIRE, SO THAT I WILL NOT STAY HERE SINKING. Twice IS, embalmer and embalmed, miracle vase of the eternal White Lady of the Legends.

"Twice IS" is, of course, Isis, or Venus, the "Eternal White Lady of the Legends." Here, her vase is associated with the embalming of corpses, both her own and someone else's. Of course, Mary Magdalene's balm was supposedly used to "anoint" Jesus for burial. "Deliver me from the mire" is perhaps a prayer from the Ark navigator, asking to be saved from the Flood, to keep him from sinking into the mud that was swallowing up creation all around him. It also may link up with the story of the children of God, Shu and Tefnut, who in Egyptian mythology got lost in the Primeval Waters, and were saved by God's eye, which was sent out to find them. In the myth, the Eye was personified as female, a precursor to the idea of the goddess Isis.

Begun in darkness, my journey could only be completed in Light.

Here is yet another reference to the opposing but equal powers of good and evil, light and dark.

At the window of the ruined house, I contemplated the trees made bare by the autumn.

This "ruined house", like the story of the ruined Temple of Solomon, or the ruined Tower of Babel, represents the loss of the Grail wisdom after the cataclysm.

At the summit of the mountain, the cross detached itself from the crest under the midday sun. It was the fourteenth and highest of all with 35 centimeters!

I have already discussed the significance of the time of midday, or high noon, in regards to the Rennes-le-Chateau mystery. As for the rest of this passage, I have been unable thus far to decipher it conclusively.

Here I am, thus, on my knight's tour, on the circuit of the divine horsemen of the abyss.

Here is an even more overt reference to the Knight's Tour. The words "divine horsemen" would also seem to correlate with the "horse of God" reference in Sauniere's second parchment. "Crossing the Abyss" may be analogous to discovering the tomb, and "reassembling the scattered stones" – regaining the Grail.

Celestial vision for him who remembers the four works of E. M. Signol regarding the meridian line;

Emile Signol was a painter who produced four paintings of the old Paris meridian line, which the Priory documents suggest has some geometric relationship to the "Roseline" meridian. Signol also painted a famous portrait of King Dagobert II. All of these works are now on display in the Saint Sulpice church in Paris.

...at the choir of the sanctuary from where this spring of love radiates towards one another, I pivot, looking from the rose from P to that of the S, then from the S to the P...

I believe this line refers to the tombs hidden beneath the mountains of Rennes-le-Chateau: the "sanctuary." The word "choir" comes from "core", indicating the inner chamber of that structure, the "heart of the sanctuary." The word "heart" in French, is "coeur", and it comes from the Latin "cor" or "cordis", from whence we get the word "cardia", designating the heart organ. These words are also related to the ancient words "kar" and "gar", the key syllables in the words "Garral", or "Grail", and "Kardo", the name given in *The Book of the Cave of Treasures* for the mountain upon which the Ark landed, which I have equated with Mt. Cardou in Rennes-le-Chateau. I have already discussed the idea that Cardou/Kardo may have been, as indicated by the Priory of Sion's own writings, the "zero point" for the ancient prime meridian referred to by the Priory as the "Roseline", and thus was literally the "center of the Earth" in ancient times.

The "rose" mentioned may be the "hidden sun" said to be within the tomb, which is referred to metaphorically in occult ritual as a rose. It may represent, in this instance, the "heart" of Mt. Cardou. If the prime meridian of the ancient world passes through this point, this may explain why it is called "the Roseline." The reference to the "heart" which "radiates the source of love for one another" identifies this "rose" with the Sacred Heart symbol as well, which was used by the Priory of Sion under their guise as the Hieron du Val d'Or, and which is discussed in Appendix C. The Sacred Heart symbol is further linked with the rose-cross, the Celtic cross, the ankh, and the Venus symbol. All of these represent this concept of the center of the Earth and the prime meridian.

The "P" and "S" represent the Priory of Sion, but also have another meaning regarding bread and salt, as explained previously.

...and the spiral in my mind becomes like a monstrous octopus expelling its ink. The tentacles absorb the light, I am dizzy.

The tomb of Marie de Blanchefort, which in its inscription reveals the coded words "Et in Arcadia Ego", also has the figure of an octopus etched down at the bottom. The octopus is, according to Priory of Sion member Paul LeCour, a solar symbol used in Atlantis. It also contains the same symbolism as Arachne, the spider goddess, in regards to the number eight and the chessboard.

"The spiral in my mind" may signify the Fibonacci spiral. On the tombstone of Marie de Blanchefort, at the top, we find the letters P and S, linked by a Fibonacci spiral. Furthermore, when an octopus expels ink into water, the ink makes a perfect Fibonacci spiral, another peculiar property of nature. Spirals in general, however, can also be seen as yet another representation of the labyrinth, or maze.

I put my hand to my mouth, instinctively biting my palm, maybe like OLIER in his coffin.

This is the Masonic "Sign of Horror", made by raising the hand over the mouth and biting the palm, a perfectly apt sign to be made if, for instance, one has just discovered a tomb. In fact, this sign is used in Masonic ritual when reenacting the discovery of Hiram Abiff's tomb. Jean-Jacques Olier was the founder of the Seminary of Saint Sulpice. "Olier in his coffin" may just be a reinforcement of the image of the divine tombs, and the involvement of the Priory of Sion in this mystery.

Curses, I understand the truth, HE HAS PASSED in doing good, as did he of the flowery tomb.

"He has passed" is reminiscent of the phrase "he is there dead" from the Sauniere parchments, which in that case referred to the remains of King Dagobert being buried at Rennes-le-Chateau. As I have said, they were probably laid there alongside those of his ancestors, going all the way back to the Cainites. The "flowery tomb" reference is in regards to the supposed "rose (or "hidden sun") within the tomb of Enoch/Hermes.

There is a grave in the church graveyard at Rennes-le-Bains which appears to links up with this line as well - or rather, two graves. For in this yard there are two gravestones bearing the name of Paul-Urbain de Fleury, grandson of Marie de Blanchefort[6]. Henry Lincoln believes that the reason for the gravestone duplication is to draw attention to the man's name, which sounds a lot like "fleurie", the French word for "flowery."

But how many have plundered the HOUSE, leaving nothing but embalmed cadavers and metal objects that they could not have taken. What strange mystery is concealed within the new temple of SOLOMON, edified by the children of Saint VINCENT?

This is clearly a reference to the sacking of Solomon's Temple, the loss of the Grail, and the "ruined house" concept discussed earlier. The "new" Temple of Solomon reference alludes to the concept of regaining that which was lost. But it may also refer to Rennes-le-Chateau, linking it symbolically with the Temple of Solomon. In other words, Rennes-le-Chateau is the *real* "Holy of Holies", where the *real* "stone from Heaven", and the bodies of the *real* "holy patriarchs" are buried: the *real* "center of the Earth", and the ideal location to build a sacred temple, which I believe also exists within the mountains. The writer seems to be describing a tomb that has been partially plundered except for the bodies, and other objects that were too heavy to carry. This may indeed be the case with the tombs beneath Rennes-le-Chateau.

The "Children of Saint Vincent" are a subsection of the Priory of Sion mentioned in the statutes written for the order by Jean Cocteau, who, according to him, number 243, and who "participate neither in the vote, nor in the Convents, but to whom the Priory of Sion accords certain rights and privileges." This subgroup was created, Cocteau claimed, on January 17, 1681.

Cursing the profaners in their ashes and those who follow their ways, I leave the abyss where I was plunged while making the gesture of horror.

Here we have another reference to the Masonic "Sign of Horror" upon discovering a tomb. The "profaners" are those who have plundered the tombs.

Here is the proof that I knew the secret of the Seal of Solomon, and that I had visited the hidden houses of this queen.

Another reference to the six-pointed star, and to the "Sleeping Beauty" hidden inside of a mountain.

Take heed, dear Friend. Do not add or remove one iota; think and think again.

This indicates that clues are hidden in the precise wording of this poem, which you will understand more clearly every time you examine it. These are the same words used at the end of the *Revelation of Saint John the Divine*, which may not, in fact, be that last words of that book in its original form. A rumor persists that the Priory of Sion (and, I suspect, specifically Jean Cocteau) was in possession of a twenty-third chapter to *The Revelation of Saint John the Divine* that contained unknown secrets about the Apocalypse which the Vatican wished to remain secret. This theory is presented in Andre Douzet's book *Sauniere's Model and the Secret of Rennes-le-Chateau*, in which he links it to the mysterious phrase "John 23" uttered by Berenger Sauniere at his death. Just a few years later, Jean Cocteau assumed the title "John 23" when he took office as the Grand Master of the Priory.[7]

The base lead of my writing contains the purest gold.

These words imply that the tomb which the poem describes contains the secrets of alchemy, which it would if it contained the tablet of Enoch (Hermes).

Returning to the white hill, the sky has opened its floodgates.

In the Bible, the "floodgates" of the "firmament of Heaven" were opened to let loose the catastrophic Deluge.

There seemed to be a presence nearby, its feet in the water like him who comes to receive the mark of baptism.

Following the Flood reference, here we have yet another reference to water, specifically baptism. This could symbolize the cleansing of the Earth via the Flood, or the "baptism of wisdom" represented by the name "Baphomet" that was taken on by Seth/Cain. It could also refer in part to Christ's baptism by John the Baptist. In those days, the ritual was performed not by an emersion of the entire body, but only the feet. Note that Jean Cocteau's mural at Notre Dame de France in London shows only the feet of Christ. But there is another mural of Cocteau's that illustrates this principle even more clearly. It is the mural in the Chapel of Saint Peter entitled *Saint Peter Walking on Water*. The painting shows Peter being held aloft by an angel while his feet are dipped into the water, as though he were being baptized.

I turn again towards the East. Facing me I see rings unrolling without end, the enormous SERPENT ROUGE cited in the parchments. Salty and bitter, the enormous unchained beast became, at the feet of this white mountain, red in color.

This passage could conceal a hidden message regarding the combination of red and white powders in alchemy. The reference to the snake being "bitter" reinforces the association with the sulfurous red element used in that process.

My emotions were rising. "Deliver me from the mire!", I said, and awoke immediately. My dream is over. I have omitted from telling you in effect that this was a dream I had this JANUARY 17th, feast day of Saint SULPICE.

January 17, as we know, is a date that recurs frequently in this Rennes-le-Chateau mystery. It is the day Marie de Blanchefort is recorded to have died, and the date on which Berenger Sauniere fell ill with a stroke, from which he died five days later. It is also the date on which Nicolas Flamel, one of the Grand Masters of the Priory of Sion, is recorded to have successfully completed his first alchemical transformation of base metal into gold, and the date upon which the Priory of Sion's "Children of Saint Vincent" were created. Furthermore, it is, as the poem notes, the Feast Day of Saint Sulpice, and we know that the Priory of Sion took headquarters in the Seminary of Saint Sulpice for some time.

Recently I have discovered even more interesting connections regarding this date. *The Birthday Book of Saints*, by Sean Kelly and Rosemary Rogers, says that January 17th is also the feast day of St. Anthony the Hermit, the patron saint of buried treasure has cropped up elsewhere in the Rennes-le-Chateau mystery. But even more astounding is that, in addition, this date marks the feast day of "St. Roseline", whose name contains an obvious connection to the "Roseline" meridian (which, incidentally, runs through St. Sulpice in Paris). According to Kelly and Rogers, she was:

"... the mind reading prioress of Provence. When she was exhumed in 1334, four years after her death, her body was perfectly incorrupt. The astonished cleric in charge was so impressed by the beauty of her eyes that he scooped them out and took them home."

The details of this story clearly mimic the legend of Venus lying incorrupt within her tomb. The bit about the eyes being taken out connects with the idea of the "Watchers", and with the story of the missing eye of Horus.

Afterwards, my trouble persisting, I wanted after some reflection to tell you a fairytale by PERRAULT.

Charles Perrault, a seventeenth century French writer and poet, was the author of the book *Sleeping Beauty*.

Here then, dear reader, in the pages that follow are the result of a dream that cradled me in the world of the strange and the unknown. To him who PASSES BY, DO GOOD!

Here the writer seems to be suggesting that we use the clues embedded in the poem to explore the "world of the strange and the unknown", and to "do good" by solving the mysteries of the Grail, and of Rennes-le-Chateau.

There are many riddles still left to be solved within this poem. This may form the basis for a forthcoming book on the subject.

Endnotes

[1] Albert Pike stated in *Morals and Dogma*: "The Ancients adored the Sun under the form of a black stone, called Elagabalus, or Heliogabulua. The faithful are promised, in the Apocalypse, a white stone."

[2] Cocteau decorated the ceiling of the Notre Dame de France with a spiderweb motif.

[3] Remember that Thoth is the same figure as Hermes, or Enoch.

[4] Aleister Crowley insisted that his student magicians construct their altars with two perfect cubes stacked atop one another, "symbolizing the Great Work... The height of the altar is equal to the height above the ground of the navel of the magician. The altar is connected with the Ark of the Covenant, Noah's Ark, the nave (*navis*, a ship) of the Church, and many other symbols of antiquity."

[5] In this context, it is also worth noting that Cocteau was one of the major participants in Hans Richter's film *8x8: A Chess Sonata*, and he created one of the film's most bizarre segments.

[6] Remember that Marie also had two graves attributed to her.

[7] Remember that, since the Cutting of the Elm, all Priory Grand Masters have taken on the title "John."

Appendix C: *Le Hieron du Val d'Or*
From *Secret Dossiers* by Henri Lobineau (attributed).
Translated by Tracy Twyman

The Greek philosophers were ignorant of the source of the knowledge contained in their mythology. Aristotle said that it came from the barbarians, and holy Clement of Alexandria expressed the same opinion. The word "barbares" is without a doubt closer to the Hebrew word "Ber." It is remarkable then that the Hebrew root "BER" means "source", an idea which is associated with that of an "origin[1]."

Cesar notes that the Welsh Druids used writing of a Greek nature. We are thus incited to see in Greek the writing of those who, along with bronze, brought to the Mediterranean basin their worship and their gods. It is also on these premises that they would have conceived of the myths collected by the Greeks.

The men of prehistory had, to our knowledge, been inclined towards the constellations of the North, and to the Great Bear (Grand Ourse[2]), the one named and illustrated by the ancients. However, the word "Aour" means light in Hebrew. The Great Bear is the great light, but what word is it in our language? The answer is rather unexpected and I give it without any reservations. Indeed, in Hebrew, as always, the name of the animal called "the Bear" is "CHR TZ", where one discovers the word Christ[3]. The astonishing mystery is a source of constant admiration when one sees the relationships between the words, or the words by which the verbs manifest!

Is it not already obvious that to speak a poor French dialect that originated elsewhere will not make mankind become one single family, and that it is the call to transformation alone which must bring together the people into a single herd, led only by a single pastor?

As for the red flag, it is that of the Sacred Heart. Previously, a red cloth was thrown derisively on the shoulders of Jesus in front of Pilate, who then scoffed at his alleged office of King of the Jews. And in the *Apocalypse, XIX, 13*, it is covered in a red cloak that Christ returns in royal majesty. Red is indeed the crimson color of the kings, this primitive race having given to the world its rules and its laws, because all the people of Europe living on the banks of the Atlantic Ocean can claim the priestly heritage.

Red is the color of the primitive solar religion. If the skeletons of the Celtic epoch were buried in red earth, then the Peaux-Bouges, who polish the body in red in certain instances, are presently heirs to the Celtic tradition.

The color red is that of Hermes (that of the kermes). The black color (of anarchy) must, in the transformations of the substance principle, transform itself into a red color. The red flag has, besides other things, a long history which is connected to the universal Tradition in general and with that of France in particular.

When the Roman Empire extended itself down into Scotland, a red standard called the "vexillum" or "cantabrun" was used as the exclusive insignia of the more venerated armies. During battle, it was carried at the head of the troops. The guard was entrusted to fifty Praetorians chosen from among the strongest and bravest men. This standard consisted of a crossed lance made from a stick, from which fell a crimson veil with fringes of gold. The pole was surmounted with an eagle made of gold. After the famous vision of the monogram of Christ (not the cross like they mistakenly say) and his apparition in the Sun - a vision of that place surrounded by Autumn, which was accompanied by a voice saying to him, "By this sign you will overcome" - the emperor Constantine placed this monogram at the top of the pole of the red standard, consequently giving it the significant name of "labarum."

In fact, the monogram of Christ, about which they little question themselves, contains the necessary elements and symbolic systems sufficient to penetrate the labyrinth. A red flag was thus the first French flag, and this idea brings to mind the famous oriflamme (golden flame) preserved in the basilica of Saint-Denis, which on many occasions led the French to victory with the cry of "Montjoie Saint-Denis"[4], and which was a red banner cut out in points at the bottom, spangled with lily of gold, and bordered with a fringe of gold

This standard was originally the banner of the Abbey of Saint Denis. Its color indicates that of the wine devoted to Dionysus, because between Saint Denis and Dionysus there is an etymological relationship. The holy Denis lost his head, having been decapitated. Dionysus lost his heart. However, he who discovers the relationship which exists between the two legends has penetrated one of the mysteries of esotericism.

Dionysus is the divine spirit of evolution throughout the universe, the radiant spirit, alive with intelligence. We know that he was torn apart by the Titans, who devoured his members and interred his heart, but that Minerva (Athena) carried this heart into the sky, captioning an entire teaching of the Orphic tradition. The word Orpheus contains "Or- phos." It is it a word composed of two words, the one Hebrew and the other Greek, and significantly both mean "light."

The Devotion of the Sacred Heart:

In reality, the devotion towards the Sacred Heart is nothing more than a popularization of a very old cult, that of the Heart of the Sky (the Sun). It is by a radiant heart that we represent the heart of Christ, that within which we do not see a gross materialization. The Church, in its psalms, glorifies it "*In sole posuit tabernaculum suum.*"[5] They thus regarded it as the gate to the vault of divinity, and, as in the famous credo, "that which is Lumen of Lumine[6]." With far less devotion to Him, such consideration gives a considerable breadth and antiquity to Him, and unites with something larger the one and single Tradition to which belongs the Christian religion.

The crowned heart figure on megalithic monuments is part of the religious tradition of solarism. It was carried to Crete on vases dated several millennia ago, and it is not without some emotion that I have seen, in the windows of certain museums, Egyptian amulets representing a heart surmounted with a cross, identical to the modern badges of the Sacred Heart.

Templars, attached to a very old Tradition, held great honor for the crowned heart. A radiant heart in front of which a character is in worship is reproduced on one of the walls of the keep of Chinon, where there were imprisoned a certain number of Templars who covered the walls with graffiti. The image of the radiant heart can be seen also in their English commanderies.

The association of the heart of Christ with the Sun appears clearly in certain marble engravings dating from the XIII century and coming from Carthusians from Saint Denis-of-Orques. The wounded heart is indeed reproduced on this marble surrounded with the planetary signs, and signs of the zodiac.

It is in France, in Paray-le-Monial, that they have given birth to the devotion towards the Sacred Heart, which is the entitlement of the Hieron du Val d'Or. In Autumn of 1893 someone found, on the tomb of a Christian woman dating from the VI century, an inscription in Greek letters (recall that the Druids wrote in Greek letters). It comprises eleven lines, and the first letter of the first five lines form the word ICHTUS.

Here is part of this inscription:

"O divine race of the celestial fish, receive with a respectful heart in immortal life among the mortals the waters of the divine ones. Friend, remake your heart with the eternal flood of the wisdom which gives treasures. It is a reservoir of nourishment, soft like the honey of the Savior of the saints. Eat with hunger: you hold the fish in your hands."

Paray-le-Monial, February 5, 1926.
Le Poulpe (The Octopus)

Notes from the Translator

This excerpt from *Secret Dossiers* was given to me by an acquaintance. The copy was very poorly produced, and the letters very small, so it was therefore very difficult to read. Any errors or omissions in translation are due to the inferior quality of the source material.

There are also many lines in this excerpt that do not entirely make sense. This document was undoubtedly written for initiates, who would have been familiar with the code words and esoteric references made throughout. However, in spite of these difficulties, there is much to be gleaned from this piece.

One of the most interesting things is the emphasis the author places on the ancient roots of words in modern languages, seeing a somewhat cabalistic symbolic connection between words that sounds similar but appear to have totally separate meanings. This shows that the approach I have taken to interpreting the language and word plays which have cropped up throughout my study was indeed the proper one. It is notable that the author seems to liken this root understanding of language to going back to the "source" of religious and mythological traditions.

That "ber" could mean "source" is an interesting idea, since this is a word that I have shown means "house" or "temple" in other languages. This brings to mind the concept that a temple, such as the Tower of Babel, could somehow embody the "source" or original language. The author's repeated emphasis on "light" and illumination indicates that he may be familiar with the concept of the language of light, and with the idea that the Grail bloodline originated with a "light race."

The author seems to see this original "source" religious doctrine of which he writes as being a "primitive solar religion", and interprets the symbol of the Sacred Heart in these terms. As we know, the Sacred Heart is essentially the same symbol as the Egyptian ankh, the rose-cross, the Celtic cross, and the sign for Venus. Such a connection seems to be drawn in these *Secret Dossiers*, where a version of the Sacred Heart is reproduced and labeled as "an Egyptian amulet." (This is also discussed in the text of the exerpt.) The image is said to have been taken from the "museum at Rennes." This links up with the assertion made by several authors that the Cathars used the Egyptian ankh symbol, and called it "the Albigensian cross." Also, it is interesting that he refers to this as a symbol of the "gate to the vault of divinity", or a gate to Heaven, as the Tower of Babel and Jacob's Ladder were seen to be.

According to Nicholas de Vere, the original Aryans descended from Cain had red hair, and many central figures that I have examined in this book, including Venus, Pyrrha, and Mary Magdalene, have had red hair. I have also discussed the importance of the association between the color red and the idea of (alchemical) "fire" which the Cainites were linked with. The link between the color of fire and the "black art" of "alchemy" (which is named after the word "khem", meaning "black") is made by the author also when he writes:

"The color red is that of Hermes (that of the kermes). The black color (of anarchy) must, in the transformations of the substance principle, transform itself into a red color."

That fact that blood is red is significant also in relation to the idea of a royal bloodline. The author's assertion here that "Red is indeed the crimson color of the kings, this primitive race having given to the world its rules and its laws" shows that he is fully aware of the royal, red-haired Aryan race, and the fact that they are responsible for civilizing the humanity.

The emphasis on Saint Denis is important as well. Denis is famous because when he was martyred, his head was chopped off. Yet like the proverbial decapitated chicken, he did not die right away, but ran madly about, for miles, they say, carrying his head in his hands. To this day, the seal of Saint Denis is a bishop holding his head, on a red field. The author of *Secret Dossiers* likens Denis to Dionysus, and indeed, other authors have suggested that Denis might have been "a Greek philosopher named Diony-sus[7]." In fact, Saint Denis is "invoked against frenzy[8]" by superstitious French Catholics, and the cult of Dionysus, of course, was known for its frenzied, drunken, orgiastic rituals. Surely, there must be a connection. *Secret Dossiers* further links these myths with that of Orpheus, for just as Denis was decapitated, and Dionysus had his heart ripped out, Orpheus "was torn apart by the Titans…" This represents the same concept as the "scattered stones" or "that which was lost" – the Grail stone, and the Grail kingdom.

Finally, the excerpt could not have ended on a better note. The author connects the cult of Christ and the solar symbol of the Sacred Heart with "the divine race of the celestial fish." He also mentions "the waters of the divine ones", and "the eternal flood of wisdom which gives treasures", seeming references to the underground stream and the secret doctrine of Satan, which is here also likened to honey. This honey then appears to be representative of the Elixir of Life, as well as, of course, the Merovingians, whose royal symbol was the bee. Clearly, my theories linking Christ and the Merovingians to the race of Atlantean sea-gods, and to the water/fish symbolism thereof, were right on track. The link between the "eternal flood of wisdom" and Baphomet (Cain/Seth), whose name means "baptism of wisdom", has already been noted.

In addition, there is a line here which appears to shed further light on certain mysterious lines from the poem *Le Serpent Rouge* (discussed in Appendix B). That poem contains references to Constantine's vision of a sign of Christ, and the message he received: "By this sign you will conquer!" It also mentions, at an entirely different point in the poem, that the narrator "contemplated the trees made bare by autumn." Although these two things are not connected in the poem, they *are* connected in this passage from *Secret Dossiers*, where it discusses the "famous vision of the monogram of Christ (not the cross like they mistakenly say) and his apparition in the Sun - a vision of that place surrounded by Autumn, which was accompanied by a voice saying to him, 'By this sign you will overcome.'" So Constantine's vision, then, took place in Autumn, something that is apparently significant to the Priory of Sion, and something that apparently has some bearing on the meaning of the poem *Le Serpent Rouge*. I have not, however, been able to fully interpret it thus far.

Endnotes

[1] In this translation, "Dagobert" would mean "source of the fish." The word "source" also indicates a stream in French.

[2] "Ourse" means "she-bear."

[3] Recall the sacredness of the bear to the Merovingian kings, who worshipped it as part of the cult of Diana. Dagobert II was probably killed during a ritual bear hunt as part of this cult, on a date very close to Christmas. Ursa Major, the Great Bear who accompanies Polaris, the pole-star, was also called "Arktos", of which the root word is, notably, "ark."

[4] This phrase originated with Merovingian King Clovis, who is said to have shouted: "Mon Jou Saint Denys!" ("My Jove shall be Saint Denis!") while charging into battle. It became the battle cry of all French kings. (Source: *The Lives of the Saints* by Sabine Baring-Gould.)

[5] This quote, from *Psalm 18*, translates, "He hath set his tabernacle in the Sun."

[6] "Light of Light."

[7] From *The Birthday Book of Saints*, by Sean Kelly and Rosemary Rogers.

[8] Ibid.

Bibliography

Andrae, Johann Valentin. *The Chymical Wedding of Christian Rosenkreutz*. Edmonds, WA, 1991.

Andrews, Richard, and Schellenberger, Paul. *The Tomb of God: The Body of Jesus and the Solution to a 200-Year-Old Mystery*. New York, NY, 1996.

Arguelles, Jose. *The Mayan Factor: Path Beyond Technology*. Santa Fe, NM, 1987.

Arguelles, Jose. *Time and the Technosphere: The Law of Time in Human Affairs*. Rochester, Vermont, 2002

Baigent, Michael, and Leigh, Richard. *The Elixir and the Stone: Unlocking the Ancient Mysteries of the Occult*. London, UK, 1998.

Baigent, Michael, and Leigh, Richard. *The Temple and the Lodge*. New York, NY, 1989.

Baigent, Michael, Leigh, Richard, and Lincoln, Henry. *Holy Blood, Holy Grail*. New York , NY, 1982.

Baigent, Michael, Leigh, Richard, and Lincoln, Henry. *The Messianic Legacy*. New York , NY, 1986.

Baring-Gould, Sabine. *The Lives of the Saints*. Edinburgh, UK, 1914.

Baring-Gould, Sabine. *Myths of the Middle Ages*. London, UK, 1996.

Barnstone, Willis. *The Other Bible: Ancient Alternative Scriptures*. New York, NY, 1984.

Besson, Luc, and Jovovich, Milla. *The Messenger: The Story of Joan of Arc*. Culver City, CA, 2000.

Blavatsky, H.P. *The Secret Doctrine*. Pasadena, CA, 1999.

Borndigital.com/tarsus.htm. 2004

Brown, Frederick, *An Interpretation of Angels: A Biography of Jean Cocteau*, London, UK, 1968.

Budge, E.A. Wallis. *From Fetish to God in Ancient Egypt*. New York, NY, 1988.

Buechner, Col. Howard. *Emerald Cup - Ark of Gold: The Quest of S.S. Lt. Otto Rahn of the Third Reich*. Metairie, Louisiana, 1991.

Butler, Alan, and Dafoe, Stephen. *The Templar Continuum*. Belleville, ON, Canada, 1999.

Cameron, Ron (editor). *The Other Gospels*. Philadelphia, PA, 1982.

Chatelain, Maurice. *Our Cosmic Ancestors*. USA, 1996.

Chaumeil, Jean-Luc. *L'Alphabet Solaire : Introduction à la Langue Universelle, avec des Textes Inédits de l'Abbé Boudet*. Paris, France, 1985.

Chaumeil, Jean-Luc. *Le Trésor des Templiers*. Paris, France, 1984.

Chaumeil, Jean-Luc. *Le Trésor du Triangle d'Or*. Nice, France, 1979.

Childress, David Hatcher. *A Hitchhiker's Guide to Armageddon*. Kempton, Illinois, 2001.

Church, J.R. *Guardians of the Grail*. Oklahoma City, OK 1989.

Clark, R.T. Rundle. *Myth and Symbol in Ancient Egypt*. New York, NY, 1959.

Clarke, James Freeman. *The Legend of Thomas Didymus*. New York, NY 1881.

Collins, Andrew. *From the Ashes of the Angels: The Forbidden Legacy of a Fallen Race*. Rochester, Vermont, 2001.

Collyer, John V. *Fringes and Snails*. http://www.bibletopics.com/biblestudy/14.htm. 1999-2003.

Cooke, Jean, Kramer, Ann, and Roland-Entwistle, Theodore. *History's Timeline*. London, UK, 1977.

Cortez, Ana, and Freeman, Charles. *The Playing Card Oracles: A Source Book for Divination*. Denver, CO, 2002.

Cory, Isaac Preston, and Hodges, Edward Richmond. *Cory's Ancient Fragments of the Phoenician, Carthaginian, Babylonian, Egyptian and Other Authors*. London, UK, 1876.

Cozarinsky, Edgardo, and Cocteau, Jean. *Autobiography of an Unknown*. Chicago, Illinois, 1983.

Crowley, Aleister. *Book 4*. Dallas, TX, 1969.

Crystal, Ellie. Crystalinks.com. 2004.

D'Anjou, Rene. *Livre du Coeur d'Amours Espris*. Vienna, Austria, 1924.

Davidson, Marshall B. (editor). *The Horizon Book of Lost Worlds*. New York, NY, 1962.

Deal, David Allen. *The Day Behemoth and Leviathan Died*. Vista, CA, 1999.

De Givry, Emile Grillot. *Illustrated Anthology of Sorcery, Magic and Alchemy*. New York, NY, 1973.

De la Vega, Garcilaso. *Royal Commentaries of the Incas, and General History of Peru*. Austin, TX, 1966.

De Sede, Gerard. *The Accursed Treasure of Rennes-le-Château*. Worcester Park, UK, 2001.

De Troyes, Chretien. *Arthurian Romances*. London, UK, 1987.

De Vere, Nicholas. *The Dragon Legacy: The Secret History of an Ancient Bloodline*. San Diego, CA, 2004.

Donnelly, Ignatius. *Atlantis: The Antediluvian World*. New York, NY 1976.

Douzet, Andre. *Sauniere's Model and the Secret of Rennes-le-Chateau*. The Netherlands, 2001.

Eco, Umberto. *The Search for the Perfect Language*. Cambridge, Massachusetts, 1995.

Emboden, William. *The Visual Art of Jean Cocteau*. New York, NY, 1989.

Ephraim, and Budge, E. Wallis. *The Book of the Cave of Treasures: A History of the Patriarchs and the Kings, Their Successors, from the Creation to the Crucifixion of Christ*. London, UK., 1927.

Evola, Julius. *The Mystery of the Grail: Initiation and Magic in the Quest for the Spirit*. Rochester, Vermont, 1997.

Evola, Julius. *The Metaphysics of Sex*. USA, 1983.

Fact-index.com. 2004

Fifield, William, *Jean Cocteau*, USA., 1974.

Filsinger, Tomas J. *The Aztec Cosmos: The Great and Venerable Mechanism of the Universe*. Berkeley, CA, 1984.

Frazer, Sir James George. *The Golden Bough*. New York, NY, 1958.

Freud, Sigmund. *Moses and Monotheism*. New York, NY, 1967.

Fulcanelli. *Le Mystere des Cathedrales*. Albuquerque, NM, 1984.

Gardner, Laurence. *Bloodline of the Holy Grail: The Hidden Lineage of Jesus Revealed*. Rockport, Massachusetts, 1996.

Gardner, Laurence. *Genesis of the Grail Kings*. Boston, Massachusetts, 2000.

Ginzberg, Louis. *The Legends of the Jews, Vol. 1 and 2*. Baltimore, Maryland, 1998.

Godwin, Joscelyn. *Arktos: The Polar Myth in Science, Symbolism and Nazi Survival*. Kempton, Illinois, 1996.

Godwin, Malcolm. *The Holy Grail: Its Origins, Secrets, and Meaning Revealed*. New York, NY 1994.

Goodrick-Clarke, Nicholas. *The Black Sun*. New York, NY, 2002.

Gregory of Tours. *The History of the Franks*. New York, NY, 1974.

Guenon, Rene. *Le Roi du Monde*. Paris, France, 1958.

Hall, Manly P. *The Lost Keys of Freemasonry*. Canada, 1976.

Hamilton, Edith. *Mythology: Timeless Tales of Gods and Heroes*. New York, 1969.

Hancock, Graham. *Fingerprints of the Gods*. New York, NY, 1995.

Hancock, Graham. *The Sign and the Seal*. New York., NY, 1992.

Hapgood, Charles. *Maps of the Ancient Sea Kings*. Kempton, Illinois, 1996.

Harrison, James. *The Pattern and the Prophecy: God's Great Code*. Petersborough, Ontario, Canada, 1995.

Hauck, Dennis William. *The Emerald Tablet: Alchemy for Personal Transformation*. New York, NY, 1999.

Helgeland, Brian. *The Sin-Eater*. USA, 2003.

The Holy Bible: King James Version. Grand Rapids, Michigan, 1989.

James, Geoffrey. *The Enochian Magick of Dr. John Dee*. Saint Paul, MN, 1994.

Josephus, Flavius. *The Works of Josephus*. USA, 1982.

Jung, C.G. *Aion: Researches into the Phenomenology of the Self.* Princeton, NJ, 1978.

Jung, Emma, and von Franz, Marie-Louise. *The Grail Legend.* Princeton, NJ, 1998.

Kaplan, Aryeh, (translator). *Sefer Yetzirah: The Book of Creation.* Northvale, NJ, 1995.

Kelly, Sean, and Rodgers, Rosemary. *The Birthday Book of Saints: Your Powerful Personal Patrons for Every Blessed Day of the Year.* New York, NY, 2001.

Knight, Christopher, and Lomas, Robert. *The Hiram Key: Pharaohs, Freemasons, and the Discovery of the Secret Scrolls of Jesus.* Michigan, 1996.

Knight, Christopher, and Lomas, Robert. *Uriel's Machine: Uncovering the Secrets of Stonehenge, Noah's Flood, and the Dawn of Civilization.* Gloucester, Massachusetts, 2001.

LaVey, Anton Szandor. *The Satanic Bible.* New York, NY 1969.

Laurence, Richard (translator). *The Book of Enoch.* San Diego, CA, 1976.

Levy, Dan. *The Alchemy Website.* http://www.levity.com/alchemy/home.html. 1996-2003.

Lincoln, Henry. *The Holy Place: Discovering the Eighth Wonder of the Ancient World.* New York, NY, 1991.

Lincoln, Henry. *Key to the Sacred Pattern: The Untold Story of Rennes-le-Château.* New York, NY, 1998.

Lobineau, Henri. *Dossiers Secrets d'Henri Lobineau.* Paris, France, 1967.

Maccoby, Hyam. *Judas Iscariot and the Myth of Jewish Evil.* New York, NY, 1992.

Mackey, Albert G. *The History of Freemasonry.* USA, 1998.

Mathers, S. Liddell MacGregor (translator). *The Key of Solomon the King.* York Beach, Maine, 1989.

Mehler, Stephen. *The Origin of the Word Pyramid.* http://www.gizapyramid.com/mehler-originword.htm. 2000-2003.

McIntosh, Christopher. *The Rosicrucians: The History, Mythology, and Rituals of an Esoteric Order.* York Beach, Maine, 1997.

Michaelson, Scott (editor). *Portable Darkness: An Aleister Crowley Reader.* New York, NY, 1989.

Oates, Joan. *Babylon.* London, UK, 1979.

Patton, Guy and Mackness, Robin. *Web of Gold: The Secret Power of a Sacred Treasure.* London, UK, 2000.

Picknett, Lynn, and Prince, Clive. *The Templar Revelation: Secret Guardians of the True Identity of Christ.* New York, NY, 1997.

Pike, Albert. *Morals and Dogma.* Richmond, VA, 1927.

Plato, Taylor, Thomas, and Taliaferro, R. Catesby. *The Timaeus, and the Critias, or Atlanticus.* New York, NY, 1944.

Raqq, Laura Maria Roberts, and Raqq, Lonsdale (editors). *The Gospel of Barnabas.* USA, 1994.

Ravenscroft, Trevor. *The Spear of Destiny.* York Beach, Maine, 1992.

Regardie, Israel. *The Golden Dawn.* Saint Paul, MN, 1994.

Reiss, Joseph. *Language, Myth, and Man.* USA, 1963.

Rest, Friedrich. *Our Christian Symbols.* Philadelphia, PA 1959.

Richardson, John. *A Life of Picasso.* New York, NY, 1991

Roberts, J.M. *A History of Europe.* New York, NY, 1996.

Roberts, Paul William. *In Search of the Birth of Jesus: The Real Journey of the Magi.* New York, NY, 1995.

Savedow, Steve. *Goetic Evocation: The Magician's Workbook, Volume 2.* Chicago, IL, 1996.

Schneider, Michael S. *A Beginner's Guide to Constructing the Universe: The Mathematical Archetypes of Nature, Art, and Science.* New York, NY 1994.

Scholem, Gershom Gerhard. *Zohar: The Book of Splendor.* New York, NY, 1963.

Schonfield, Dr. Hugh J. *The Passover Plot.* New York, NY, 1965

Simpson, D.P. *Cassell's New Latin Dictionary.* New York, NY, 1959.

Sitchin, Zecharia. *The Twelfth Planet : Book I of the Earth Chronicles.* USA, 1999.

Springmeier, Fritz. *The Bloodlines of the Illuminati.* Westminster, CO, 1999.

Smith, Paul. *The Rennes-le-Chateau Papers of Paul Smith.* priory-of-sion.com, 2003.

Smith, Morton. *Jesus the Magician.* San Francisco, CA, 1981.

Spacedaily.com. "World will See Computers in Whole New Light." 2002.

Starbird, Margaret. *The Woman with the Alabaster Jar.* Rochester, VT, 1993.

Steegmuller, Francis. *Cocteau: A Biography.* Boston, Massachusetts, 1970.

Steel, Duncan. Marking Time: *The Epic Quest to Invent the Perfect Calendar.* New York, NY, 2000.

Stewart, Prince Michael of Albany. *The Forgotten Monarchy of Scotland.* Dorset, UK 1998.

Still, William T. *New World Order: The Ancient Plan of Secret Societies.* Lafayette, Louisiana, 1990.

Talbott, David N. *The Saturn Myth.* Garden City, NY, 1979.

Tenen, Stan. *Geometric Metaphors of Life.* Sharon, MA, 1989.

Thompson, James. *Nicolas Poussin.* New York, NY, 1992.

Urwin, Kenneth. *Langenscheidt Standard Dictionary: French-English, English-French.* Berlin, Germany, 1968.

Von Eschenbach, Wolfram. *Parzival* (excerpt). From *Transformations of Myth Through Time: An Anthology of Readings.* Orlando, FL, 1990.

Waddell, L.A. *The British Edda: The Great Epic Poem of the Ancient Britons on the Exploits of King Thor, Arthur or Adam and His Knights in Establishing Civilization, Reforming Eden & Capturing the Holy Grail About 3380-3350 B.C.* London, UK, 1930.

Waddell, L.A. *Egyptian Civilization: Its Sumerian Origin and Real Chronology, and Sumerian Origin of Egyptian Hieroglyphs.*

Waddell, L.A. *The Makers of Civilization in Race and History.* London, UK, 1929.

Waite, Arthur Edward. *The Rider Tarot Deck.* Stamford, CT, 1971.

Waite, Arthur Edward. *A New Encyclopedia of Freemasonry.* USA, 1970.

William Collins Sons & Co. Ltd. *Collins Gem German-English/English-German Dictionary.* UK, 1978.

Wilson, Colin, and Flem-Ath, Rand. *The Atlantis Blueprint.* New York, NY, 2000.

Wood, David. *Genisis: The First Book of Revelations.* Illinois, Tunbridge Wells, UK, 1985.

Wood, David and Campbell, Ian. *Geneset: Target Earth.* Sunbury-on-Thames, UK, 1994.

Woodrow, Ralph. *Babylon Mystery Religion.* USA, 1966.

Printed in the United States
22708LVS00003B/253-285